The History And Antiquities Of Dartford: With Topographical Notices Of The Neighbourhood

John Dunkin

Dartford:

J. & W. DAVIS,

PRINTERS AND

PUBLISHERS.

———

RE-PRINTED 1904.

THE

HISTORY AND ANTIQUITIES

OF

DARTFORD.

Engraved by I. I. Pennstone   from a Photograph by h. ard.

yours truly,

Jno: Dunkin.

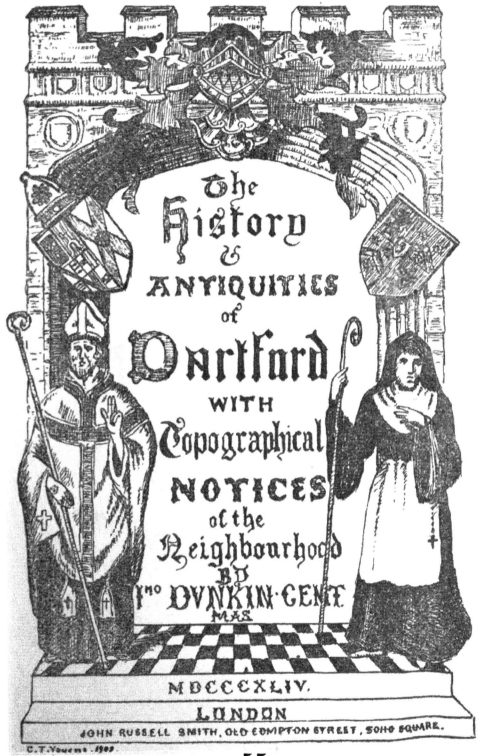

The History
&
Antiquities
of
Dartford
with
Topographical
Notices
of the
Neighbourhood
By
Jno Dunkin Gent.
M.A.S.

MDCCCXLIV.

LONDON

JOHN RUSSELL SMITH, OLD COMPTON STREET, SOHO SQUARE.

C.T.Vacent. 1901.

55

TO THE RIGHT REVEREND GEORGE MURRAY, D.D.

PATRON OF THE CHURCH OF DARTFORD,

THIS HISTORY

OF

THE PARISH OF DARTFORD,

IS

[WITH HIS LORDSHIP'S PERMISSION,]

MOST RESPECTFULLY INSCRIBED,

BY HIS MOST OBEDIENT HUMBLE SERVANT,

THE AUTHOR.

DARTFORD, MAY 1st, 1844.

PREFACE.

THE late Mr. Robert Pocock some years since circulated Proposals for a History of Dartford, which his death, and then the dispersion, if not destruction, of his Collections, prevented ever being fulfilled. In consequence of several members of the literary world having expressed considerable regret that the intended Work was never published, the present writer was induced to attempt to supply the hiatus.

In accordance with this resolve, soon after his son settled in the town of Dartford, he issued a prospectus, and the readiness with which many individuals responded, stimulated his efforts to render the book worthy their patronage. In this endeavour he was particularly assisted by the well known liberality of the Right Reverend Father in God, the present BISHOP OF ROCHESTER who kindly exerted his influence with the Keepers of the Archives of the see to allow him to examine their records; Messrs. TWOPENNY and ESSELL then liberally and gratuitously opened all their stores to the writer's inspection. He has also to acknowledge the extreme kindness of JOHN HAYWARD, esq., who permitted him access to the

several manorial Court Rolls and other valuable
documents in his possession; and also his gratitude to the Vicar of Dartford, the Rev. F. B.
GRANT; and Mr. SNOWDEN, the vicar's-warden for
their permission to allow him to make unlimited
extracts from the Registers, Churchwardens',
Overseers', Vestry, and other Parochial Books,
and Documents in their custody, of which it will
be found he has made ample use. He also here
takes the opportunity to thank the Rev. T. HARD-
ING, the vicar of Bexley, and the other Clergymen
in the neighbourhood who have permitted the
inspection of their Registers, or whose great kindness induced them to verify his extracts.—And,
while he deeply deplores that calamity, which
deprived him of the further valuable assistance of
the erudite and highly-talented JOHN CALEY, esq.,
F.A.S. the Keeper of the Records at the Augmentation Office, he can never be sufficiently
thankful for the information derived from the
stores of that office, which have added a permanent value to the work, it was incapable of
deriving from any other source. His best thanks
are also due to the *Keeper of the Lambeth Library;
the Keepers of the Records at the Rolls Chapel; the
Tower of London; and the Librarians of the British
Museum* who have all readily assisted him in his
researches. Nor must his obligations be forgotten

for the valued information respecting the Priory, rendered him by L. P. STAFF, esq., the worshipful the Mayor of Gravesend; WILLIAM CRAFTER, esq., the resident chief of the Engineering department at Tilbury and Gravesend Forts; J. B. GARDINER, esq., who, favoured him with some unique and curious extracts from Wills in the Prerogative Office, London; Dr. POTTS of Vanburgh Castle, Blackheath, to whom he is indebted for the plate of the Camp on Dartford-Heath; ALFRED JOHN KEMPE, esq., F.A.S. who kindly revised the account of the discovery of the Cemetery on East Hill, favoured him with drawings of the stone sarcophagus, and the measurement of the Watling street, on Dartford-Brent; and, also generally, to the gentlemen inhabiting Dartford and its vicinity, most of whom have been very communicative; thus evincing the interest they took in contributing their share towards the publication.

He has also to acknowledge his special obligations to Mr. JARDINE, who has favoured him with several valuable Lithographic prints of antient structures, engraved by his own hand, the remembrance of which, would have otherwise perished.

The writer is aware that no work that ever appeared was absolutely perfect; but to those who may cavil at the present performance, he has

no hesitation in saying, that considerable pains
have been taken throughout the volume to procure
documental authority for the statements that have
been advanced, and he hopes that future generations will find the book worthy of implicit credit.

LIST OF ILLUSTRATIONS.

Illustrative Vignettes in Letter-press.

NOTICE TO SUBSCRIBERS.

———————

AS far as possible, this re-issue of "𝔇𝔲𝔫𝔨𝔦𝔫'𝔰 𝔥𝔦𝔰𝔱𝔬𝔯𝔶 𝔞𝔫𝔡 𝔄𝔫𝔱𝔦𝔮𝔲𝔦𝔱𝔦𝔢𝔰 𝔬𝔣 𝔇𝔞𝔯𝔱𝔣𝔬𝔯𝔡" will be a *fac-simile* of the original edition. This will account for the old-fashioned style of expression and spelling. Where, however, palpable mistakes have been made, they have been corrected. Subscribers knowing of anything of interest relating to the past history of Dartford, or having old illustrations, deeds, leases, or documents relating to the same, are earnestly requested to communicate with the Publishers, or Mr. E. C. Youens, Photographer, Tower Road, who will gladly acknowledge the same in the appendix when published.

A

INTRODUCTION.

A series of papers having lately appeared in the Dover Chronicle under the title of "The Chronicles of Kent," as well as an article in the Gentleman's Magazine which throw light on the hitherto unnoticed British Antiquities in the neighbourhood of Dartford, I have thought it right to give extracts therefrom, in an introductory chapter to this History.*

The writer states "that after the conquest of the British fortress on Chartham Downs,† Cæsar marched

---

* Articles in that publication, by Alfred John Dunkin, from Jan. 1844, to April of the same year. Gent's Mag. April, 1844. To the articles in the Chronicle, Lambert Weston, esq., in an interesting Lecture at the Dover Institution, March 24th, acknowledged himself principally indebted for his observations " On the Remains of British Antiquities."

† " Ipse noctu progressus millia passuum circiter xii, hostium copias conspicatus est. Illi equitatu atque essedis ad flumen progressi (the Stour), ex loco superiore nostros prohibere, et prœlium committere cœperunt. Repulsi ab equitatu, se in sylvas abdiderunt; locum nacti, egregiè et naturâ, et opere munitum: quem, domestici belli, ut videbatur, causâ, jam antè præparaverant: nam crebis arboribus succisis, omnes introitus errant præclusi. Ipsi ex sylvis rari propugnabant, nostròsque intra munitiones ingredi prohibebant. At milites legionis vii, testudine factâ, et aggere ad munitiones adjecto, locum ceperunt; eòsque ex sylvis expulerunt, paucis vulneribus acceptis: sed eos fugientes longiùs Cæsar persequi vetuit; et quòd loci naturam ignorabat, et quòd magnâ parte diei consumptâ, munitioni castrorum tempus relinqui volebat. *Cæsar, lib. v. ¶ 8.* For had

by the great British trackway* to Debtling, where he
encamped for the night, and prepared to pass the river,†
which he miscalls 'the Thames,' regarding the Medway
as that river—instead of being only an arm‡ thereof.

"Arrived at the ford,¶ Cæsar found the Britons in
great force determined to dispute his passage; to render
which more difficult, they had driven down sharp
stakes into the bed of the river. Here, Cæsar was
necessitated to fight a terrific battle, but at length,
his legions wading through the water up to their necks,

Cæsar crossed the Medway, he would not have totally omitted to
mention his passage thereof, inasmuch as it was a river of much greater
extent and magnitude than the Stour, as it then covered the whole of
the valley between the rising grounds.

* It led by the great Druid altar vulgarly called Kit's Coty House.
The Romans used these roads where they could. *Fosbroke's Ency.* ii.
578.—In Kent however, they afterwards deviated from the ford, and
crossed the river at Rochester.

† About two miles from Debtling, in the direction of Medhurst, a few
years since some entrenched embankments were discovered which
formed nearly a square, with a double vallum on the north side. *Lam-
prey's Maidstone.*

‡ Cæsar, cognito eorum consilio, ad flumen Tamesin, in fines Cassivellauni, exercitum duxit; quod flumen uno omnino loco pedibus, atque
hoc ægre, transiri potest. Eò quum venisset; animum advertit, ad
alteram fluminis ripam magnas esse copias hostium instructas: ripa
autem erat acutis sudibus præfixis munita; ejusdemque generis sub aquâ
defixæ sudes, flumine tegebantur. *Cæsar, lib.* v. ¶ 14. It does not
appear that the stakes were shod with metal, or in fact were any thing
else but "sharp stakes," which in process of time, by the action of the
current would necessarily be swept away.

¶ Elesford, the ford of Eccles; an antient village near Aylesford,
called Aiglessa in Domesday book. Tradition still speaks of it as having
been a strong and populous town; the cottages occupying its site being
chiefly built of stones from the foundation of its primitive houses.
Allport's Maidstone. p. 17.

forced the ford. Adjacent, was the town where dwelt the Cenimagni, in whose territories were comprised the grand Druidical fanes on the banks of the Medway.* An immediate consequence of the victory, was, that the tribe yielded allegiance to the conqueror, and sent in their adhesion to his standard.†

"Caswallon‡ the British leader, in consequence of the defection of some of his allies, was then compelled to retreat to his town and fortress, (the remains of which,

---

* The Druidical erections on the banks of the Medway, were as magnificent and imposing as any in the world. There, was found every appliance and ornament that the Druid religion demanded to awe and alarm its superstitious votaries.—Prominently on the brow of the hill, stood the altar, from whence, the Arch-Priest while offering to heaven the victim's reeking heart, declared the decrees of fate.—By the side of this CROMLECH stood a Meinigwyr, used, at times, as a gorsedd to explain the law to the assembled thousands—at the foot of the hill in the deep recesses of the SACRED GROVE was reared the HOLY OF HOLIES ; adjacent to a KISTVAEN, were the LUSTRATING SPRINGS. *Chron. of Kent.* Dov. Ch. Nos. 472 & 473.

† "Cenimagni legationibus missis, sese Cæsari dediderunt. Ab his cognoscit, *non longe ex eo loco oppidum Cassivellauni* abesse, sylvis paludibúsque munitum, quò satìs magnus hominum pecorisque numerus convenerit." *Cæsar,* lib. v. ¶ 17.

‡ Geoffrey of Monmouth says, 'Caswallon was second son of Heli, king of Britain ; that his elder brother who succeeded him enlarg'd and wall'd Trinovant his capital, and called it after himself Cær-Lud or Lud's town, (now London).' 'This,' Gildas says, 'caused great dissention between him and Nennius his younger brother, who took it hainously that the name of Troy thir antient country should be abolish'd for any new one. Lud was hardy and bold in warr, in peace, a jolly feaster.' He was buried by the gate, thence called Ludgate. His two sons, Androgeus and Theomantius, were not of age to govern, and so their uncle Caswallon obtained the crown. In the 8th year of his reign, Cæsar invaded Britain. *Chronicles of Kent,* lib. i., *Legendæ.* Dov. Ch. No. 420.

still exist about Dartford,*) in the centre of his own territories, (the Cassii†) where he was followed by Cæsar, and again defeated, for

> " Treason like an old and eating sore
> Consumed the bones and sinews of their strength."

This British town was extremely large, as its boundaries can now be traced extending into no less than five parishes, Wilmington,‡ Dartford, Bexley, Sutton-at-Hone,‖ and North-cray.

"Cæsar, then (lib. v. ¶ 17.) says 'From them, (the 'Cenimagni,) he had intelligence, that he was not far

---

* "A British town although very populous, is little more than a wood with a number of straggling groups of houses in it, surrounded with a ditch and earthwork." *Cæsar, lib.* v. ¶ 17. The houses themselves were circular huts half buried in the ground, formed of wattled poles driven into the earth round a circular hole, fastened together at top, and covered with grass, sods, or reeds, to exclude the rain. *Strabo* says 'The fortresses of the Britons are their cities, for when they have enclosed a very large space with felled trees they build within houses for themselves, and hovels for their cattle.'

† *Cæsar, lib.* v. ¶ 21. Segonax one of the four chiefs of Kent enumerated by Cæsar, doubless governed the Segontiaci. By analogy Caswallon ruled the Cassii. When Cæsar invaded Britain he found the whole country divided among numerous chieftains each of whom assumed the high sounding title of king.

‡ In a meadow not far from Ruehill are several tumuli.

‖ The British road runs by Cold-Harbour in this parish. Sir R. C. Hoare states, that he always found this name in the vicinity of old high roads. *Col* in the British language signifies an eminence, summit, peak or head; and *arbhav* in the Gallic a host, army, &c. Cold-Harbour therefore properly designates a statio militaris or resting place. *Anc. Wilts.* ii. 96. Perhaps the spot where Cæsar or Plautius encamped to rest their legions, wearied after crossing the Darenth, previously to their attacking the city of the Cassii.

'from the capital of Caswallon, which was situated 'amidst woods and marshes, and whither great num- 'bers of men had retired,' this description precisely applies to this spot, which is guarded in its front by the marshes of the Darenth, and in the rear, by those of the Cray. 'Thither he marched with his legions, 'and although the place appeared exceedingly strong 'both by art and nature, he nevertheless resolved to 'attack it.' Now, within but a short distance of the road by which Cæsar marched from Elesford, (the capital town of the Cenimagni,) which road is still in existence, and partly used to this day,* stands a most conspicuous circular mound,† at present covered with trees and shrubs, and called "Ruehill Wood."‡

---

* The miserable condition of this road nearly entailed upon the parish of Dartford an outlay of upwards of a thousand pounds for repair during the past year. H. Lowe, esq., of North Cray and Mount Mascal, having purchased considerable property in the neighbourhood found the value thereof would be much increased by the restoration in a serviceable condition of this one of the earliest of British trackways. Thereupon, he instituted legal proceedings against the parish of North Cray and compelled its Surveyors to renovate their portion of the road. After this success, Notices were served upon the proper Dartford parochial authorities, who called a Vestry to consider the demand, at which, 'it was resolved to be opposed' on the plea, that the right had been so long in abeyance as to be now lost. The death of Mr. Lowe in February, 1844, prevented litigation.

† On the southern side of Dartford Heath.

‡ Ruehill is evidently a corruption of the old Celtic word Tyrru, which is from Twr, a heap, an accumulation. Thus, its modern name with the merest alteration has descended to our time in utter defiance of the various languages imported by the different masters of the land, Romans, Saxons, Danes and Normans. The name too is expressive of accumulation of material, or the formation of an ar-

This was undoubtedly the position to which Cæsar alludes, as admirably defended both by nature and art, and certainly still exhibits a splendid specimen of early British military strategy and skill. Even Hasted, *(note to p. 234,)* but a slight observer of these subjects, says, 'in the woods hereabouts there have been found quantities of bricks and other building materials,' which he hints to have been 'perhaps the remains of depopulation occasioned by the Wars between the houses of York and Lancaster,' had this latter hypothesis been at all founded in fact, tradition would most certainly have handed down some legendary tale, of the annihilation of a town so recently as the wars of the Roses. But, Hasted has himself, in the preceding page, utterly disproved the conjecture, by stating that the manor of Ruehill or Rowhill, 'was, in the reign of King Edward, in the possession of the family of Gyse,' and concludes the paragraph by giving its descent through the different lords to 1778; when he published

---

tificial mound, or earthwork. The artificial portion has been heaped on the summit of a lofty natural elevation, and forms nearly a complete circle. The vallum and foss by which it was environed have been obliterated by the plough. It stands in a wood now containing upwards of an hundred acres, and is supposed to occupy about six acres of land at the base. This mound from its great altitude was in the present century, selected by the Government, (who purchased an acre on the top,) and used it as a position for the site of a telegraph.—Adjoining to the mound, but quite detached, is a smaller earthwork or fortalice, on the summit of which is a deep round excavation like a well, which a labourer, on the 18th of March last, informed me, at the bottom extended for some distance, and was strongly arched; it had then been, but a few weeks before, wattled round, to prevent accidents.

his History of Kent. That there are great quantities of Roman bricks and other building materials, and nearly one hundred finely formed British excavations or pits scattered through these woods, I have the confirmatory assurance of S. Landale, esq., a fellow labourer in the archæological vineyard, who has repeatedly noticed them while there shooting, and who moreover informed me, that I should find a mass of antient brickwork, in a court lodge at Hook Green Farm, (a building not a quarter of a mile from Rue-hill). It is therefore most probable that a villa was there erected some years after the conquest of Kent; since the city of the Cassii was not at once destroyed after the victories of Aulus Plautius, (A.D. 43,) but, by degrees fell into decay, after the divergence of the road from the sea coast into the better formed and more direct Watling Street, aided by the establishment of the station of Noviomagus [Dartford], which, (as shown in a subsequent page,) attracted and absorbed the aborigines, and gradually caused the desertion and final total abandonment of the British city.

"However, after the fall of his fortress of Tyrru, that brave commander Caswallon, changed his tactics, and incited the chiefs in Cæsar's rear to attack the camp on the sea coast.* Cæsar was then compelled to retrace his steps, and, as in the year before, was in such haste to embark and return, that he crowded his men (nothing

---

* Although the Segontiaci had made a peace with Cæsar (lib. v. ¶ xxi.) yet, Segonax joins (lib. v. ¶ xxii.) Cingetorix, Carmilius, and Taximagulus, in Caswallon's new confederacy to destroy the Roman invaders' fleet.

loth) into what ships he had and sailed away.* According to the best expositors upon Cæsar's Commentaries,
he could not have been more than thirty-two days
in Britain. From this, we must deduct sixteen required
for the reparation of the fleet after being damaged by the
equinoctial tides, and to which Cæsar had to return from
Chartham Downs after fighting his first battle with the
Britons. Thus, Cæsar had only sixteen days left for his
incursion, conquest, and return ; hence it becomes almost a
physical impossibility for Cæsar to have marched in eight
days so far as Coway Stakes, through, to him, an entirely
unknown, wild and bitterly opposed country, where, every
minute and hour of the day he had to endure the vexatious
skirmishing of the Essedarii,† (who never remained
long enough to be beaten,) that Caswallon had pur-
purposely retained to harass his foes. Besides, he not only
had to remove day by day the *materiel* of his invading
forces, but also to construct a camp,‡ which although
only an earthwork, yet was necessary to be done by his

---

* Tacitus, writing more than a century after Cæsar, distinctly says,
that even Cæsar, the first who entered Britain with an army, although
he struck terror into the islanders by a successful battle, could only
maintain himself on the sea coast ;—that he was a discoverer rather than
a conqueror. In fact, that he only saw a small portion of the island.
So, also Lucan, (lib. ii. v. 572.) reproaches Cæsar with running away
from the Britons ; Dion Cassius (lib. xxxix et xl.) also says " the Roman
infantry were entirely routed in a battle by them, and that Cæsar retired
from hence without effecting anything."

† Lib. v. ¶ xix.

‡ Sed eos fugientes, longiùs Cæsar persequi vetuit, et quòd loci
naturam ignorabat, et quòd magnâ parte diei consumptâ, munitioni
castrorum tempus relinqui volebat. Lib. v. ¶ viii.

wearied legions during day-light, else they would have been subjected to a night-attack similar to that Q. Laberius Durus* met his death endeavouring to repel. I also think it most probable, that the state of the Trinobantes was in the hundred of Hoo, because how otherwise could it have been possible for Cæsar during his rapid march to have received ambassadors, who had then to return and collect forty hostages, and procure from perchance north, east, west, and south, sufficient corn for the sustenance of the Roman troops and convey it across a mighty river like the Thames? Now, it is quite clear, that the extremely brief stay of Cæsar utterly precludes him from having delayed his march anywhere to wait for supplies. The road by which these exactions reached him is still in existence near Higham.

"The great road however continued over hill and dale to the city of the Cassii, which, it entered at the south-eastern extremity, [Stanhill]; and by Cauden's wood proceeded to North-cray. Prior to its entrance, it threw off two branches, one to the chief fortress, Tyrru; and another† to Stankey, the extreme northern point of the city.

---

* Q. Laberius Durus was buried at Chartham Downs. Mr. Fagg in the eighteenth century opened the barrow, and was rewarded by finding many relics. (Douglas, Nenia Brit.) Eo die Q. Laberius Durus tribunus mil. interficitur: illi, pluribus submissis cohortibus, repellentur.

† When Mr. Elliott, the present tenant, first occupied the farm, this road was perceptible — the track gradually disappeared and merged into the arable land by continual ploughing, that the slightest depression is all that now remains. Mr. Elliott in whose veins flows true British blood and who is a stanch conservator of old

"To protect the main road, and the southern end of the city was erected an artificial earthwork, which might have been also used as a mound, whence

'Flaming beacons cast their blaze afar
The dreadful signal of invasive war.'

On the south-western side of this earthwork may clearly be seen developed the broad terraces*, by which, it was erst surrounded. The modern name of the mound, which comprises about two acres, is Greenhill,† corrupted from the Celtic word Cruan‡, the summit, the topmost height,

---

privileges, has lately caused a waggon and team to traverse the field to prevent the right of road-way being lost to future generations. *Ex inform. R. Allen, Armig.*

* The British Kings lived apart from their subjects on lofty eminences.

† Length across E = W. 112 paces; N = S. 110.

‡ Bishop Percy states, that in England 'although the names of the towns and villages are generally of Anglo-Saxon derivation, yet the hills, forests, rivers, etc., have almost universally retained their old Celtic names. This neighbourhood presents most strikingly confirmatory examples of this statement; as shewn in *Twyrru*, Ruehill; *Cruan*, Greenhill; *Gogr*, Cau, or Cawden's, or Jorden's, or Joyden's Wood, (for it has all these variations.) *Jones on the Origin of Language and Nations.* The Anglo-Saxon name of the city, at the commencement, is *Stane*-hill; and at the end, *Stane*-key. Because, although *tan* is a Celtic particle, like *cau*, which, as previously shewn, signifies, to shut or enclose, yet, the Saxon names to these two spots, seem to have clung to the present day. *Tan*, is primitive, "spreading, an expansive principle, or continuous." *Owen Geiradur.* Stan-key is immediately corrupted from Stán-scylie, stoneshally, stony. Again, it is evident, Cauden's is from the Celtic word *Gogr*, which is derived from *cau-o-cau'r* the inclosures, or holes from shutting or keeping. A great number of the excavations are in that portion of the wood, attached nevertheless, termed 'College Land,' from whence the city proceeds to Stankey. Nor is Stankey

the crown, derived from the primitive *cau-ar-en*, an enclosure shut, or covering on the highest end.

"The city of the Cassii was somewhat in the shape of an irregular triangle, and commenced at the southern point at Stanhill, in the parish of Dartford, and extended directly north-westward to Stankey.

"At the southern end of the city traces are everywhere found of former habitations, and even in a field at the back of Mr. Allen's homestead at Stanhill, during the growth of a crop of peas, where a plough and team passed over but a few days previously, the ground, this spring tide has given way, and left gaping, a frightful hole, considered to be 60 or 70 feet in depth;—about twenty yards from this, in a direct line in the adjoining field, is the clear mark of another pit, partly filled in, many, many years ago, and now grown over with greensward, and I stated to the pro-

---

distant more than two miles, as the crow flies, from Crayford, where, *Hasted*, i. 24, says, there are in the heaths, 'fields and woods many' similar pits, 'or artificial caves, some of which, are ten, some fifteen, and others twenty fathoms deep,' which, he describes, as being also 'at the mouth, and thence downward, narrow like the tunnel of a chimney, or passage of a well, but at the bottom they are large and of great compass, insomuch that some of them have several rooms or partitions one within another, strongly vaulted and supported with pillars of chalk.' *Tacit. de Mor. Ger. c.* 16., writing of the Germans, whose habits were similar to the Britons, says, 'they were accustomed to dig subterraneous caverns, and then cover them over with much loose mould, where they lay up provisions, and dwell in winter; into these receptacles they also used to retire whilst their enemies were plundering the open country.' *Diodorus Siculus* also states that the Britons laid up their harvest in subterranean repositories.

prietor whilst going over the farm in April 1844, that there could be little doubt in the pit which this season had exhibited itself, being the centre of three, and moreover pointed out a depression in the pea-field, where I supposed was the vent, and which, in the course of time might give way, when between the three would be found a connection for the purposes of adition. Mr. Allen declared, that had the ground but sunk whilst ploughing, the accident must have been most serious, as nothing could have saved one of the horses, and most likely the lives of two would have been sacrificed.

"Distant barely a quarter of a mile from these remains, on the same farm, are three other excavations in an angle, which have now *all* fallen in, and, at the very least, comprise a quarter of an acre of ground. When the present proprietor obtained the premises, he imagined, like his predecessors, that the entrance to the largest was nothing but a rabbit burrow, till, one day, coney shooting, he slipped in, and was unable to extricate himself without assistance, he then procured a pole and tried to sound for the bottom, in which he failed. Shortly after this, the land around gave way, exhibiting a vast bowl-shaped hollow, into which upwards of two hundred loads of soil have been thrown, in the vain hope of levelling it with the surrounding field.

"Within sixty yards of these hollows is a protecting earthwork; the preceding proprietor caused the roots of the trees and shrubs that grew on either side to be grubbed up. In fact, in consequence of the value of the land, an unremitting warfare against these British vestiges, has been levied by every successive cultivator of the ground from the period of its abandonment as a city—and were it not, that a great portion of these remains are in woods, retained in their normal uncleared condition not a trace would have been left, save the artificial mounds, to mark the spot where Caswallon made his glorious stand

' To stay the progress of th' invading foe.'

but alas! the axe of the spoiler is still wielded, and although Mr. Allen, the present possessor of a great portion of the territory, would gladly preserve these relics; yet, a higher power has issued its fiat of destruction, and the progress of dis-forresting owing to the declining value of woodland is rapidly proceeding. During this process in January, 1844, was discovered another pit, and, at about the usual distance is visible, a corresponding sinking of the ground, shewing that there, the archway was not strong enough to support the superincumbent weight of soil. As within the last four years, no less than six of these covered excavations have developed themselves, may not the conclusion safely be deduced, that, whilst Time for nineteen centuries has been relentlessly fulfilling his devastating destiny hundreds of these caverns have given way and been filled in by the farmers. Because it is now only in woody recesses, such as Cawden's wood the most western, and Stankey the most northern, that these excavations exist in numbers; there indeed, they are, to use the game-keeper's expression, 'as thick as rabbit-burys.'

' Mind creates and re-creates,
Bids cities, long destroyed, resume
    Their pomp of pride, and all life's stir,
Then leaves them once more to their doom
    Engulphed in Time's vast sepulchre.' "   *Keane.*

AFTER these extracts from Mr. Alfred John Dunkin's articles in the Gentleman's Magazine and his "Kentish Chronicles," probably the reader will expect some reasons should be assigned for considering DARTFORD the antient Roman station of NOVIOMAGUS, especially when the discovery of the remains of a Roman temple, tombs, etc., at Keston, by that able antiquary, A. J. Kempe, esq.,* under the auspices of the Society of Antiquaries, seemed to have settled the site past conjecture; sanctioned as that opinion was by the establishment of the Noviomagian club, which for some years commemorated the discovery by an annual dinner at Keston-Mark, and also, by the adoption of the same theory by the Society for the Diffusion of Useful Knowledge; as shewn in their map of Roman Britain.   Yet, having at that time, the honor of a personal intimacy with Mr. Kempe, the writer well remembers his remark that his opportunities of obtaining satisfactory indications of the former existence of the streets or public buildings of a Roman town were not sufficiently conclusive to produce a decided conviction.

The remarks of that gentleman, combined with the discovery of stone coffins,† and numerous graves‡ on

---

* The researches at Keston, originated in some remarks in a small Tract written by Mr. Kempe, which induced the writer to apply to the Rev. Sir C. F. Farnaby, to obtain permission for Mr. Crofton Croker to make the excavations in June, 1828 ; Mr. Kempe continued them in the following October.

† Three stone coffins have been already taken up, and probably others remain in the same ground.

‡ The graves were all found to be north and south, like those at the War-bank, Keston. In one was found a lachrymatory, and in another a præfericulum. *Vide* p. 93.

East Hill, amidst which, many crumbling urns, fragments of pottery, and glass vessels were found, led
the writer to submit several of them to the inspection of
some eminent antiquaries whose opinion perfectly coin-
cided with his own, that they were decidedly Roman.
His attention was next called to the antient Roman plan
of the streets at Dartford crossing each other nearly at
right angles. Further investigation, aided by a series of
coins, discovered on the spot,* once a Roman cemetery,
enabled him clearly to retrace the town through the
Saxons to the Roman domination. And although a
comparison of the distances of the Roman stations from

---

* Coins in the possession of Mr. Landale, found in the Roman Burial-
place on East Hill.

Vespasian. One specimen in second brass, badly preserved.

Trajan. A denarius—*Reverse*, Titles.

Faustina. Ditto.

Lucilla. One specimen in large brass, much worn.

Diocletian. One specimen in third brass,—*Reverse*, IOVI. CY. AVGG.

Maximian. One ditto,—*Reverse*, GENIO. POP. ROM. ; in the area B, and a
star in the exergue, TR.

Postumus. A denarius,— *Reverse*, VIRTVS. AVG.

Gordianus Pius. Ditto,—*Reverse*, AETERNITATI. AVG.

Constantine and family. Three or four of common types.

Constantinopolis One specimen.

Thus, from the few straggling specimens recorded above, we safely
conclude that at the time of Constantine or later, the Cemetery was
resorted to by the neighbouring people for the burial of the dead. Had
other coins been preserved, they would probably have shewn that it was
in use up to the period when the Romans departed from Britain. *Letter
from Mr. Charles Roach Smith to the author.*

A*

London as given in the different versions of the Roman Itineraries,* shew that no decided evidence of their precise situation can be obtained from those records, yet if any reliance may be placed on that of Richard de Cirencestre, (according to Stukeley, the best authority,) who places the Roman station of Noviomagus† at 15

---

* The following discrepancies appear in the various Itineraries.

ANTONINUS.	RICHARD OF CIRENCESTRE.
ITER II.	ITER XV.
A Londino ad Portum Ritupis.	*A Dubris ad Londinium.*
Noviomago M.P. x.	Rhutupium x.
Vagniacis M.P. xviii.	Cantiopolis Stipendiaria
Durobrovis M.P. ix.	Durolevum
Durolevo M.P. xvi.	Madum xii.
Duroverno M.P. xii.	Vagniaca xviii.
ad portum Ritupis M.P. xii.	Noviomagus xv.
	Londinium Augusta

In Iter XVII. *(R de Cirencestre)* the distance is also stated at 15 miles.

† Dr. Stukeley says, we hereby correct Antoninus, in the distance between London and Novoamagus, xv. miles, ; whereas in the other it is but x. Yet Stukeley following Camden, places it near Croydon, *Itinerarum Curiosum,* ii. 135. *Lon.* 1776.

In Burton's Commentary on Anto- *ninus the distances are thus given*	William Harrison *states the dis- tances and affixes the stations to the following places :*
Noviomago m.p. xii.	Noviomago m.p. x. *Leusham*
Vagniacis m.p. vi.	Vagniacis m.p. xviii. *Maidstone*
Durobrovis m.p. v.	Durobrovis m.p. v. *Rochester*

The site of the Noviomagus of Antonine, or the Noiomagus of the Greek geographer, Ptolemy, has long been an undecided point among antiquaries, although many high authorities concur in placing it near Holwood-hill. Camden assigned its situation at Woodcote, near Croydon, which very ill agrees with its distance from Vagniacæ, near Maidstone, as marked by the imperial Itinerary. *Kempe's Account of some*

miles distance from London, on the road to Rutupium or Richborough,* it affords convincing proof that the site of Dartford must have been the original Novioma-gus. If it be objected that there is no historic record of any tesselated pavements or other Roman remains discovered in Dartford, let it be remembered that the site of the town has been subjected to the incessant alterations incident to the caprices of a changing popu-lation for 1,400 years at the least, and then let the reader imagine how few relics of such a distant period could possibly exist, besides, the general incompetence and reluctance of residents to investigate and record such matters as are, from time to time developed, is evinced by the circumstance, that *no account* of the discovery

---

Discoveries at Holwood-hill. Archæl v. xxii. Burton, in his commentary on Antoninus's Itinerary says, it is most probable the name of the place was brought out of Gallia Belgica, and is very ancient, for Ptolemy reprehends Marinus Tyrius for placing the Noviomagus of Britain considerably northward of London. He further adds, some placed it at Chester, Sir Thomas Eliat at Buckingham, Humphrey Lluid at Guild-ford. William Harrison derives the town's name from Magus, the son of Samothes, the son of the second king of the Celts that reigned in this island. Magus among the old Gauls signifying oppidam, or a town. p. 176. In this instance, as Noviomagus was found to be gradually supplanting the *adjacent city* of the Cassii, is not the Roman name literally significant of its being the NEW LARGE TOWN?

* Somner says, he cannot conceive how writers have made the Noviomagus which was evidently *a stage* on the road, *leading from* London to Richborough, *so many miles* out of the *direct line*, and therefore, looking along the Richborough road, he, (in accordance with the distance of miles from London given by Antoninus) is inclined to place it at Crayford, although, as Hasted rightly says, there are neither foundations, tiles, urns, nor other vestiges of antiquity to confirm its having been a Roman station.

of a Roman burial ground in this place, has appeared in any previous publication. Additional proof of its being Noviomagus may be found in the latin termination of its name, which, says Somner, "according to Claverius, (Germania Antiqua, I. i. p. 64. 37.) shews the town to be situated near a ford or river."

Besides, it has the general marks of a Roman station as enumerated by Fosbroke: 1st, It stood on the line of a great Roman road, (the Watling street); 2ndly, a number of others pointed to it, especially one along the line of the Darenth, which abounds with Roman remains;* 3dly, it stood at the precise distance (fifteen miles) from London, named in the Roman Itinerary of Richard de Cirencestre, on the direct road to Rutupium; whereas, there is no evidence of any great road ever passing by Keston from Maidstone, and thence in a straight line towards London.†

---

* Mr. Carlos is decidedly of opinion, that the walls of Darenth church are Roman, (*Gent's Mag. Sept.* 1838); and my friend Mr. Cresy, informed me that he discovered the remains of a Roman edifice near his residence, South Darenth.

† Even Mr. Kempe in endeavouring to reconcile the distance of Keston from London at ten miles, as Noviomagus is described by Antoninus, states his "measurements were accomplished by applying the compasses to the Ordnance map of Kent, by the scale, and measuring from the south side of London bridge in the direction of Holwood 10 miles according to Antonine, and thence in the same manner 18 miles, when the point falls at Maidstone."

Memoranda

of

Dartford.

DARTFORD.

———

ETYMOLOGY.—The celebrity of the ford over the river Darenth, imparted its name to the adjacent town, which in most of the ancient instruments was written Daɼenꞇɼoɼꝺ.   The Norman scribes, however, at the compilation of Domesday-book entered it in that record *Tarentford*, either from ignorance, or a wilful design to disguise its Saxon origin.

SITUATION AND BOUNDARY.

Dartford and Wilmington though now constituting a Hundred of themselves in West Kent, were anciently comprised in that of Axtane, and dissevered by some of the early kings after the conquest, in consequence of being a royal demesne.   It is comprehended in the Lathe of Sutton-at-Hone.

The parish of Dartford lies on the high road from London to Dover, and is entered a few yards on the

B

western side of the fourteenth mile-stone. Its boundaries stretch along those of Crayford, by the junction of the Cray with the Creek to the Thames; and then proceeding along its banks for about two miles, suddenly turns to the south-east—when, passing to the left of Littlebrook over the hill of Temple farm, again crosses the Dover road near the sixteenth mile-stone: from thence after going over Trendly-down, turns round and crosses the Darenth above the powder mills, and running in a westerly direction over the turnpike-road leading from Dartford to Sevenoaks, proceeds along the boundaries of Wilmington to Baldwins, which it includes; then stretching along the western edge of Dartford heath, goes north-east until it reaches the before mentioned point of the Dover road near the fourteenth mile-stone.

Hasted describes "the upland parts of this parish" as "thin and gravelly," but says, the crops were greatly increased by the culture of turnips; that the vallies more than the upland were inclined to loam—that behind Baldwins and towards Stanhill, there was a stiff clay—that part of the priory farm bordering on the marshes was a good mould, and that the northern part of the parish containing eight hundred acres reaching to the Thames is wholly marsh land, none of which is ever ploughed.* He adds, forty acres of this land lie on the western side of the Creek next Crayford, and about one hundred acres of meadow on the side of the river:—that, above the town are three hundred acres of wood, and there are about five hundred acres of waste on Dartford Heath, and fifty on the Brent.

---

* Since this publication, some parts have been placed under culture.

In the survey and valuation of the houses, mill, and machinery property in the parish of Dartford, made by order of the Board of Guardians of the Dartford Union, in the months of November, December, January and February 1837 and 1838, and finished in May, by T. W. Carter, surveyor, Maidstone, the total amount of the Net Rent as passed by him, is stated at £15,986 8s.

And in the survey and valuation of the arable, meadow, plantation, wood, orchard and other lands, including the Rectorial and Vicarial Tithes,* made and delivered by James Russell of Horton Kirby, June the 23rd, 1838, the gross estimated rental is stated to be £7,296 5s. and the rateable value £4,923.

The survey and valuation of the parish made by Messrs. Russell and Elliott, in 1840, for the tithe apportionment, gives the following summary,

	A	R.	P.
Land—Arable, Meadow, etc.	3724	2	39¾
Houses, Buildings, Yards, Gardens, etc.	46	0	21½
Dartford Heath—Common and Waste Land‡	329	3	38
TOTAL	4,100	3	9¾†

---

* The Rectorial Tithes are thus stated. Gross value £694. Rateable value £425. Vicarial, Gross value £528. Rateable value £337 13s. 4d.

† The loose nature of former estimates, is thus shown by facts. From a survey made in 1626, there appeared to be 2,883 acres of land in the parish; Hasted says it contained 4,300; but Mr. Landale avers that by a return made to the House of Lords in 1827, they are only given at two thousand seven hundred and twenty-four and a-half acres.

‡ Dartford Brent is stated to contain 42A. OR. 36P. of pasture and furze, and entered among the lands of Messrs. Pigou.

		£	s.	d.
Rent charge payable to the Vicar	560	10	0
Rent charge payable to the Rector	807	4	10*

In May 1841, the *occupied premises* were estimated at a Net Rental of £18,947 3s. 6d., and a Poor Rate granted thereon at nine-pence in the pound, which was expected to produce £710 11s. 4¾d.

The supplemental appendix to the Poor Rate returns, states that the sum raised for that purpose in Dartford A. D. 1816, was £1,532 14s.; in 1817, £2,026 7s.; in 1819, £1,937 12s.; in 1820, £2,068; and in 1821, £2,076 7s. 0d.

POPULATION, ETC.

The Census being directed by Act of Parliament to be taken in one day, June 7th, 1841, the parish was divided into districts for that purpose, and the following are the returns of each district:

DISTRICT 1. That part of the parish from the Turnpike gate, on the north and south sides of the road leading to Maiden lane, and all that part on Dartford Heath and Stone Hill. Length, 5 miles; breadth, 1 mile, 4 furlongs. Computed distance as traversed by the enumerator, 7 furlongs. Contains 118 inhabited houses; 2 uninhabited, and 9 building; 271 males, 316 females; Total 587. Persons not enumerated, 23 males, 32 females; Total 55.

---

* The Rent Charge is calculated upon the following estimate:

	s.	d.	Bush.	Decim. pts.
Price of Wheat *per bushel*	7	0¼	1,298	14,580
Barley *per ditto.*	3	11½	2,203	56,491
Oats *per ditto.*	2	9	3,315	73,137

DISTRICT 2. That part of the parish lying on the south side of the road from the Turn-pike gate, to the One Bell corner, and all that part of the parish which lies from the One Bell corner on the west side of Low-field to the Orange Tree. Length, 1 mile, 4 furlongs; breadth, 7 furlongs. Computed distance as traversed by the enumerator, 3 furlongs. Contains 147 inhabited houses, 4 uninhabited and 0 building; 419 males, 409 females; Total 828. Persons not enumerated, 3 males.

DISTRICT 3. That part of the parish lying on the south side of the High street from the Bridge to the Town-pump, and all that part of Lowfield street on the east side from the Pump to the Orange Tree; and all that part of the parish which lies between the Orange Tree and the river Darenth. Length, 1 mile, 4 furlongs; breadth, 5 furlongs. Computed distance as traversed by the enumerator, 2 furlongs. Contains 130 inhabited houses, 7 uninhabited houses, and 1 building; 363 males, 400 females; Total 763.

DISTRICT 4. All that part of the parish which lies on the north side of the High street from the Bridge to the Waterside street and all that part of the east side of Waterside street to the Creek's mouth. Length, 1 mile, 2 furlongs; breadth, 6 furlongs. Computed distance as traversed by the enumerator, less than 200 yards. Contains 151 inhabited houses, 6 uninhabited, and 0 building; 426 males, 404 females; Total 830. Persons not enumerated, 6 males, 0 females; Total 6.

DISTRICT 5. That part of the parish lying on the north side of the road down Spital street to the chemist's shop; and all the west side of Waterside street from the chemist's shop to the Creek's mouth; and all that part of the parish on the west side of the Creek. Length, 1 mile 4 furlongs; breadth, 7 furlongs; computed distance as traversed by enumerator, 3 furlongs. Contains 205 inhabited houses, 19 uninhabited, and 0 building; 517 males, 550 females; Total 1,067. Persons not enumerated, 11 males, 14 females; Total 25.

DISTRICT 6. That part of the parish lying on the east side of the river Darenth, from the bottom of Overy street to the Powder mills, and all that part of the parish on the Brent, and all the marshes on the east side of the Creek in the parish. Length, 5 miles; breadth, 1 mile. Computed distance as traversed by enumerator, 7 furlongs. Contains 206 inhabited houses, 17 uninhabited, and 0 building; 584 males, 556 females; Total 1,140. Persons not enumerated, 35 males, 52 females; Total 87.

This Census therefore makes the following as the total return of the population and number of houses in Dartford. Inhabited houses, 957; uninhabited 55; buildings, 10; males, 2,580; females, 2,535; Total 5,215. Persons computed not to have been enumerated in the foregoing list, 78 males, 98 females. Total 176.

DESCRIPTION OF THE TOWN.

The town of Dartford built on either side of the great road leading from London to Dover, is situated in a valley between two hills which rise abruptly at both extremities. On the western hill is the handsome residence of Mr. Landale, to whose valuable labours the Inhabitants are indebted for the judicious "Abstract of wills, leases, and legal documents, relating to the several public charities and endowments of the parish." The brow of the hill is crowned by the turnpike, and on the left are a row of houses, chiefly erected by the before mentioned gentleman, and Mr. Robert Okill. Further down are chalk pits, which, having been worked for ages, present rather a fearful and dangerous appearance to travellers. Below is the National School, erected in 1826, a somewhat tasty structure;—and nearly contiguous are the Spital Houses, re-founded by John Beer in the reign of queen Elizabeth as a substitute for a more ancient hospital for leperous persons, which gave name to the street,—the present building was erected by Mr. Twisleton in 1704; on the opposite side of the road is a deep and sandy loam, where, on a plot formerly called *Lurchin's Hole*, in 1728 the parish erected a commodious workhouse by public subscription, which has since given place to the Union house. Here is the principal road which led to the Priory, the grand entrance to which was situated on the southern side of the quadrangle. On the top of this road, amid some ruinous buildings nearly opposite the workhouse, is *Zion* Chapel, an edifice of humble pretensions, belonging to the Independents, now chiefly supplied with preachers either by Lady Huntington's connection, or the London Itinerant society.   As we descend Spital street, Dartford assumes the appearance of a handsome and wealthy town, having the residence of Mrs. Stainton Hall on the left,* and the dwellings of some very respectable tradesmen on either side.   Opposite Hithe street† is the Bull Inn or Victoria Hotel,‡ an excellent

---

* Dr. John Latham, the celebrated ornithologist, resided in a mansion upon this site. He was born at Eltham, studied Anatomy under the famous Dr. William Hunter, and commenced medical practice at Dartford in 1763, at the age of twenty-two. A few years after he became noted for his collections in Natural History, and devoted much attention to his favourite pursuit. He stuffed and set up with his own hands almost every animal in his extensive museum, and when he commenced his elaborate work on ornithology, made his own drawings, and actually etched every copper plate. Notwithstanding his correspondence and numerous avocations he was one of the most punctual men of business, and ever attentive to the duties and courtesies of life. A practice of thirty-two years realised a handsome fortune. He left Dartford in 1795, and retired to Romsey in Hampshire; but at the age of eighty a series of calamities plunged him in utter destitution. All his valuable library was sold, and his copy of Hasted's Kent enriched with his own notes and drawings of places in Dartford and its neighbourhood, purchased and carried by a baronet to his seat in Hertfordshire, where it remained until 1839, when it was once more sold to the present writer, in whose possession it now remains. Dr. Latham died Feb. 6th, 1837, at the advanced age of ninety-seven. His remains are deposited in the abbey church of Romsey.—He left a history of that place in manuscript.

† The waters of the Cranpit, issuing from beneath the arch of the bridge opposite the Bull, formerly gave this part of the town a very romantic appearance in the estimation of strangers.

‡ Lady Fermanaugh presented to the Bull Inn, a very large mirror that had been brought from Bowman's Lodge on the heath, once the

THE "BLACK BOY" INN.

THE "ONE BELL" INN.

establishment, the chief posting house in the town, kept by Mr. Potter, and at the corner of Lowfield street, is the One Bell.

Here the High street assumes a wide and noble appearance, chiefly occasioned by the removal of the shambles and market-house in 1769 to their present situation,* and may be considered the principal mart for business, abounding with handsome shops, well stocked with a choice assortment of goods tastefully displayed. At the corner of Lowfield, is an ancient mansion, although the present front in the High street is modernised, erected by the heirs of John Martin in 1591,† (34 Elizabeth,) on the site of one

property of the Prince of Wales afterwards George the Fourth. *Mrs. Pott's Moonshine.* iii 347.

* The butcher's shambles nearly occupied the entire space from the end of Lowfield street to the Cranpit which runs under the east side of Mr. Taylor's shop. The market-house stood at the end of the shambles, and reached from thence along the front of Messrs. Hill's Bank. The structure consisted of a long room supported by stone columns, originally designed for a Town Hall, but latterly used for the purposes of the grammar school. The open space beneath, afforded shelter for the corn pitched for sale, and other commodities brought to the market. These buildings thus standing on the south side of the High street only admitted a narrow passage between themselves and the houses, rendering the high road exceedingly inconvenient and dangerous to vehicles passing each other. On market and fair days the street must have been absolutely choked up.

Near this spot also stood a Market Cross, erected after the model of the cross in the market-place at Sevenoaks, in the reign of Henry VI., by John Sherborne, pursuant to the will of John, his father, who gave a messuage in Dartford for that purpose. *Reg. Lib. Test. Roff.* i. 8.

† John Martin, the ancestor of the family, one of the king's

heretofore inhabited by that family for many generations; a part is now occupied by Mr. Hodsoll, a coach-maker, and another portion constitutes the King's Head public house*; adjoining is Mr. A. J. Dunkin's residence†; opposite is the Bull's Head; at a short distance the Black Boy; and nearly contiguous the Post Office.

---

justices, temp. Henry the sixth, founded a Chantry in Our Lady's chapel in Dartford church, where he was buried. His descendants possessed considerable estates in the neighbourhood. Margaret, a daughter of Edward, the great grandson of John Martin, carried it in marriage to William Brown of Horton Kirby, who seems to have been the builder of the present mansion. The front in Lowfield street has undergone little alteration, and may be regarded as a specimen of the domestic architecture of that age. The pointed-arch doorway now blocked up, led immediately to the hall near the centre of the edifice, a considerable part of which still remains, and is used as the kitchen of the King's Head. The noble arched window divided by stone mullions, and the expansive fire-place still attest the importance of the edifice to which they belonged. The back of the premises extended to the Cranpit.

* In the reign of Henry the eighth, a cottage held by one John Bodemay, clerk or priest (for Andrew Dolbing), stood on the site of the King's Head public house; it is described in a rental of St. John's Preceptory as "a cottage in the market-place of Dartford betwixt the messuage of John Martin on the sowthe and west, and a cartwaye leading to the messuage of the said John Martin on the est;" it paid 14d., quit-rent to the Knights of St. John yearly. *Vide Rentale de Dertforde cum Sutton-at-Hone, renovatum xx die Marcii, anno primo Henrici viij., tempore venerabilis Fratris Domini Thomi Docwra, prioris Hospitalis S. Johannis Jer' l'm in Anglia.* MSS. Addit. No. 9,493. Brit. Mus.

† The same rental says, that the cartway of the said John Martin (now the site of Mr. A. J. Dunkin's residence), had, sometime previously, namely in the reign of Henry VII., constituted part of a messuage of John le Berr [of Horsman's Place], and that it also

The Town Hall, Market-house and Cage are situated about the middle of the High street*. The former are enclosed with gates, and standing somewhat behind the houses, are not visible to strangers passing through the town. In the Town Hall the justices of the peace hold their petty sessions every fortnight for the district; and on the third Friday in every month the commissioners of the Court of Requests, hold a sitting for the recovery of debts under five pounds.

Opposite is a large inn and posting house called the Bull and George; and on the adjoining site of some new shops, formerly stood the mansion of the manor of Charles, built by William D'Aith in the reign of queen Elizabeth. On the other side of the street is the residence of Mr. Fleet, late that of Mr. Caldecott†; and a messuage now in the occupation of Mr. Kemp as a butcher's shop, was used during the greater

---

paid a quit rent to St. John's of 2s. 4d. per annum. In after ages, the messuage built thereon was a public house, and known as "the Butcher's Arms." Ex origin penes J. Dunkin. The Dunkins are descendants of an Oxfordshire family settled at Merton from the time of Queen Elizabeth. Many particulars appear in the History of the Hundreds of Bullington and Ploughly, ij 48—54.

Between Martin's cartway and the Cranpit stood four shops, part of the endowments of the chantry of our blessed lady of Dartford, these paid 9d. quit rent and suit of court.

* The pillory stood nearly opposite the present market-house; and one Lawes and his wife were nearly the last who stood in it for keeping an house of ill fame in Spital street.—They resided in a part of the house lately occupied by Mr. Kingston.

† Mr. Caldecott was the representative of the family of Senhouse of Nether-Hall, Cumberland. Burke's Genealogical Hist. i. 216. He was a noted collector of old English Books.

part of the seventeenth century as the House of Correction.

The house at the east corner of Bullis lane now occupied by Mr. Stidolph an upholsterer, was the dwelling of John Groverste in the reign of king Edward the fourth; that gentleman in 1465 obtained permission of the vicar and churchwardens of Dartford, to erect a chimney (still standing) on a part of the church yard,* and in acknowledgment thereof provided a lamp to burn perpetually, during the celebration of divine service in the parish church. The house has undergone many alterations, yet its overhanging upper floors convey a very fair idea of a mansion in the fifteenth century, and the warehouse or shop still exhibits all the interior appearance of the ancient hall; the original arched entrance is apparent in Bullis lane.‡

---

* Regist. Roff. 314. Chimneys were not common in private dwellings in the reign of Hen. VIII. Even Leland when he visited Bolton Castle was greatly surprised at the novelty and ingenuity of the contrivance, "one thing" says he "I much notyd in the haull of Bolton, how chimeneys was conveyed by tunnills made in the sydds of the waulls betwixt the lights; and by this means is the smoke of the harthe wonder-strangely convayed." The front of St. John's Hospital, Litchfield, erected 1475, presents one of the most curious ancient specimens extant of this part of our domestic architecture. Gents. Mag. 230, March, 1829.

‡ The principal apartment in the upper floor (a room about 25 by 20ft.), was originally hung round with tapestry, said to be worked by the nuns at the priory, who were occasionally permitted to visit at the mansion. The principal figures were in armour, and two of them as large as life, latterly called Hector and Andromache; in the back ground was the representation of a large army with inscribed banners. The colours of

In 1792 the western corner of the north aisle of the church was rounded off, and a portion of the church-yard added to the highway, which by their projection had heretofore been rendered narrow and dangerous. Nearly adjoining to the end of the south aisle, pursuant to an order of vestry, the parish officers erected an engine-house, but a subsequent vestry refusing to sanction the expense it was almost immediately after, taken down.*

A commodious bridge crosses the Darenth; on the right is the Vicarage, and nearly adjoining, anciently stood a fulling mill† on the site of the present corn mill occupied by Messrs. Hards and Hills.

On the acclivity of the east hill, on the left side of the Darenth road, are two rows of houses erected by Mr. Landale, called St. Ronan's and the Crescent.

The steep ascent of the Dover road leading towards the Brent, was in ancient times called *St. Edmunde's weye*, from its leading to a chapel dedicated to that saint, situated near the middle of the upper church yard.

---

the worsted remained quite brilliant although the tapestry itself was decayed ; it was taken down by Miss Mary Brand about 1817, and no part is now in existence. The "blue room" was supposed to have been an oratory. Old legends say, a ghost was laid under one of the floors and that when the floor was taken up the inmates were terrified by unearthly noises. His ghostship, however, has long fled before the increased intelligence of the age. The Rev. Mr. Currey always main-tained that the footpath leading into Bullis lane was a private road from the nunnery to the church.

* The expense thus thrown upon Mr. William Shepperd, the church-warden, together with the costs of a lawsuit thereon, amounted to £550 which the first vestry proposed to raise by annuity, 29th June, 1827, but the order was rescinded and the mockery of a *subscription* recommended. *(Vestry Book.)* It is said to have broken his heart.

† *Ministers' Accompt Roll*, 32. *Hen.* 8.

Near the foot of the bridge running northwards is
Overy street ;* in every age studded with habitations of
wealthy persons.   Portions of former mansions still remain and impart thereunto an air of venerable antiquity.†
The two tenements on the left hand, called "the
church" or "parish houses,"‡ as well as the house
to which the adjoining gateway was attached, were
evidently dwellings of the gentry or substantial yeomen
in the fifteenth century; and the gothic brick-work

---

* Overy or Over-ey, *over the river.*   Rea, or Ray, is an appellative for
a river. *Kennett's Glossary.*

† Vide *Parish Books, Wills and other Documents.*

‡ Thomas Taylor of Dartford, by will, dated 16th Feb. 1476, gave the
house where he dwelt in Overy, to Beatrice, his wife, for her life, and,
after her decease, directed that it be sold by his executors, and "with
the money thereof be fownde a priest singing in the church of Dertford
by half a yer, praying for" his "sowl and for all" his friends; and the
residue of the money to be distributed in deeds of charity to the most
worship of God, and profit of" his "soule" *Reg. Test.* iii. 568.

John Morley of Dartford being sick, by his last will and testament, dated 10th November, 1533, gave the tenement wherein he
lived and the garden belonging to the same in Overy-street, after
the decease of Denys his wife, to Robert Derby, to cause a four-
pound taper of wax to be set before the sepulchre in the church of
Dartford at Easter every year, for ever, at his sole cost, and charges
out of the house; and if the said Robert Derby to whom the house
is given for that purpose, did not cause it to be done, then, the
churchwardens of Dartford, for the time being, should enter upon
the same, and hold them for the finding of the said taper: the adjoining house (of which the gateway remains perfect) he directed to
be sold, and one half of the proceeds to be given to John Morley
his son and the other half expended in deeds of charity.   His son
was constituted overseer and executor of this will. *Reg. Test. Ep.
Roffen.* ix. 111.   Eventually the churchwardens did enter upon and
retain the tenement, but as the provision of finding a taper was
only an incidental charge and not the value as a rental, and as there

niches in the chimney of the cottage lower down, once

---

was no specific appropriation of the remainder of the proceeds, the churchwardens of that day very properly allotted the premises for the habitation of the poor and destitute in all succeeding ages. At the Reformation this charge of a taper was extinguished, and the estate would have escheated to the crown as lands given for superstitious purposes (Stat. 1 Edw. VI. c. 14), had not their assignment to the relief of the poor prevented their being seized by the king's commissioners. Although all record of this benefaction has *disappeared* from the parish archives, for more than three hundred years successive generations of the poor reaped the benefit of this provision—and each successive parish officer amidst all the changes of religion and politics scrupulously fulfilled the obligations imposed upon him by his Roman catholic predecessors. Overseers of the poor were first appointed in 1597, 39 Eliz; but at what time the churchwardens of Dartford permitted them to place indigent poor in these houses is not clear: the retention of three pounds a year rental, notwithstanding the continued appropriation of the premises to proper purposes, was an acknowledgment of the trusteeship being vested in the churchwardens alone. In 1840 the vicar and several influential individuals projected the erection of an Infant School on the site, and the poor inmates were removed into other habitations; but when the *new* scheme was mooted in vestry, Mr. A. J. Dunkin courageously denounced the misapplication of the benefaction. The materials were, however, advertised for sale, when sundry newspaper paragraphs and an Address to the parishioners, induced the exertions of Mr. Barrell, and other gentlemen to prevent their demolition. Mr. Storey of Horseman's Place actually offered ground for the erection of an Infant School, rent free for twenty years, and to repair the houses at his own expense. The houses were preserved; and it is most creditable to the churchwardens to add, that *they* repaired them and reinstated the poor persons. Posterity will, however, be surprised to learn that Resolutions condemnatory of the individuals who resisted these innovations disgrace the vestry book of Dartford. Vide. *Tracts.* Parish houses, Overy street, *versus* the Infant School. *Nos.* 1 & 2. Dartford, 1840.

The tenement in question is a fair specimen of the timber buildings of the fifteenth century, inhabited by the substantial yeomen of the country; and by a singular fatality, has undergone little alteration

the "guild of All Saints," betoken the edifice of still earlier erection.*   From the reign of Charles the first to nearly the middle of the next century, the family of Rogers† inhabited a mansion in this street.   A fell-monger's yard is now replaced by the handsome residence and grammar school of Mr. Barton.   The upper floors of the cottages adjoining the pipe-manufactory, once overhung the path-way so low, that the fronts were necessitated to be re-built.   Fifty years since the upper part of the street near the bridge was so deep and miry, that it was nearly impassable in winter and frequently overflowed by the floods.

About the centre of the town, and nearly opposite the Bull inn, branches off towards the north a street

---

except in the form of the windows.   There was no staircase, but the two solars or upper rooms were ascended by a ladder.   The chimney seems an appendage of later construction.

* John Ockhurst left 6s. 8d. "to the sustentation of the guild of All Saints in Dertford" by will dated 15th Oct. 1440, Reg. Test. i. 2. Gothic niches executed in brick, are extremely rare at this early period; possibly those which appear on the outside these chimneys were intended for statues, and were among the first in the country. Dr. Littleton says there were no brick buildings except chimneys before the reign of Henry the seventh.   Archælogia, i. 140.   The tenement of All Saints, Overy Street, is noticed again in the Minister's Accompt Roll, 32 Hen. VIII.   Addit. MSS.   No. 5,535, Brit. Mus.

† One John Rogers seems to have acquired some of the confis-cated church property and settled at Dartford, his name first occurs

THE CHURCH HOUSES, OVERY STREET.

ROMAN COFFIN, &c.

anciently called Hithe street, from its leading towards the haven, but latterly from the Cranpit flowing down the middle, usually known as the *Waterside.* Stepping blocks banded with iron, are inserted at intervals in the bed of the shallow stream, to enable the inhabitants to cross. In the reign of Henry the eighth, an elm tree stood just at the corner of the Waterside, between the Cranpit, and a messuage on the site of the chemist's shop, now occupied by Mr. Edwards. At the back of that messuage toward Spital street, evidently on the site of the coach office and premises occupied by Mr. John Willding, was a "connie ground" or rabbit warren, on which stood *the Pillory* for the punishment of offenders.* At that period there were few houses in Hithe street, except on the western bank; and of

---

in a latin deed, (No. 13) in the parish archives, A.D. 1566. His descendants remained till near the middle of the last century.

* "Item. Walter Clement for Walter Roe, which holdeth a messuage at the elm lying betwixt the hieway on the south, and the running water called the Cranford on the est, and a garden of the prioress of Dertford sometyme of Walter Roe on the north, and the connie ground wherr the pylary is set, on the west, and owes 1d. per ann." Rentale de Dertford (Temples). From its central situation, contiguity to the market place, and place of punishment of offenders, that elm tree in ancient times was doubtless the chief place of resort for all the idlers of the town.

Another of the tenements held of the same community was near the wharf. "Robert Lang for Richard Sumy, holds a messuage at Hithe betwixt a shop of William Rotheley and a messuage of the p'oress of Dertford, and a messuage of the said Robert sometyme the Bishop of Rochester's south, and the weirs of the lordship of Dertford and of William Rotheley, and the rivulet called Robins dyche on the west, and the way to the said wharf on the north and owes . . . d." Ib.

C

those, six were held of the Knights Hospitalers of St. John, Sutton-at-Hone, and ten belonged to the prioress of Dartford.*

A brewery is built in the garden at the back of the late Mr. Hards' cottages.

The Wesleyan-Methodist chapel is situated in the Waterside.

About 1792, the late Mr. Hall obtained some premises for carrying on the business of a millwright, and subsequently erected a factory and iron foundry in this street,† which eventually became an establishment of the first magnitude, and very materially contributed towards the prosperity of the town; at one period upwards of three hundred men were constantly employed. In 1825, Mr. Hall erected the long row of cottages opposite, called Hall-place, upon part of the garden constituting the manor of Charles, principally for their accommodation.

Opposite Mr. Hall's factory is Spare-penny lane, leading by a narrow causeway between two ditches into Bullis lane.‡

---

* Register Munimentorum Nominum Prioratus Hospitalis S. Joan Jerusalem in Anglia. Cotton MS. Nero E. vi. Valor Eccles. i. 114.

† The prioress of Dartford had a house on the site of Mr. Hall's foundry, described in a terrier of the lady Elizabeth Cressener, 24 Hen. VII. as a "tenement, abutting on the highway to the east, to the lane leading to the monastery of the prioress and convent against the south; and towards the fountain vulgarly called the horse pool against the west, to the garden formerly William Pultes and now of Robert Blagges against the north; the which tenement...............widow, now inhabits, and renders 8s. 4d. per annum." Arundel MSS. No. 61. Brit. Mus.

‡ 1788. April 3rd. "The foot-path leading from Waterside to

The Phœnix mills are situated at a short distance below, and farther down are the wharfs of Mr. Philcox and Mr. Hammond.

Contiguous to the priory garden are the Gas-works.

Southward from the High street, runs another called *Lowfield*, from remote antiquity. It is now the turnpike road to Farningham, Sevenoaks, etc. On the eastern side of this street are the breweries of the Messrs. Fleet and Messrs. Tasker, and nearly opposite is the Independent chapel erected in 1819, now under the pastorate of the Rev. Mr. Harris. Higher up is a large edifice erected for a Bridewell, but latterly converted into a beer shop, and across the road are four Alms Houses, built and endowed by John Beer, in the reign of queen Elizabeth. Adjoining is

---

Bullock's lane and so to Dartford church, being stopped up by persons unauthorized, the surveyors directed to open it, the parish undertaking to indemnify them." Vestry Book, sub ann. Again in January 1821, on the representation of certain inhabitants, the magistrates of the district were induced to issue an order for stopping up this causeway; and on the 22nd of the same month, a vote in vestry declared "the footway in question not only unnecessary but a public nuisance, affording facilities from its situation and course to nightly depredations and other illegal and immoral practices, and therefore, that it will be a great benefit if the same be stopped up." Seventeen persons signed this resolution, many of whom had property in the immediate vicinity; but the dissentients, with the vicar at their head, inserted a protest against the measure "considering the footpath in question of public benefit." A strong opposition ultimately prevented the measure being carried into effect. Ibid. sub ann.

Horsman's place, built by Mr. Storey, on the site of an ancient mansion bearing the same name, formerly the residence of the Twisletons. At the extremity of the street is a messuage called Bugden hall, now inhabited by Mr. Whitlock a farmer,* and about a quarter of a mile further the handsome residence of Mrs. Cresy.

In Lowfield were three tenements, held of the commandry of St. John's, Sutton-at-Hone, several belonging to the priory of Dartford, and one to Lesnes abbey.

Anciently the entrance to Lowfield from the High street was extremely narrow and confined. For ages a branch of the Cranpit flowed down the centre, leaving an unprotected causeway barely sufficient for a single foot passenger, which was most dangerously elevated nearly two feet above the horse road. This highway in its turn would not admit of one carriage passing another. The street was widened at the expense of the parish about 1792,† and the Cranpit is said to have been confined to its original channel by Messrs. Tasker for the supply of their brewery toward the latter end of the last century; but the waters are now disused.

---

* Streams from the Cranpit were originally turned into Lowfield for the supply of Horseman's-place, and Bugden-hall.

† In January 1792, a treaty was entered into with Mr. Tasker, for the purchase of Mr. John Plaisket's house and the old houses up Lowfield street to the Bull back gate, and part of the ground upon which they stood, in order that the street might be widened and rendered commodious to the public. The sum required was £450, about £340 had been raised by voluntary subscription, and the remainder of the purchase money was ordered by vestry to be paid out of the Highway rate. Parish archives.

THE PARISH CHURCH.

The situation of the parish church, at once blocking up the end of the street and the approach to the bridge, is so manifestly inconvenient, as to convince the most incredulous that the selection of the site, must have arisen from conviction that no other possessed corresponding advantages.

The ford of the Darent was too important to be overlooked as a military post during the murderous incursions of the Saxons and Danes; consequently a strong massive fort or tower was erected on the banks of the river immediately contiguous to the Watling-street, to serve at once as a defence of the ford, and a strong-hold for the inhabitants of the town.—On the southern side of this tower, the people, very naturally, afterwards erected their church, and in times of war and depredation carried thither their valuables as a place of complete security. When tranquillity prevailed, the tower became the campanile of the parish church.

The first Saxon edifice may be reasonably supposed to have consisted of a nave and chancel only, yet standing according to the cardinal points, the south western corner necessarily projected itself upon the line of the Watling-street.—In those ages, the presence of the sacred edifice was considered an ample counter-balance to any little inconvenience arising from a slight inclination in the road.

At a very early period, the Saxon kings, then lords of the domain, gave Dartford church towards the endowment of the see of Rochester, and it is entered among those possessions in Domesday Book.

A.D. 1220. Immediately after the canonization of Becket, vast multitudes of all classes flocked on pilgrimage to his tomb, and Dartford became the first resting place from London to Canterbury :* this evidently led, in the time of Henry the third, to the erection of a chapel on the southern side of the chancel, and to the *dedication of an altar therein to St. Thomas of Canterbury*, for the use of the pilgrims. In the same reign, the emperor of Germany, was married by proxy in this church to Isabella, the king's sister.†

The ancient fabric having fallen to decay, or been adjudged too mean for the magnificent ideas of the age; the present greatly enlarged edifice, was projected in the reign of Edward the first. The church was proposed to consist of a nave, three chancels and side aisles, although it was evident this object could not be accomplished without carrying the western end of the south aisle right athwart the ancient road, and thereby apparently blocking up the street. This inconvenience, however, seems to have been considered subordinate to the advantages of having a church worthy of the town, and calculated to arrest the attention of strangers. The ecclesiastics pressed forward the re-building, and the south aisle was evidently completed in the time of the first Edward, from the character of the architecture of some of the windows. The great western window of the middle aisle, clearly bespeaks itself to have been constructed in the reign of his son and successor Edward the second; while the records of the

---

* From this period, Dartford became noted for its numerous Inns. The feast of St. Thomas of Canterbury was held 12th July.

† Lamb. Dict. 94.

church of Rochester, state those at the east end of the three chancels to have been inserted by the bishops Thomas de Woldham, and Hamo de Hethe, temp. Edward the third;* the arches of the nave are about the same age, and the north aisle windows display tracery of a somewhat later period.

It was on the addition of this northern aisle to the church, that the architect entertained the bold conception of exhibiting St. Thomas's altar to the devout pilgrim, by cutting lofty arches through the eastern, western, and southern walls of the ancient Saxon tower. Since the removal of that altar at the reformation, and the conversion of the chapel itself into a *vestry room*, those arches have been blocked up, but the solidity of the edifice they uphold, and the symmetry of their several architectural members still attest the care and skill with which the design was carried into effect.

The principal repair during the following century was that of re-covering the church with lead, circa 1470, and easily effected by the voluntary offerings and donations of the faithful.†

---

* 7 Edw. III. On Monday before the nativity of the blessed Mary, the bishop, Thomas de Woldham, went to Dartford to view the window in the chancel of the church which Hamo de Hethe his chaplain had made, and returned to his new house at Stone, called La Plâce. Wharton's Anglia Sac. i. 372.

† 1444, Richard Rokesle of Dertford, by will, directs his body to be buried in the church of Dertford near his father, and gives to the works of the church and tower, 23s. 4d. Reg. Test. i. 30.

1453, William Rokesley of Dertford, by will dated, 8th Oct. 1453, directs his body to be buried in the cemetery of St. Trinity (lower

But towards the latter end of the reign of Edward the fourth, the ancient campanile was so much decayed as to call the special attention of the parishioners to the subject, and by the aid of donations and benefactions,* the repair was not only effected, but *another story added to heighten the tower*, thereby divesting it of its former heavy, squat, military character.

---

church-yard), near the sepulchre of his father; wills to the high altar for forgotten tythes, 12d.; to making the fabric of the church, 20d.; to John his son, a chalice of laten; to Joan his wife, etc.   Ib. Regist. i. 142. Latten was an alloy of copper and zinc.

Richard Miles of Wise, called Mysok of Stoneham, in the parish of Dertford, directs his body to be buried in the church-yard of Dertford, and wills to the works of the parish church, 6s.   Ib. Regist. 60.

Roos Pitt of Dertford, by will dated 4th July 1470, commends her soul to Almighty Ih'u, to our blessed lady his modyr, to all the saynts of heven and her body to be buried in the churche-yarde of the holy trynitie aforesaid, beside the sepulchre of her husbonde; to the haulter of the parish church there in recompence of offerings and tythes, 20s.; to the helying of the said parish churche with lede when nede ys, 13s. etc. Ib. Regist. iii. 84.

John Tottenham of Dertford, by will dat. 22nd Jan. 1474, directs his body to be buried in the cemetery of St. Edmund (upper burying ground); for forgotten oblations, 6s. 8d.; to repair the parish church of Dertford, wherever defective, 5 marks sterling; to repair the chapel of St. Edmund, 9s.; to an honest priest to celebrate daily for himself and all his benefactors for . . years . . ; to John Wells to pray for his soul, 6s. 8d. etc.   Ib. iv.   He resided in Overy.

Nicholas Baker of Dertford, smith, will dated last day of October, 1476; his body to be buried in the cemetery of the church; to the fabric of the church, 20d.,; to John Wells to pray for his soul, 6d. etc.   Ib. iv. 175.

* 18 Edw. IV.   John Bamberg of Dertford, will dat. 21st Aug. 1478, "to be buried in the church-yard of the holie Trinitye of Dert-

DARTFORD PARISH CHURCH, FROM THE BRIDGE

The edifice having thus assumed its present form and projecting far into the road, the foot-path was carried round the north side of the church, and the *Cross* erected hard by, to excite the devotion of the passenger. There was a turn-stile at each end of the path.

———

No further external alteration of importance was effected from that period until 1792; when the commerce of the country having greatly increased, it was adjudged advisable to widen the road, by taking down the western corner of the south aisle, and re-building it in its present circular form.—At the same time the foot-path was made on the south side of the church, and the turn-stiles leading into the church yard removed.

INTERIOR OF THE CHURCH.

In Catholic times the whole body of the church was open, and all classes of individuals knelt indiscriminately amongst each other for divine worship. There

———

ford, at the west door nigh the holy water stoppe; to the high altar for tythes and oblations forgott, 3s. 4d.; I will, that when the steeple shall be in making, my wife reward the churchwardens unto the said stepul, after her good discresion, plesing to God and profitable to my soul; the residue of my goods and chatels I bequeath to Jane my wife." etc. Ib Regist. iii 246.

John Smith, by will dat. 2nd Oct. 1417; his body to be buried in the cemetry of St. Edmund, king and martyr; to the altar of the holy Trinity, 12d.; to the reparation of the campanile of the parish church, 12s. etc. Ib. Regist. iii. 29.

* Joane Calver, widow of Dertford, will dat. 1533; "my body to be buried on the north side of the church yarde *beside the cross* of the parish church." Ib. Regist. ix. 72.

were in Dartford church as least four altars. The *High Altar*, dedicated to the Holy Trinity* occupied the place of the present communion table, and the window above, probably from a painting therein, bore also the name of "St. Trinity window." *St. Thomas of Canterbury's altar†* stood against the east wall of the north chancel, now called the parish vestry; and *St. Mary's altar* occupied the space below the painting of St. George and the dragon in the Virgin's chapel. In the great chancel also stood an image of the Virgin

---

* Richard Bolton of Dertford, by will dat. 3rd Feb. 1465, after providing for the burial of his body in the monastery of Dertford, gives 20s. to the altar of St. Trinity in Dertford; 12d. for the day of his month's mind; 10s. to the window of St. Trinity. Ib. Reg. ii. A month's or year's mind was the performance of a requiem at the period specified by the testator, when a dole was given to the poor present. Private masses were celebrated without pomp or attendant except the priest's boy, unless any of the relatives of the deceased chose to be present. Peck's Desiderata Curiosa, 38.

Richard Fagg also buried in the cemetery of the same monastery, gave 20d. to the Altar of St. Trinity. Ib. Reg. ii. 129.

† Sir John Bruer vicar of Dartford, was buried within the great chancel before the high altar, 1534. Ib. Reg. 175. Undergraduated priests were entitled " Sir," but graduates were called " Master."

Margaret Sherman, widow, by will dat. 7th Dec. 1460, desires to be buried in the church-yard of St. Trinity; gives to the light before the altar of St. Thomas of Canterbury, 4s. ; to the fabric of the church, 26s. ; and six marks for vestments. Ib. ii. 200.

Thomas Mynt, 7th Aug. 1498, wills to be buried in St. Trinity church, Dertford, to the high altar 8d. ; to St. Thomas, martyr in the said church 8d. ; residue to Agnes his wife. Ib. Reg. v. 338.

John Gulby of Dertford by will dat. 4th Jan. 1454, directs his body to be buried in Dartford church, and gives to the light of St. Thomas, 3s. 4d. Ib. Regist. ii.

called *our lady of pity*,* and in the north wall an arch called the *Sepulchre*, in which the crucifix was laid from Good-Friday to Easter-day, and in reverence

* Thomas Barnard of Dertford, 3rd Dec. 1492, directs his body to "be buried in the church before the ymage of our blessed lady of pity; to the jayte light in Dertford 20d.; to the taper light of our lady of pity, 12d.; to the rode light 20d.; to the light of St. Antonie 12d.; to every light in the said church, 2d.; after his decease a trental of masses at the Grey friars in London, wherefore he bequeaths 18s.; to the friars in Greenwich, 12d.; to the Charterhouse 20d.; to each of his daughters Alice and Margaret, 4s.; residue of his goods, etc. to his wife." Reg. iii. The trental was founded by pope Gregory the great, and consisted of thirty days masses.

Stephen Round, by will dat. 28th March, 1494, directs his body to be buried in the church-yard of Dertford, and "wills to the high awter 8d.; to our lady light in the chancel one pound of wax; to Roger my son to his marriage, 20s.; to Richard on his marriage 20s. to Margaret Blad-wyve my daughter 20s." Ib. Reg. v. 236. The statue of the virgin in the chancel seems to have been called indifferently, "our lady" and "our lady of pity."

Joan Calvert of Dertford, widow, in 1533, directed her executors to make a three pound taper of wax to be set before our lady of pity in the parish, and there to be lighted every Sunday at high mass. Ib. Reg. ix. 72.

William Parker of Dertford, Innholder, by will dat. 2nd Jan. 1534, directs his body to be buried in the church of Dartford, before the image of our lady of pity, beside Anne his first wife, *to the Candle before the Rood* as much as will perform the whole sute.

Agnes Parker, widow (late wife of William Parker), being sick in body, by will dat. 27th August, 1535, bequeaths her soul to God her maker, and to his mother our lady St. Mary, and all the company of heaven; her body to be buried before the image of our lady of pity, beside the grave of her husband, etc.; wills to the fryars of the abbey, 3s. etc. Ib. Test. ix. 154. Probably one of these friars of Dartford was her confessor. Brethren of the different orders were frequently selected for those offices by their affectation of superior piety; hence they were hated by the secular clergy.

whereof John Morley caused a "taper of four pounds of wax to be provided to be set in the church of Dartford before the sepulchre at Easter every year."* An image of *St. Anthony* and a *light* burning before it, is mentioned in the will of Thomas Barnard;† and the *altar* of *St. Ann* in that of William Ladd, who gave 3s. 4d. thereunto in 1504.‡ A *rood loft* or narrow gallery stretched across the east end of the nave just above the present screen; upon it was placed a *lofty* crucifix called *the Rood*, and before the Rood hung a lamp or candle called the *Rood-light*.¶ The staircase and a doorway leading to it still remain.—There was also the *guild of All Saints* remembered in the will of John Oakhurst,‖ to whose sustentation he gave 6s. 8d.

---

* For a provision for this benefaction see Morley's will under the account of the Church houses, Overy street.

In 1368 W. Shepherd of Dertford charged a messuage in Lowfield with providing seven flaggons of oil yearly, for the perpetual sustentation of the lamp in the bosom of the church before the high cross, and constituted Thomas Lecheford the vicar of Dertford, Richard Dove, John Depple, and Robert Hostler, trustees. Parish Archives. No. 22. Landale, 3. The house escheated to the crown as a "light endowment." 1 Edw. VI. John Dowse also gave four acres of arable land in 1465 in Southfield to buy wax lights for the use church of Dertford for ever. No. 36. Landale. 8. The land was settled upon the reparation of the church and therefore preserved.

† To the rode light 20d. ; to the light of St. Antonie 12d.

‡ To St. Ann's awter within the parish church of Dertford, 3s. 4d.

¶ "To the candle before the rode as much as will perform the whole suite." *Vide* will of William Parker, Innholder.

‖ John Oakhurst of Dertford by will dat. 15th Oct. 1440, gives to the altar of the blessed Trinity in the parish church......; to the hospital of leperous 12d.; to the sustentation of the guild of All Saints in Dartford 8d; Ib. Reg. i. 2. The situation of the mansion is still

A.D. 1440; and a "Freretre" mentioned in the will of Thomas Chapleyn. 34 Hen. VIII.* A.D. 1542.

A cross or crucifix also stood in the south side of the church.†

CHAPEL OF THE BLESSED VIRGIN.

12 Edward III. After the formation of the priest's vestment room, Thomas de Dertford, alias Stampit then vicar of Dartford, enclosed the south chancel with screens of elegant open work, and founded therein *a chantry in honor of the blessed Virgin*, for the health of his own soul, the souls of his ancestors, and all the

---

marked out by the gothic arches in the chimney and the following entry in the Accompt Roll of tenements in the hands of the king, 32 Hen. VIII. under the head "Redd' lib' Tenent' in Dertford." *Translation.* "Of 10d. rent for a tenement and garden formerly in tenure of Thomas Judd, situate near the tenement of ALL SAINTS in Dertford." Addit. MSS. No. 5,535, Brit. Mus.

* Ib. Regist. ix 402. Freretory. The stall or desk occupied by the fraternity of clerks or singers, who assisted in chanting the services of the church: probably persons of this class constituted the guild of All Saints in Overy Street, and the guild of the blessed Virgin in Spital Street, and supplied the pilgrims of St. Thomas with crosses and religious toys. In some places gentlemen fond of church music, enrolled themselves members of the singing brotherhoods, and wore surplices during service. Hawkin's Mus. iii. pass.

† Richard Pinden, by will, dat. 6th May, 1 Hen. VIII. "my body to be buried in the church of holie trinitie in Dertford, beside the cross in the south side of the church; my executors to distribute for my sowl at my burying in costs and alms dedes, 20d.; at my month's mind, 40s.; residue of my goods and chattels to Joan my wife." Ib. Reg. vi. 147. Richard Pinden held a messuage in Overy Street. Addit. MSS. 5,535.

faithful departed this life which he endowed with lands in perpetuity.*

St. Mary's Chapel was regarded in subsequent ages with high veneration:—the piety of individuals enlarged the window contiguous to the altar in the reign of Richard the second, and provided a succession of lights and lamps as long as the chantry was permitted to exist.†

1485. In the reign of Henry the seventh,‡ or perhaps earlier, the glory of this chapel was completed by the painting of the story of St. George and the dragon in fresco, on the whole width and height of the east wall of the chapel.

---

* Reg. Roff. 302. This Thomas de Stampit, like other ecclesiastics, relinquished his paternal name and assumed that of his benefice.

† Thomas Underdown, by will dat. 12th Nov. 1462, directs his body to be buried in the chapel of St. Mary the virgin, in the church of Dertford, and that an honest priest celebrate therein for one year. Ib. Regist. ii. 251.

Roger Rothely of Dertford, by will, dat. 6th May, 1468; his body to be buried in the chapel of St. Mary, at Dertford, near the sepulchre of his wife, and his executors to put a stone above the bodies of them; to the altar for tythes and oblations, 6s. 8d.; to be given for masses on the day of his exequies, 6s.; to the reparation of St. Edmund's chapel, king and martyr, 6s. 8d.; he wills his anniversary to be kept for twenty years in the parish church, when 6s. 8d. is to be given to the choir and poor; to John Wells, chaplain and his successors ten marks, if such remain, after the before mentioned payments, *vis*, yearly for three years, 40s.; to the prioress and convent, five marks, on condition that the said prioress, and their successors perform divine offices for him in the convent, for ten years after his decease. Ib. Regist. iii. 9.

There is a brass in this chapel for W. Rothele of Dertford, who died in 1464, and his wives Betrix and Joan and their children.

‡ Gentleman's Magazine

As the open work of the screen afforded a complete view of the high altar, many of the parishioners selected it for the performance of their devotions, and some of the more opulent erected seats therein, before which their bodies were afterwards buried.*

---

* Thomas Bond of Dertford, by testament dat. 27th Jan. 1500, "I will, that my bodie be buried in our lady chancel, *afore my sete;* for the breaking of the ground there 6d.; to the awter 2s.; to the light, a taper of 50lb weight; at the burying of me .... and for me and Johan my wif, half a trentall of masses; and at my twelve month's mynde anoder half trentall of masses; to Alis my wife my best fetherbedde, etc. I woll it to be given to the chantry of Stampitt, for to pray for the souls of my fader and moder and my wif, all by name a 51d.; that all the wool that is above the chamber of my house, be sold to pay my debts; to William my ghostly fader to pray for my soul ....; Alis my wif to have twenty nobles in money; residue of my goods to John my son." Ibid. Regist. vi. 46.

William Kingham of Dertford, yeoman, being sick, makes his testament, 1st Jan. 1545. 37 Hen. VIII. "I will my body to be buried in o'r lady chapel, in the parish church of Dertford, againste my *pew and seate,* and I give to the reparation of the said church, 6s. 8d. to the high altar, 8d.; to poor people, where most need be, 20s. sterling: *i.e.* 6s. 8d. at my burial, at my month's mind, 6s. 8d., and at my year's mind, 6s. 8d.; I will have to be said and done in the parish church of Dertford, thirty masses and three diriges, *i s.* that is to say, on the day of my burial one dirige and ten masses, on my month's day one dirige and ten masses, and on my year's day, one dirige and ten masses; to Alice Maston, my old servant, six pieces of my old pewter vessells, and twenty pence in money, which I now owe unto her of her waige; to Elizabeth my daughter, the wife of Nicholas Gadeling, three pounds sterly, upon condition that it shall be to relief of the same Elizabeth upon such condition that the said Nicholas shall suffer the said Elizabeth to be put forth to be nourished in some honest person's house, unto such time she may be better comforted and nourished whereby she may the sooner attain unto her health; or otherwise the said Nicholas

There was a tenement in Up-street called the "Guild of the blessed Virgin" belonging to this chapel.*

1545. The stability of this chantry was threatened by an act passed 37 Henry VIII. for valuing and sur-rendering all colleges, hospitals and chantries; but it continued to survive two years longer, when it was finally suppressed 1 Edward VI. A.D. 1547; the lamps were then taken away, the figure of the virgin removed, and the altar pulled down. A small part of the stone work is, however, still visible against the east wall, and the piscina remains on the right hand.

At the same time also in pursuance of the order for the removal of all images, pictures, etc., from parish churches, the niche was blocked up and the painting of St. George covered with whitewash.

————

In the church was also a chantry called *Martin's Chantry*, founded about the time of Henry the sixth by John Martin, a judge of the Common Pleas,† but at

————

will not suffer the same, then the seyd three pounds, nor one penny they shall not be paid or dely'n; the residue to be divided between my children, John Everest and Beatrice his wife; John Brett and Alice his wife; to John Everest and Beatrice his wife, my meadow called *Harp Hawes*, lying in Billet's, [Bullis] lane; to John Brett and Alyce his wife, all my orchard and little parcel of land in Overy street; and all my other parcel next the church yard and my close lying in the town field called p'yery feld." Ib. Regist. vol. ix. 172.

* Rentale de Dertford. [Temples.]

† John Martin the judge of the Common Pleas, was the eldest son of Richard Martyn of Dertford and his wife, buried in the chancel of the church. The justice increased his patrimonial posses-sions by purchasing the manor of Franks in Horton-Kirby, where he settled, and a moiety of the manor of Chartons adjoining, in Farn-

what altar the priest celebrated does not clearly appear,

---

ingham parish; to these he subsequently added the manor of Chepsted in Kingsdown. He had also sundry lands and tenements in Dartford, and a large mansion at the corner of Lowfield which he frequently inhabited. He deceased 15 Hen. VI. A.D. 1436, and was buried in St. Mary's chapel wherein he had founded the above chantry. He left two sons, Richard and John, and two daughters, one of whom married Richard Cobham. Richard Martyn settled in Dartford, and in 1500 was constituted a trustee with William Ladd and John Miller of Orpington for a messuage in Lowfield five years afterwards settled upon the church. No. 29. Par. Arch. Landale. 9.

John Martyn a younger son who inherited the principal estates, also chiefly resided in the family mansion at Lowfield street. He sold the manor of Chepsted in the parish of Kingsdown, to the beforementioned John Underdown of Dertford, 33 Henry VI. He died 4 Hen. VIII. and in his will dat. 27th Dec. 1512 (wherein he describes himself as John Martyn of Dertford in Kent, gent) desires his body to be buried in the chapel of our lady in the church of Dertford; wills "to high altar 3s. 4d.; £3 13s. 4d. to be disposed of for the health of my soul by Edward Barnard, vicar of Dertford, by the space of seven years, each year 10s., the last year 13s. 4d.; all my woodes, Frank's park, and Weltec, to be sold as much as is able of the said woods by my executors within the space of ten years; whereof Ann my wife to have £3 6s. 8d. and my debts to be paid and bequests fulfilled: the residue of my monies, etc., divided between my daughters: the lands which his mother now hath of her jointure in Kent, my son Edward to have after her decease; Robert my son to have all my land in parish of Ludward; William my son to have half my manor of Franks after the decease of my wyff which she hath now in her jointure; also I will when he cometh to age of fifteen that he have my tenement of Calvestock; and in the space I will that my executors receive the profit in behoof of my daughters; also I will that if my wife fortune to marry, then I will that all such money as shall be in her hands then to remayne unto my brother Edward Cobham, and she to be discharged clere of my will; to each of my sisters 20s.; my executors to have all their costs borne about my business touching my will, etc.; two horses to be sold by my executors in performance of my will, etc., residue

D

although the desire of his descendant to be buried in the chapel of our lady, may induce the supposition that it was at her altar.

———

The piety of the parishioners also provided vestments for the priest.* In 1504 William Ladd, by will, gave two pair of sheets to make surplices, and four marks to buy an altar cloth, on which should be embroidered a prayer for the soul of himself and other benefactors to the same. This altar cloth, doubtless, continued to be used until the reformation.

———

of my goods to Ann my wiff whom I make my executor with my broder Edward Cobham. Ib. Regist. vi. 359.

Edward Martyn his eldest son sold the manor of Franks in Horton, and Chartons in Farningham, temp. Eliz. to Launcelot Bathurst an alderman of London. He left issue two sons, Francis and James, (the latter of Farningham,) of whom we hear nothing, and a daughter, who married William Brown of Reynolds Place, Horton Kirby. The Martyns bore for their arms, gules, three bezants, a chief or.

* William Ladd of Dertford, by testament dated 20th Nov. 1504: wills to be buried in the church yard of Dertford by his wife; gives to the altar for forgotten oblations, 6s. 8d.; to church work in the said church, 3s. 4d. "I will two payer of shets to make two surplices; four marks to buy a cloth according to the best sute of carro' if the money could so far extend, for the high altar of the same church; in the which cloth I will that there be made the words in carving pro p' x't'x with a ▨. J. et benefactor' ejusd'; I will to the abbey of Boxley my great chest bound with yron to set afore the rode of grace, &c.; to Magdalen College 40s. for the fellows to pray for me; to St. Ann's awter within the church of Dertford, 3s. 4d.; to our lady in the new work chapel in Crayford, 6s. 8d.; to William Cooke a chantry priest of Stampit to pray for me and such as I am bound to pray for 3s. 4d.; to my god-children 3s. 4d.; the residue of my goods, &c., to Charles Barnard, vicar of Dertford." Ibid. Regist. vi. 117.

Cysley Jhonson, widow, by will dat. 1533, gives to the high altar

About 1532 William Cook, by will, vested his lands and tenements, after the death of his wife, in certain feoffees to found an YEARLY OBIT in Dartford church, for the souls of himself, Joan his wife, and Thomas and Felice Cook his father and mother,* but as no account

---

her best corporal kercher, to make a corporal cloth, and further directs that William Morris, her executor, do find a taper of 3lb. weight to burn before our lady, in the chapel in the church of Dertford, as long time as he hath wherewith to maintain it, &c. 1b. ix. 94.

* William Cook of Dertford, ill, but whole in minde, by testament dated 6th March, 1532, 24 Hen VIII. wills his body to be buried in the church yard of Dartford; "to be said in the parish church at my FORTHFARE, one night *placebo* and *dyridge*, and *five masses*, next day; and in like manner and forme at my MONTH'S DAY *dyridge*, sixty nights, and *five masses* on the morrow, and *5s.* in bred bestowed and distributed amongst poore peple at the end of the seyd days; the residue of my goods, and movables, &c. debts payd, &c. to Joan my wife to dispose to the health of my soul, &c. my wife to have during her natural life all lands, rents, and tenements, afterwards my feoffees to stand seized of the repairs, payments to the lords of the fee, &c. to FIND AN YEARLY OBIT to *sing and say one night* and on the *morrow following*, masses for the soul of *Thomas Cooke, Felice Cooke* his wife, my father and mother's souls, *Joan* my wyfs sowl, and *all christen sowls* to be bestowed to prests and clerkes of the same p'she of Dertford; and the residue of the profits to be *distributed in brede yerely among poore people in Dertford*, at the said obit; and the church-wardens of the parish for the time being to have for their labour in three distributions, 16d. yerely equally between them. And the same my tenement, little croft, orchard and appurtenances, always to continue in feoffment; the feoffees to sell all my chief messuages after the decease of my wife Joan, and after payments of debts, &c., of the remainder, £6 13s. 4d. parcel thereof to be distributed among poor young wives, and maidens marriageable; *livery* in the seyd parish church, every of them, 6s. 8d., as long as the seyd £6 13s. 4d. will endure. And the residue, after the seyd moneys received, to go towards the buying of a chalice and a suite of vestments, to be bought by the

of these lands appear in the Chantry Roll, it is possible
that the settlement might not be legally effected through
the longevity of the widow.

In September, 1538, injunctions were issued for the
abolition of numerous holidays, and every parish priest
required to procure an English Bible of the largest
print at the joint expense of the parish and himself;
this Bible he was directed to set up in the most convenient situation in the church, and admonish his parishioners to diligently read. At the same time, for avoid-
ing idolatry, he was directed henceforward to suffer
no person to set any tapers before any images or pictures, "but only the light that goeth commonly about
the cross of the church by the rood-loft, the light before
the sacrament of the altar, and the light about the
sepulchre, which shall remain for the adorning of the
church." He is also to provide a book for registering
therein all births, marriages, and christenings in the
parish. It is also enjoined that "as the *goods* of the
church are the goods of the poor, every parson *non-resident*
shall spend the *fortieth part* of *his benefice among his poor
parishioners.*†

About the same time the king ordered all pilgrimages to cease; Becket to be declared a traitor instead
of a saint, and his tomb at Canterbury destroyed. Hereupon his altar was removed from Dartford church, his

----

advice of my supervisors and churchwardens for the time being." Ib.
Reg. ix. 71. Placebo was taken from the anthem "Placebo Domine"
etc. with which vespers for the dead open. The dirige is the 5th psalm.
Fosbroke Encycl. Antiquit. *v.* Funerals. ii. 668.

  † Fox's Acts and Monuments of the church.   *v.* 169. Lond. 1838.

festivals abolished, and the towns-people's trade in his images and trinkets totally ruined.*

1541. Notwithstanding these injunctions it appears that if any copy of the Holy Scriptures was provided for the use of the parishioners it was small or unfit for public use, for, four years after, Robert Dove of Stanham bequeathed "to the parish church of Dartford one Bible of the greatest volume to be set up where it shall please John Brett and John Kettle" his executors.† The practice of praying for the dead continued during the whole of Henry the eighth's reign.‡

---

* It is not improbable that a painting of the martyrdom of St. Thomas may exist under the whitewash in his chapel. A representation of the subject has been recently discovered on the eastern wall of the nave in Preston church, Sussex. temp. Edward I. Ever since the opening of the shrine of Thomas à Becket had rendered pilgrimages common, the town of Dartford as the first stage to Canterbury, had become the resting place for pilgrims, who usually paid their devoirs at St. Thomas's altar. It was noted for its inns, and a considerable traffic arose from the strangers' temporary accommodation. The sudden cessation of pilgrimage must have greatly injured Dartford.

† Will dated 18th Novem. 38 Henry VIII. probate 14th April. Ibid. Regist. ix. 115.

‡ Christopher Emerson, 7th May, 1541. "I will my soul to Almighty God; my body to be buried in Dertford parish churchyard; to the high altar for my oblations negligently forgotten 4d.; I bequeath at my burial for the wealth of my soul and in remembrance of the passion of Christ, to be sung or said in the parish church of Dertford, eight masses and dirige, and every priest to have eightpence; and likewise at my month's mind the same to be done: my house and lands in Yorkshire to be sold. etc. Ib. Reg. 348.

Sir John Farrer of Dertford, priest, 1541: his body to be buried in the parish church; wills to the parish church of Crayford a pair of sheets; "I woll at my burial a dirge to be song with masses on the morrow, each of the priests to have for the lab'r 12d." etc. Ibid.

1547. 1 Edw. VI. All the remaining images in the church destroyed; the altar of St. Mary pulled down, her chapel despoiled, and the revenues seized by the commissioners appointed by act of parliament for the suppression of all chantries, guilds, etc.* The same year the churchwardens were enjoined to set up a Pulpit,† at the cost of the parish, and provide a strong Chest with a hole in the upper part, having three locks and keys, that the parishioners may therein put their alms and oblations for the relief of the poor and necessitous.‡ The mass also ceased, the service was

---

Dyryck Rowland of Dertford; will dat. 5th Aug. 1540: "First I bequeath my soul unto the merciful hand of o' savy'r Jh'u, and our lady his mothyr, and to all the company of heaven, and my body to be buryd in church yard of Dertford aforesaid, Item. to the high altar of the same for tythe and offerings by me negligently forgotten 8d.; I woll that my executors do dispose in dedes of charytie for the welthe of my soul to the pov'tie 3s. 4d." etc. Ib. Regist. x. 2.

Sissily Frende of Dertford, widow, will dat. 2nd Aug. 35 Hen. VIII. "to be buried in church yarde beside my husband John Frende; to high altar, 4d.; to Sir Raff, p'yshe prest, my goostly father for his paynes taken, and to pray for me, one pewter dyshe: a sawter sylt' sargey; one salt seller of tyne and tyne goblett to drynke; and one candlestick; all the residue to be sold." etc. Ib. Regist. x. 47. Metal articles were then extremely rare; the most substantial persons dined off wooden trenchers, ate their pottage with spoons of the same material, and drank out of hooped tankards, or horn vessels.

* Chantry Roll, co. Kent, in Augmentation Office.

† Sermons had previously been delivered from the Rood-loft or steps of the altar.

‡ Thomas Haule, will dat. 4th April, 2 Edward VI.; "my soul to Almighty God, my body buried in the church of Dertford." Ib. xi. 25.

William Fuller of Dertford, by will dat. 8th Nov. 1552, gives to the poor man's box, 2s. Ib. Regist.

William Ensell, will dated 24th May, 6 Edward VI., gave to God's chest for relief of the poor, 4s. 4d. etc. Ib.

performed in English,* all the altars taken away, and a table provided for the holy communion.

In July 1553 king Edward the sixth died, and the following year the mass was again set up, the high altar restored,† and the ancient ceremonies performed by order of queen Mary.‡ These practices continued for upwards of five years,¶ when the accession of her

---

* In ages when few persons could read, and the ritual was in latin, the priests taught the people the "Pater-noster" and "Ave Maria" as the chief form of individual devotion. Their prayers being thus limited, they were told that a repetition of them in decades was equivalent to certain offices in the church. Peter the Hermit instructed his followers to say ten Aves to every Pater-noster, and these repeated three times were called the Psalter of the Virgin Mary. But, as persons of the most fervid piety were liable to miscount, while they drowsily repeated words they did not understand, he invented a mode of praying, by beads strung in tens, so that they might drop one after every "Ave," and when they came to a larger, know it was the proper place to say a "Pater-noster." Butler's Lives of the Saints. i 23, *note*. In Fox's Acts and Monuments, numbers of the worshippers in churches are shewn with beads in their hands thus performing their devotions; for as latin was understood by few persons in the congregation, the priest usually recited the offices in a low tone that he might not disturb the faithful in their prayers. Du Cange. *v.* Rosarium. Fosbroke. *v.* Beads.

† But it does not appear that the altar of St. Mary, St. Thomas, or that of any other saint was rebuilt. during this reign, as there was no support for a priest.

‡ John Smithe of Dertford (testament dated 27th August, 1555), bequeaths his soul to Almighty God, St. Mary, and the company of heaven, etc. Ib. Reg. xi. 350. Clearly a return to the ancient catholic testamentary form. Queen Mary died 16th Nov., 1558.

¶ The wills made in the time of Edward the sixth, queen Mary and until the final establishment of protestantism by queen Elizabeth

sister Elizabeth led again to the pulling down of the
altar, and substitution of the communion table. The
latin service also was superseded by the Common Prayer,
the Rood-loft removed, and the Queen's Arms affixed
to the wall nearly on the spot heretofore occupied by the
Rood.

---

convey a vivid portraiture of the distracted state of men's minds in
matters of religion. The majority were evidently attached to the ancient
faith, and sought provision for the weal of their souls only in masses,
requiems, and other services of the catholic church. And so deeply were
they prejudiced in favor of that creed, that it is highly probable nothing
short of the extreme cruelties of the bigoted priesthood in the reign of
queen Mary, which endangered the personal safety of every one they
might please to accuse of heresy, could have awakened the bulk of the
people to the dangerous powers of the clergy. Hence, submission to the
alterations of Elizabeth was regarded as necessary to individual security.
We can now scarcely conceive how indelibly the recollection and hatred
of these cruelties were impressed upon the minds of the people by the
publication of Fox's Martyrology, embellished with such singular
engravings of events to which many must have been eye-witnesses.* By
order of archbishop Parker the book was placed in the most conspicuous
part of every church for all to read; what resistance it offered to the
progress of the Roman-catholic missioner is best shewn by their anxiety
to answer it. The sufferings and death of the victims could not be
denied, father Parsons therefore was driven to ridicule their motives and
misrepresent their conduct. Modern investigations have verified the
general accuracy of Fox, notwithstanding the vast mass of biography
rendered him liable to be misled by corrupted or incompetent authorities.
Parsons' boasted "Examen" will grievously disappoint the reader who
expects to find Fox refuted by facts and documentary evidence; many of
the actors in those dismal tragedies were then alive, and it was very easy
to collect the persecutors' exculpatory version of their own conduct, and

---

* Particulars of the condemnation of Nicholas Hall, and the burning
of Christopher Wade on Dartford Brent, 12th of July 1555, will be given
in a subsequent page.

The processions about the church seem to have been the only intelligible part of the ceremonies of divine worship in the ancient religion wherein an ignorant populace could join; but these having ceased with the introduction of the English liturgy, seats became necessary for the convenience of the parishioners and were speedily introduced.

---

their criminatory anecdotes of the sufferers. Silence on these points, proves there was little exaggeration; the Jesuit's book was nearly forgotten until the late Eusebius Andrews re-printed the substance with a sketch of Catholic Missionary priests. On the alleged authority of Anthony Wood (?) Roman-catholic writers tell with glee how a minister in the reign of Elizabeth, relying upon the statement of Fox, illustrated God's judgments by the horrible death of one of the persecutors of the protestants in queen Mary's time—how the person so alluded to, happened to be present at the sermon—and how he commenced a prosecution against the preacher for calumny! In subsequent editions, errors concerning Merbeck and others have been corrected.* The original Collections of Fox now constitute Nos. 416 to 426 Harleian MSS.; they have been carefully examined by the present writer and abound with unpublished matter.

The following is one of the squibs against Fox's works in a blank leaf of a MS. entitled the "Pricke of Conscience," in the Bodleian Library, Oxford. John Day was Fox's printer.

> The grave counsell of Gravesend barge†
> Gevethe Jhon Daye a privylege large
> To put this in prynt for his gaynes
> Because in the Legend of lies he taketh paynes
> Commanding other upon pyne of slavery
> That none prynt this but John Daye the
> prynter of FOXE HIS KNAVERY.

---

* The burning of Merbeck is given in the first edition; he was condemned, but saved by Gardiner in consequence of his great skill in music; he lived more than thirty-nine years after his condemnation, and was the first person who attempted making a Concordance to the Bible. Wood's Fasti Oxonien, i. 130.

† The heterogeneous company of the Gravesend Tilt-boat gives additional point to the satire, in connection with the pricke of conscience.

The nave of the church is divided from the north
and south aisles by three similar rows of lofty arches
of the early part of the fourteenth century, supported
by octagon pillars, having slightly ornamented capitals.
On either side it is lighted by clerestory windows of
anomalous character, constructed in the repair of 1792,
when the walls of the nave were heightened, the sharp
pointed roof lowered, and the church ceiled. The
eastern part of the chancel has a coved roof, with oak
panels and carved bosses, formerly painted azure and
studded with gilt stars. The western end is merely lath
and plaister. A very handsome oak Screen of the Decorated character divides the nave from the chancel, and
once sustained the rood-loft. Fears are entertained that
it is irreparably injured by wanton mutilation, although
as a better era has arrived, it is devoutly hoped the parish
will attempt something towards its restoration. The
same screen is continued across the end of the southern
aisle, and heretofore divided it from the Virgin's chapel.
This part is still perfect, and being glazed is both useful
and ornamental.

The length of the church is 109 feet 6 inches, inclusive
of the chancel. The breadth 67 feet including the nave
and side aisles.*

The present pulpit and reading desk were constructed
in the reign of James I.

Between 1702 and 1704 very extensive repairs,† altera-

---

* The north aisle is 18 feet 6 inches wide, the south aisle only 13 feet
in the clear; the base of the columns, 2ft. 9. in diameter.

† In the earliest Assessment extant for the repair of the church,
A.D. 1635; every one was rated "according to their abilitie." Lady
Spilman, 13s. 4d.; John Spilman, 6s. 8d.; John Twisleton, 30s.; etc.

tions, and improvements were effected in the interior of the fabric. The pavement within the altar-rails was renewed, and the altar-piece restored, at the expense of Charles Manning, gent.

In September, 1704, the six old bells were taken from the steeple, and recast with additional metal into eight. In November they were re-hung, and near the same time the roof of the nave and south aisle re-laid with lead.

1748, May. The church of Dartford improved by the suspension of two brass branches of twelve lights each, bequeathed by the late vicar, Charles Chambers, one of them hung below and the other above his grave. He also gave £18 to set up four distinct Tables of Bene-factions in the Church, which, however, were not erected until 1754.*

Total of Rate, £47 15s 8d. The yearly assessments up to 1694 seldom exceeded three-pence in the pound, and averaged little more than £26 per annum; but the following year it being necessary to relay the roof of the north aisle with lead, and undertake some extensive reparations for the stability and ornament of the edifice, a rate of 1s. 6d. in the pound was granted, (estimated to produce £142 4s.) although Mr. C. Manning and others resisted payment. On May 13th, 1696, upon a view of the dilapidated and dangerous state of the church, the inhabitants of Dartford being assured that the necessary repairs would amount to £150 again ordered a rate to be made at 1s. 6d. in the pound. The renewal and repair of the church windows for fifty years previous, were effected by contract at £2 per annum. Vestry Book, sub. ann.

Five pounds was given by Joshua Allen 1739 for purchase of a piece of communion plate.

* Will dat. 1 Oct. 1745. Besides the above benefaction he gave £25 toward the casting the Communion plate anew; sums for the relief of the poor, and the establishment of a charity school.

1763. Several of the pews lowered and made more uniform, and three new seats erected on the south side.

1766. A great flood; the church and many of the houses in the neighbourhood above a foot under water.

1773. A gallery erected on the south side of the church for the better accommodation of the parishioners. By order of vestry the churchwardens restricted to an expenditure of £100; in consequence, the building of the eight new pews were paid by subscription, and an exclusive right thereto settled by vestry upon the subscribers and their respective families, so long as they remained inhabitants of the parish. The gallery in the north aisle had been built some years previous.*

The institution of a Charity School was effected in 1748, and directed to be held in the north chancel, (heretofore the chapel of St. Thomas of Canterbury); in 1751 a chimney was built therein and the school ceiled.

1748, May 30th. "Whereas many complaints and disputes have arisen from the customary practice of the churchwardens to expend considerable sums of money in the repair of the church, without order of vestry; for the remedy thereof and for the greater satisfaction of the parish, the subscribing parishioners agree it shall not be lawful to lay out or expend for the repair or decoration of the church any sum exceeding forty shillings." Vestry Book sub. ann.

A new King's Arms painted on canvas put up in 1750; in 1753 and 1754, the old lead spouts altered and brought down into proper drains to carry off the water, and in 1769, a new dial plate affixed to the clock. The church rates were 9d. in the pound upon full rents in 1752; but in 1760 advanced to one shilling.

* 1773. The costs of building the eight new pews in the gallery were paid by the under-named persons, and allotted to them in the following order: (No. 1) to Edward Rawling; (2) John Latham; (3) Richard Hulse, esq.; (4) William Pope; (5) Thomas Brandon;

1783. The chancel repaired, and the great eastern window erected by Hamo de Hethe tastelessly changed into its present form. Previous to this alteration the lower part formed into five divisions by stone mullions, was glazed, but the upper part filled with tracery had been long stopped up. The head of the bishop occupied the uppermost central compartment. The window was originally filled with painted glass. There is a representation of it in Thorpe's Custumale Roffense plate xxxix, taken just before its demolition.

1784. This summer "the vestry ordered the pulpit to be removed to the north east pillar of the church and the donation tables into the centre of the arch" leading into the chancel.

1792. A general repair of the church. The nave ceiled, the walls raised two or three feet and new clerestory windows inserted. The roof lowered and covered with slate, and the western angle of the south aisle rounded; the whole repairs and alterations effected upon a plan furnished by Mr. Searle,* and estimated at

---

(6) William Tankard; (7) Catherine and Jane Tasker; (8) George Blackburne. On the 12th May, £30 was allowed Mr. Sharp to repair the steeple; the fourth bell ordered to be recast, and an engine house built at the east end of the church yard.

* Vest. Book. Anciently the nave was covered by an open timber roof, slightly ornamented with gothic work, and spanned with large beams; but the incongruous flat ceiling with which it was replaced, and the wood-frame windows which disfigure the southern aisle, were totally destructive of the original architectural character of the sacred edifice, and evince the depraved taste of the age. During these repairs divine service was performed in the chancel. A parishioner, Mr. W. L. Pearce, remarks "I was then a boy, but well remember going under the scaffold to church, and that there happened an

£1,200. The sum authorised to be raised upon annuities for life. The following year the whole of the outer walls from the small tower on the south side including the buttresses on the north, were also repaired.

1793. George Mason of Horton-Kirby, sold the parishioners an organ for the church for £150, upon condition of taking it back within one year, if not approved by vestry, and repaying the money. He proposed also to accept the office of organist at a salary of £26, which terms were accepted. The organ was erected in July the following year.* In May 1817, £211 10s. was subscribed for a new organ, which Mr. Russell

---

explosion at the powder mills (Dec. 31) which threw down a part of the ceiling."

19 Nov. 1792. Stephen Martin ordered by vestry "to be paid for ringing the eight o'clock bell to Christmas next and no longer, the parish considering it unnecessary; and he is ordered not to ring the four o'clock bell after to-morrow morning, 23d instant."—The sound of the curfew bell in winter has oftentimes preserved the life of the benighted and bewildered traveller when the country was open, and the deep sloughs and ruts compelled him to leave the highway for a lonesome and unfrequented track.

* Mason held the office three years; when the subscriptions became insufficient, payment of the salary was objected to by vestry; and in 1797 John Warcup, jun. became organist at £12 10s. per ann. In 1801 his salary was increased to £15, and ordered to be paid from the poor rate; but the following year the churchwardens were directed to allow the organist thirty guineas yearly, he undertaking to keep the organ in repair

1807. The church bells ordered to be put in proper order by Mr Mears, bell-founder, for £55 10s. according to his offer. Except the re-casting of the 4th bell in 1773, nothing had been done since they had been formed into a peal of eight, upwards of 100 years back.

† Sept. 4th, 1817. "The present organ-gallery being insufficient in strength and size to receive the new organ now building, and

undertook to build with a trumpet stop for £267, adequate to the size of the church, and allow £30 for the old organ. The churchwardens were directed to make proper alterations for its reception in the loft, and seats for the children. The new galleries were erected in 1818, and with the enlargement of the upper burial ground, cost £900.

1833. The Reading-desk placed in its present situation* and the pulpit removed to the north east corner of the nave. The church lighted with gas, and warmed by a stove placed in the middle aisle.

---

having in view the accommodation of the inhabitants by removing the children of the Schools from the body of the church to seats in the said gallery: on April 16th the churchwardens were directed to raise £900 on life annuities to discharge the expense, and to accept the offer of Mr. Ayres of £600 at ten per cent. as part of it."

* "On Tuesday, 18th June 1833, some workmen removing the Reading-desk and making alterations in the church, about four feet below the surface broke into a coffin covered with velvet, enclosing one of lead 6ft. 6in. long, within which was another of oak an inch and half thick, containing the body of a man of large proportions. The coffin had been evidently too short, for the vertebræ of the neck had been much bent forcing in the corpse. By its side lay a circular piece of dark glass, somewhat like talc, about one inch and a half in diameter. This was given to the Rev. F. B. Grant, vicar of Dartford, but is now in possession of the author. On the right side of the coffin lay another, which, like the former, had been also covered with velvet, and enclosed one of lead, filled with saw-dust. The corpse was cased in cement, apparently poured in hot, and become so hard that it could only be broken with a pick-axe. On the removal of part of the cement, the body of a female was disclosed wrapped in cerecloth, which adhered so closely to the flesh, as to bring away a portion of the breast on attempting its removal. The effluvia was so offensive, that it was judged prudent to close the coffin immediately." *Information of Mr. W. Brand, jun.* Adjoining was a large stone slab, once inlaid with a lofty cross fleuri, mounted

Near the same time also the workmen employed in repairing and cleansing the church discovered a fresco painting of St. George and the Dragon on the eastern wall of the south aisle, entirely covered with white-wash,* which they succeeded in removing but not without injury to the design. The picture occupies the whole width of the wall, being 19ft. 8in. and in height about twelve feet. The upper part reaches to the roof and its distance from the pavement is twelve

---

on a gresse, enclosing apparently the figure of an ecclesiastic. The form of the cross indicates it of the fourteenth or fifteenth century. The coffins may have been those of William Death and one of his wives, from their contiguity to the brass memorials of that family.

* The following particulars are copied from the Gentleman's Magazine. "The picture appears to be of the time of Henry the seventh or earlier. The foreground exhibits St. George mounted on a white charger, with scarlet caparisons: his lance couched, having transfixed the Dragon through the mouth and neck. The Saint is habited in plate armour of a brown colour, covered with a white surcoat, on the breast of which the red cross is displayed. Round the skirt of his vest are three bands of black, and the sleeves are open and flowing behind. In his girdle is a dagger. His helmet is of the same colour as his body armour, and appears to be united to the corslet by a gorget of mail. It is adorned with a plume of three feathers, and the visor is raised. The Dragon, which is of a green colour (except the under part of the wings, which are brown), is issuing out of a black pool, or stagnant lake, wherein we are informed by the Golden Legend the Dragon abode, and in which are seen bones and vestiges of his ravenous appetite. The back ground of the picture displays a hilly country, with the city of Sylene in the distance, and on the side of the hill stands the King's daughter, in her bridal dress of crimson, trimmed with ermine; her head uncovered, but adorned with flowing hair, after the usual fashion of virgins; by her side is the lamb by which she is always accompanied. Behind the holy champion is a castle with towers, having numerous loopholes, and between them an arched gate; and in a turret

W. B. Barker del.

PAINTING FOUND IN DARTFORD CHURCH, KENT.

feet. Under the centre of the painting was a shallow niche 3ft. 8in. high, and 18in. wide, having a trefoil head; it was painted red, and from an interval in the colouring had evidently contained a statue. In the south wall of the same chapel a wide recess was also opened, which had been blocked up, and adjoining it toward the east is a holy water stoup having a cinque-foil headed canopy.

THE ARMORY.

Above the vestment room on the south side of the chancel is an upper apartment formerly called the parish armory, wherein had been preserved from time

---

above are the King and Queen, anxiously watching their daughter's fate. The upper centre of the painting is charged with a shield, containing the arms of England and France quarterly."

Dr. Milner, a bishop of the church of Rome, gives the detail of the legend of St. George thus, "The common story is that a dragon or winged serpent of prodigious size and fierceness, the breath of which alone caused death, took up his residence in a lake near the city destroying men and beasts; nor was any other method discovered of restraining its devastations, than by exposing to it a tender maiden to be devoured. At length it came to the turn of the king's daughter to be sacrificed for the general welfare; to which measure he and his royal consort were obliged to submit, at the earnest request of the magnanimous heroine herself, and in consequence of a sedition amongst their subjects. She was accordingly led out of the city at the usual hour to the fatal lake, stained with the blood of her companions, and left exposed to the monster's unrelenting fury. At this critical moment, before the monster had emerged from his watery den, the invincible Red-cross Knight happens to arrive at the spot where the innocent princess is patiently expecting her devourer; and having learned the cause of her being thus left

E

immemorial considerable portions of ancient armour. It was little noticed except by casual visitors, but many of the parishioners recollect it to have consisted of helmets, breast-plates, gauntlets, greaves, etc., together with some pieces of chain armour.* Probably it had originally belonged to some of the gentry buried in the church, been hung over their graves, or laid upon their tombs, like that of Sir John Peche at Lulling-stone, or of the Sedley family in Southfleet church. The slight attention paid to this armour by the successive parish officers, and easy access of strangers, had rendered it liable to abstraction for many years; insomuch that when it came under the care of the present parish and vestry-clerk there was no complete suit, but only detached pieces. Mr. Brand says "being fond of these sort of things, I looked out a parcel of them, furbished them up, strung them together with wires and hung them against the wall over Beer's tomb in the south chancel. The suit, if it may be so called, was of nearly similar character to that represented upon the effigy of Sir John Spilman on the

---

alone and exposed, he undertook her deliverance, vowing to conquer or die in her cause." *Carter's Ancient Sculpture and Painting.* The story resembles that of Perseus as told by Ovid.

* Mr. John Hall informed the writer (1841,) that about thirty years ago two brass Mail Shirts originally purchased from this collection were in possession of his father; the shirts were very heavy and the rings about three eighths of an inch in diameter, interlaced something after the manner of a steel purse. Mr. Hall long kept them by him, and his son has had them on scores of times. They reached just below a man's waist, and extended from the shoulder half down to the elbow. The value of the brass at last consigned it to the melting pot.

tomb in the chancel, and having its tassetts formed of overlapping plates and straps attaching them to the taces complete, speedily attracted the attention of strangers." A dealer in those articles from Fetter Lane made the churchwardens repeated offers for the purchase of the armour, and about 1814, under the pretence of contributing towards the establishment of a parochial Sunday School, the whole of this collection (the finest in any church in the kingdom), was sold to this dealer* by Simmonds Hammond and Henry Morris the churchwardens, for the paltry sum of twelve guineas, to the inexpressible regret of every lover of local antiquities.

In the same armory was also a large mass of accoutrements, said by Mr. Currey, the late vicar, to have belonged to a company of Train Bands raised in the town and neighbourhood of Dartford, during the civil wars in the time of Charles the first.† The apartment was fitted up with shelves, etc., whereon they were deposited ready for any emergency; but during the long period which has since elapsed, and the change which has taken place in military equipments, the whole mass becoming neglected, gradually decayed, and were removed. At present there are only a few holsters and remnants of scabbards.‡ There were no military weapons preserved in this armory within recollection.

---

* Mr. W. L. Pearce says "the steel armour was sold to one Lazarus or Harris, a jew, and he told me he sold it afterwards for £200!" It subsequently formed part of Mr. Bullock's Collection.

† "In 1644 there was a magazine at Dartford, which was seized July 26th, by the Kentish, 6,000 strong." *Mercurius Aulicus*, 13th week.

‡ The holsters, etc., must have belonged to a Troop of Horse.

MONUMENTAL INSCRIPTIONS.

In the Nave, on three adjoining gravestones are inscriptions for Henry Manning, who died 5th October 1725, aged 72 years; Sarah, the wife of Henry Manning, who deceased 16th October, 1718, aged 58 years; and —lann Manning, who died May 12, 1769, aged 64.

In the south aisle, on a large flat stone bearing the effigies of a man in brass between his two wives, and having underneath them fifteen children, is inscribed in black letter;

𝕳ere under lyeth buried the bodye of 𝖂illiam 𝕯eath, gentylman, 𝕻ryncipall of 𝕾tapyle 𝕴nne, and one of the 𝕬ttorneys of the 𝕮omon 𝕻leas at 𝖂estminster, who had two wybes, 𝕰lizabeth and 𝕬nne; and had yssue by 𝕰lizabeth ten sonnes and six daughters: which 𝖂ylliam beying of the age of sixty three yeares, deceased the firste of 𝕸arch, 1590. 𝕬nd 𝕰lizabeth being of the age of xl yeares deceased the xiii of 𝕬pril, 1582, unto whose soules almighty 𝕲od grant a joyful resurrection.

ARMS, Six coats quarterly. 1st, A Griffin passant between three crescents. 2d, a chevron between three children's heads couped at the shoulders, enwrapped about the neck with as many snakes. 3rd, a chevron. 4th, is not now discernible. 5th, three lions rampant. 6th, as the first.

A Cross anciently stood on the south side of the church, and in the aisle were inlaid gravestones, the brasses are now lost.*

In the north aisle are memorials for the following individuals, but part of the inscriptions are covered by the pews.

Here lyeth the body of Iohn Round, late of Dartford in Kent, who departed this life 24th October, 1682, in the 76 year of his age.

John Round, citizen and clothworker of London, who died 26th August, 1701, aged 53 years and three months.

---

* Possibly the slab with brasses was a monument for R. Pinden, vide p. 29.

Sarah Woodin, departed this life 12 March, 1723, aged 71 years.

Joane, daughter of Thomas Round of this parish, by Joane his wife, departed this life 10th December, 1632, in 12th year of her age.

Israel Round died 24th August, 1682, aged 37.

Here lieth the body of Anthony Poulter who died July——aged——

Elizabeth Round, daughter to the aforesaid Anthony Poulter, deceased 7th January, 1681, in the 67th year of her age.

Olive, son of Mr. Henry Woodin of this parish, died August 13th Anno Domini 1716, aged 41 years.

Nicholas Chambers, late of this parish, gent dyed 11th October, in the year of our lord 1685.

Mary his first wife, daughter of Samuel Dalling of Westerham, in the county of Kent, gentleman.

Elizabeth, his second wife daughter of Richard Porter of Crayford, gent. and his daughter Mary, whom he had by Mary his first wife.

In the great chancel, on the northern side of the altar, is a handsome monument erected by Sir John Spilman, for lady Elizabeth his first wife, enclosed with iron railings. Upon it is his effigy in armour, together with that of his lady, kneeling at a desk, each with a book open,* and over their heads on a tablet of black marble the following German inscription in gilt letters,

Alhie Ruehet in Christo Jesu

Frauw Elisabeth H. Nicolai Mengels Burgers, undt dess Raths der Stadt Nuernberg Tochter H. Johan Spilmans Rittern, Ehliche Hausfrauw. welche nach dem sie mitt Jhrem Ehman from, Gottesfurchtig, und getreuw 35 Ihar gelebet, Endtlich in abuehmung Ihres Leibs Seliklich entschlaffen.

Ihres alters 55 Jhar den 10 May, Ano 1607.

Under the above is the following trilinguar verse.

Non licuit pro te conjunx extrema subire,
atque tuam mortem, morte piare mea ;
quod licuit feci, tumulus lachrimæque secutæ,
quisquid et mariti continet alma fides.

Thee to release, giving my life
For the was not God's will, deare wife ;
What must be is, that this tombe will
Declare my love, and dvetie still.

---

* The books are lost: and the lady's hands are gone. Sir John Spilman died in November, 1626, *vide* Manor of Bignors.

Mein leib Leben, liebs Weib hett ich,
Gern geben umb zueerretten dich;
Weils so must sein, soll doch diss Grab,
Kundt thuen mein treuw gmuet so ich hab.

Von Lindow } H. Johan Spilman Ritter, hatt dieses seyner lieven
am Bodensee } Hausfrew zue guetter gedechtnes, auffrichten lassen
anno 1607.

On a small tablet between two escutcheons on the base of
the tomb is this inscription in Roman capitals.

Auf den 31 dac. . Jul. an. 1607. ist in Got verscaiden der junge gesel
Hans Buoschor von Lindow am Bodensee.

On the top of the monument are these arms. Or, a serpent wreathed in pale azure, crested
gules, on a mount in base vert, two flanches gules, each charged with three lions passant, or.
Crest, a savage wreathed about the temples and loins, with ivy: the motto, "Arte et
fortuna."

Beneath, on the tomb, are two coats;—Spilman as above, impaling argent, a man cloathed
sable, with a long cap on, holding in his hand an olive branch proper, and standing on a
mount inverted gules.

On the south side of the chancel, an altar tomb enclosed
with iron rails thus inscribed.

Here lies interred the body of Clement Petit, Esq. of Joyes, in this
parish, whose paternal seat was of *Dentelion*, in the Isle of Thanet., in
this county; who departed this life the 23rd of March, Anno Domini,
1717, aged 73 years.

Before the rails of the altar inlaid in a large stone slab,
are the effigies of a man and woman in brass, in the
costume of the age, under an ogee crocketed canopy,
with labels issuing from their mouths in black letter
viz. from the man's 𝕮𝖗𝖊𝖉𝖔 𝖖𝖚𝖔𝖉 𝕽𝖊𝖉𝖊𝖒𝖕𝖙𝖔𝖗 𝖒𝖊𝖚𝖘 𝖇𝖎𝖇𝖊𝖗, 𝖊𝖙 𝖎𝖓
𝖓𝖔𝖇𝖎𝖘𝖘𝖎𝖒𝖔 𝖉𝖎𝖊 and from the woman's 𝕰𝖙 𝖎𝖓 𝖈𝖆𝖗𝖓𝖊
𝖒𝖊𝖆 𝖇𝖎𝖉𝖊𝖇𝖔 𝕯𝖊𝖚𝖒 𝕾𝖆𝖑𝖇𝖆𝖙𝖔𝖗𝖊𝖒 𝖒𝖊𝖚𝖒. Round the verge of
the stone is an inscription in brass, in part torn away, for
Richard Martin and his wife:

𝕳𝖎𝖈 𝖏𝖆𝖈𝖊𝖓𝖙 𝕽𝖎𝖈𝖆𝖗𝖉𝖚𝖘 𝕸𝖆𝖗𝖙𝖎𝖓𝖎 𝖉𝖊 𝕭𝖊𝖗𝖙𝖊𝖋𝖔𝖗𝖉, 𝖖𝖚𝖎 𝖔𝖇𝖎𝖎𝖙 𝖚𝖓𝖉𝖊𝖘𝖈𝖎𝖒𝖔
𝖉𝖎𝖊 𝖒𝖊𝖓𝖘𝖎𝖘 𝕬𝖕𝖗𝖎𝖑𝖎𝖘, 𝕬𝖓𝖓𝖔 𝕯'𝖓𝖎 𝖒𝖎𝖑𝖊𝖘𝖘𝖎𝖒𝖔 𝖖𝖚𝖆𝖉𝖗𝖆𝖌𝖎𝖓𝖙𝖊𝖘𝖘𝖊𝖒𝖔
𝖝𝖇𝖎𝖎𝖎 𝖉𝖎𝖊 𝖒𝖊𝖓𝖘𝖎𝖘 𝕱𝖊𝖇𝖗𝖚𝖆𝖗𝖎𝖎, 𝖆𝖓𝖓𝖔 𝖉𝖔𝖒𝖎𝖓𝖎 𝖒𝖎𝖑𝖊𝖘𝖘𝖎𝖒𝖔
𝖖𝖚𝖆𝖉𝖗𝖆𝖌𝖎𝖓𝖙𝖊𝖘𝖎𝖒𝖔 𝖘𝖊𝖈𝖚𝖓𝖉𝖔𝖘. 𝕼𝖚𝖔𝖗𝖚𝖒 𝖆𝖓𝖎𝖒𝖆𝖇𝖚𝖘 𝖕𝖗𝖔𝖕𝖎𝖈𝖎𝖊𝖙𝖚𝖗
𝕯𝖊𝖚𝖘, 𝕬𝖒𝖊𝖓.

Inlaid in an adjoining stone are the figures of a woman and six children, habited in the fashion of the reign of James I. The effigy of the man is lost.

The inscription reads thus:

Here lieth the body of Captaine Arthvr Bostocke, gent. who maried Frances, the second davghter of Francis Rogers, Esq. and had issve by her two sonnes and four davghters, and departed this lyfe the 7th of Ivly, 1612.

On a stone formerly inlaid with the effigies of a priest, with his name and time of his decease inscribed around the verge but now entirely lost—are these lines;

[Hic jacet Johannes Hornley, theologie baccal   qui obiit mcccclxxvii.]

Si flerent artes, Hornley tacuisse Johannem
    Non possent ista, qui tumulatur humo.
In septem fuerat liberalibus ille magister;
    Prudens et Castus, maximus atque fide.
Doctrine sacre tunc bacchalaureus ingens.
    Oxonie cunctis semper amatus erat.
Consilio valuit, sermones pandere sacros
    Noverat, et Doctos semper amare viros
Pauperibus largus fuerat; quos noverat aptos.
    In studiis paciens, sobrius atque fuit.
Moribus insignis cuncta virtute refulgens,
    Pro tantis meritis spiritus astra tenet.

The cavity once filled by a figure and inscription-plate in the adjacent stone, now offers no indication of the party sought to be commemorated.

On the left of Martin's monument, before the altar is a slab containing the upper part only of a female figure in brass, wearing a head dress of the time of queen Mary, with a small ruff round the neck in nebule folds, and a long stomacher. There is no inscription.

Against the vestry door a black marble slab inscribed

Spe Resurgendi sub hoc marmore Lapide reponitur quiquid mortale erat Nich'i Tooke de Dartford, gen' qui obijt Dominica xxij die Decembris, Anno Domini 1672, Ætatis suæ 90. Vivit post funera.

Arms, Tooke, argent on a chevron sable, three plates of the field between three greyhounds heads erased sable coloured or. (Incorrectly engraved.)

Upon a stone inlaid with brass, before the step of the altar, is the figure of a woman, her hands joined in prayer, and beneath, this inscription :—

Hic jacet Agnes, filia Joh'is Appelton qu'dm ux' Willi' Hesilt, uni' Baronii' de S'cc'io d'ni Regis Henricii Sexti, & postea ux' Rob'ti Molyngton, fr'is Thome Molyngton, milit'· Baronis ie Memme, q' obijt xxix die Augusti Anno Domini Mccccl:iij. Cui' a'i'e prop'icietur deus, Amen.

Affixed to the north wall over Lady Spilman's monument is a painting on canvas, in black frame, Escott impaling Spilman, underneath, this inscription without date :

Here Lyeth the Body of Mistris Katherin Estcott, Daughter of Sir Iohn Spillman of this Parrish.

On black marble slabs south side of the great chancel :

Here lieth the body of William Tasker of this parish, who departed this life, 10th May, 1732, in the 72 year of his age.

Elizabeth, wife of the above named William Tasker, who died October 25th, 1740, in the 81st year of her age.

Also the body of William Tasker, jun. 2d son of the abovesaid William Tasker, who died 27th of March, 1733, aged 35 years.

On adjoining slabs :

Also Henry, the 3rd son of William and Elizabeth Tasker, died 3rd day of August, 1746, aged 48 years.

Sarah, relict of Henry Tasker above mentioned, 22nd November, 1774, aged 66 years.

John, their 5th son, April 25th, 1736, in his second year.

Thomas, their 2nd son, 5th January, 1760, in his 32nd year.

Henry, their eldest son, 12th July, 1766, in his 40th year, leaving issue by Jane his wife, Jane and John.

Jane, relict of last named Henry Tasker, 24th February, 1790, aged 66.

William, 4th son, 11th June, 1738, in his fifth year.
Matthew, 3rd son of Henry and Sarah Tasker, 9 Feb. 1786, aged 53.

On a similar slab at the foot :

Here lyeth interred the body of William Burges, late Cittizen and Salter of London, bee deceased the 26th August, 1640, Anno Ætatis, 54, he left issue two sonns and one daughter.   Vivit post funera vertus.

ARMS.   A fess fret between three rooks.

On a black marble slab, north side :

Here lyeth the body of Mark Feilder, died 17 May, 1753, aged 91.
Also of Mrs. Elizabeth Feilder, who died the 9th Feb. 1743, aged 68.
Also Mr. Samuel Feilder, who died the 13th Nov. 1760, aged 47.
Likewise Mr. Mark Fielder, who died May 10th, 1782, aged 76.
Also Mary Henley, who died 5th July, 1799, aged 80 years.

Upon the north wall of the chancel near the entrance, a mural monument of white marble, with a bust in profile of Mr. Currey, and beneath, a tablet with this inscription :

Sacred to the Memory of the Rev. John Currey, A. M. forty-seven years Vicar of this Parish, Rector of Longfield, and formerly fellow of St. John's College, Cambridge, who departed this life on the 18th day of October, 1824, aged 89 years, and lies buried in Northfleet Church.   For a perpetual remembrance of his virtues : to record their deep sense of his worth, and their heartfelt sorrow for their loss, his parishioners have caused this monumental tablet to be erected.

We saw in him benevolence tempered with discretion, zeal controuled by sober judgment, and piety adorned with a simplicity approaching almost to that of the apostolic age.

Beneath are his arms.

Near it, a gothic mural tablet, with pinnacles :

In memory of Joseph Jardine, who died March 14th, 1832, aged 75.
Sarah Jardine, died December 17th, 1816, aged 49.

They lived in usefulness and honour : they died in peace.
As a tribute of filial affection to departed worth, their sons caused this tablet to be erected.

F

On the entrance into the vestry is a board thus inscribed:

DARTFORD PARISH.

A table of Fees settled at a publick Vestry 16th day of June, 1825.

Burials.	Vicar,	Clerk,	and	Sexton.
Little Bell	2s. 6d.	3s.		
Fourth Bell	2s. 6d.	4s.		4 ft. grave.
Sixth Bell	2s. 6d.	5s.		
Eighth Bell	2s. 6d.	7s. 6d.		

To the Clerk and Sexton for every foot additional to a grave above 4ft.

For the first foot .... 1s.
For the second in addition to the first ...... 2s.
For the third in addition .... 3s.
And so on 1s. for every additional foot.

Marriages by Banns.	Vicar.	Clerk.
For the Banns	1s.	
For the Marriage	6s.	3s. 6d.

In the *South Chancel* beneath the ancient painting of the story of St. George and the Dragon, is an altar tomb formerly enclosed with wood rails, bearing the following inscription on the south side:

John Beer of Dartford had issue, Nicholas, Ann, and Dorothy Beer.
Nicholas Beer had issue, Clement and Edward Beer.
Clement Beer had issue, John & Clement Beer, both died without issue.

Edward Beer their Onckle, was their heire, and lived onmarried 59 ieares, and died abovt the 14th March, 1627.

ON THE NORTH SIDE—Christofer Twisleton, of Barley, in the county of York, esqyier, married with Ann Beer, and had issue George Twisleton; George Twisleton had issue John Twisleton; and Edward Beer dying without issue gave all his land in Kent to John Twisleton, who erected this monument in memory of the said Edward Beer in the ieare 1628.

On the west side are two shields; one quarterly 1st, and 4th, quarterly a canton ermine 2nd and 3rd, on a fess three garbs; the other the same arms impaling a chevron.

On a black marble slab at the north entrance;

John Twisleton of Horseman's Place, died 28 July, 1721, aged 72.

---

* The Vicar's fee for a brick Vault is eight guineas; for a grave bricked up to the top of the coffin and then arched over three pounds ten shillings, but in a recent instance [G Cann's,] where the grave was dug twelve feet deep and bricked up to the surface, six guineas has been demanded. For putting down head and foot stone, one guinea. In each of the above cases, the Clerk's fee is five shillings.

At a little distance a grave stone having a brass plate thus inscribed in black letter:

Here lyeth John Beer somtyme of Dartford, esqye, and Alyce, and Johane his wyves, also Henry Beer his sonne and heir, who had to wife Anne Beer, sometime wife to Richard Howlett, gent. deceased, and had by her a son named William Beer deceased: which said John died Ap. 25. 1572, and the said Henry, 26th May in 1574.

Above are two coats in brass, both a bear rampant, on a canton five escalop shells.

This tomb stands upon an ancient monumental slab.

On the east wall a mural monument inscribed:

Near this place lies interred John Twisleton of Horseman's Place, in this parish, Esq. son and heir of John Twisleton of Drax, in Yorkshire; who was uncle and heir to Sir George Twisleton, Bart. of Barley in that county the ancient paternal seat of the family. This John had fouer wiues, the 1st. Elizabeth, dau. and heir of Augustine Skinner of Tolsham, in yt county; 2d. Lucy 5th dau. of S. Dunch, of Baddesley, co. Berks. buried near this place: 3rd. Elizabeth, eldest dau. & coh. of the Rt. Hon. James, Viscount and Baron Say and Seale, by whom he had issue two sons and a daughter, who died shortly after, and also a daughter now living; 4th Ann, dau. & heir of John Christofer Meyern, a German, who survived him. He departed this life 4th December, 1682, in the 69th year of his age.

Anne, his last wife died 19th of November, 1717, aged 88.

On a large stone inlaid with engraved brass plates were formerly the figures of a man and his two wives with four children, and their shield of arms; but the whole are lost, excepting the second wife, who appears clad in the costume, temp. Henry VI. wearing a heart shaped head-dress, with her hair enclosed in net-work. The monument anciently was thus inscribed:

Hic jacent Willielmus Rothele de Hertford, que obiit primo die mensis Augusti anno domini Mcccclxiiii, necnon Beatrix et Johanna uxoris ejus ac puerorum eorundum. Quorum a'i'abus propicietur Deus, Amen.

On a gravestone of black marble near the former.

Here lyeth the body of Prosper Browne, Esq. of Horsman's Place in this parish, who departed this life, Sept. 20th, 1739, aged 56 yrs.

ARMS. On a bend cotised, three lions passant impaling a chevron between three eagles' heads erased.

Inlaid on a large slab are the effigies of a man and woman in brass, in the costume of the age, (temp. Hen. VII.) the gentleman wearing a long gown, and the lady a pediment head-dress partly covered by a long veil. She is habited in a close gown buckled round the waist with a broad girdle of wrought work hanging down to the skirts; their hands joined in prayer:

𝕺 pytefull creatur co'cernyng erthly sepulture
𝕺f 𝕶atryn burlton subterrat ix day w'yn 𝕵une
𝕿howsand iiij 𝕮.lxxxxbi yer accurrent
𝖂't' rychard burlton jantilma' spows to the katryn
𝕰xpy'ed thowsand b'
𝖂'hyer thus cumbent ask criest ma' gre' yt' is urgent
𝖂her thorow y' prayour of theys tweyn schall he be
        sabyour.

On a gravestone near the former were the effigies of a man and woman with four escutcheons in brass now lost. The figure of the man only remains.* Round the verge of the stone was an inscription in brass in black letter, of which the following portion existed in the last century—but the whole is now missing:

domini millessimo quingentessimo octabo, et 𝕰leanor uxor ejus, que obiit quinto die mensis 𝕱ebruarii, anno domini mb'lxxbij. 𝕼uorum animabus propicietur 𝕯eus. 𝕬men.

The characters between each word of the above inscription were somewhat singular, each consisting of a bell, tun, leaf, rose, trefoil, slipped dog, mullet, leopard, head, crescent, cross, form, horses head, &c. although they were only designed as ornamental points. Two of the escutcheons were v parted per chevron, in the first eight crosses formeè: the 2nd coat the same impaling a chevron, three leopards heads in chief.

---

* He is habited as a gentleman of the fifteenth century in a long gown bordered with fur, which reaches to his feet, having large sleeves down to the wrist; to his girdle on the right side hangs a purse or pouch worn on the outside for convenience. A brass plate in Penshurst church represents Thomas Yden, Esq (who died 1564,) in a dress similar to this effigy: and Agnes his wife in a costume much like that of Katryn Burlton.

Richard Burlton held lands at Lampytt, of Temples Dartford manor, for which he paid 2½d. quit rent. Rentale de Dertford, Addit. MSS. 9493. They were in possession of William Heynes, 1 Hen. VIII.

There were several other brass figures and inscriptions formerly in this chapel, but the whole are lost.

A mural white marble monument affixed to the south wall is thus inscribed :

Sacred to the memory of John Williams heretofore of this place, and late of Wilcroft, co. Hereford, Esq: who having throughout the early period of life, (ever assiduous and intelligent,) successfully pursued his profession of the Law, and having, with acquired and hereditary affluence, in retirement and amidst his family, during the remainder of the days allotted to him, been long occupied in the pursuits of agriculture, and ever in extensive acts of benevolence and charity, under severe bodily infirmity, but supported by christian faith, religious hope, and rational piety, closed an active and useful life on the 14th day of August, 1823, aged 69.

On a gravestone of black marble on the south side :

Here lies interred the body of Mrs. Margaret Pitt, the relict of John Pitt, Esq. late president to the Honorable South Sea Company, at Vera Cruz, who died 22nd February, 1731, aged 49 years.

Arms. A fess checky between three besants, impaling a chevron engrailed between three eagles' heads erased.

On the eastern wall of this chapel is an oval tablet

Sacred to the memory of the Rev. James Harwood, M.A. Rector of Cliffe, and Vicar of this parish twenty two years. Who died February 15th 1778, aged 63.

And also of his deceased daughters, Charlotte, Mary, and Frances, whose Remains together with His are interred in a vault in the west side of the Upper Burying Ground.

The Righteous shall be had in everlasting Remembrance.

———

A diminutive modern font in total discordance with the architectural character of the edifice, stands in this chapel, and is the only one now used for the sacred rite of baptism.*

* These modern tasty fonts only accord with the china basons used by the Independents, Wesleyans, etc. who consider that "sprinkling" constitutes baptism. Their size prevents the officiating minister from complying with the injunctions of the rubric, "to DIP the child in the water discreetly and warily" whilst he repeats the baptismal form, unless the godfathers and godmothers "certify the child is weak." The

In the vestry are a series of Oxford Almanacks from 1732, to the present time in black frames.*

———

The TOWER of the church has been already noticed in its conversion from a fortress to a campanile; but if it is admitted that the basement may partly be of Norman re-construction, its proportions were vastly improved by the erection of the additional story which now contains the bells, about the time of Edward IV. or somewhat later. The edifice is seventy-four feet in height, and twenty-two feet square; it consists of three stories, having the clock and chimes in the second, and a good ring of eight bells in the third, hung therein A.D. 1704.† Fears of the stability of the tower were entertained a few years past, but upon a careful survey by Mr. Cresy the architect, August, 1836, it was ascertained that with the adoption of a few slight precautionary measures there was no danger to be apprehended.‡

———

practice of immersion is still sanctioned by the highest authorities in the church, even in the baptism of persons who are of riper years; for "on Tuesday the 30th December, 1829, (a bitter cold day,) a young lady was baptized by immersion in St. Martin's church, Oxford, who from conscientious motives had desired this mode of baptism, the bishop of London having directed that her wishes should be complied with." *Jackson's Oxford Journal, Jan. 2d.* 1830. In the performance of this ceremony it seems a large wood vessel was prepared; the lady stepped in and was immersed in a similar manner to that practised by the Baptists.—It is hoped the correct feeling which pervades the age will re-place the venerable parochial font of *Dartford* on a proper pedestal and restore it to its original use.

* The late Lord Harcourt's Collections for Oxfordshire (now in possession of the writer) contain the whole series of engravings from their commencement. Numerous drawings, prints, etc. have lately been added thereunto.

† Vide p. 24. p. 27. ante.   ‡ Vestry Book sub ann.

THE CHURCH-YARD.

On the north side of the CHURCH-YARD anciently stood a stone Cross, in catholic times an appendage to almost every cemetery.* The period of its demolition is unknown.

On the 20th Feb. 1465, (5 Edw. IV.) John Hornley the vicar, Richard Hert, and William Stockmede, the church-wardens of Dartford, by an instrument under their hands granted license to John Groverste whose house bounded the north-western side of the church-yard, to take from the said cemetery two feet of assize, build thereon a chimney, and carry the wall of his dwelling house in a straight line. This license was confirmed by the bishop, and the prior and convent of Rochester: the chimney exists to this day.†

The church-yard anciently extended to the present kerb stone of the pavement on the south side of the church, and was enclosed by a flint wall: but on the erection of the new bridge in 1754, that portion was given to widen the approaches thereunto.‡ Some years after the whole of the southern side was open to the highway. The inscription on the tomb against the wall¶ is said to have been then legible, but idle boys playing thereon it became utterly effaced.

---

* Joan Calvert of Dertford, widow, by will dat. 20 April, 1535, desires her body to be buried on the north side of the church yard, beside THE CROSS of the parish church. Regist. Test. ix. 72.

† Act. Cur Consist. f. 241. ‡ Vest Book. f. 202. The bishop's faculty and license, dat. 25 Sep. 1754, grants seven superficial rods.

¶ Some years ago a report prevailed that a ghost might nightly be seen perched upon this old tomb, which on a passenger's approach glided away and disappeared behind the church. Timid persons

The present iron railing was erected in 1827.

Gravestones and tombs in church-yards do not occur earlier than about the middle of the seventeenth century. The graves of the most wealthy were only indicated by small mounds of earth up to that period.*

---

would not pass. At last Mr. Brand's father (who had been on the watch) caught it in its accustomed position, and striking it with his rule discovered its humanity by its scream: then dragging it down found it no other than Sarah, daughter of Mrs. Brewer the parish clerk, wrapped up in a sheet gathered at the head like a shroud, with her face whitened with powder. The young lady afterwards married, and was many years landlady of the Eight Bells in Dartford.

The church gates were ordered by vestry to be removed to the south end of Mr. Cranwell's house (now Stidolph's) in 1756, and to be spiked to prevent a passage.

* In Dunkin's Oxfordshire, ii. 184, is a memorandum by the rector of Wendlebury in his Parish Register, that "the gravestone of one Richard Dawson who died Feb. 1667, was the first ever set up in that church-yard." Bloxham also intimates that no headstones existed in church-yards before the early part of that century, and if there were any other monuments, they had originally been placed in the church Mon. Archit. 262. Yet Laborde, in his recent journey through Arabia Petræa, found at Sarbout el Cadem a deserted Egyptian burial place of remote ages, about seventy-five paces in length and thirty-five in breadth, having much the appearance of a ruined church-yard. The stones are exactly the shape but higher than the head stones in a country church-yard in England; they vary in height from 5 to 8ft.; in breadth from 18 to 20 inches, and from 14 to 16 inches in thickness. The gravestones, about 14 in number, are partly thrown down; a few are standing, and their fronts are covered with hieroglyphics, which will be easily read should the key be ever discovered. Among them are the remains of a small Egyptian temple. The preservation of these monuments, amidst the storms of wind and weather is attributed to the purity of the atmosphere. ib. 87. Lond. 1838. As there never was any town in the vicinity, the author supposes it a cemetery of the Egyptians who worked the copper mines at Sarbout el Cadem. No similar ancient memorials are known.

As there are few gravestones in the eastern part of this cemetery, it is tastefully planted with shrubs and flowers, and kept in the neatest order.

———

The following is the substance of the inscriptions now legible.

North-west, and North side of the Church-yard.

Gravestones. Elizabeth Walker, died July 14, 1718, aged 81.

John Walker, died March 6th 1716, aged 70.

John Wood, died 20th March, 1826, aged 83.

Ann, his wife, 4th May, 1821, aged 64.

On a tomb. Sarah Loft, of this parish, died 23 Nov. 1806, aged 68

Gravestones. Henry Swaisland, died 13 July, 1746, aged 65.

John Barnard, Elizabeth Swaisland, and Susanna Loft, also lieth here interred.

John Loft, of this parish died 10th July, 1754, aged 61.

Mary his wife died, June 4th, 1775, aged 68.

John Kempton, sen. late of this parish, died 12th April, 1792, aged 68.

John his son, died 17th Feb. 1792, aged 23.

Mary, widow of above, died   1796, aged

Richard Cacket, died 29th Feb. 1788, aged 37.

Mary his wife, dau. of John and Mary Kimpton of this parish, died 15th July, 1780, aged 36.

Mary, Sarah, and John, their children, died infants.

Samuel Cacket, son of above, died 7 July, 1806, aged 23.

Samuel Sedgwick, died 20th Aug. 1780, aged 38.

Elizabeth his wife, died 21 Nov. 1797, aged 58.

William Newton, sen. died 21 Dec. 1800, aged 64.

Elizabeth his first wife sist. of S. Sedgwick, died 17 Sept. 1788, aged 53.

Jane his 2d. wife, died 16 March, 1795, aged 44.

Jane Sedgwick Newton d. 15th Jan. 1796, aged 7 weeks.

Charles Gregory died 25th December, 1750, aged

Elizabeth his wife, died 25th December, 1750, aged 25.

Robert Pearcey late of this parish, d. 27 Oct. 1765, ag. 39.

William son of Rob. & Eliz. P. died 11 Jan. 1766, aged 18.

Also William, Elizabeth, Anna, and Elizabeth.

Robert Child, of this parish, died 28 Aug. 1752, aged 52.

Peter C. his nephew, died Dec. 3d. 1771, aged 36.

Margaret wife of John Day, died 5th March 1821 aged 42.

Ann Pennington wife of Thomas Metcalf, d. 18th August 1821, aged 68.

G

John Buttinger, late of this p. died 18 Nov. 1781, aged 66.

Ann, his wife, died 8th Feb. 1798, aged 71.

John, son of the above, died 11 June, 1784, aged 39.

Anna Maria, wife of the Rev. Thomas Deacon, of this parish, died 23rd July, 1815, aged 36.

Anna Maria, only daughter of the above, died 4th August, 1826, aged 11.

John, son of John Garrett, died 6th July, 1773, aged 18.

John Garrett, Sen. died 15th June, 1777, aged 89.

Mary Garrett his wife, died 11th June, 1772, aged 72.

Catherine wife of Matthew Waterhouse, died 29th September 1790, aged 69.

Colonel George Saxon, late of the Honourable East India Company's service, died 23rd April 1821, aged 66.

Thomas Hall died 11th June, 1815, aged 75.

Sarah his wife, died 2nd May, 1825, aged 67.

James Lawford, died 13th September, 1788, aged 83.

James, son of the above, died 23rd Oct. 1769, aged 31.

An altar tomb to the memory of the Woodins has only the following portions of inscription legible.

William Woodin, who died............................. 1760
.... 1760

Gravestones. Elizabeth Barton, relict of Mr. William Barton, of this parish, died 13th July 1831, aged 85.

Richard Brandon died 14th April, 1786, aged 35.

Thomas Brandon his son died an infant.

William Barton, butcher, of this Parish, died 1st Dec. 1796, aged

Ann, wife of Robert Young, died 28th April, 1813, aged 30.

Ann Young, daughter of the above, died 15th September, 1804, aged 4 months.

John Brown, died October 7th, 1764, aged 60 years.

Grace his wife, died Feb. 29th, 1768, aged 55.

Richard Dumright died Nov. 8th, 1758, aged 60.

East of the Church.

Richard Theobald, many years doctor of physic in this parish................................

Mary, his wife, died June 1st, 1740, aged 56.

Catherine wife of James Prescott, died July 16th 1759, aged 70.

A broken stone. Charles Fry, died October 11th, 1754, aged 41. Vivit post funera vertus.

> Truth and integrity amidst temptation,
> Exemplified beneath you lies,
> A publican, a friend to the nation,
> Beloved he lived, lamented died.

CHANTRY OF St. MARY AT STAMPIT.

1338. Thomas de Dertford alias *At Stampit** vicar of Dartford founded a Chantry in the south aisle of the church of Dartford, in honor of the Virgin Mary the Mother of God, for the health of his own soul, his ancestors, and all the faithful departed. He appointed master Robert Felthorp first chaplain, and endowed it with about one hundred and twenty acres of land and sundry lands and tenements; viz., *one messuage* and garden which was formerly Alexander's at Stampit, situate at *Rokemary lane;* the *whole of the moor* which was Alexander's, and *another* which the founder had acquired of Thomas Henton, senior; a *messuage* in *Hithe street* with its curtilage; a *garden* with its appurtenances in *Hithe street; two messuages* with their appurtenances in the *High street of Dartford,* which are now held of William Newcock and Letitia who was the wife of Gilbert Taverner, lying between the messuage formerly John Este's against the east, and the messuage of John Pilcher† against the west; the head to the King's way [High street], and opposite the Cranford water to the north:—a *garden‡* lying near to the *manse of the vicar* of Dartford to the east, and the curtilage of master Richard Rogers, chaplain, to the west, and between the two running streams south and northward; three acres and a rod of land in the field

---

* A *surname* derived from *Stampit* or *Stanepit*, the stone-pit above the priory near which he was born. He assumed that of his benefice.

† The printing-office of J. Dunkin and Son stands on the site of the messuage belonging to *Pilcher* in the *time of Edward III.*, and the Eight-Bells public house on that of *John Este.* The *Cranpit* stream is an ineffaceable locality.　　‡ Now the site of Mr Hurst's garden.

called *Kyland;* one acre and three rods in *Highfield;* an acre and a half of land with appurtenances in *Castle- field* in two places there, together with *pasturage for three cows* in Eastlease-pasture at *Stoneham.* The houses, woods, etc., constituting this endowment the chaplain and his successors were enjoined to maintain and on their cession or decease leave   store, and lands sown as the aforesaid Ralph the chaplain received of the founder; viz, *three cows* of the usual value and *thirty sheep;* and if the land is not sown, sufficient *seed to sow the same,* or if it remains unsown until after Easter, then he shall immediately give his successor *four quarters of corn* for the subsequent year. Every year within the octaves of St. Andrew in winter the chaplain was bound to celebrate in the church of Dartford solemn exequies with mass for the soul of bishop Hamo, and his successors in the see of Rochester, Thomas the founder, and all the faithful departed this life. The said chaplain was also bound to pay twelve pence yearly in token of subjection or recom- pence yearly to the vicar of Dartford and his successors. The founder gave the patronage and nomination of the chaplain in future to the bishop of Rochester and his successors. The endowment was *dated at Dertford, on Thursday, the feast of St. George the martyr,* 1338, and subsequently confirmed by the bishop and prior of the church of Rochester.*

1338   Ralph de Felthrop. Presented by the founder Thomas de Dertford,
                                                 alias At Stampit.

---

* Thorpe's Registrum Roffense. 309. 112. Lond. 1788.

CHAPLAINS.   PATRON, THE BISHOP OF ROCHESTER.

1396 John Standon, he resigned the chaplaincy to Robert Grape, vicar
      of Dertford, brother John Sill of the order of preaching
      friars, and Henry Walpole and Jacob Bere, clerks of the
      church of Rochester, when John Faconer was admitted,
      10 Oct.*

1400 20 Sept. John Delve or Drew, collated to chantry of the blessed
      Mary of Dertford.†

1401 28 Jan. Thomas Gibbs instit to chantry of Stampit on death of
      John Drew.‡

1422 31 Dec. John de Asney, chapl. presented to the same ¶

1424 22 Dec. John Arney, or Elmey, exchanged the chantry with
      Thomas Merhaant for the rectory of Hever, in this county.

1425 8 Oct. John Burford, appointed chaplain to chantry of blessed
      Mary on dismission of the former and demanded possession
      in person.‖

1433 4 Aug. John Bloss appointed chaplain ;** five years afterwards he
      obtained license (dated 9 May, 1498,) to celebrate certain
      divine offices yearly in consequence of the revenues of the
      chantry being diminished to six marks per annum.††

1448 26 Dec. Master John Sherborne presented to the chaplaincy of
      Stampit on death of John Bloss or Bloir.‡‡

---

* Reg. Will. de Botelsham. MS. Archiv. Ep. Roff.f.90.   † Ib. 150.

‡ Ibid. f. 184.

¶ Act. Cur. Consist. f 21. MS. Ib. 20 July 1422. Andreas Sondre,
clerk, vicar general to John, bishop of Rochester, granted license to John
Elmey [Arney] chaplain of the chantry called Stampit, to celebrate
certain special divine offices yearly, for nine years, in consequence of the
house being greatly ruinated   Ibid. sub. an.—Probably the scanty
revenues precluded the chaplain's repair of his residence and the chapel;
both were expected to be accomplished by oblations of the faithful.

‖ Ibid. f. 184.   ** Ibid. f. 97.   †† Ibid sub ann.   ‡‡ Ibid. f. 220.

1458. John Elmful, chaplain.*

1493. 1 Oct. Thomas Vernon instit. chaplain of the chantry of Stampit, on the free resignation of John Newman late chaplain, and collated to the same by the bishop on swearing to observe the statutes and ordinances of the chantry.†

1494. 18 Nov. The rev. father [the bishop] in his mansion at Lambeth Marsh, presented Simon Alleyn, priest, to the perpetual chantry of Stampit, on the free resignation of John Cokkes last chaplain ‡

1499. Will. Gawen pres. on resig. of Mast. Thos. Worsley.¶

1504. William Cooke chaplain ;‖ he held it eight years

1512. 26 Nov. Master Thomas Pelton presented to chantry of Stampit on death of William Coke ; to be resident therein according to the form and foundation of the said chantry.**

1514. 13 Nov. Master Nicholas Hall chaplain, presented to chantry of Stampit on death of Thomas Pelton.

—— John Blower.††

----

* Regist. Testam. ii. f. 129. Joan Fagg gave a tenement called Corsinghead at Rochester by will to this chantry.

† Episc' Cur. Munim. f. 6. This MS. comprises transcripts of charters, endowments of churches, and official transactions of the diocese of Rochester, interspersed with presentations to benefices from 1492 to 1542.   ‡ Ibid. f. 15.   ¶ Ibid. f. 23. b.

‖ See William Ladd's will, p. 34. Cooke held also a cottage and lands of the prioress of Dertford in Hithe street, temp Hen. VII.

** Epi. Cur. Mun. f. 61. The *chamber* constructed *above the vestiment room in the church* was the chaplain's *habitation*; the chimney is still visible. According to modern ideas it must have been an uncomfortable dwelling; for the *walls* were *unplaistered*, and the windows *unglazed*, although they had shutters. Two apertures in the walls afforded a view of the high altar and St. Mary's chapel. In the seventeenth century the room was converted into an armory.

†† John Blower chantry p'st of o'r Lady of Dertford, holdethe bi ye seyd chantery iiij shoppis in the Hie strete of Darfort, w'ch werr

1535. 3 Nov. William Hale [or Hall] priest, presented on death of
         Robert Johnson.*

1539. John Stacey chantry priest of Stampit.†

1545. Robert Baken [or Bacon].

By an Act passed 37 Henry VIII. for valuing and sur-
rendering all Colleges, Hospitals, Chantries, etc. the
following account of this endowment was taken.

(*Translation.*)

THE CHANTRY OF OUR BLESSED LADY THE VIRGIN OF
STAMPIT IN THE VILL OF DARTFORD.

*Farm or rent of divers tenements in the town aforesaid, in tenure of
divers persons at will, videlicet*—A tenement in Hythe street
adjoining the bridge, called the Orchard in the occupation
of Thomas Smith, 8s. 4d. A tenement in Hythe street in
tenure of William Potter, 13s. 4d. A tenement situate near
.....................Ib'm in tenure of Richard William, 10s.
Another tenement.......................20s. A garden plot
situate between one formerly the Cowmede in tenure of
Robert Duly, 3s. 4d.   Total -   60s. 0d.

A farm or tenement called the cherry orchard in Hythe street
aforesaid, with 6 acres of land adjacent in Stoneham field,
as let to Alexander Baker by indent. dat. 35 Hen. 8. for a
term of seven years at 53s. 4d. per ann.   •   •   •

A farm or tenement with shop near the market place as let
to John Cottman by indent. dat. 35 Hen. 8. aforesaid, for a
term of 21 years at 40s. per ann.   •   •   •   •

---

sometyme a messuage of Gilb't Cam'r [Taverner] and after of Thomas
Ancelme, to wit, betwix the runnyn Ryver called Cramforde on the est,
and the messuage of John M'rtyn on the southe and west, of the Kyngs
strete to the north ; and owes per ann. ixd. [quit rent] and suit of Court.
Rentale de Dertford [Temples]. temp. Hen. VIII.

  * Epi. Cur. Muniment. f. 184.

  † In a roll 22 Hen. 8. he is named as a tenant at will holding a garden
in Dartford of the crown at 20s. a year. No. 5535 Add. MSS.

A farm or tenement with shop let to Thomas Parrett by
    patent, dated 34th of the aforesaid king, for a term of
    21 years at 10s. per ann.   Total   -   103s. 4d.

              Total of the whole   -   £8 3s. 4d.

Reprises or Payments to divers persons underwritten, viz,
To the king by a former grant coming out of the aforesaid
tenement in the market-place 2s. To the king out of the
aforesaid premises 6d. To the king for a tenement in
Hithe street 2s. To Roger Appleton for rent coming
from the land in Stoneham-field 20d. To John Bere, gent.
for rent coming from a parcel of orchard at Stampit 20d.
To the same John Bere for rent for a tenement at [Stone-
ham] aforesaid 8d.- - - p an 8s. 10d. To Thomas Moile
for Grandison's rent 12s.   Total - £7 13s. 10d.

         Clear value beyond reprises - £... ... ...

MEMORANDUM. *There is a certain land called Oxenlease or* Estlease *now in
the tenure of* Thomas,* *fermour to the king's majestie of his manor and
demeynes of the late Pryorye of Dertford now dysolved of the yerely value of
13s. 4d. whych hath been delayned and not payed to the seyd Chuntye priest
sythens the Dysolution of the s'd pryorie; and also that Syr Robert Bacon
(Baken), is the Chuntry priest there:---and one Syr Thomas Darteford
late vicar of the parysh church was founder thereof as by the copy of the
foundacon remayning appeareth.†*

Notwithstanding the preceding valuation gave clear
intimation of approaching ruin, the foundation continued
to linger on until the 1 Edward VI. when its revenues
were seized by the king's commissioners, together with
all Obits, and Lands for providing Lights in churches,

---

* Afterwards Sir Thomas Walsingham.

† Chantry Roll, co. Kent. No. 89, dated 14 Feb. 37 Hen. VIII. in the
    Augmentation Office. It is written in latin upon paper.

pursuant to an Act passed for the Dissolution of all Colleges, Free Chapels, Guilds, Brotherhoods, Stipendages, with other like, given unto the king's majesty.

(Entry in Chantry Roll. 1 Edw. VI.)

THE CHANTRY OF O'R BLESSED LADY THE VIRGIN OF STAMPIT' founded by one Thomas de Dertford to thintente and purpos that one prest shuld celebrate dyvine service there for the soul of the s'd founder and all Christian souls.

The yearlye value of the landes and tenements of the same belonging - - - - - - -		£8 3s. 4d.
Rent resolut' - - - 8s. 9d. ⎫	. -	17s. 11d.
Perpetual Tenths upon - 9s 2d. ⎭		
so remaynes clere to the use of the chunt'y prest	-	£7 5s. 5d.

Robert Baken, clk. is incumbent there, of thage of 63 yeres, of indifferent learning and qualities: and the said Robert hath one yerely pencion of Cs. by the yere out of the chauntry of Northflete within the county of Kent.*

There was a vicarage already endowed within the parish church, the vicar's name is James Goldwell, and there are of howsling people within the s'd parish vij hundred.†

There heth not been any Grammar scole kept, preacher maintained, or poor people relieved by the same chauntry.

There hath not been any sale of land or tenement, spoyle or waste of woods, or gifte goodes appertayning to the late chauntry.

Goods there be none ‡

———

King Edward VI. granted to George Blagge, Nicholas Goodrych and their heirs, the Chantry of the blessed

———

* Robert Bacon was living 1553, and had a pension of £6 a year.

† Howseling people, *i.e.* persons capable of taking the sacrament.

‡ Chantry Roll. 1 Edward VI. No. 104. Augment. Office.

Mary of Stampit, with other lands and tenements, in Kent and in the city of London, 8th February, 1551.* On the death of Robert Blagge his son† they passed to Henry his son and heir, who sold them 24 Eliz. to Richard Burden, yeoman, he disposed of them the next year to Thomas and Andrew Asheley.   On the division of the property the several parcels passed into unknown hands.

MARTIN'S SALARY CHANTRY.

In this church was also another endowment called Martin's Chantry founded by John Martin, of Horton, probably the Judge of the Common Pleas, in the time of Henry the Sixth.

(Translation of Valuation, 26 Hen. VIII.)

The CHANTRY in the Town of DARTFORD called MARTIN'S SALARY, for one priest to celebrate divine service there for the Founder's soul and all Christians' souls for ever.‡

Imprimis.   A farm of 59 acres of meadow or marsh in divers places in Dartford ; within the salt marsh 1½ acres ; near the river called Thames 5 acres of land ; 1 acre in another part ; a piece of land called *Rodys* 8 acres, and 1 acre near the *Stone pitts ;* 4 acres called *Kingesland* in Dartford ; 4 acres called *Costerdowne* in Dartford aforesaid as let to John Rogers by indenture : Edmund Parker incumbent of the same and other feoffees of the same aforesaid, dated 36 Hen. VIII. for a term of 20 years at £9. per annum.

Reprises.   A payment to Thomas Moyle for 40 yeares called *Brasson-rent* coming out of the said premises 12s.

Value beyond reprises £8 8s per ann.

---

* Originalia. 4 Edw. VI. p. l. r. 26. No. 6367. Addit. MSS.

† Hasted's Kent. i. 230.   ‡ Chantry Roll, co. Kent.

MEMORANDUM. That one Sir Edmund Parker ys Salary pst there and one John Martin, late of Horton, founded the same as by the copie of the Founder remaininge appeareth.

CHANTRY ROLL, I EDW. VI.

A PERPETUAL SALARY founded by one Thomas (John) Martin, to thentente and purpose that one preste should celebrate Divine Service there for the Founder's soul and all Xt'n souls for ever.

Yerely value of land and tenements appertaining to the same place	-	-	-	-	-	£9	0s.	0d.
Reprises	-	-	-	-	-	-	12s.	0d.
Remayneth clere to maintenance of the s'd prest					-	£8	8s.	0d.

Edmund Parker is incumbent or Salary priest there of the age of xliiij. yeres of humble qualities of learning, and hath not any other lyving but only his fyne in the same salary.

As for the endowments of a Vicar it is answered in the title heretofore.

No spoile or waste of lands, etc. *

LIGHT LANDS.

LIGHT LANDS were given and bequeathed to the Parish Church [of Dartford] by the last will and testament of John Groverste for the finding of a perpetual Lamp Light for ever. They are of the yerely value of 13s. 4d.; and chargeable with a payment of 3s. 4d. Clere yerely value 10s.†

Also, there were LAMPE LANDS given to the seyd Parish Church, by whom unknown, the profit always employed to the finding and manufacture of a Lamp within the said church of the yerely value of 18s.‡

---

* Chantry Roll. 1 Edw. VI. 104. † These lands appear to have been given by Groverste in recompence of permission to build his chimney, etc. on the church yard, 6 Edw. IV. The will is not to be found.

‡ These could not have been Douce's, the valuation is too high.

ECCLESIASTICAL MATTERS.

This parish is the head of the Deanery of Dartford, and within the jurisdiction of the diocese of Rochester.

The church anciently paid 9*d.* chrism rent to the mother church of the diocese.

The church was granted by the Saxon kings to the see of Rochester, and recognised as held by the bishop at the compilation of domesday-book: *viz.* "The bishop holds the church of this manor, and it is worth sixty shillings: beside this, there are now three chapels.

Of the chapels nothing further is known: but one is presumed to have stood in the upper burying ground afterwards known as St. Edmund's; another was appendant to the king's manor house, and eventually merged in the priory chapel;* and the third was an appurtenance to the parish church.

THE RECTORY.

It appears that in the time of the Conqueror this church was seized by the king; but Hamo his steward re-settled it upon the church of St. Andrew at Rochester.† Gundulph the celebrated bishop of that see, on the separation of his own maintenance from that of the monks, allotted it among others to the support of the *almonry of the convent.* This appropriation was, however, annulled by bishop Gilbert de Glanvill who obtained the see 32 Hen. II. 1185, on pretence that his predecessor had impoverished the bishoprick by his too large donations to the priory;‡ he therefore divested

---

* The zig-zag and hatched mouldings of the priory church diffusively scattered in every part of the garden walls incontestibly prove it an Early-Norman edifice. † Text. Roff 158. ‡ Reg. Roff. 35.

the convent of its right to this church, and restored it to the see, only confirming the ancient pension therefrom to the monks.

In 1253 Bishop Laurence de St. Martin demised this church, and all the small tythes, oblations, and obventions, together with the tythes of sheaves in gardens and curtilages not ploughed, to the convent of Rochester, for three years, at a rental of thirty-eight marks per annum, on condition that they supplied the cure, and deducted their pension of ten marks from the same.

He afterwards upon complaining to pope Innocent IV. that his table was so slenderly provided for, that himself and his family had not at times common necessaries for food, obtained leave from the pontiff to appropriate the revenues of the church of Dartford to the supply of his board during life. This appropriation Alexander IV. and Clement IV. confirmed to the bishop and his successors on condition of their endowing a vicarage for the perpetual celebration of divine service in the parish church.*

In a very ancient valuation of the bishop's revenues Dartford rectory was stated at £40, and the bishop's *mill* and rents belonging thereto, at one hundred shillings yearly. [The mill is now the property of Mr. Colyer.]

In the 15 Edward I.† and 33 Edward III.‡ the rectory was valued at £25 per annum.

1536. At the general ecclesiastical survey in the 26 Hen. VIII., Dartford rectory and the rents belonging thereunto were entered at 45 marks.¶

---

* Reg. Roff. 66. It was usual to alledge some strong reason for seeking the appropriation; the record adds that the bishop's whole receipts were only 300 marks a year, insufficient for half his expences.

† Stev. Mon. i. 456.　‡ Reg. Roff. 129.　¶ Valor. Eccles. i. 229.

In 1613 the parsonage was valued at £160 per ann. and was then let to Francis Rogers, gent.*

The rectory still remains part of the possessions of the see of Rochester. The venerable archdeacon King, is the present lessee.

The rectorial tythes are commuted at £800 per ann.

THE BISHOP'S LIBERTY.

Bishop Laurence de St. Martin seems to have purchased several of the rents which now constitute the greater part if not the whole of the *Manor of Dartford Rectory* from Robert and Richard de Ripa, John Badcock, William de Wilmington and others in the reign of Henry III.

1292. In the 21 Edw. I. on a writ of quo warranto the jury found that the bishop was seized in right of his church of a view of frankpledge, and assize of bread and ale of his tenants in Dartford and Stone; and that the bishops, his predecessors, had been possessed of the same, time beyond memory.

The manor of Dartford Rectory extends over both sides of the high-street, from the site of the old market place to the church, and southward in Lowfield, as far as the late House of Correction. The whole of this is called the *Bishop's Liberty*. At the leet of this manor a constable and borsholder are annually chosen for the liberty. There are several tenants which hold of it in soccage at small quit rents.†

---

* In 1628 the parsonage was held by Mark Fielder, who resided in the Waterside; in 1685 by William Tasker and assessed at £30, but in 1693 raised to £60 although still in his occupation. Vest. Book.

The Dormans were lessees during great part of the last century and sold it to the archdeacon. Information of J. Dorman, Esq.

† MS. Notes by Dr. Latham to Hasted's Kent, in poss. of the writer.

The manor of Charles is included within the manor of Dartford Rectory, and pays a quit rent of 8s. 4½d. per annum. The houses and breweries of Messrs. Fleet, and Messrs. Tasker together with the premises used for the Bank, etc., are comprehended in the *twenty-eight tenements* charged with suit and service at the bishop's court, and are held freely by the payment of a small quit rent, and a third part of a year's quit rent, on death or alienation for a relief. The quit rents amount to something more than forty-two shillings per annum.*

THE VICARAGE.

Circa 1258. The endowment which bishop Lawrence ordained for the support of a vicar consisted of *two acres of arable and one of meadow land : the small tythes of the parish,* excepting hay; *the tythe of sheaves* growing from land in *gardens* and *curtilages dug up with the foot :* and *all oblations and obventions made to the church.* Out of these revenues *the vicar was to discharge* the ordinary burthens of his vicarage, and the pension of ten marks per annum to the monks at Rochester.

In 1299, bishop Thomas de Woldham confirmed this approbation, and granted the vicar an house standing on the soil of the church for a *vicarage* for himself and his successors; and as a farther endowment he added *the tithe of twenty-one acres of meadow* called *King's Marsh* in Dartford, heretofore taken by the bishops of Rochester; and he decreed that the vicar and his successors should *keep and maintain the books, vestments,* and *other ornaments* of the church in a *proper state* and

---

* Court Rolls. The Rental will be given in the Appendix. John Morgan, Esq. was lessee of this manor in 1790; Sir Charles Morgan in 1793; but in 1796, it had reverted to the bishop of Rochester.

order; and should sustain and acknowledge all other ordinary burthens to which it is liable.*

Archbishop Robert Winchelsea further endowed this vicarage with the tithe of hay to the value of forty shillings, in commutation of which *the whole tythe of hay arising in the great salt marsh* in Dartford, (excepting a payment of *4s*, due from the knights Templars to the bishop of Rochester as rector of the church,) was decreed to the vicar, by definitive sentence of Walter archbishop of Canterbury 1315, as an augmentation of his endowment.

In the 15 Edward I. the vicarage was valued at an hundred shillings. *Stev. Mon.* i. 456.

At the general valuation of ecclesiastical benefices 26 Hen. VIII. the vicarage was thus entered:

DECANATUS DE DERTFORD.†

Dertford. Vicaria ibm val p annu cu xxs. de firma mans' & gardini vi*li:* In feno xls in lan' & agnis & xvi*li.* xs. iiij*d.* de omnibz al' decimis and oblacoibz xxv*li.* xiijs. iiij*d.* Inde alloc' de vi*j̇li.* ijs. ij*d.* cu vj*li.* xiijs. iiij*d.* solut' an'ti p'ior de Rochister p pens' sua xvj*d.* in reddu rec' dne de Salisbury & vjs. vj*d.* solut' annuati' p le pxes. Et rem' clare. . . . .

	£	s.	d.
	xviij	xi	ij
Xᵃ inde . . .	xxxvij	j	ob.

---

* Reg. Roff. 294. The profits of the vicarage were then found by a jury to be worth 40 marks per annum.—Other documents reciting further particulars of a messuage in Overe, in Dartford, [the vicarage]. which Thomas de Woldham had purchased for £50 ready money of Robert de Levee of Frindsbury, and settled in mortmain on Robert Levee vicar of Dartford, and his successors, describe it as having the running stream from the *Breden-mille* [Bignors] west, the way to *Orchard's-mede* east, a curtilage formerly Boyden Rufi's in the south, and the way near *Orchard's-mille* north. † Valor. Eccles. i. 117.

1540. On the dissolution of the priory of St. Andrew, 32 Hen. VIII. the above pension of ten marks was given by the king among other premises towards the endowment of the dean and chapter of Rochester.

By virtue of a commission of enquiry in 1650, Dartford was returned as a vicarage with a house and glebe all worth with the privy tithes £70 a year. Master Charnock then incumbent.*

In queen Anne's reign the following account of the endowment of the vicarage was taken, and together with the benefactions to the parish, registered in the archives of the diocese.†

Amount of the glebe belonging to the vicarage. 1712.

Imprimis. A vicarage-house and piece of land thereunto adjoining, from north to south 174ft., and about 6ft. distant from the piles in the north adjoining the said glebe land; in breadth at the south end thereof 113ft.; on the north side thereof 65ft. It abuts and bounds on the south and west on the lands of John Twisleton, Esq. now in the occupation of William Sawell, miller, and to the river against the common highway north, and holds of the manor of Dartford Priorie at 1s. 2d. per ann. quit rent.

Item. One acre and one rood lying together in Dartford Fresh-Marsh, bounding on the common sewer south and east, on the lands of Thomas Gough, Esq. north, and on the lands of Mr. Myles and Mr. Wilkinson west.

Item. A piece of glebe heretofore in the occupation of Dorothy Weller, widow, and now in the occupation of Henry

---

* Parliamentary Surveys. MS. vol. xix. Lambeth Library.

† Regist. Temporalium Roffen. By some mistake the whole of the benefactions of the parish have been inserted in this instrument and made to appear as the endowment of the vicarage in the records of Rochester.

Woodin, brewer, in a field called . . . . . . belonging to the paper-mill-farme in Dartford aforesaid, and buts and bounds on a field called Broomfield east and west, on the queen's highway leading from Dartford to Darenth, and on the north on a field called the sixteen-acres, and on the south on a field called Chalkdale.

Item. An acre of glebe lying in a field heretofore of Mr. Thomas Rogers, now of Charles Manning, gent., at the end of Bowling-alley lane.

T. Price, *Vicar.* W. Clare, H. Pierce, *Ch.-Ward.*

In Sept. 1725 many disputes having arisen respecting vicarial tythes, the Rev. Charles Chambers and the parishioners agreed upon the following arrangement :

The Vicarial Tithes to be discharged of all taxes, assessments, and rates, so long as the Rev. C. Chambers continues vicar of Dartford, and of all arrears of former assessments, *upon condition* that THE VICAR shall agree to *bury all the parish poor without his fees,* and to *accept the same consideration in lieu* of certain *vicarial tithes* which are now, or at all times hereafter shall become due to him, as his late predecessor the Rev. Thomas Price did receive for like tithes ; i. e. for every acre of hops 10s. ; for every acre of pasture lying between the river Darent and the highway to Wilmington 1s. yearly ; for each and every acre of pasture in any of the fresh marshes 1s., and 4d. for each and every acre of hay and pasture land in the salt marshes ; and if enclosed 1s 10d. yearly, and if in common 1s. 4d. yearly ; for every calf 1s. ; for every lamb 6d. ; for wool the 10th part of the money it shall be sold for ; for Mr. Thomas Durrant's corn mill 30s. a year payable in equal payments quarterly, namely, Christmas, Lady-day, Midsummer, and Michaelmas ; for Mr. William Sowell's corn mill 30s. a year, payable quarterly at the said four usual feasts ; for Mr. Richard Archer's paper mill 20s. a year payable quarterly, etc. ; for Mr. Charles Manning's iron mill £3 a year, payable quarterly, etc. ; for each and every acre of woodland so many shillings as the wood shall be of yearly growth, at the felling thereof ; and for all other small and vicarial tithes according to the value thereof, and agreement with the vicar. In testimony of which agreement, etc. *Signed,* Geo Swift, *Ch-warden* and twenty-nine inhabitants, and *counter-signed* by the vicar.

The vicarage was in 1736 augmented by Queen Anne's bounty; when the Rev. Charles Chambers as vicar of Dartford contributed £100 for that purpose.

It is endowed with £200 private benefactions.*

The tithes of this vicarage are now commuted at about £540 per annum.†

The vicarage house was rebuilt A.D. 1831.‡

RECTORS. *Patrons*, THE PRIOR AND CONVENT OF ROCHESTER.

Adam. temp. King John.
Peter de Rupibus.
Ralph de Wengham : he died 1176.
Roger ——

Bishop Glanville restored the patronage to the see of Rochester A.D. 1185 ; and the bishops became patrons.

Thomas Chewte.
Lawrence de St. Martin, 1249.

The Vicarage instituted about 1258, by Bp. Lawrence.

VICARS.

Walter, 1299.
Robert Levee, 1308.
Thomas de Dertford alias Stampit, 1338.¶

---

* Vestry Book. Dr. Latham's MS. notes to Hasted's Kent. i. 230.

† Information of J. Dorman, Esq. A vast increase in the living ; compare the benevolence of former vicars with *their* scanty pittance.

‡ Reported to have been chiefly effected by a loan from Queen Anne's bounty, which the incumbent engaged to repay by instalments.

¶ Reg. Roff. 506. p. 10. p. 291. p. 303. p. 297. p. 309.

Thomas Lecheford, vicar, 1368.*

Robert Grope, (or Grape,) 1386.†

William Page, presented to vicarage, 4 July, 1390, on exchange with Robert Grope for rectory of Burnstede.‡

Richard Witch.¶

Andrew Sanders, exchanges the vicarage of Dertford with John Smith for vicarage of Edly'ng, 3 Octob. 1431.||

John Warren, presented to vicarage 21 June, 1441, on resignation of John Smith.**

John Croke present. to vicarage 6 Dec. 1437, on exchanging his rectory of Staplehurst with John Warriff [Warren].††

John Hornley, pres. 1441, on d. Croke, bur. at Dartford, 1477.‡‡

Edward Barnard, collated 25 Sept. 1501, on the decease of John Gurnes.

John Rogers, pres. 29 July, 1515, on d. of Edw. Barnard.

Thomas Wadesuff, pres. 16 June, 1526, on d. of J. Rogers.¶¶

Sir John Bruer, vicar, died 1534.||||

---

* Parish Archives. No. 18. see p. 31. *ante*.

† Regist. Will. de Botelsham, f. 90.   ‡ Ib. f. 4.

¶ Afterward vicar of Hansworth, Middlesex, and burnt on Tower hill for heresy, June 17, 1440. Stowe says many persons believed him to be a good man, and came the night after his execution to make their prayers where he suffered, and carry away some of his ashes as relics. This devotion being observed by the vicar of Barking, a coveteous designing priest, (in whose parish the execution had taken place) he went and strewed powdered spices on the spot, and pretending it was a sweet savour issuing from the martyr's remains, induced great numbers of persons to come thither by night and make offerings of money, wax, etc. for the space of eight days, when they were restrained by the city magistrates and all persons found there, committed to prison, together with the artful priest himself. *Annales.*

|| Act. Curia Consist. f. 91.   ** Ibid. f. 93.

†† Regist. Chichle. Abp. Cant. No. 6078. Addit. MSS. Brit. Mus.

‡‡ Act. Cur. Consist. He was the first president of Magdalen Hall, Oxford, very learned and pious. He resigned that office and retired to Dartford, where he resided till his death. *Wood's Coll. & Halls.* 314.

¶¶ Epi' Cur. Mun. f. 27. f. 73. f. 136. |||| Reg. Test. ix. 175.

Sir John Bartlett, 1540.*

Sir Ralph ———— 35 Hen. VIII. 1543.†

Edward Xyval, 1546 ‡

James Goldwell, 1547.¶ probably a relation of bp. Goldwell.

Edward Browne, clk. presented 2 May, 1559, by Elizabeth, queen of England, on vacancy of the see of Canterbury.∥

Richard Turner, 1565.**

John Browne, B.D. 1575; buried 15 Feb. 1601.††

Richard Wallis, 1623: buried 8 May, 1632.‡‡

John Denne, sequestered, 1642 ¶¶

---

* Reg. x. 2   He subscribed as a witness to Dyryok Rowland's will.

† Ibid. x. 47. p. 41. *ante.*

‡ By will, dat. 6 May 1546, (38 Hen. 8.) William Alexander left him 20s. to sing for his soul. Reg. Test. ix.

¶ Chantry Roll. co. Kent, 1 Edw. 6. No. 104.—Edmund Parker is named in the same record (*vide* p. 76 *ante*) as Martin's Salary priest, his burial is thus entered in the parish Register. 1560. *Edmund Parker, priest in Dartford 42 yeares was buried 8 November. He was made vicar (priest) ye 18 Henrici octavi: died 11 Eliz.*

∥ No. 6087. f. 561. Addit. MSS. Brit. Mus. Ducarell's Excerpts.

** He was prebend of Windsor at the latter end of Edward VI. time; a voluntary exile for religion in queen Mary's reign. In 1560 Archbishop Parker appointed him a visitor for reformation of Canterbury and Rochester dioceses.   He was an able zealous protestant divine. *Strype's Parker,* i. 144. 151. *Oxf.* 1838.

†† This vicar, somewhat of a puritan, was remarkably conscientious in the discharge of his clerical duties. The following is an example of his mode of entering Christenings in the parish Register: "1591. *Browne, Ellen, the daughter of John Browne, preacher and vicar of Dartford, was christened the 12 March; godfather, Christofer Lamb, gent. and grandfather to her godmothers Ellen Rogers and Ann Death, gentlewomen.*" Genealogists only can truly estimate the value of such records. His own funeral is thus entered 1601. "*John Browen bachelor of Divinitie, & preacher of the word of God, & Vicker of Dartford 26 yeares, buried the xv day of February.*"

‡‡ Parish Register, sub anno.

¶¶ John Denne, vicar of the church of Dartford, a common ale-house and tavern haunter, and commonly drunk on the Sabboth-day

Vavassor Powell, resigned 7 January, 1646.*

used to sit till 12 o'clock at night sending for bottles of wine; and in sermon described a drunkard to be such a one as lies in the cart-way foaming at the mouth, and not able to remove himself from the cart wheels; he refuseth to preach on the Lord's day, and on fast days, and is unwilling to suffer any to do the same: he hath expressed great malignancy against the parliament and the proceedings thereof. *White's Centenary of Scandalous Ministers p.* 21.

* Vavassor Powell a talented Welchman of very considerable eminence among the nonconformists, was ordained in the established church and left his cure at Clun, in Shropshire, and came to London to avoid suspension for some irregularities in preaching in fields and unlicensed places, where he arrived in 1642. Patronised by some of the most popular men of the day for his abilities and zeal in religious matters he was settled at Dartford on the expulsion of Denne, where he remained about three years, according to his adversary " cheating and seducing poor souls," *(Griffith's Strena Vavassoriensis.* 3.) but if we believe his friend " to the building them up in faith in Christ Jesus." When he had resided at Dartford about two years and a half, the plague broke out violently in the town, many houses were shut up, and the dead bodies carried out by his chamber wall and windows, yet he did not discontinue his labours, but preached constantly three times a week; and though some of them that had the sickness upon them came publicly to hear, yet both he and his family were preserved from the contagion! " After a while the plague ceased, but it pleased God to visit me," he writes, " with a very dangerous fever and ague, insomuch that in the physician's judgment I could not live; yet God gave me faith to be healed by the means prescribed James, v. 14. 12. Then I sent unto some godly preachers in London desiring them to come unto me to perform the duty of anointing me with oil." Though he doubted whether they would have faith and freedom to practise the same, he felt convinced their unbelief would not make the work of God of none effect, and thereupon was confirmed in the belief that God would recover him. He adds "accordingly after a strange and sudden trance, which I fell into, and continued in for about six hours, where I did sweat abundantly, yet discerned not at all what was done for me, my sickness presently abated and I recovered." *(Life of V. Powell,* 18.) Tradition

Symond Rumeney, 1646.*

Robert Charnock, vicar, 1650.†

Robert Powell, 1655.‡

John Powle, vicar, 1663 : 1685.¶

Thomas Price, vicar, 1712.‖

Charles Chambers, inst. 30 Sept. 1718: ob. 22 Feb. 1746.**

John Lewis. A.M. resigned, 1755.††

James Harwood, A.M. induct. 6 Nov, 1755; ob. Feb. 1778.‡‡

John Currey, M.A. presen. Apr. 1778; ob. 18 Oct. 1825.¶¶

Walker King, pres. to vicarage on death of J. Currey, 1825. He resigned the following year.‖‖

George Heberden, vicar, 1826 ; died, 1830.***.

Edward Murray, present. on death of G. Heberden, 1830. Resigned the same year.†††

Francis Bassett Grant, 1830.

---

relates that he often preached to the parliamentary army on Dartford heath, and some have said that he erected a Baptist chapel near the Orange-tree gate on the Wilmington road ; this, however, is an error, for he did not become a Baptist until 1654. On the reduction of Wales by the parliament in 1646, he was removed to exercise his gifts in his own country, where he frequently preached in churches, chapels, town-halls, fairs, markets, and mountains. During the protectorate of Cromwell he purchased much sequestered property belonging to the church and crown, but on the restoration was stripped of the whole and imprisoned for nonconformity. He died in the Fleet prison. London, Oct. 25. 1671 æt. 53. *Athen. Oxon.* iii. 911.

* Assessment 8 July sub ann. Churchwarden's Book.

† Parliamentary Survey, MSS. vol. xix. Lambeth Library.

‡ Churchwarden's Book, f. 62.   ¶ Parish Register.

‖ Regist. Temporalium Roff. He seems to have been curate from 1678 until he obtained the vicarage. He was buried in the south chancel. *Memorand. of Rev. C. Chambers.*

** See his benefactions, p. 43. and tithe arrangement, p. 82.

‡‡ Memorandum in Parish Register.

‖‖ Archdeacon of Rochester, and rector of Stone.

*** Son of the celebrated physician of king George III.

††† Brother to the present bishop of Rochester.

ROMAN BURIAL-GROUND, EAST HILL.

The stone coffins, lacrymatory, urns, skeletons, and other vestiges of sepulture found upon East Hill on the southern side of the public road, combined with the very ancient burial ground opposite, incontestibly prove that a numerous and wealthy population inhabited the site and vicinity of Dartford from the Roman times* to the final establishment of Christianity among the Saxons; and, that conformably to the custom of those ages they buried their dead on either side the highway† (then called the "Watling-street,") which

---

* An elegant unbaked Roman urn strongly indented with the marks of the turner's lathe, was found by Mr. Dunkin, November, 1833, on laying the foundation of his house in the High street, Dartford.

† Notwithstanding there is certain record of Dartford existing as a Saxon town, and its Roman origin is clearly indicated by the streets crossing each other at right angles, yet it seems unsuspected of having been a Roman Station. Antiquaries place their Vagniaca at Southfleet, merely on the discovery of a tomb, which, after all, seems only the sepulchre of a family which occupied an adjacent villa; while there are no wells nor extensive foundations to indicate the presence of a town. The number of interments on this hill just without Dartford, with the discovery of coffins and other vestiges incontestibly of Roman character, prove it must have been the cemetery of a large population. Like that of Dunovara, (Dorchester) all knowledge of its existence had perished, until digging accidentally disclosed a number of skeletons, urns, etc. Like that at Dunovara, a christian church (St. Edmund's,) had been built contiguous to its very site which thereafter attracted the burial of the christian population. See *Achæolog.* xviii. *Gent. Mag.* 527. 1830.

About 1792 Mr. Thomas Brandon, a grocer at the corner of Overy street, then owner of the east-hill field, opposite the upper burying ground, observing that his hedge across the field uniformly withered

ran from the Ford up the steep acclivity, nearly on the
site of the present turnpike road.

---

away whenever the roots struck the gravel, determined upon rooting it
up, removing the cause of complaint, and planting a new one. On
opening the ground about four feet below the surface, the labourers
dropt upon a huge stone which all their power could not remove, and
upon being dug round was discovered to be a large sarcophagus The
noise of the discovery brought multitudes of spectators; it was opened,
and found to contain the skeleton of a human body and some particles of
dust, but all traces of its envelopes are said to have perished. The bones
were re-interred in the upper church yard; the coffin was taken to Mr.
Brandon's premises opposite the church, and eventually broken up.
Some have said it had a recess for the head, etc., but the description
is vague and contradictory.

Quantities of broken pottery were also found, but the fragments
escaped investigation.

Circa 1797. About five years after, the same proprietor causing a pit
to be dug in the upper part of the field to bury a favourite horse, discovered another stone sarcophagus of larger dimensions. In this instance
greater care was taken in investigating its contents, and a good antiquary, the Rev. Samuel Denne, vicar of Wilmington, was present,
together with a number of persons still living. The lid of the coffin was
found strongly fastened down with iron cramps; and upon being forced
open, broke in sunder. The whole of the body excepting the head was
enveloped in a chalky cement evidently poured in while in a state of
fluidity, from its retaining the impress of the grave clothes. Mr. W. L.
Pearce says "the white cement gave the corpse somewhat the appearance
of having a ruff round the neck." When the coffin was first opened, the
face, though of a dark mahogany colour exhibited all the lineaments of
the deceased, but, upon the nose being touched by a person named
Watson, it trembled for an instant, then fell to dust. The accident
precluded the possibility of ascertaining whether there was any cob-
weblike appearance of the sudarium, or face-cloth. The bones were
buried in the upper church yard, but the skull was long kept in
Mr. John Brandon's parlour: all the teeth were perfect. — This
coffin also was taken to Mr. Brandon's yard [now Colyer's], where

As a chapel existed on the brow of the hill beyond
all record, the probability is that it originated in some

---

it long served for a horse-trough, and was broken up about Whitsuntide,
1810, by order of Mr. J. Brandon for materials to pave a cowhouse in
Overy street. One Thomas Blere, and Job Ufford, the Dartford sexton,
were the persons employed in its destruction. Ufford says it was shaped
somewhat after the modern form.

A few years later A.D. 1804, Mr. Brandon employed among others an
intelligent workman named Massingham to dig gravel in the same field,
who informed the writer, that they found many relics of human skeletons
apparently buried side by side in wood coffins similar to those in our
church yards, only laid north and south. He said the wood of the coffins
had entirely perished, yet the earth around bore that dark impress
peculiar to decayed coffins in burial grounds which no one can mistake:
besides, among the bones were found fragments of corroded iron, evidently the nails which had once fastened them together. Striking his
pickaxe into one of those hollow masses, Massingham unfortunately
shattered to pieces the body of a vessel formed of clear green glass, [*a
lachrymatory,*] which upon collecting the fragments, he found to have
been circular, about two and a half inches in diameter in the globular
part, and five inches in height, elegantly formed with a long narrow neck
and handle. The upper part being perfect he carefully preserved, and
has given it to the writer, in whose possession it remains. Massingham
also found an earthen vessel in one of the graves, [*a præfericulum*] with a
narrow neck two inches long; the body about three inches diameter, and
somewhat in form of a vase. It stood six inches high.

After the death of Mr. John Brandon the field was sold to Mr.
Landale This gentleman upon trenching the ground about 1822 found
another storie coffin which, says Mr. L. "contained a female skeleton,
"with remarkably small bones. When the coffin was first opened, the
"hair appeared of a light brown colour, apparently clubbed on the
"crown of the head, and fastened with a brooch or bandeau of pearls:
"but in a few moments the whole fell to dust: the pearls rubbed like
"soap to the touch and only a few pieces of the broken metal ornaments

sacred edifice connected with Roman funeral rites. The

"remained. The body had been swathed in linen some of which was "visible, and covered with cement" formed of chalk and coarse grit of great hardness Mr. L. says "a coating of gum strongly adhered to the "larger bones, which retained an aromatic and pleasant smell, and in "the coffin was found a copper coin of Constantinopolis in good pre-"servation." He adds "the stone is similar to those in the quarries of "Candebec, in Normandy, and the coffin when found was estimated "above two tons in weight. The lid had been evidently broken before "it was placed on the coffin from the circumstance of fibres of plants "and roots of grass being found in the interstice." The bones were re-buried in the field with many others found during these excavations, but the coffin was removed to Park-place where it remained several years, and was seen by A. J. Kempe, Esq. F.S.A., Messrs. Nichols, and other eminent antiquaries, who pronounced it decidedly Roman. The coin found therein, however, shows that the interment must have been after the time of Constantine. Mr. Kempe made a drawing of the coffin and when kindly favouring me therewith writes, "in it was part of the "cement which covered the body; it was like plaster of Paris. Some of "that cement I brought away to my museum in the New Kent Road, in "it were the impression of the linen habiliments of the body. The stone "of the coffin, if I remember right, was like that of the coffin at Keston "of a close texture mixed with small sea shells. The lid was chiselled "across diagonally, as you see in the drawing, and I think the sculptor "intended that the lines should have returned in the hatched form" [crossing each other] "but his material being brittle he could not cross "the lines without the stone breaking away. That was my impression at "the time. It is singular that the cross lines are now made on the "lids of leaden coffins as an ornament. Let me observe that this "hatched ornament was common on Roman urns, etc., and that the "Roman milestone lately in the grounds of the Rev. Mr Rashleigh "of Southfleet, [now at the Rectory, Horton-Kirby], was chiselled in "that way." The coffin is rounded at the head, and measures 7ft. 4in. in length; the width at the broadest part of the head 2ft. 10in.; and 1ft. 10in. at the foot. The sides are about 3½ inches thick; it

circular Temple discovered at Keston, stood immediately

---

is 22½ inches deep, and the lid is 5 inches in thickness. The coffin lay north and south. It is now on Mr. Landale's premises, West Hill.

Mr. Landale adds that while trenching the ground "they also found "within the compass of a quarter of an acre numbers of distinct skele- "tons, but in no instance did it appear that wood had been used as "coffins; they all laid east and west with a layer of fine gold coloured "sand underneath them. The bones of one of these was so large, that it "was thought the individual must have been upwards of seven feet in "height. Mr. Brand and others who were present, observed the teeth "were of immense magnitude. There were also several square pits dis- "covered wherein apparently bodies had been burned, containing pieces "of charcoal, pottery, etc. The fire at bottom had burnt the sides and "given them the appearance of red brick."

"On lowering the point where Park place now stands about seven feet "for building, we came to a foundation between three and four feet in "thickness, formed chiefly of Normandy burr" [something like mill stone], "and various small diaper foundations as if they had been cells. "One floor of plaster was firm as stone until exposed to the air, when it "became soft as ashes. On this lay a coin of Agrippa, about the size of "a penny piece. In the above cells were many broken urns, of very "rude workmanship and various forms. There were also pieces of pot- "tery of a green colour and glazed. In front of these foundations was a "gravelled path whereon a silver crucifix of beautiful workmanship was "found." On it is faintly inscribed the date 1140; but being engraved in Arabic numerals [which were not permanently fixed until the end of the fifteenth century], the inscription conveys no evidence of its age. Mr. Landale closes his account of the discoveries by saying that "in "digging and trenching nearly one hundred coins had been found at "various times, some of which are Roman silver coins of extreme "rarity."

The broken urns being found in the same burial ground with the coffins is indisputable evidence that the latter was deposited after urn burial had ceased. There was little burning of the dead after the time of the Antonines in consequence of the progress of christianity.

contiguous to some tombs, and the exuviæ* of the sacrifices were found on the spot. May not an heathen temple at Dartford have been changed into a christian church on the conversion of the Saxons?

In A. D. 742, Cuthbert archbishop of Canterbury introduced the formation of *church-yards* from what he had seen at Rome, but they were not universal until long afterwards, and many legends had been invented to show the advantages of burial in consecrated ground.

After the canonization of king Edmund, murdered in 870, a new chapel was erected, and with the surrounding cemetery now known as "the upper church

---

Mr. Landale also found on the site of the Crescent an enchased silver cup with two elevated handles enclosed in an earthen vessel. Also a medal of William the conqueror deposited in an urn, together with a shilling of Edward VI. and another of Queen Elizabeth.

The ancient road which led from the Brent south of this field, towards Dartford, was thought by some, to have been once the main highway between Dover and London. The road, however, was one formed in the middle ages after the Watling street became impassable from want of repair, or to avoid the steep acclivity of the hill. Another branch-road formed for the same purpose, wound round the upper burying ground and descending the lane into Overy street, passed on to the Ford and thus entered the town.

* The mass evidently *consists of a burnt animal substance mingled with ashes and cinders;* Mr. Kempe has also a deer's horn deeply notched, supposed to be done by a missing blow of the *victimarius*, when the animal was brought for sacrifice at the altar before the temple at Keston.—The present writer introduced Mr. Crofton Croker to the Rev. Sir C. Farnaby, Bart. and obtained permission to make the excavations. The first day, June 17th, 1828, most of the gentry in the neighbourhood were present, and John Ward of Holwood, Esq. sent seventeen labourers to assist in digging. For the final result of the researches at Keston, see *Archæolog.* vol. xxii. 336. 339.

yard," enclosed and dedicated to that saint.*   And there can be no doubt, that from the additional interest and sanctity thus conferred on the spot, all funerals entirely ceased on the opposite side of the highway, if they had not done so a century before.   The burial ground, however, so long hallowed by the ashes of the dead was settled as an appanage to the chapel,† and passed with it to Dartford priory where it remained until the fall of that house.   In the middle ages the celebrity of this chapel gave name to the ancient road itself, which is called in many records 𝔖𝔱. 𝔈𝔡𝔪𝔲𝔫𝔡𝔢𝔰 𝔥𝔦𝔤𝔥𝔴𝔞𝔶.

ST. EDMUND'S CHAPEL AND CEMETERY.

This burial ground was the site of one of the three chapels enumerated in domesday book.   In the reign of Edward II. it was included it the knight's fee belonging to Warren de Montchesnie, and held of him by Peter de Amersham, Roger de Bykenore and others.

---

* St. Edmund was crowned king of the East Angles at Bury, A.D. 856. He reigned fifteen years, and in 870, was taken prisoner by the Danes on an invasion under Hinguar and Hubba, in a village called Hoglesdune ; and being a christian as well as an enemy, was first scourged, then bound to a tree and his body pierced with arrows. His head was then cut off and thrown into a wood. *Saxon Chron.* The legend says the body was found, but the head remained undiscovered forty days, when it was seen between the fore paws of a wolf, who immediately resigned it unmutilated and fled into a wood. The head being placed in contact with the trunk, which was not in the least decomposed, is said to have reunited so closely that the separation was scarcely visible. *Caley's Dugdale,* iii. 99. For fifty years East Anglia remained under the Danish dominion, when it was rescued by Edward the elder and joined to the West-Saxon kingdom.

† Una acra terre jacente ex opposito (capell') beati Edmundi regis et martiris. Act. Curia Consist. f. 240.

About 1346, 20 Edw. III. John de Bicknore then lord of the manor of Portbridge or Bicknor's, endowed the chapel of St. Edmund standing hereon with five marks per annum, payable out of his lands and tenements in Dartford for the support of a chaplain.

On the death of Robert de Bicknore, the manor of that name together with the advowson of the chapel escheated to the crown; and with its endowments, were settled upon Dartford priory by the foundation charter of king Edward III.* The appointment of a chaplain thenceforward vested in the prioress and convent.

The Records at Rochester contain the following entries of chaplains presented thereunto :

(Translation.)

1399. 10 Feb. John Symonds, chaplain, presented to the perpetual chantry of St. Edmund at Dertford, by the religious women, Joan prioress, and her convent, at Dartford.†

1422. 24 Dec. John Blier, chaplain, instituted to the perpetual chantry of St. Edmund on the presentation of the prioress and convent of Dertford.‡

1432. 10 May. John Derby admitted to the perpetual chantry of St. Edmund, king and martyr, within the parish of Dertford, on death of master Edmund, late chaplain, to which chantry he was presented by Rose, the prioress, and her convent of Dertford, and instituted within the same ¶

---

* Pat. 40 Edw. I. m. 26.

† Regist. Will. de Botelsham. f. 142. *Dertford.* Custos Capell' Sc'i Ed'i ib'm John Symons. Pat. 19 Ric. II. m. 3.

‡ Act. Curia Consist. f. 20. called by Thorpe Regist. Spiritual.

¶ Ibid. f. 95. Among the numerous notices of this chapel in the Registry of Wills at Rochester are the following.—Joan Moonlight of Dartford, formerly wife of Robert Moonlight by will dat. 28 Sep. 1444. desires her body to be buried in the church of St. Edmund.

1446. 6 Oct. Thomas Ingesdell presented to the perpetual chantry of St. Edmund, on death of brother William Crowland, by Margaret de Bellomonte the prioress, and her convent of Dertford.*

1462. 4 July. John Wells presented on death of Thomas Yngeldell, by the lady Alice Brainswaite, prioress of the monastery of the blessed Virgin Mary at Dertford, and her convent.†

In 1448, Robert Taylor of Dertford gave by will to the high altar of St. Edmund's church where he desires to be buried, 6d. *Landale.* 9.

* Act. Curia Consist. Thomas Ingesdell by will dat. 20 Jan. 1462. directs his body to be buried in St. Edmund's chapel, before the high altar, and ten marks to be distributed among the poor according to the discretion of John Hornle and master Richard Maresh. Regist. Test. ii. 253.

† Act. Curia Consist. f. 235. f. 239.

By will dat. 20 Aug. 1466. Christiana at Dene directs her body to be buried in the cemetery of St. Edmund, near the body of John her son; gives to the light of the crucifix, 12d, Reg. Ib. ii. f. 262.

By will dat. 4 Feb. 1466, Thomas Neuman of Stoneham, within the parish of Dertford, directed his body to be buried in the chapel of St. Edmund, king and martyr, near the sepulchre of Ade Corby. Lowe's Regist. f. 309. Margaret his wife was also buried there.

1468. Edmund Chymbham gave by will 8d. to mend the great window of the chapel of St. Edmund king and martyr. Reg. iii. 9.

Roger Rotheley, will dat. 6 May, (same year,) gave to the reparation of the chapel of St. Edmund, king and martyr, 6s. 8d.; to John Wells, chaplain of St. Edmund, and his successors, 10 marks, if such remain after sundry payments, viz. yearly for three years, 40s.

John Hammond of Dertford by will dat. 11 May, 1572, gave to John Wells and John Skebborne (chantry priest of Stanpit,) "to every of them 5d. to pray for my soul, and everich of them to say thirty *masses of the name of John;* to Jone my daughter 5 marks, etc. Residue of goods that my wife have them." etc. Ibid.

John Taylor by will, 1476, directed his body to be buried by the sepulchre of Joan his wife (vide Priory annals); as did John Smith and Katherine his wife. Regist. Test. 568. 229.

On the application of Wells for admission, some doubts arose respecting his title, and an enquiry was instituted by the bishop's officers sitting at the adjoining abbey of Lesnes. It then appeared that the prioress and convent having deferred presenting the said chaplain for more than six months from the decease of Ingledew or Ingesdell, the last incumbent, the presentation had lapsed to the bishop of the diocese, who hereupon presented the said John Wells, and he was admitted 3 June, 1463.*

Afterwards the said John exhibited copies of the donation to the said prioress, and the concession of Master Ralph Felthorpe, consisting of *five marks issuing out of the seld* which is called *Tannersfeld*, and also the whole of the *tenement with the buildings*

---

* *Institutio Capellani et Dotatio Capella S'ti. Edmundi de Dertford.*

Tercio die mensis Junij, coram eodem reverendo patre in abbacia de Lesenes dominus Johannes Well Capellanus exhibuit domino quandam literam domine priorisse et conventus monalium de Dertford, sigillo suo communi sigillatam, ex donacione et concessione v. marcarum, et certarum terrarum, ad celebrandum in capella sancti Edmundi de Dertford, vacante per mortem domini Thome Ingeldwe, vel alibi ad libitum suum, durante vita sua Unde idem reverendus eundem capellanum admissit. Sed quia dicte priorissa et conventus, patrone distullerunt presentare dictum capellanum domino episcopo, vel literas presentacionis ad capellam predictam dicto reverendo patri dirigere, prout ab antiquo consueverunt. Idem reverendus pater, lapsis vi. mensibus eandem capellam dicto domino Johanni contulit jure sibi devoluto. Et ipsum institutit etc.

COPIA DONACIONIS V. MARCARUM.

Et postea idem dominus Johannes Well exhibuit copias donacionis dicte priorisse, et concessionis domini Radulphi Felthorpe, de v marcis annui redditus, capiendis de quadam selda que vocatur Tannersfeld et ecciam totum illud tenementum cum edificijs, et alijs pertinencijs quod est jacens inter messuagium

and appurtenances, which lies between the messuage of William de Brenchesle on the east, and the messuage of the heirs of Thomas Squynore against the west, with the whole meadow in fresh and in salt pertaining to the said tenement: the one containing two and a half acres of land at *Fullewych*; and *one acre lying opposite the chapel of St. Edmund, king and martyr,* with all rights whatsoever appertaining to the aforesaid five marks of the donation of John Bicknore to sustain a priest to celebrate divine service in the chapel of St. Edmund, king and martyr, in the parish of Dertford, etc., like as is contained in the records of the Register remaining.

Willielmi de Brenchesle versus orientum, et messuagium heredum Thome Squynore versus occidentem, cum toto illo prato in frisco, et salso, dicto tenemento pertinente, una cum duabus acris terre et dimidio apud Fullesuych, et una acra terre jacente ex opposito (capell') beati Edmundi regis et martiris, cum omnibus juribus, predictis v. marcis quovismodo pertinentibus, ex donacione Johannis Bykenore de Dertford, ad sustentacionem ejusdem ad divina celebrand. in capella beati Edwardi regis in parochia de Dertford, etc. prout in eisdem continentur penes registrum remanentibus. Act. Curia Consist. f. 240. Regist. Roff. 314.

The following extract exhibits a curious instance of an individual directing the celebration of her exequies by the same priest in two distinct chapels. Probably John Sadler was a relative.

Johanna Holt, alias Sadler, widow, by will dated 23 Sep. 1473, directs her body to be buried in the cemetery of St. Edmund next her husband; gives to the altar for forgotten tythes and oblations 6s.; to an honest priest to celebrate her exequies and pray for her soul and the souls of all departed, for three years, ten marks,—in this form—three days in the week in the chapel of St. Edmund, and with the permission of the vicar, the other days in the church of St. Trinity; to the fabric of the said church 20s.; to John Sadler a canon of the monastery of St. Thomas of

John Wells died in 1477, leaving by will 3s. 4d. towards making a window to the chapel.*

I have been unable to discover any further memorandums relative to this chapel in the archives of the see at Rochester, but in a terrier of the lands and possessions, of the priory of Dertford taken by order of the prioress, 24 Hen. VII. is the following memorandum under the head "MANOUR OF BICKNORS. *Item.* The advowson of the chapel of St. Edmund, king and martyr, together with all the lands and tenements of the said chapel pertaining to the manor aforesaid." It is therefore probable Wells was the last priest who was regularly presented and admitted. Few persons ever attending divine worship therein from its inconvenient situation, the daily service was discontinued; the prioress and convent of Dartford appropriated the revenues to the use of the monastery, and it was henceforward used only occasionally as a chantry chapel.

Lesnes five marks of money to pray for her; the residue of her goods she leaves to John Wells chaplain of St. Edmund. Regist. iv, 59.

William Johnson by will made 25 April, 1474, desires his body to be buried in the church of St. Edmund; gives all his goods to Jone Morton, and his house in Upstreet to Jone Satyll, till the time his daughter comes to years of marriage. Ibid. 135.

John Tottenham of Dertford by will dat. 22 Jan. 1474, directs his body to be buried in the cemetery of St. Edmund, etc.; gives towards repairing the chapel of St. Edmund 9s.; to an honest priest to celebrate daily for himself and all his benefactors for .. years ..: to John Wells to pray for his soul 6s. 8d. etc. Ibid. 188.

* John Wools, or Wells, vicar of Wilmington, and chaplain of St. Edmunds in Dertford by will dat. 29 Oct. 1477, gives 3s. 4d. to make a window for the chapel of St Edmund, and also gives all his faggots now *in his Chantry-House of St. Edmund* to be distributed among the poor. Regist. Test. iii. 213.

The following extracts from the testaments of individuals throw some incidental light upon the structure after the death of Wells, but no chaplain is mentioned.

Thomas Wearing, by will dat. 22 Dec. 1494, directs his body to be buried in the cemetery of St. Edmund, near the sepulchre of his son ; desires eight honest persons, his labourers, to carry his body to be buried, gives to each 3s. 4d. ; to his brother Roger Waring twenty pounds, etc. Regist. v. 263.

Katerine Sampson, widow. 19 Oct. 1496 ; her body to be buried in the cemetery of St. Edmund.   Ibid. 363.

Richard Pinden, will dat. 6 May, 1 Hen. VIII.   "I bequeath to the most needful reparation of St. Edmund's chapel 3s 6d.   iv. 147.

The subsequent items shew that within this chapel stood an *image of the patron saint;* at the east end above the high altar, *a large rood or crucifix,* and underneath it an *image of the Virgin Mary;* in other parts of the chapel were *images of St. John Baptist, St. Peter,* and *St. James,* before each of which were lights burning during the celebration of certain divine offices.

Hugh Serle of Dertford, by testament dat. 20 Oct. 15, Hen. VIII. directs his body to be buried in the chapel of St. Edmond before his image ; he gives to the rode light 12d. ; to our lady light under the rode 12d. ; to St. John Baptist, St. Peter, and St. James 12d ; for a taper before St. Edmond in the chapel 12d. ; wills that a marble stone to his memory be placed there, etc. ; he further gives after the decease of Alice his wife, half of the yearly profits of his two tenements in Overy street to the prioress of Dertford, and the other half to the repair of St. Edmond's chapel for ever.   Lowe's Regist. f. 213. 214.

William Parker of Dartford, innholder, 1534, wills (inter alia) to the raparacion of St. Edmund's chapel 6s. 8d. ; to the reparacion of the charnel-house if the paryshe will repair it 10s. etc.   Reg. ibid.

1535.   Philip Ockford wills to be buried in St. Edmund's cemetery.

It is clear from the conditional donation in Parker's will towards the repair of the charnel house beneath

St. Edmund's chapel "if the parish will repair it" that the chapel itself as well as the cemetery belonged to the parish; and that the *advowson* only vested in the prioress and convent.   And it is also clear from that community not claiming to be allowed the stipend of five marks for the support of a priest at St. Edmund's chapel in the general ecclesiastical valuation, 26 Hen. 8. A.D. 1535, that they had ceased to present thereunto.   When therefore, at the suppression of the priory the endowment passed to the crown, the parishioners continued to exercise their proprietory rights over the chapel and burial ground. This statement is corroborated by the following extract, which also shows that *the chapel had then been recently rebuilt,* or undergone most extensive renewals or reparations.

Thomas Worship, chaplain, of Dertford, by will, dated 31 May, 1546, directed his body to be buried at the door of the chapel newly built in the cemetery of St. Edmund above the charnel, at the western entrance of the same.   Lowe's Regist. f. 214.

In the next year (1547) 1 Edw. VI. an Act was passed for abolishing all Chantries, Free Chapels, Guilds, etc.*   When prayers for the dead ceased, there were no longer religious services performed in this chapel; and being immediately stripped of its crucifix, images, chalices, and other paraphernalia of the ancient worship, its gloomy and repulsive interior was altogether deserted.   The violation of its sanctity also induced all the opulent and most respectable inhabitants of Dartford to inter their dead in the parish church or adjacent church yard; insomuch that hardly a solitary instance occurs in the Registry of Wills at Rochester,

---

* Stat. 1 Edw. VI. cap. 14.

of any person desiring to be buried in St. Edmund's chapel or cemetery for a long period after the Reformation.* As *there were no tombs or gravestones in those days* the hillocks of the dead were speedily trampled down, and its doorless, roofless chapel, gave the spot a most melancholy and forbidding aspect. Added to this, credulity was so rife with tales of shadowy forms seen constantly flitting about the deserted walls by moonlight, and of heart-thrilling moans of the dead nightly heard in the stormy blast, that the stoutest shuddered and avoided the pathway after day had closed.† Upwards of a century elapsed—and the over-filled churchyard was found incapable of receiving more interments. The parishioners were therefore necessitated once more to carry their dead to the upper burial-ground. Fortunately about the same time, gravestones were introduced, and the convenience of erecting these memorials in the open space, materially tended to reconcile the friends of the deceased to the change of sepulture.‡ Another hundred years rolled on, and in the interim, vast masses of the walls of the chapel had fallen down and broken through the vaults of the charnel house, so that, though they were nearly level with the sod in some parts, the area presented a frightful cavity partly choked up with flint and stones.¶ About 1780 the parish officers began to bury their poor therein,

---

* Vide Liber Testam. xi. xii. passim.

† "Prodigies and Apparitions seen and heard at Darford, and other places in Kent, etc." London, 1646.

‡ The oldest gravestone stands near the middle of the upper church yard and inscribed *Mr. Thomas Kemp, died June* 24, 1696, *at.* 65. Like all ancient stones, it is low; and sculptured with an hour-glass.

¶ It has only been filled up a few years since, and is now hardly level. Temp. 1841.

and since that period the remaining masses and foundations have been removed, insomuch that interments are now made throughout the ground indiscriminately.

In 1817, the burial ground was enlarged by the addition of upwards of an acre of land.*

The lichen gate or porch was constructed in 1826.†

The festival of St. Edmund‡ was held on the 29th day of November.

―――

The chapel is said to have stood nearly in the centre of the burial ground; it was constructed of flints, with

―――

* The following extracts convey some minute information.

1732. A parochial Visitation.—"Ordered to make good the fence of the upper churchyard.—All the old elm pollards round it remain, but they were all lopped this year by the vicar, as they were fifteen years ago." Regist. Temporal. in archiv. Epi' Roffen.

1733. "The churchwardens ordered to make a footway to the upper church-yard that the minister and inhabitants may with safety pass and re-pass to bury the dead." Vestry-Book, sub an.

1734. "The churchwardens ordered to prosecute any person digging or carrying away any earth or sand from the upper church yard, or bottom of the same place next the road." Ibid.

† 1825. Oct. 5. "The alteration in reducing the high road having done away with the old road to the upper burial ground, a new carriage road ordered to be made to the said cemetery in the most convenient manner." Signed, J. H. MANTELL, Curate, Chairman.

‡ Might not the foundations discovered on the site of Park Place have been those of St. Edmund's chantry-house noticed p. 99?

In a terrier of the priory lands 27 Hen. VII., the site of the Roman burial ground is called Broomhill; Mr. Landale says it is designated Hillifield in other evidences, but for the last twenty years has been known as Brent Park.—Similar corroded coffin nails with heads upwards of an inch and half in diameter as found by Mr. Massingham in the graves at East Hill, are said by Stowe to have been discovered in the Roman cemetery in Spitalfields, temp. Eliz.

stone facings round the doors and windows. Part of the foundations remained within the recollection of persons still living. Thorpe, who wrote in 1788, says "nothing "now appears of it above ground, the walls having been "thrown down many years since; and the flints which "composed them converted to other uses. However the "foundations may be traced by the edges or rising of the "ground, and fineness of the turf; which I measured May "24th, 1784, and found the contents to be in breadth "from north to south thirty-nine feet from outside to "outside; in length from east to west fifty-two feet. "There are many graves within its area the parish poor "having of late been there interred." Thorpe adds, the vicar receives 6s. 8d. annually for the two and a half acres of land which formerly constituted part of the endowment; and concludes by stating that "this church-yard is considerably elevated above the top of the tower."

———

On a handsome lofty tomb decorated with sepulchral emblems, elevated four degrees, and surrounded by iron rails, is this inscription on a marble tablet.

To the Memory of
JOHN HALL,
who, for upwards of half a century, resided in this parish.
He was born at Whitchurch, in Hampshire, September 5th, 1765;
possessing a vigorous mind, and a habit of untiring application,
He acquired considerable celebrity in his profession as a
Millwright and Engineer.
In disposition he was humble, kind, and affectionate,
And his life was marked by a high regard for the interests of Religion
and devoted Piety to God.
He died on the 7th January, 1836, aged 71 years.

———

The memory of the just is blessed. Prov. x. 7.

Near the north-western corner of the cemetery is a noble square tomb, surrounded with iron railing, and inscribed on the west side:

JOHN PARDON, GENT.
Late Treasurer for the county of Surrey,
Died 21 March, 1803, in the 70th year of his age.*

On the south side:

ANN, wife of JOHN PARDON, Gent.
Died the 4th July, 1787, aged 57.

East side:

EDWARD BILKE, ESQ.
of Hertford-street, May Fair, co. Middlesex,
Died 5th April, 1828, aged 68.
His widow MARY BILKE,
Died 28th February, 1840, aged 82.

North side:

ELIZABETH MIDDLETON,
Of Hertford-street, May Fair, Middlesex,
Died 23rd May, 1830.

In this burial ground are tombs and memorials of the families of Brames, Brandon, Budgen, Callow, Cresy, Deane, Dorman, Gardiner, Hall, Hammond, Hards, Harwood, Jardine, Latham, Loader, Manguad, Parkhurst, Pearce, Pierce, Quelch, Sears, Sheppard, Sharp, Sherren, Terry, Tippets, Umfrey, Warde, Walker, Wellard, Williams, and many others. The substance of the inscriptions will be given in the appendix, in the alphabetic order of names, together with some slight occasional

---

* Mr. Pardon, by his will, charged the repairs of his vault upon his estate in Spital street, Dartford. Mr. Fooks purchased the premises and resided therein till his death in 1841. Near the middle of the last century the adjoining property belonged to Ellis Bostock and Dudley Marshall.

historical or genealogical notes, explanatory of the connexion of individuals with different families.

The following inscription, now almost obliterated by moss, upon a gravestone near the entrance of the burial ground, has often attracted the attention of strangers.

Here lyeth the body of
MRS. ELIZABETH QUELCH,
of this Parish, she died in April, 1741.

———

Here lies interred Elizabeth Quelch,
  A Maid not Twenty-three;
In Dartford born, and there she died,
  As you above may see.

For in that fatal April month,
  Upon the Nineteenth day,
A sore distemper then did rage,
  Which took her life away.

In youthful years she left this world,
  Within this grave to rest;
That she a Virgin pure might rise,
  To dwell among the blest.

THE KING'S MANSION, OR CASTLE.

From a very remote period, beyond existing records, Dartford was the demesne of the Saxon kings, and they had a mansion on what was afterwards the site of the priory. Whether, however, there is any foundation for the tradition, that Ethelbert under the auspices of Austin founded here a " Seminary for noble Virgins " is perhaps questionable; although the legend states somewhat circumstantially, that the Danes in one of their piratical excursions to the coast pursued their depredations up to Dartford,* and falling upon this community, then under the government of Editha the daughter of a Saxon king, first treacherously ravished, and then barbarously murdered the holy inmates. This tale has been made the groundwork of a short poem invoking and celebrating Offa's vengeance on the delinquents; and the author argues that "the tradition shews the high antiquity of the place, because we know that very few of the fables of early ages either floated on the pinions of local tradition, or were chained to the desks of monastic libraries except they were in some degree supported by facts."

An historical gloom darkly illumined by the archives of Rochester, and the rays reflected from the accidental discovery of coins, fragments of armour, and other vestiges of antiquity, rests upon this domain of the Saxon kings until the days of Edward the Confessor, when we gather from Domesday book that it was

---

* The tower at the ford of the Darent was erected to check the Danish incursions, vide p. 24.   † Offa died A.D. 774.   *Sax. Chron.*
‡ European Mag. lvii. 360.

valued at sixty pounds, and at the compilation of that record possessed three chapels besides a church, one of which may be fairly presumed to have been attached to the king's mansion.

It was customary with both the Saxon and Norman kings to move with their courts from one estate to another, and consume the produce on the lands where it was raised; and there can be no doubt that the convenient situation of this palace on the high road led to its being frequently visited on their journeys to Canterbury or the coast, although no event of sufficient importance occurred during their stay to call the historian's attention to Dartford. The marriage of Isabella the sister of Henry III to the emperor of Germany in this town A.D. 1235, may be presumed to have occurred in consequence of the English sovereign residing temporarily at Dartford. Doubtless the contiguity of this mansion also led Edward III to select this place for holding that splendid military spectacle, the tournament, in April, A.D. 1331, during which he made the palace his abode.

The necessity of guarding this mansion against surprise in those turbulent ages gradually conferred upon it the characteristics of a fortress, insomuch that in the time of Edward III. it was called "the Castle;" the precincts around "the castle place," and the adjacent hill "castle hill."

---

* Stow's Annales.

† Priory Foundation Charter, Pat. 46 Edw. III. p. 2. m. 28.

THE PRIORY.

A.D. 1344. In conformity with the spirit of the age, which strangely blended military ardour with devotional feeling, Edward III. determined upon founding a monastery for Sisters of the order of Preachers, at Dartford; but owing to his numerous political undertakings and the process necessary to secure the sanction of the various ecclesiastical authorities interested in the parish, much time elapsed before he could carry his design into effect,* so that the first patent does not bear date until 1349,† when it appears he installed his new community in the ancient buildings of his castle. That community consisted of twenty-four sisters and six brothers,‡ for whose maintenance he allotted two hundred marks annually to be received

---

* The following process seems to have been adopted.—King Edward addressed a letter dated 5th Oct. 1344, to Hamo, bishop of Rochester, announcing his intention to found a House of Sisters of the Order of Preachers, with a church, etc , soliciting licence for the same. A second letter dat. 28th Jan. the following year, produced an epistle from the archbishop of Canterbury to the same bishop, dat 21 Oct. ; whereupon Hamo issued a mandate to the prior and chapter of Rochester, requesting their consent to the same, provided it be not to the injury of the church of Dartford, of which they were patrons and impropriators. He also directed another to the vicar of the parish to the same purport. The certificate of consent from both parties, securing the pension payable to the church of Rochester, together with the rights of the rectory and vicarage ; is dated, 13th Nov. 1243. The letter of Hamo de Heth authorising the foundation "as far as in him lies" is dated 3 non Feb. 1345. *Reg. Roffm.* 312—314.

† The year of the great pestilence which raged throughout England. ‡

‡ Tanner's Notitia, Dugdale's Monasticon, *Caley.* vi. 226.

at his exchequer for ever,* or until such time as other provision should be made for the supply of their wants.

Thus fostered by the king, benefactors speedily arose; and among the earliest names which appear, is that of Matilda Walys, who, in 1356, gave certain tenements in London towards its endowment; most likely at the same time she took the veil, and was appointed the first superior of the house. She appears to be the same person who is called MATILDA, *the prioress,* in the great charter of endowment granted in the forty-sixth year of that monarch's reign.†

Shortly after the king granted the prioress and convent licence to acquire lands to the amount of three hundred pounds per annum in mortmain;‡ and the same year the convent was licenced to appropriate the church of Whitley, in the county of Surrey.¶

In consideration of one thousand marks paid to the prioress of Dertford, by Sir Peter de Braose, the king granted to him and Joanna his wife, and the heirs male of the body of the said Peter, the manors of Wistneston, Ashhurst, Chillington, Sloughter, Hene and Iringham with remainder to the right heirs of Sir Peter, for ever.‖

1358. Grant of the manor of Shibborn, co. Kent; and near the same time, the community obtained the reversion of the manors of Norton, Bilney, Emwell, and Trowe then in possession of Sir Roger de Bavent Knight, and Haweis, his wife.**

---

* Pat. 23 Edw. III. p. 2. m. 9.   Cart. 30 Edw. III. No. 2.
† Claus. 30 Edw. III. m. 7.   ‡ Pat. 30 Edw. III. p. 3. m. 5.
¶ Pat. 31 Edw. III. p. 2 m. 12.
‖ Collectanea Topographica et Genealogica. vi. 420.
** Pat. 32 Ed. III. p 2. m. 2, et m. 13, et m. 25, 26, vel 27.

1361.   Certain tenements in Billingsgate, Pudding lane, etc., in London, bestowed on the convent.*

1362.   Haweis, relict of Sir Roger de Bavent, knight, releases to the prioress and convent of Dertford, all right and title to the manors of Norton-Bavent, Fifehide, Knowle, Belegh, Trowe, and Witehall in the county of Wilts.; Burton and Nash, Dorset; Pitford, and Halesham, Surrey; Shibborne, Kent; Brandiston and Combes, Suffolk; and Colveston, Glamorgan.†

1363.   The king confirms the manor of Bradnestone Hall in Wingfield-Magna, com. Suffolk, to the prioress and convent.‡

About the same time the convent also acquired other tenements in the city of London.¶

1366.   The entire manor of Portbrugge, [Portbridge,] one knight's fee belonging thereunto, together with the advowson of the chapel of St. Edmund, king and martyr, which had escheated to the crown on the death of Robert Bicknor, given by patent to the monastery; and also certain other lands and tenements with their appurtenances, heretofore the property of William Clapte and Joane his wife in Dertford, Wilmington and Stone settled upon the prioress and convent by John Bond, chaplain.‖

Certain woods in Dertford, Wilmington, and Stone, given to the convent.**

1369.   The sisters obtain confirmation of the manor

---

* Pat. 35 Edw. III. p. 2. m. 10.   † Claus. 36 Edw. III. m. 43.
‡ Fin. Suffolk. 37 Edw. III. No. 208.
¶ Pat. 37 Edw. III. p. 2. m. 4.   Claus. 37 Edw. III. m. 3.
‖ Pat. 40 Edw. III. p. l. m. 26.   ** Ibid. p. 2. m. 10.

of Hailsham, and by the same instrument acquire sixteen acres of land in Dertford.*

The same year Thomas de Bridport dying without heirs, his estates in Dorset, escheated to the crown,† and were given by the king to Dertford priory.‡

These various acquisitions having secured an ample provision for the religious community, the royal founder consolidated the several grants into one charter of endowment, therein reciting the names of the different benefactors, with their specific benefactions; which instrument he granted to the prioress MATILDA and her convent in the forty-sixth year of his reign, A.D. 1372.

FOUNDATION CHARTER.

Cart 46 Edw. III. No. 2. Pat. 46 Edw. III. p. l. m. 28. Cart. 1 Hen. V. p. l. m. 8. per Inspexim.

(TRANSLATION.)

Edward, by the grace of God, king of England and France, and Lord of Ireland, to all to whom these present letters shall come, health. Know ye, that we of our special grace have given, granted and assigned for ourselves and our heirs to our beloved in Christ, MATILDA, prioress of the monastery of *St. Mary and St. Margaret the Virgins* in Dertford, by us founded, and the convent of sisters of the *order of St. Augustine* according to the institutes and under the *cure* of the brethren of the order of Friars Preachers¶ of the monastery aforesaid, TO WIT, *The mansion, site* and *appurtenances*—the

---

* Claus 43 Ed. III. m. 6. Ibid. m. 16.

† Esch. Dorset. 43 Edw. III. No. 4.

‡ Pat. 45 Edw. III. p. 2. m. 6. Claus. 45 Edw. III. m 6.

¶ The notice of the founder having thus changed the order of the sisters from that of St. Austin to the Friars Preachers, may somewhat countenance the before-mentioned tradition of the monastery having been originally a Saxon foundation. If so, it was not unlikely subject to Danish violence.

DARTFORD PRIORY. TEMP. HEN. VIII.

which mansion, the prioress and convent now inhabit. The manors of *Shibborn* and *Portbrugge*, with their appurtenances in the county of Kent, with one knight's fee, and all other things to the same manor belonging or pertaining; the advowson of the *chapel of St. Edmund, king and martyr in Dertford;* and all *lands and tenements* with their appurtenances which the said prioress and convent hath of *the gift of John Brond*, chaplain, and which were *William Clapte's* and *Joan* his wife's in the parishes of *Dertford, Stone, Wilmington* and *Southfleet.* A messuage with its appurtenances which was *John de Chertsey's*, in the said vill of *Dertford;* and three messuages with their appurtenances in the same vill, which were *Simon Kagworth's.* One messuage, one pigeon house, thirty acres of land, three acres of meadow, fifteen acres of pasture, and twenty shillings rent, with their appurtenances in the same vill which were *Robert Mount's;* thirty-four acres of land, five acres of meadow, and six shillings rents with their appurtenances, in *Dartford* and *Wilmington*, which were *William de Wilmington's;* seven messuages, two tofts, four gardens, one hundred and fifty-eight acres and a half of land, forty of meadow, thirty of pasture, twenty of marsh, and fifty shillings rents with their appurtenances; and the reversion of a messuage, eight acres of land and a half with their appurtenances in the vill of *Dertford*, which messuage and land formerly belonged to *William de Newport*, citizen and fishmonger of London, but it is now held by *Margaret Mitchell* for life. One messuage and seven shillings rent in the vill of *Dertford* which were *Nicholas de Crofton's.* Two messuages and one garden in the same vill of *Dertford*, which were formerly *Alexander Folke's.* One messuage with appurtenances in the same vill which was *John Lambyn's;* three roods of meadow and pasture, and two oxgangs with their appurtenances in the same vill which were *John Michell's;* sixteen acres of land in the same vill which were *John Chepstede's* and *John Wallworth's* citizens of London; thirty acres of land with their

J

appurtenances which were *Alice Perrer's*,* in the said vill of Wilmington, now *John Pikeman's*. Two messuages and all the lands and tenements, rents and services with their appurtenances, which were Alice Perrers, in the parishes of *Dertford*, *Wilmington*, *Southfleet*, and *Marsh*, in the county aforesaid, and the *Place land* with its appurtenances called LE CASTEL PLACE; also five shillings and three pence rents with appurtenances in the same vill, which were *William Morgaunt's*. One messuage or tenement with its appurtenances in our city of *London*, which belonged to *Robert de Burton*, and *John de Letton*, executors to the testament of Robert de Harwood, formerly citizen and trader in London; and all tenements with their appurtenances in the same city in the parish of St. Martin, without Ludgate; in Fleet street; in the parish of St. Mary de Orgar, near Estgate; and in the parish of St. Catherine, below the cemetery of the great Holy Trinity near Aldgate, which were *Augustine Waley's*.

All the rents and services with their appurtenances coming from two messuages and three shops in Cordwainer street, in the same city, which Jacob Andrew held for life of the prioress and convent, with the reversion of the said messuages and shops, with their accessions; and sixty six shillings and eight pence rent with their appurtenances in Tamorsfield, and Westcheap, in London, which rents pertain to the manor of Portbrugge, which formerly were Robert Bicknore's. The manor of *Great Belstede*, with their appurtenances, with the church of *Washbrook* and *Velechurch*, to be held to their proper use, and the *advowsons* of the same churches; and also the advowson of the church of *Alterton*, and the vicarages of

---

* Alice Perrers the mistress of king Edward the third. She afterwards became the wife of Sir William de Windsor, and is mentioned as then being such in the will of Bishop Hatfield of Durham, 1381. She dabbled much in ecclesiastical preferments, as is evident from the celebrated William of Wickham negociating with her for the see of Winchester. Vide, *Testamenta Eboraciensia*. London. 1836.

the said churches of Washbrook and Velechurch, with their appurtenances and liberties in the county of Suffolk.

The manor of *Brandiston*, with rents and services and all other things pertaining to the said manor in *Herkenstede* in the same county, with rents and services and all other things pertaining thereto in the town of *Goffield* in the county of Essex; and the manor of *Combes* with the *site of the chapel*, and all rents, services and whatsoever belongeth to the manor and site of the chapel in the said county of Suffolk; the manor of *Hecchesham** with its appurtenances in Surrey and Kent, with all our [the king's] lands and tenements and their appurtenances in *Putfold* in the said county of Surrey, with the church of *Witteleg*, and chapel of *Horslee*, to hold to their proper use, and the advowson of the church and chapel with all the liberties thereunto appertaining: the manor of *Norton* with its appurtenances, the advowson of the *church* of the manor with the *chantry* in the church, and certain members to the same manor belonging, to wit: *Silleigh, Ernewell, Trowe,* and *West-Withhill.* And also all rents and services with the appurtenances of all *our* tenements in the parishes of *Weremenetre, Rolveston,* and *Madyngton,* with their appurtenances in the county of Wilts; and all rents and services which they hath in *Burton-atte-Nashe,* and *atte-More,* with all the appurtenances of our manor of *Norton,* in com. Dorset. The manor of *Fiffehide* with its appurtenances, lands, tenements, rents, services, escheats, reversions, and all other things pertaining to the said manor of Fiffehide which were formerly belonging to the prioress and convent in *Gerardston, Wilton, Digehampton, Foulston* and *Little Derneford* in the county of *Wilts;* and all lands and tenements, meadows, rents and services with their appurtenances, which they have in *Purbeck,* in co. *Dorset,* pertaining to the same manor, of Fiffehide with all other manors of this manor, and the advowson

---

* Hecchesham, or Hatcham, a manor in Deptford, Kent.

of the church of Fiffehide and St. Michael, in West street, in Wilton, also the knight's fee, and all other lands and tenements belonging to the same.

And the manor of *Colwenston*, with its appurtenances in the county of *Glamorgan*, in Wales, together with all lands and tenements with their appurtenances, in *Woldeston*, in the marches of Wales, in co. *Hereford*, with the knight's fee, belonging to the manor of Coldwenton or appurtenances, to have and to hold all the aforesaid manors, lands, tenements, rents and services, fees, reversions and liberties as is aforesaid, with appurtenances; and the advowsons to the said prioress and convent, and their successors in dowry and foundation of the monastery aforesaid as the same were anciently delivered to our hands, to hold of the same lord by the same services by which they were anciently held and by our hands given for ever—notwithstanding the statute of mortmain; in testimony of which we have made these our letters patent. Witnessed at Westminster, the 20th day of July, in the forty-sixth year of our reign over England, and thirty-third of our reign over France.

A.D. 1373, an inquisition was taken of the prioress' manors of Fiffehide, Wilts; and of Bradele in Purbeck com. Dorset.* And the same year, the churches of Bokesworth, Skydmore, and Chiltern Langley, were appropriated to the Prioress and Nuns of Dertford, for the support of the brethren who exercised the spiritual government and direction of that community.†

1375. A confirmation of certain shops and messuages in Cordwainer street, London.‡

---

* Esch. 47 Edw. III. No. 4. Dorset and Wilts.
† Pat. 47 Edw. III. p. 2. m. 3. m. 32. and m. 34.
‡ Pat. 49 Edw. III. p. l. m. 3.

About this time Catherine widow of ———— Brewes or Braouse, of Salle, in Norfolk, and daughter of Sir Thomas de Norwich, took the veil in Dartford priory;* this lady having become the heiress of the family of De Norwich, procured her estates to be settled on the convent.

King Edward the Third died in June, 1377, (five years after he had granted Dartford priory the great charter of endowment,) at his palace, at Shene, in Surrey, with Alice Perrers for his sole companion, who having drawn some valuable rings from his fingers, abandoned him before life was quite extinct.†

1379. King Richard II., confirmed his grandfather's benefactions in Dartford to the nunnery.‡

About a fortnight before Whitsuntide, 1381, Wat Tyler began his resistance to the poll tax, which

---

* Sir Walter de Norwich, lord of ...., left by Katherine his wife, three sons, John, Thomas, and Roger. Sir John the eldest 4 Edw. III., settled certain estates on himself, and Thomas and Roger his brothers in tail. Sir John had by Margaret his wife, a son Walter, who died before his father, leaving a son John by Walleon his wife, daughter of Sir Miles Stapleton, and heir to his grandfather. By an inquisition taken at Walsingham on Thursday next after the feast of St. Luke the Evangelist, 48 Edw. III. Sir John de Norwich was found to have died on the Feast of the Circumcision then last past, possessed of the Lordships of ...., and Catherine Brewes daughter of Sir Thomas de Norwich, Son of Sir Walter and Catherine and brother of Sir John, was his cousin and heir—This Catherine the widow of .... Brewes, of Salle, in Norfolk, was now a nun at Dartford.—Bloomfield's Norfolk. vol. iii. 846. [1769.] In vol. v. p. 267. under the head of "Ravenham College," Sir John de Norwich is mentioned as the last heir male of this family, and it is stated that the lordship of Kemborley was about 1374 conveyed to this lady, Catherine Brewes, by Sir Roger de Norwich, who was her uncle.

† Stowe's Annales.

‡ Claus. 49 Ed. III. m. 34. Cart. 3 Ric. II. No. 1. Pat. 4 Ric. II. p. 2. m. 29.

imposed six shillings and eight-pence upon all religious
men and women, and four-pence upon every male and
female above the age of fifteen.*

1384.   The convent having lately built a new chapel in
the infirmary, king Richard II. gave the manors of Massingham, West and East-Wrotham, in Norfolk, etc. for the
support of a chaplain, to perform divine offices daily
therein, for the benefit of the said sisters, by the following
charter.

(Translation.)

Richard, by the grace of God, King of England and
France, and Lord of Ireland, to all to whom the present
letters shall come, health. Know ye, that whereas formerly John Daventre, parson of the church of Brom,
Walter Berkeley, vicar of the church of Kimberlee, John
Cranhouse, Edmund Lakingheth, and Richard Nooth,
enfeoffed us of the manor of Massyngham, with their
appurtenances in com. Norfolk, with all fairs, markets,
waifs, strays, and all other liberties to the same manor
appertaining, and that John Bacon, Henry Boghay,
Thomas Godelake and John Appleton, conceded and confirmed to us the reversion of the manor of West Wrotham, East Wrotham and Elyngton, in the county aforesaid, which the said John Daventre, Walter and Richard,
John Snoreing and Stephen Langham held for the life of
Katherine Breouse, and for a year after the decease of the
said Katherine, to have and to hold after the said year is
complete to us and our heirs.   We of our special grace to
the honour of God and in devotion to our monastery of
sisters of the order of Friars Preachers founded in Dertford by the charity of our lord and grandfather, give,
grant and assign for ourselves and heirs, to the beloved
in Christ, the prioress and convent of the monastery aforesaid, the said manor of Massingham with its appurtenances, with the fairs, markets, waifs, strays and all other

---

* Stowe's Annales, 285.

liberties to the said manor belonging, to have and to hold of us and our successors for ever.

Also in like manner, we grant the manor of *West-Wrotham* with its appurtenances, with the aforesaid *lands and tenements*, in *East Wrotham* and *Elyngton*, as before recited, to the said prioress and convent and their successors, that a chaplain may come every day to perform divine offices in the chapel of the infirmary of the monastery aforesaid, newly erected, to celebrate for the relief and sustentation of the infirm sisters and brethren, and that he may continue to pray for their good estate, and for our health while living, and for our souls after we have left this light, and also for the souls of the founders and benefactors to this monastery; and for the prioress and convent aforesaid and their successors, and all the faithful departed for ever. In testimony whereof, etc. Witness ourself at Westminster, 8th September, in the eighth year of our reign.*

1392. The king granted the prioress and convent certain messuages in Dertford, together with others above the Haysourf [Haywharf] of London.†

1393. The church of Wylde, near Baldock, appropriated to the use of the brethren of Chiltern-Langley, in connexion with this house.‡

---

* Pat. 8 Ric. II. p. l. m. 25.   † Pat. 16 Ric. II. p. 2. m. 31.

‡ Pat. 17 Ric. II. p. 2. m. 35. Hence it is evident the Preaching Friars of [King's] Langley, in Hertfordshire, who were appointed by the founder's charter *superintendants* of this community, deputed some of the brethren to reside in Dartford priory, and that they had apartments within its walls. In 1396, the principal resident friar was brother John Sill. His name occurs in conjunction with Robert Grape, vicar of Dartford, and others, as one of the commissioners appointed by the bishop of Rochester to receive the resignation of John Staundon the chaplain of St. Mary Stampit, and appoint his successor. Vide. *Reg. Botelsham. f. 90.*

1395. The king granted the prioress and convent a charter of confirmation of the custody or advowson of the chapel of St. Edmund, at Dertford.*

1398. The manors of Preston, Overland, Elmston, Wodeling, Pakemaston, Herelesham, Godmeston, etc., granted to the prioress and convent of Dertford for the use of themselves and the Friars Preachers of Langley, by the king's grandfather, Edward III. confirmed to those communities by the reigning monarch.†

1399. JOAN the prioress, daughter of lord Scrope, together with her convent, present John Symonds to the chantry or chaplaincy of St. Edmund.‡

This sisterhood was equally favoured by the House of Lancaster; and Henry IV. in 1399,¶ and 1404‖, granted fresh charters of confirmation for their estates. Willing further to increase the revenues of this house, the new monarch enjoined an inquisition to enquire whether it would be to the prejudice of the crown if certain lands in Bexhill or Bexley and Dertford were settled by Walter Makenade, the proprietor upon the convent. The jury having returned, that no damage could result thereunto, the said lands were conveyed to this monastery.**

---

* Pat 19 Ric. p. 2. m. 3.   † Pat. 22 Ric. p. 3. m 15.

‡ Regist. Will. de Botelsham. Epis Reff. 142. This prioress was the daughter of Richard lord Scrope, of Bolton, memorable for his long suit in the court military with Sir Robert Grosvenor, respecting a right to certain armorial bearings. Richard, the brother of the prioress, was archbishop of York. *Dugdale's Baronage.* i. 154.

¶ Cart. 1 Henry IV. p. 2. m. 14.   Pat. 1. Henry IV. p. 5. m. 2.

‖ Pat 6. Hen IV. p. 1. m. 15.

** Inquisit. ad quod Damnum. 6 Hen. IV. No. 33.

1405. Certain lands and tenements in East and West Wrotham, com. Norfolk, settled by fine upon the convent,* and confirmed to the sisters by the king the following year, A.D. 1406.† And about the same time Walter Makenade and others gave the prioress and nuns of Dertford some lands and tenements at Sutton-at-Hone,‡ which donation the king confirmed by patent, together with the adjoining manor of Portbrugge at Dertford.¶

1422. Dec. 4. The prioress and convent present John Blice, to the perpetual chaplaincy of the chantry of St. Edmund, king and martyr.∥

King Henry VI. in the first and third years of his reign, A.D. 1422**, and 1422††, confirmed the possessions of the priory with all their rights, and repeated the confirmation in 1437.‡‡

1432. Rose the prioress and her convent present John Derby to the perpetual chantry of St. Edmund, on death of master Edmund, late chaplain, to which he was instituted the tenth of May.¶¶

Shortly after, John Martin, late judge of the Common Pleas, with others, gave the same house of "Sisters of the order of Preachers, Dertford," eleven acres of wood,

---

* Fin. Norfolk 7 Hen. IV. No. 61. † Pat. 8 Hen. IV. p. 1. m. 22. Inquisit. ad quod Damnum. 6 Hen. IV. No. 2.

‡ Pat. 8. Hen. IV. p. 1. m. 22. ¶ Ibid. p. 2. m. 14.

∥ Act. Curia Consist. f. 206. in Eccl. Roffen.

** Pat. 1 Hen. VI. p. 5. m. 32. †† Pat. 3 Hen. VI. p. 1. m. 13.

‡‡ Pat. 16 Hen. VI. p. 4. m. 30. These repeated confirmations were considered necessary to give stability to the original grants in those confiscating ages.

¶¶ Act. Curia Consist. f. 95.

and briers [underwood], with their appurtenances in Dertford, and also a messuage together with six acres and a half of land, and seven acres of wood with their appurtenances in Bexley, to hold to themselves and their successors for ever.

Circa 1439. John Osborne, mercer, and John Selby, citizens of London, gave two messuages, and a moiety of twenty others in London to the same sisterhood in Dertford, and their successors.*

1441. William, bishop of Rochester, on the receipt of twenty pounds sterling, grants the prioress and convent an acquittance for the "manor and demaynes" of the rectory of Dertford, which they now held of him to farm, in full payment of all rents and fines, from Easter to the nativity of John the Baptist. Dated the nineteenth day of June.†

1442. The prioress and convent pay the bishop a further sum of ten pounds, and receive another acquittance for the "rectory-farm and lordship" of Dertford, from the Nativity. The instrument is dated Trottesclyve, 11th February.‡

1446. Oct. 6. MARGARET DE BELLOMONT,¶ prioress of Dertford, and her convent present Thomas de Inges-

---

* Inquisit. ad quod damnum.   18 Henry IV. Nos. 9 et 10.

† Act. Cur. Consist. 160.   ‡ Ibid. sub ann.

¶ This prioress was daughter to Henry, lord Beaumond, or Bellomont and Elizabeth daughter of William lord Willoughby ; her father died, 1 Henry V. A.D. 1413, and her mother, 19 Henry VI. 1439. Her brother John, lord Beaumond, was created Earl of Boloine [Boulogne] by letters patent, dated 27th July, 14 Henry VI while proceeding to relieve Calais.   Four years after he was advanced to the title of Viscount, and was the first person in England that bore

dell or Ingledew, to the perpetual chaplaincy of St. Edmund, on death of brother William Crowland.*

1453. This year died Richard Miles of Stoneham, the husbandman to the prioress and convent; he gave by will six shillings towards repairing the parish church of Dartford.†

1455. Certain payments made from the king's exchequer to the prioress.‡

1456. Richard Bolton of Dertford, by will dated 3rd of February, this year, directs his body to be buried within the monastery of Dertford, or in whatsoever place it shall please God; giving to the altar of St. Trinity, (in the parish church,) for forgotten tithes and offerings twenty shillings; keeping the day of his month's mind twelve pence, and sixty shillings to be distributed amongst the poor who attend on that solemn occasion; to repairing the window of St. Trinity in Dertford ten shillings; to the prioress and convent of Dertford twenty shillings; to the same community for exequies and masses twelve pence, etc. He constitutes Joan his wife and William his son, executors.¶

1457. King Henry the Sixth, grants a confirmation of all the lands and tenements in Preston, Ash, Slape,

---

that dignity. (Pat. 18 Henry VI.) His lady Elizabeth, daughter of William Phelip, lord Bardolph, died in 1440. John lord Beaumond was slain in the battle at Northampton, 10th July, 1459, in the forty-ninth year of his age. *Dugd. Bar.* ii. 54.

* Act. Curia Consist. sub ann.

† Regist. Lib. Testam. in Eccles. Roffen. ii. f. . .

‡ Receipt. in S'ccar. 37 Henry VI. Trin. rot. 22.

¶ Regist. Lib. Testament ii. f. 101.

Wingham, etc., for the use of the priory of Chiltern-Langley, in connexion with this religious community.*

1451. Agnes wife of Richard Fagg of Dertford, by will dated 22nd of January this year, directs his body to be buried in the cemetery of the blessed Mary and Margaret virgins of Bellomont,† (i. e. the burying ground attached to the church of the monastery,) and besides sundry pecuniary donations to her relatives, gives a tenement at Rochester, called Corsingham, to John Elmful, chaplain of Stampit, towards a further endowment of that chantry founded in Dertford church.   The residue of her goods she gives to John Martyn.

The same year certain tenements in the parish of St. Mary de Arcubus, London, were given to the prioress and her convent,‡ and the benefaction confirmed by the king.

1461.   The prioress lady ALICE BRANSWAITE,¶ and

---

* Pat. 36 Hen. VI. p. 2. m. 7

† Regist. Testament. ii. f. 129.   Possibly lady Margaret Bellomont formed the cemetery of the priory, and effected so many alterations or additions to the monastic edifice as to induce contemporaries to honour it with her name.

‡ Pat. 36 Henry VI. p. 1. m. 18.   Claus. 37 Henry VI. m. 7.

¶ There is a book in small folio beautifully written on vellum, with the first page illuminated, which once belonged to this lady, and no doubt was afterwards preserved in the conventual library until the dissolution of the society.   On the first blank leaf at the beginning are the following memorandums, "Thys Boyk longyth to Dame Alys Braintwaith the worchypfulle Prioras of Dartford.   Jhesu mercy ;" underneath are the following words,

"Orate pro anima Dominæ Elizabith Rede hujus loci . . . .
"Orate pro anima Johanne Newmarche."

The last two names are written in a superior manner to the former, but whether earlier or later may be doubted.   From the word

her convent present John Wells, chaplain, to the chaplaincy of St. Edmund, July 4th, on the death of Thomas Yngledew.*

1462. John Millman of Dertford, by will dated 21st April, directed his body to be buried in the [priory] church of the blessed Mary and St. Margaret, and on the day of his funeral three shillings and four-pence to be given in doles: and twelve pence to the clerk.*

On the establishment of the House of York upon the throne, this priory being under the immediate patronage of the reigning monarch immediately experienced his fostering influence; and in 1465 the

---

Dominæ prefixed to the name of Elizabeth Rede, it is not improbable that she was prioress, and Johanne Newmarche, one of the nuns. There was a family of the name of Rede, lords of Borstal, in Buckinghamshire, from the reign of Henry the sixth, until long after the suppression of the monasteries; many particulars of them occur in Kennett's Parochial Antiquities, and Dunkin's Oxfordshire. The Redes were great benefactors to the religious orders.

The volume in question now constitutes the Harleian MS. No. 2254, in the British Museum. It is a theological work, and at its conclusion thus entitled "The Treetis that is kalled the Prelynge of Love made bi a Frere Minour, Bonaventure, that was Cardinal of the Courte of Roome." —In the same volume is another treatise, imperfect at the beginning, having likewise, its title at the conclusion. The first chapter is thus headed, "Incipit tractatus cuius titulio Cratur Stimulus amoris," and the first sentence runs thus: "How a man shall have Cristis passion in mynde." At the bottom of this folio are the arms of Shirley and Breuis (or Brewes) quartered.

The writer of the catalogue of the Harleian MSS. says he "has not now conveniences for ascertaining whether both the treatises or either of them are a translation of Bonaventure's Stimulus divini Amoris" or to whom else one of them may belong.

* Act. Cur. Consist. f. 235.   † Regist. Test. ii. f, ,

beforementioned charter being laid before him, received a most ample confirmation.*

1467.   Some imperfections being found in divers of the grants of preceding monarchs, Edw. IV. issued a new instrument of incorporation to this community, including a confirmation of all their lands, revenues and privileges.†

1468.   Roger Rothley of Dertford, by will dated 6th of May in this year, gave to the prioress and convent of Dertford, ten marks, upon this condition, that the said prioress and convent and their successors should perform in the said monastery, a yearly service (mass), for the repose of his soul for ten years after his decease.‡

Roos Pitt of Dertford, by will dated 4th July, 1470,¶ gave to the prioress and convent of Dertford, thirteen shillings and four-pence, to pray for her soul; to Jone

---

* Cart. 5 Edw. IV. No. 1. Preter confirm. quod ipsa per nomen priorissæ Monast. S. Mariæ and Margaritæ virginum de Dertford et ejusdem loci conventus sororum ordinis S. Augustine secundum instituta et sub cura fratrum ordines prædicat. sint habiles, etc.

† Cart. 7 Edw. IV. Nos. 1 et 5.   See also Lambarde.

‡ Regist. Testament. Roff. iii. 9.

¶ This is the laste wille of me the said Roos Pittes, made the day and yere above wreten, that is to sey, that Master John Hornley, Jehn Groveherst, Thomas Stockton and John Barbour, my feyffees dely'r in lawful state when they shall be required, to Thomas Stockton, fishmonger and citizen of London, the place that 'ey dwell yn, and the littel house beside yt with the appe'tences thereto longyng.   And with 'y money thereoff received I will that th' be fownde an obitt preste to pray and syng dyvyne s'vice in the p'ish church of Dertford by the space of on yere, for my sowl and the sowls of my fader and moth' and for all my gode doers.   And the residue of the money I wull that Betr' my sust' myne executor dispose and fullfill my last will and ...... wryten.   Also I wolle that

Stokton in the abbey, twenty-pence; to Jone Mores in the same place, twenty-pence and a candlestick.* As both these were evidently nuns, it is clear that the religious were permitted to receive and expend small benefactions for their own individual use although contrary to the strict rule of their profession.

---

the p'ioress and co'vent have *xiijs. iiijd.* to pray for me. Further more I woll that ij acres of my lond lying in the est of Grenestrete be sold by my feoffees and the money thereof received to be delyvred to the said Betric' in performing my last will aforesaid specified and delv'd." *Reg. Test* iii. 65. This will is registered as a sort of codicil to a former containing the above benefactions, wherein also John Groverste is stated to be Roos Pittes' brother, and given a brass pot containing six gallons.— Beatrice and Joan her sisters are therein named, and xxd. willed to the reparation of the glass window of St. Edmund's chapel. The Groverste family were the principal inhabitants of Dartford, and the nuns were occasionally permitted to visit them; there was an oratory in their mansion, and a room hung with tapestry, said to be *worked by those ladies*. The road from Hithe street through Bullis lane was made for their accommodation. Vide p. 14. 20.

* The Stockton's were resident gentry in Overy street, Dartford, from the reign of Edward IV, to that of Henry VIII. The family of Joan Mores is unknown. Instances occur in which guardians grossly abused monastic institutions by placing the younger sisters of families, (co-heiresses,) in nunneries at a very early age, and inducing them to take the bonds of a religious profession when only twelve years old, that the elder married sisters' husbands might entirely have the inheritance; yet so indelibly did these obligations impress the minds of youthful females, that they generally resisted every attempt to remove them from the convents. Nuns relinquished all property on admission and were punished for the *receipt of letters* or *presents* without the permission of the superior. There was frequent preaching in the Dartford priory; and besides fasting on Fridays, the sisters were required to abstain from animal food from Holy-rood day till Easter.

1471. The king's escheator held an inquisition of certain lands at Crockenhill, in the parish of Eynesford, in the county of Kent, to enquire if it would be to the prejudice of the king and kingdom if the manor of Crockenhill were granted to the prioress and convent, when a jury having returned that no injury would occur, the said manor and lands were settled upon that community.*

Thomas Taylor of Dartford, by will dated 16th Feb. 1476, gave to the prioress and her convent a legacy of twenty shillings.†

1478. John Joynor of Dartford, by will dated 18th

---

* Inquisit. ad quod Damnum. Kane. 11 Edw. IV.

† As the items of this will are somewhat curious, a few are subjoined. John Taylor of Dertford, gives his soul to almighty Jesus, to our blessed lady his mother, and all the saints in heaven; his body to be buried in the church yard of St. Edmund king and martyr, beside the sepulchre of Joan his wife. "Item, to the vicar of Dertford to pray for me ijs.: to iiij men beryng my body to my sepulture, each of them for their labour iiijd; to the prioress and convent of Dertford xxs.: to Richard Taylor my brother, my best gown; the residue of my goods and chattels after my debts are paid, I will to Beatrice my wife, who I will be my executor. The howse where I dwell in Overy the which Thomas Wiltshire [afterwards Sir Thomass Wiltshire, of Stone place,] and Beatrice his wife standeth feoffed in, the said Thomas to release by deed sufficient in law to the said Beatrice her heirs and assigns, to the intent that the said Beatrice shall have that dwelling during her life, and after her decease if none issue there be, then I will that the said place and its appurts be sold by her executors, and with the money thereof to be found a priest singing in the parish church of Dertford by half a yere, praying for his soul, and the souls of all my friends; and the residue of the money to be distributed in deeds of charity to the most worship of God and profit of my soul." Regist. Test. iv. f. 568.

July of that year, after commending his soul to God, the blessed virgin, the holy company of heaven, and directing his body to be buried in the church yard of Dartford, bequeaths "unto o'r lady light in the abbay iiij*d*.; 'unto the prioress and convent in the abbay of Darford aforesaid, my grete bras potte;—the residue of alle my goods unto Dyoness my wyffe that she dispose for me as she seemeth best God to please, etc."*

1479. An inquisition taken of the lands belonging to the convent at North-Cray, Wilmington, etc.†

1490. In the sixth year of the reign of Henry the Seventh, the princess Bridget, third daughter of king Edward the Fourth, by his queen Elizabeth Wydville,‡ was placed in Dartford priory on the retirement of her mother to the monastery of Bermondsey. The princess was then about ten years old, and having been destined from infancy to be a nun, entrusted to the

---

* Regist. Test. iii. f. 244.   † Esch. com. Cant. 19 Edw. IV.

‡ The princess Bridget was born 9th November, 1480, at the king's palace at Eltham, where she was christened in the chapel by the bishop of Winchester. *Stowe's Ann.* 431. She lost her father when not more than two years and a half old. In February, 1483, she was sick being then lying in the wardrobe, and in consequence there was delivered for her use, from the king's stores in that place, "two long pillows of fustain stuffed with down, and pillow beres of hollond cloth unto them." *Wardrobe Accounts. Antiq. Repert.* i. 51. She was taken by her mother into Sanctuary on her uncle's usurpation, and remained there till Feb. 14th, 1485. She was six years old at her sister's marriage with Henry the Seventh, and it is probable remained with her mother about the court, until her retirement to Bermondsey monastery A.D. 1490, when, being intended for a nun, she was sent to Dartford and placed under the tuition of the prioress, where she remained a constant resident.

K

care and instruction of the·prioress. She remained an
inmate of the convent until the alarming illness of the
queen dowager induced the prioress to permit the
young neophyte to visit her mother's death bed.* Not-

---

* Nearly every incident in the life of this queen is tinged with
romance. She was married at an early age to John, lord Grey of
Groby, a zealous partizan of the house of Lancaster. Her husband
fell fighting for Henry VI. in the battle of St. Albans, and the
victor confiscated his estates. Reduced to the extremity of distress,
she seized the opportunity of king Edward's visit to Whittlebury
forest in the neighbourhood of her residence at Grafton, for the purpose of hunting, to throw herself at his feet and sue for mercy to
herself and children. Her surpassing beauty shone resplendent
through her widow's weeds and melted the heart of the amorous
monarch. Her suit was granted and he in return became a peti-
tioner. Her virtue resisted his blandishments, and her high-spirited
reply to his overtures, that "though she felt herself unworthy to
be his wife she would not stoop to be his concubine," so inflamed
his passion that he determined to raise her to his bed and throne,
and they were privately married at Grafton, in Northamptonshire,
May 1st, 1464. This marriage so displeased the potent earl of
Warwick, Edward's strongest supporter, that he immediately changed
sides, raised an army, drove her husband from his kingdom,
and compelled her to flee for safety to the Sanctuary of St. Peter
at Westminster. The chances of war re-seated Edward ' in the
government ; and she bore him two sons and several daughters. Her
husband suddenly died of repletion April 9th, 1483; Richard duke
of Gloucester seized upon the person of the young king at Stoney-
Stratford on the 30th of the same month, and the next night when
rumours of the proceedings reached London, the queen hastily fled
from the palace of Westminster to the Sanctuary of the abbey,
carrying with her the young duke of York and her daughters. She
took up her abode in the abbot's house, and here desolate and dis-
mayed she was found *seated on the rushes of the floor* by the archbishop of York sometime before *day-break*, May 1st., in the utmost
alarm for the safety of herself and children, *(Stow's Ann.* 439).

withstanding the king's displeasure clouded the latter
days of the royal sufferer "she expired in the monastery

Misfortunes now thickened around; on the 16th of June the duke
of York was taken from her, under the pretence of carrying him to
the king his brother; on the 21st, Edward was set aside from the
crown, and on Thursday the 26th, Richard, his uncle, assumed the
throne of his inheritance.   Her sons, lodged in the tower, fell by
the hands of the assassin, or constitute the historical problem that
can never be satisfactorily solved in the person of Perkin Warbeck.
And to complete her misery, a servile parliament, declared her
marriage invalid and bastardised her issue. (*Rot. Parl.* vi. 241.) Yet
amidst all these misfortunes, aggravated by the seizure of all her
property, the queen and her five daughters continued to live in comparative personal safety beneath the protection of the church for
nearly a year and three quarters.   Dark rumours then floated upon
Richard's ear of a projected invasion by the Earl of Richmond,
supported by the Yorkists under an engagement of the earl to
marry Elizabeth the eldest daughter of the late king.   The policy
of Richard the Third then changed; he courted the smiles of the
late queen, settled estates upon her of considerable value, and proposed in case his queen, then ill, should die, to marry his niece.
The proposal is said to have met her concurrence and not proved
disagreable to the young lady.   Edward's daughters were delivered into his hands and the queen herself left the Sanctuary in
February, 1485.   The following month Richard's queen died, and
news of the projected alliance being carried to the earl of Richmond
the expedition was precipitated.   The battle of Bosworth decided the
fate of Richard on the 12th of August, 1485, and the victor, pursuant
to his engagement, married the lady Elizabeth, 18th January, 1486,
then in her twenty-first year.   Polydore Virgil (p. 571,) says that
Henry the Seventh was greatly irritated by the knowledge of the
apparent facility with which the queen had listened to his rival's
overtures, and suspecting afterwards that the exclusion of herself
and friends from power had induced her to abet the rebellion of
John, earl of Lincoln, A.D. 1487, he caused her to be suddenly
apprehended, confiscated the estates, which Richard had given, and
imprisoned her in the monastery of Bermondsey where she remained

"of Bermondsey, in the arms of her daughters *all of*
"*whom were present* at the mournful scene with the
"exception of the queen, who was precluded by her

---

in solitude and wretchedness for life. This statement is however
contradicted by Sir Nicholas Harris Nicholas who, while he admits
that Henry seized the lands, nevertheless endeavours to prove her
in favour, by shewing that on the 4th of March, 1486, Henry the
Seventh granted her certain lordships for life of the annual value
of £102, though he owns there was a rumour that some regarded
it as a bribe to prevent her divulging the secret which she had
somehow penetrated into, *that her second son was still living.* Nicholas
also states, that in the following November, Henry proposed her
marriage with James the Third, king of Scotland, and that the completion of the marriage was frustrated only by the death of that
prince in July, 1488. Hence he contends, that if the king had felt
any apprehensions of her enmity, he would not have permitted her
to enter an independent kingdom where her machinations might
have been attended with fatal effects to his government. Nicholas
further says, that she remained about the court subsequent to that
year, was present at the audience of the French ambassador, and
in November, 1489, when Elizabeth took her church after her confinement with prince Arthur, stood godmother, and attended at the
font. The same writer, however, informs us that on the 19th of
June, Henry repossessed himself of the estates and assigned her
a pension of £400 in lieu thereof. It may be safely concluded
that she soon after retired to the monastery of Bermondsey. Her
will is dated 12th of April, 1492; she therein styles herself
queen of England, and orders her body to be buried at Windsor
with her late husband king Edward, but forbids any pomp or great
expense, adding "Whereas I have no worldly goods to do the
queen's grace my dearest daughter a pleasure with, neither to reward any of my children according to my heart and mind as is to
me possible, I give her grace my blessing and all the aforesaid my
children." Such small stuff as she possessed she desired might be
appropriated to the payment of her debts and the health of her soul
as far as it extended, but if any of her blood wished any part of her
property she ordered them to be allowed the preference. She con-

"approaching accouchement.   Queen Elizabeth Wyd-
"ville was buried privately at Windsor, on Whit-sunday,
"A.D. 1492, at eleven o'clock, without ringing of bells;
"but on Tuesday came by water king Edward's three
"daughters lady Ann, lady Katherine, and the *lady*
"*Bridget;* * that night began the solemn dirge, and all
"the queen's daughters† offered."   At the close of this
mournful ceremony the princess Bridget returned to
Dartford, and it is presumed, under the influence of
high-wrought feeling shortly took the veil.   This event
is believed to have occurred in the eleventh or twelfth
year of the reign of Henry the seventh, and as the professed was the reigning queen's sister and daughter
of a monarch it is affirmed this splendid sacrifice of
royalty to religion was celebrated with all the imposing
pomp of the catholic church, and attended by the
nobility and gentry of the neighbourhood.   The princess
never attained any higher rank than that of a common nun.   She seems, however, during her whole life to

---

stituted the prior of Shene, and doctors Sutton and Brent, her
executors, and she entreated her dearest daughter the queen, and
the marquis of Dorset, to assist in seeing her wishes fulfilled.   It
is witnessed by the prior of Bermondsey, John de Merlow. *Introd.
to Nicholas's Privy Purse Expences of Elizabeth of York.* lxxx. 1821.
Manning's Survey. i. 202.   * M.S. Herald's College.

† This queen had seven daughters; 1st, Elizabeth, queen of Hen. VII.
2, Mary, died unmarried at Greenwich, 1482; 3, Cicely, married to
viscount Wells; 4, Margaret, born 1472, died in infancy; 5, Ann, in
1425 became the wife of Thomas, lord Howard, the date of her decease
is unknown; 6, Katherine, at 17 married to Lord Courteney; a month
after her husband's death, æt. 33, she made a *vow of chastity* before the
bishop of London; she survived the earl 16 years; died 1527, and her
effigies adorn her tomb at Tiverton; 7, Bridget a nun.

have been occasionally visited by her family, and kept
up an active correspondence with the queen, since the
"Privy Purse Expences" of the latter in September,
1502, contains an entry of a person being paid for
going from Windsor to Dartford to the lady Bridget
with a message from Her majesty.   And in another
part of the same document occurs the following, "Item,
"paid to John Weredon for his costes riding from
"Windsore to Dartford to my lady Brigget by the
"space of too day at *xijd.* the day, *ijs.*" The sum of
three pounds, six shillings and eight pence was paid
yearly to the convent for her maintenance; and in
1502, it evidently appears the queen charged herself
with the payment of this annuity, by the following entry
"Item, the vj day of July delivered to thabbasse of
"Dartford by thands of John Weredon towards such,
"money as the said abbasse hath laid owt towardes
"the charges of my lady Brigget ther, *lxvjs. viijd.**

1503. Feb. 11th.   Elizabeth queen of Henry the
Seventh and sister to the princess Bridget, died nine
days after giving birth to a daughter, at the age of thirty-
eight.†   The process of embalming commenced as soon
as the queen's body was cold.‡

* Privy Purse Expences of Elizabeth of York, from March, 1502, to
Feb. 1503. *Harl. MSS.* 4780.

† Little is known of the acquirements of the queen of Henry
the Seventh, except on the doubtful authority of Brereton, who represents her as able to write French and Spanish.   It is remarkable
that not one of her letters are known to be preserved, and even her
autograph is rarely to be met with.   One piece of her writing before
the death of her father Edward IV. which once occurred in a book
belonging to her is bound up in a volume of the Cotton MSS.
marked Julius. B. XII. f. "Thys Boke is myn Elysabeth the kyngs
dawghtyr."   ‡ MS. in the College of Arms.

In 1508 a Rental of all the lands and tenements of the lady Elizabeth Cressenor,* prioress of St. Mary and St. Margaret virgins of Dartford, and her convent, was taken by examination of all the farmers, and other tenants.† From that document, the following summary of their possessions in Dartford is deduced:

In the Hythe street; nine tenements with gardens, and two cottages.‡

In the main street¶; fifteen tenements, of which four

---

* There was a Thomas Cressenor, lord Fitzwalter, John Ratcliffe and others, who were suddenly arrested and committed to prison in 1495, as some of the principal supporters of Perkyn Warbeck.

† Arundell MSS. No. 61, Brit. Mus. A document invaluable to the local antiquary, but generally inaccessible and unknown when reposing on the shelves of the Royal Society.

‡ Four were below the entrance to the Gas Works; one on either side of the priory lane, now the site of Messrs. Hall's Iron Works. Above the tenement on the north side was the horse-pool, and opposite a pasture of the prioress. The former tenement let for 8s. 4d., and the latter inhabited by William Rogers, William Churchgate, and Thomas Foy, with three gardens, was let to each individual at a separate rental of 6s. 8d. per annum. The prioress held two other tenements on the eastern side of Hithe street severally inhabited by Thomas Hepgode and Dyoniss Burgess.

¶ "Sum'us Vicus" evidently included Spital street and High street:—In these were the hostel called *le Hole Bull*, inhabited by Richard Fyke, baker, it stood on the site of the present Victoria hotel and let for 40s. per annum; above, immediately contiguous, was another called *The Hart*; on the east, a tenement belonging to Cobham College: and at the corner of Lowfield another hostel of the prioress known as *le Bell*, held by Clace Cordyn, at 40s. Nearly opposite, extending to the Waterside, stood another called THE KING'S INN, otherwise *the Crown*, held by Nicholas Cordyn, at 6os. *The Swan*, a tenement of Christopher Todde's adjoined. Near the site of the present *Bull's Head* stood another bearing the same name,

were hostels or inns, besides several parcels of land and the manor of Aleyns.*

(the gift of John Wodrow clerk,) inhabited by William Longe, fuller, who rendered 53s. per annum rent, and three large gardens at the back thereof. Below, between the hostel called the *Cock-on-the-Hoop*, (belonging to heirs of Thomas Cooke) and the *Sarazen's Head*, stood another belonging to the prioress called *le Maiden-Hedde*, in occupation of Beatrix Cowley, with two other tenements extending to a back lane on the north, and the High-street on the south, which were severally inhabited by Anmichiot Giles, barber, at 26s. 8d. ; Thomas Palmer, parish clerk of Dertford, at 20s. 4d. ; and Alice Tibott, at 6s. 8d. per annum. Probably these occupied the site of Mr. Hammond's premises. Three others on the same side were private houses, and let at 26s. and 20s. per annum. A fourth in the occupation of William Pesok nearer the church, was let for 20s. ; and another abutting eastward against the garden of William Stockmede, on the opposite side of the street, was let on a repairing lease for twenty-one years at 8s. 4d per annum. The parcels of garden lying at the back of the Bull's Head adjoining the manor of Charles, (part the gift of William Claptus at the foundation of the priory,) were held by Jenkyn Corbyn, Christopher Todde, and Richard Sterne, tailor. A small portion of land extended to the High-street. Several of the ancient hostels still exist, and though somewhat modernised may be easily known by their overhanging stories, and gables, fronting the street. The Harp is nearly perfect. The King's Inn or Crown, is or lately was a grocer's shop in the occupation of Mr. Dove. The Bull's Head is now the residence of Mr. Kither, gunmaker. The other four tenements may be sought amongst the ancient houses near the church.

* The south side of the manor of Aleyns abutted on the main street; the east, on a tenement of Andrew Auditor; and the west to a tenement of William Pynson, of London, dyer. The mansion comprised a hall, kitchen, oriels or upper rooms, stable, grange, and cow-house, with kitchen garden, etc ; attached to this was also a pasture of two acres. The *Rookery* in Spital street seems to have been a remnant of the mansion.

In Overy; two tenements with gardens,* a garden adjoining the river, and a piece of land adjoining the Fulling mill and the Tenters.

In the manor of Bignors; the mansion, the water-mills, the advowson of St. Edmund's chapel with all its lands and tenements, south of the high road leading from Wilmington to Shinglewell-wey, and 299½ *acres,* 9 *virgates,* and 25½ *days'-work* of land.†

---

* One tenement stood on the eastern side of Overy street, adjoining a grange of William Bolling, one of the barons of the Exchequer, in right of his wife, formerly .... of Nicholas Goldwyn, the other at the corner of Darenth road. The garden adjoined the river; the Fulling mill belonged to the heirs of Edward Bamme, who also owned lands in nearly every part of the parish. The Tenters, were divided between the prioress, and Sir Thomas Wiltshire, of Stone, also a large holder of lands and tenements in Dartford.

† *Shingle-Well* seems to have been a spring or well near the Darenth road. Shinglewell-wey, a road running by it towards the Brent. The head of the manor house of Bignors faced the road leading from Wilmington towards Shinglewell-wey; the mansion comprised a hall, two oriels, with a stable and appurtenances; attached were the water-mills, three acres, and six days'-work of land. *Rayfield,* which extended from the One-acre appertaining to St. Edmund's chapel along the Rochester high road to the Brimpth or Brent, was included in this division; the upper part belonged to Martin's Chantry, the remainder to the prioress. Three acres and a virgate, called Tirling, on the eastern side of the Brent, were given by John Aleyn, late proprietor of the manor of the same name, to the convent. In the high grounds overlooking Bignors, called Bromehill, Checker, Denelsdene, Bicknorsdene, Calamonte, etc, were 130 acres the property of the prioress. The manor, with other lands and premises therein belonging to the convent were then held to farm by William Mason, at £6 6s. 8d. per annum. The other landholders in Bignors were John, lord Cobham; the abbot of Lesnes; Thomas Stockton, gent.; lord de Saymer; John Hart of London, beer-brewer; John Aleyn

In the eastern part of the parish of Dartford; viz.´: on the north side of the highway leading to Shinglewell-way,* *49 acres, 1 rood, and three days' work.*

In the northern part of the parish; viz: meadows, fresh marshes, and pastures, lying east of the river running towards the Thames, 56 *acres, 17 virgates, and 45 days' work.*†

---

a descendant of the late owner of the manor of Aleyns; William Fullesclough, the vicar of Dartford; and Roger Appleton, the latter an extensive proprietor of lands and tenements throughout the same vill. The prioress had also eleven acres in Kingsland field.

A *Virgate* or yard-land, varied in different counties from fifteen to fifty acres. At Chesterton, in Oxfordshire, in Henry the third's reign, it was forty-five; at Wimbledon, Surrey, it was only fifteen at a later period.— A *Day's Work of land*, was estimated at the quantity which could be ploughed up by one plough in one day. Kennett's Glossary, *verb.* Virgata terræ, et Dayeria.

* This part included Highfield, (now the site of St. Ronans and the Crescent,) the lower part of which, then called Fullers-earth-field was bounded on the west by the high road leading from Dartford towards Shinglewell; the eastern abutted upon the road leading from Fulwich toward Tirling. The prioress' lands in Fulwich croft adjoined part of the endowment of St. Edmund's chapel. Those called *Broadfield,* lay interspersed around the manors of Joie and Temples, and extended to Mersh-gate. The other proprietors were John Norborowe, who held land and tenements in many parts of the parish in right of his wife the daughter of William Millet; the heirs of Thomas Cooke, Nicholas Goldwin, John Blackhall, John Buckland, the prior of St. John's, Sir T. Wiltshire, etc.

† In addition to the meadows and fresh marshes, the prioress had pasturage for three cows in *Gorless* or *Morshamtesless* near Templefield. But the prior of St. John of Jerusalem, in right of his manor of Temples was the principal landed proprietor in this northern division, and his quit-rents or lands extended their ramifications nearly into every other part of the parish. There was a

In the salt marshes . . . acres . . . .

In the southern part of the parish including Lowfield; viz. western from the stream called the Cranford, to land in Bexley and Crayford, south side the highway, (London road,) 346 *acres,* 11 *virgates, 8 roods and* 36½ *days work.*†

---

large sheet of water in these marshes called Bigpoole, in which all the prior's tenants were privileged with right of free fishery. The other holders and proprietors were John Algood, the heirs of John Aleyn, Roger Appleton, Robert Baker, John Bere, the Vicar of Dartford, the wardens of Rochester Bridge, the master of Strood Hospital, the late prioress of Higham, (whose estates were now seized into the hands of the king for arrears of rent,) Richard Lakyn, etc.

* Many of the prioress' lands in the Saltmarsh and else where "*of the foundation,*" were *tithe free*; portions of the marsh were allotted to several of her upland tenements or farms. The prior of the Hospital of the Leperous at Dertford, Martin's salary priest, the chantry priests of St. Edmund, and Stampits, the prior of St. John's, the abbot of Lesnes, and most of the religious, and lay proprietors in Dartford, had lands in the Saltmarshes. Here also Sir Edward Poynyng the lord of Rokesle, in right of his manor, claimed pasture in Longswathe.—Annually a Guardian of the Marshes was appointed, who in virtue of his office, held certain lands at Pittegrownde or Comutemede.—On the verge of the Saltmarsh was a large stagnant pool called Stynkinglake.

† In this southern division among the lands adjacent to the road leading from Lowfield towards Sutton, the prioress had two acres of pasture extending from Wilmington-well to the Cranford; and eighteen acres adjoining the common Loam-pits. She had also a wood of five acres called Highgrove, and upwards of 200 acres of briers named *Closeheth,* situated near the heath, as well as lands adjoining the Crayford road and nearly surrounding a small estate attached to the support of the Hospital of the Lepers, called *le Olde Spital Lande*.—The other principal proprietors were the heirs of

In the western part of the parish; viz, north side of the highway leading towards Crayford,* [*about*] 56 *acres* 30 *virgates, and 28 days'-work.*

———

1510. King Henry the Eighth in the second year of his reign confirms the manors of Massingham and West-Wrotham to the prioress and sisters.†

Circa 1517. (8 Hen. VIII.) Bridget, daughter of the late king Edward the Fourth, after a life chiefly spent in contemplation, in this convent, dies at the age of thirty-seven, and is buried within the priory church.‡

1518. King Henry the Eighth in the eighteenth year of his reign confirms the whole of the estates belonging to this monastery to the prioress and her community.¶

———

Robert Blagge, of Horseman's Place, Roger Appulton, the heirs of Edward Bamme, Galfred Crowshawe, William Haynes, William Lakyn, William Person, John le Bere, John Whittock, etc.

* This part comprehended the lands adjoining the priory.—*The Cook's Garden* contained half an acre, therein was a dove-house and *the Ortyard. Ropescroft* lay opposite the western gate of the priory; and an enclosure called *the Lyme-hill acre* adjoined the lane leading from *Spital hill* toward *Stampits.* The mansion called *Stoneham place* was furnished with oriels, stables, and granary, and seems to have been a retreat occasionally for sick or aged nuns. The prioress had also a *Wharf* and garden in the tenement called *la Hegge (f.* 48) probably the town wharf, and that occupied by Wilks and Temperley. The other landed proprietors were the Duchess of Somerset the king's mother, ; the heirs of Robert Blagge, who possessed most of the late John Martin's estates; the lord of Newbury; John Greenwood in right of his wife; John Marshall, Richard Sale, and others.

† Priv. Sigill. 2 Hen. VIII. p. 2.

‡ Weever's Funeral Monuments. Nicholas's Introduction to Privy Purse Expences of Elizabeth of York.

¶ Letters Patent, in the King's Remembrancer's Office.

1519. December 8th. Elizabeth Woodford takes the veil in this nunnery: this lady at the dissolution went into Flanders, and in 1540, became a nun in the convent of St. Ursula, in Louvain, where she died 25th Oct. 1572, having been fifty-two years professed, twenty-four of which she lived at St. Ursula's.* Cole is of opinion she is the same person whose name appears as Elizabeth Woode, in the subsequent list of the religious who obtained a pension of forty shillings at the surrender of the priory.

1522. Brother Robert Mylys, S.T.P. provincial of the English order of the Preaching Friars, prior of King's Langley (Linc. dioc.), and Elizabeth prioress of our Blessed Mary and St. Margaret virgins of Dertford, (Roff. dioc.) and her convent, present Thomas Bartlett, to church of Elmeston, on resignation of John Parnell, and he was admitted to the same 26th of November.†

---

* Excerpts from a MS. History of the monastery of St. Monica, in Louvain, of English Nuns, Regular Canonesses of the order of St. Austin, quoted by William Cole in his MSS. vol. xii. p. 53. to which he subjoins the following particulars.—"This Elizabeth Woodford educated mother Margaret Clement, daughter of Dr. John Clement, who was elected prioress of the monastery of St. Ursula in 1552, and governed thirty-eight years until she was blind, when mother Margaret resigned. The present prioress (17---) of St. Monica in Louvain, is mother Delphina Sheldon, daughter of Edward Sheldon, of Steeple Barton, in Oxfordshire, Esq., and Catherine his wife, daughter of Sir Philip Constable, of Evringham, co. York. Bart. She was elected on the 12th of Nov. 1715, and hath professed fifty-six nuns and four lay-sisters."

† Reg. Wareham, archiep. Cantuar. f. 334. vide Ducarell's Transcripts from the Lambeth Registers. No. 6084. Addit. MSS in

1523. Hugh le Serle of Dertford, by will dated 20th Oct. 15 Hen. VIII. gives, after the decease of Alys his wife, to the prioress and convent of Dertford, the half of the rents of two tenements in Overy street, in the town aforesaid; and the other half yearly to be bestowed about the repair of St. Edmund's chapel for ever. In this chapel he directed his body to be buried before the image of the said St. Edmund, and a marble monumental stone to be placed over his remains. He gives a taper of 12d. value, to be placed before St. Edmund in the said chapel; to the rode-light 12d.; to our lady light under the rode 12d.; to St. John Baptist, St. Peter, and St. James 12d. etc.*

1526. Dame Catherine, widow of Sir Maurice Berkeley, late governor of Calais, dies, and is buried in the chapel of our lady in the priory, and a tomb erected over her remains.† Her will bears date 5th Sept. 1526, and was proved on the 25th of the same month by John Whitton. The testatrix desires to be buried in the chapel of our lady in the monastery of Dertford: also wills that a tomb, price £13 6s. 8d. should be constructed there to her memory; she gives to the said monastery, a suit of vestments price £20; wills that a priest be found to sing mass there for her soul for four years, for which she gives £32; to wit £8,

---

Brit. Mus. That joint patronage of the prior of King's Langley with the prioress of Dertford in the church of Elmeston, originated in its appropriation to the maintenance of the brethren of that house, resident in Dertford nunnery. Pat. 19 Ric. II. p. 2. m. 3.

* Lowe Episc. Roffen. Lib. Test. f. 213, 214.

† Information of Elizabeth Cressenor the prioress. Weever.

per annum; she also gives a suit of vestments to the church of St. Nicholas, at Calais, where her late husband was buried, price £13 6s. 8d.;* and directs that a tomb should be erected over her mother's grave at St. Augustine's, Bristowe, price £13 6s. 8d.; she gives £13 6s. 8d. to the black friars of the same place towards building their cloister: she gives trifling bequests to her nephew John Berkeley, to Mary Berkeley, and a few others; and constitutes John Whitton, gent. aforesaid, executor and residuary legatee.

---

* Reg. Test. Prerog. Offic. Cant. 10 *Porch*. Catherine, lady Berkeley was daughter of Sir William Berkeley of Stoke Gifford, co. Somerset, she left no issue. Her husband Sir Maurice Berkeley, was the eldest son of Maurice Berkeley, and Isabel, daughter of Sir Philip Mead, of Bristol. He was made knight of the Bath in 1509; knight for the body of king Henry VIII 1512; was sheriff of Gloucester, 1516 and 1517; lieutenant of Calais castle, 1517; summoned to parliament, 14 Hen. VIII, 1523: died the 12th September following, and buried in St. Nicholas' church, at Calais. His will bears date 1st May 1520; he therein describes himself as of Yate, in the county of Gloucester, knight, and desires to be buried in the church of the Augustines at Bristowe, if he should die in England. He made a codicil when near his death 11th Sept. 1523, as Maurice lord Berkeley, and desires to be buried in the church of St. Nicholas at Calais. In the codicil, he provides for the application of five hundred marks for the use of his bastard son Humphrey Berkeley, but the greater part of both will and codicil consists of provisions in reference to divers wardships, etc, which he had purchased from the king. The manor of Tetbury is mentioned as the property settled on his wife, dame Catherine, in dower. Property at Margotsfield, and that of Yate, is also referred to, and John Whitton seems also to have been connected with the testator's establishment. The will was proved the 29th November, 1523. (14 *Bodfelde*.) by--Cowick, notary, acting for the executors, viz: the testator's brother-in-law William Denys, esq. and John Fitzjames, esq. attorney to our lord

William Maykins of Dertford, by will dated 2nd April
1530, gives sixteen-pence to one of the friars of this
monastery.* Probably he was his confessor, for the
affected sanctity of the friars' lives often induced
individuals to select them for that office, and the parochial clergy mortally hated them for thus abstracting their
emoluments.

1533. King Henry the Eighth privately married
to Anne Boleyn on January the 25th, by Dr. Henry
Lee. She was openly shewed as queen on Easter-eve,
12th April, and crowned on Whitsunday following.†

1534. The parliament sitting in February pass
an act affirming the king is supreme Head of the

---

the king. The overseer was William lord Sandys.—I am indebted to
my excellent friend John Bull Gardiner, esq. for this communication ; a
gentleman of unparalleled industry in the investigation of Oxfordshire
Genealogical Antiquities—a portion of which it is hoped he will at some
future time communicate to the public.

* Reg. Test. Episc. Roffen. ix. f. 24. Maykins directs his body to be
buried at the high altar end of the church-yard of Dertford ; gives to the
priest at his burial 20d., and to the clerk 16d. Beside the donation to the
friar, he gives to poor people in bread and drink at his burying
6s. 8d ; The other things to be done for the health of his soul, to be at
the discretion of Joan his wife, to whom he wills his land in Dertford
for life, and after her decease, to remain to Nicholas Maykins his son,
and the heirs of his body ; Dorothy his daughter, to have land, etc.

† The devotion of the religious orders to the Roman see induced
them strongly to oppose Catherine's divorce and the king's marriage
with Anne Boleyn. In the Observant Friary church, in the king's
own palace at Greenwich, friar Peto threatened his sovereign to his
face with the fate of Ahab, unless he took back his wife. Though
indignant, the king suppressed his resentment, but finding that
Elstow another friar of the same house repeated the threat the follow-

Church of England, as recognised by the prelates and clergy of the realm in convocation; which is followed up by another declaring the king's marriage with Catherine to be void, and that with Ann valid, and settling the crown on his heirs by that lady. To these acts all the king's subjects being required to swear on pain of misprision of treason, commissioners are dispatched into all parts of the kingdom for this purpose.

The following is the Acknowledgement of the Supremacy and Right of Succession under the seal of the prioress and convent of Dartford assembled in chapter, May the fourteenth.

Quum ea sit non solum Christianæ Religionis et pietatis ratio sed nostræ etiam obedientiæ Regula, ut Domino nostro *Henrico,* ejus nomine *Octavo,* cui soli post Christum Jesum servatorem nostrum debemus universa, non modo omnimodam in Christo et eandem sinceram integram pertuamque *Animi, Devotionem, Fidem,* Observantiam Honorem, Cultum, *Reverentiam* præstemus, sed etiam de eadem Fide et Observantia nostra Rationem quotienscumque postulabitur reddamus et palám omnibus si res poscat libentissime testemur.

Noverint universi ad quos præsens scriptum pervenerit quód, Nos, Priorissa et conventus de Dertford in comitatu

---

ing sunday, the whole fraternity were removed, August 11th, 1534. Shortly after Peto's insult the religious orders being found actively exciting the people to resist the king's divorce, and the consequent ecclesiastical innovations, the court party blazoned the peccadillos incident to a monastic life with so many exaggerations, that a violent hatred was excited against them.

Kantiæ Ordinis Sancti Dominici Roffensis Diœcesis, uno ore et voce atque unanimi omnium, et singulorum consensu et assensu, hoc scripto nostro sub sigillo nostro communi in Domo nostra Capitulari Dato, pro nobis et successoribus nostris omnibus et singulis imperpetuum *profitemur* testamur ac fideliter *promittimus* et *spondemus*, Nos dictos *priorissam* et *conventum* et successores nostros omnes et singulos, integram, inviolatam, sinceram, perpetuamque *Fidem observantiam et obedientiam* semper præstaturos erga Dominum *Regem nostrum Henricum Octavum*, et erga serenissimam *Reginam Annam* uxorem ejusdem, et erga castum sanctumque matrimonium nuper non solum inter eosdem juste et legittime contractum ratum et consummatum, sed etiam tam *in duabus Convocationibus Cleri, quam in Parliamento Dominorum Spiritualium et Temporalium atque communium* in eodem Parliamento congregatorum et præsentium determinatum, et per *Thomam Cantuariensem Archiepiscopum* solemniter confirmatum, et erga quamcumque aliam ejusdem *Henrici regis nostri uxorem* post mortem *prædictæ Annæ* nunc uxoris ejus legittime ducendam, et erga *sobolem dicti Domini Regis ex prædicta Anna* legittime tam pro quam progenerandam, et erga *sobolem* dicti *domini* Regis ex alia quacumque *legittima uxore* post mortem ejusdem *Annæ* legittime progenerandam, et quod hæc eadem populo notificabimus, prædicabimus et suadebimus ubicumque dabitur locus et occasio.

Item, quod confirmatum Ratumque habemus semperque perpetuo habituri sumus, quod *prædictus Rex noster Henricus* est CAPUT ECCLESIÆ ANGLICANÆ.*

---

* Stat. 25 Hen. VIII. c. 22. The title of "Supreme Head of the Church," first appeared in a petition of the Convocation of the province of Canterbury, for relief of the penalties of premunire, by pardon for acts committed under Wolsey's Legantine power, and was only intended as a compliment to the king. *Burnett* 112. *Wilkin. Concil.* iii. 745.

Item, quod *Episcopus Romanus*, qui in suis Bullis *Papæ Nomen usurpat et summi Pontificis Principatum* sibi arrogat, nihilo majoris neque Authoritatis aut jurisdictionis habendus sit quam *cæteri quivus Episcopi* in Anglia vel alibi gentium in sua diœcese.

Item, quod soli *dicto Domino Regi* et successoribus suis adhærebimus, atque ejus Decreta ac proclamationes, in super omnes Angliæ leges, atque etiam statuta omnia in Parliamento et per Parliamentum decreta confirmata stabilita et ratificata perpetuo manutenibimus, *Episcopi Romani* legibus decretis et canonibus, si qui contra Legem Divinam et sacram Scripturam esse invenientur, perpetuo renanciantes.

Item, quod nos *Priorissa et conventus prædictus*, et successores nostri conscientiæ ac juris jurandi Sacramento Nosmet firmiter obligamus, quod omnia et singula prædicta fideliter et imperpetuum observiabimus.

In cujus rei testimonium huic instrumento vel scripto nostro sigillum nostrum commune appendimus.

Dat in Domo nostra capitulari decimo quarto die mensis Maij, anno Christi millesimo quingentessimo tricessimo quarto, et regni vero regis nostri Henrici Octavi vicessimo sexto.

ET MEMORANDUM *quod prædicti* Priorissa et conventus de Dertford quartodecimo die Maij anno presenti, coram præfatis Commissionariis in Domo sua Capitulari personaliter constituti, recognoverunt scriptum ac omnia et singular in eodem contenta in forma prædicta.*

This instrument remains in the Chapter House, Westminster, and attached is an impression of the Common Seal in red wax, the subject of which is, St. Margaret, and under her the royal founder, Edward III, bearing a shrine. On each side these figures, is a shield emblazoned with the royal arms.†

---

* Rymer Fœd. xiv. 490, 491.   † Caley's Dugdale. vi. 538.

In the next session of the parliament which met in November following, the authority of the pope was abrogated in England, and his spiritual powers, together with the *First Fruits* and the *Tenths* of *all ecclesiastical benefices*, given to the king.*

It appears that about this period the aged prioress Elizabeth Cressenor resigned, perhaps from aversion to taking part in the innovations in religion now pressed forward by the king, and JOAN FANE,† (or Vane,) was appointed to her dignity.

26 Hen. VIII. 1535. Early in the spring the commissioners appointed for the new Ecclesiastical Survey entered the possessions of this house as under.‡

(Translation.)

PRIORY OF St. MARY AND St. MARGARET VIRGINS OF DERTFORD,

CO. KENT.

Rents, Lands, and Tenements lying in DERTFORD, WILMINGTON, SUTTON-AT-HONE, CRAYFORD, BEXLEY, NORTH-CRAY, and SOUTHFLEET, in the County of Kent.

IMPRIMIS; *From an examination of the common Compotus* [Accompt Roll] *of the said monastery*—75s. 0½d. from Rents of Assize in *Dertford*; 46s. 4d. of farm lands in *Dertford* the gift of William Millet, yearly; £6 5s. 8d., of farm lands and tenements in the street called the *High-street* in *Dertford*;

---

* Stat. 25 Hen. VIII. c. 22.   Stowe's Annales. 571.

† Probably a daughter of Humphrey Fane of Hildon, near Tunbridge, and sister of Sir Ralph Fane, knighted at the siege of Boulogne.

‡ The commission for taking the *Valor*, dated 26th Jan. 26 Hen. VIII., was returnable on the octaves of the Holy Trinity that year.

£31 8s. 9d., from farm lands and tenements in *several streets* in Dertford ; 12s. 6d., from lands and tenements in *Bullet's Lane in Dertford ;* 42s., from farm lands and tenements in the street of *Overy*, in *Dertford ;* 39s. 8d., of farm lands and tenements in *Loffhilde* per ann., in *Dertford ;* 20s., of farm lands and tenements in *Upstrete* per ann., in *Dertford ;* £12, of the farm of the manor of *Bignors*, and mills, with all lands there ; £20 20d., of the farm lands and tenements in *Stoneham*, per ann. ; £6 10s. 8d., of the farm lands and tenements in *Wilmington*, per ann. ; 28s. 4d., of the farm lands and tenements in *Crayford*, per ann. ; 40s. of the farm lands in *Northcray*, per ann. as in preceding ; £4 13s. 4d., of the farm lands in *Gildon Hill*, per ann. ; 7s. 4d., of the farm lands in *Southflete*, per ann. ; 20s. of the farm land of *the gift of Thomas Wem*, per ann. ; 16s. 8d., of the farm lands in *Fletewall*, per ann. ; 46s. 8d., of the farm of the *Tilekill* at *Bexley*, per ann. ; 30s. of rents and farms formerly *perquisites of William Wiggane*, clerk, supervisor of this monastery.

Sum total of the same . . . . . . £102 11s. 0½d.

From which allow for Outgoings, as appears upon examination of the aforesaid Compotus—£8 9s. 10½d., payable to divers persons, viz. : to the Lord the King, to his manor of *Swanscombe*, 12s. ; issuing out of the manor of Bignors, 17s. 8d. ; to the Duchess of Richmond, from the manor of Dertford, 13s. 7d. ; to the Lady of Salisbury, 33s. 4d. ; to the College of Eton, out of lands in Stoneham, 11s. 3d. ; to the Archbishop of Canterbury, 20s. 10½d. ; to the Bishop of Rochester, for lands in Wilmington, 31s. ; to the manor of Sutton, 19s. ; to the manor of Northcray, 8s. 4d. ; to the manor of Newbury, 21d. ; to Master Appulton with 12d., as paid to Sir Henry Isley, knight ; and also allow 18d., further of rents of certain lands in Dertford, for divers years elapsed, of which, nothing is left whereon to distrain ; and also allow 66s. 8d., for travelling expenses to John Hollingworth, our collector of rents, because of the troubles of his office yearly; and allow of 100s. stipend, for *one chaplain to celebrate divine offices* in the monastery aforesaid, for *the soul of John Chertsey and his parents*, given in lands and tenements *in the other street of Dertford* aforesaid, for this use to the monastery; and allow £4 for the *annual obit* of the same John Chertsey, in the said monastery, by lands noted in the second preceding particular; and allow 100s. 10d., in land, with 60s. 10d., for a *stipend* for *one chaplain* to *celebrate* divine service in the same monastery for the soul of *William Sedley*, with 40s. *for a yearly obit*, which the said William himself gave in lands for this use; and also allow 40s. *for Masses twice a week*, celebrated *for the soul of John Millet*, given for this use to the said monastery; and also allow £4 yearly, for the expenses about the *obit of John Needham* and other charitable *gifts* issuing out of the manor of *Stoneham*.

And remains....................

Manors, Lands, Tenements, and *other premises* with their appurtenances in the Counties of *Kent, Dorset, Wilts, Surrey, Suffolk, Norfolk, and Wales.*

And also as appears upon examination of the Compotus afore-said,—£9 0s. 7½d., of rents of assize from divers parcels of farm in *Norton Bavent* with its members, per ann. in co. Wilts; £6 11s. 11d., of rents by copy-lands and tenements in co. Wilts., held at the will of the lord called *yerd land;* 74s. 7½d., of rents by copy at the will of the lord called *small lands*, per ann., in the county aforesaid; £20 of the *manor farm* of Norton Bavent, in the said county; £11 1s. 1½d., of the *Rectory farm of Norton Bavent* aforesaid; 33s. 4d., of the *New farm*, there in the said county; 5s. 10d., of perquisites of court there, per ann.; 22s. 5½d., of increments of the farm there, per ann.; £20., of the manor farm of *Fifhide Bavent* in the county aforesaid, per ann. Also £6 2s. 6d., of the *Rectory Farm of Whitley*, per ann., in

the county of Surrey. Also £33 6s. 8d., of the Manor
farm of *Belsted Magna* in co. Suffolk, with £13 6s. 8d. the
money price of forty quarters of bread corn valued at
6s. 8d. per quarter; 8s. 4d. of a meadow farm there in the
said county of Suffolk; 2s. of the perquisites of court
there; 113s. 8d., of the farm of *Belsted parva*, in the county
of Suffolk aforesaid, with 26s. 8d., the money price of four
quarters of bread-corn at the rate aforesaid; £8., of the
farm of *Bavent*, in *Combes*, in co. Suffolk, per ann.; £13
6s. 8d., of the manor farm of *Bramston-Hall*, co. Suffolk,
yearly. Also £13 7s. 3d., of the manor farm of *Thorpe-
Hall*, and demesne lands in *Est Wrotham*, *West-Wrotham*,
Yllington, in co. Norfolk, yearly; £13 6s. 8d., of the manor
farm of *Great Massingham*, in co. Norfolk, aforesaid; Also
£25., of the manor farm of *Hacham* in co. Surrey, yearly;
£6 7s., of rents of assize of the manor of *Shipborne*, in co.
Kent, yearly; £13 9s. 4d., of the farm of the demesne land
aforesaid, in the county aforesaid this year; 40s., of the
farm lands, and tenements, called *Isborows*, co. Kent,
yearly; 113s. 4d. of the farm lands in *Cronk-hill* [Crocken-
hill], yearly in co. Kent., £19 13s. 5½d., of rents of assize
in *Colwynston*, in *Wales*, yearly. A money payment of £16
per annum granted by our lord king Henry VIII, *in lieu
of Four Hogsheads of Wine* payable for ever.* Also 100s., of
the outgoings and profits of 100 acres of wood, growing
upon the joint lands and manors of *Fifefield* and *Hacham-
bernys*, rated at £100 value every twenty years.

> Sum total of the same, two hundred four score
> and twelve pounds, fourteen shillings.

From which allow for Outgoings, *as appears upon examination
of the Compotus aforesaid.*—£7 7s. 0½d., rents paid to divers
persons,—viz: 23s. 4d., issuing out of the lands and tenements in *Crockenhill*; 7s., out of the manor of *Massingham*; -

---

* Given by a former monarch.

13s. 4d., out of the manor of *Little Belstede.*   Also allow
6s. 8d., paid to the bishop of Salisbury for his visitation at
Norton; 6s. 8d. to the dean of Salisbury for visitation at
Norton aforesaid: 12s. 6d. to the archdeacon of Salisbury
for proxies and synodals for the same manor and its members: 2d., paid to the bishop of Winchester for the manor
of *Pitfold*; 3s. 4d., for the collection of the rents of the said
manor; 33s. 4d. to the *castle of Dover*, for *Castleward*, out of
the manors of *Bramston* and *Hatcham*; 18d., to the county
of Wilts. for the manor of *Shipborne*; 15d., to John Colton,
esq. out of the same manor; 13s. to the lord the king out
of the manor of *Pettiscourte*; 6s. 4d., to the lord the prior
of St. John of Jerusalem in England from the manor
aforesaid; 16d., to the Hundred of Milton; 8d. paid to
the prior of Puckvale for the manor of Pettiscourte aforesaid.   Also 6s. 8d., paid to the Castle of *Oxmore* out of the
manor of *Colwynston.*   And also allow 30s. 8d., tythe rents
of certain lands and tenements aforesaid for deficiencies
as taken in preceding accounts; and allow £10 13s. 4d.,
for the fees and journies of divers bailiffs, stewards,
collectors of rent, and other officers and ministers,
employed in collecting rent, supervision of farms, lordships, and manors, within the counties aforesaid like as
has been accustomed to be allowed in former accounts;
and allow 40s., for the fee of John Roper, esq., *Capital
Seneschal* of Colwynston; and 13s. 4d., for the fee of
Nicholas Fitzwilliam, *Sub-seneschal* there; and allow of
£10, paid out of the manor of *Massyngham*, for the *sententa-
tion of two Chaplains to celebrate Divine Service in Dartford
monastery aforesaid for the soul of King Richard* II., constituted and ordained for the same.   And also allow 20s.,
for the fee of Master Hungerford, *Seneschall of Norton-
Bavent* aforesaid.   And allow £6 13s. 4d., paid yearly out
of the manor of *Pettiscourt*, and *Parva-Belsted*, for *two obits*
within the said monastery *yearly kept for the soul of John
Raynard* for certain lands given for that use.

And so remains £255 11s. 0½d.

Divers *Tenements* within the *City* of LONDON.

And also as appear upon examination of the Compotus of this Monastery—£9 5s. 4d., of a farm tenement in the parish of *St. Katherine, Christechurch,* per ann.; £4 14s. 8d., of a farm tenement in the parish of *St. Martin Orgar,* called Maydenhedde, per ann.; 46s. 8d., of a farm tenement in the parish of *St. Peter de Power* yearly; £11 6s. 8d., of a farm tenement in the parish of *S. Maria de Arcuibus,* [Bow Church, Cheapside,] yearly as in the preceding; £7 9s. 4d. of the farm of divers tenements in *Wood-strete* yearly as before; £8 3s. 10d., of the farm of divers tenements in the parish of *All Saints the great,* yearly; £7 5s. 4d., of the farm of tenements in *Fleet street* yearly as in the preceding.

Total Sum there £60 1s. 10d.

Of which allow for Outgoings—£6 2s. 7d., for rents paid to divers persons as in the preceding—viz.: 10s., to the lord of St. John of Jerusalem in England from a tenement called *The Bell* in *Fleet-street* yearly; 30s. rents paid to the prior of Merton in the county of Surrey, for a tenement in the parish of S. Maria de Arcuibus; 46s. 8d., paid to the prior of the Charter House, London, for a tenement in *Wood-street*; 30s. to the king for a tenement in St. Catherine, Christe-church, with 6s. 8d., paid to the sheriff of London for *Soccage* due from the lady prioress yearly. And also allow 60s. for the troublesome office of collecting the arrears of these farm-rents as allowed in the Compotus of preceding years. And allow 20s. yearly paid for an *obit* of *Master John Exmewe** for the tenement of St. Katerene aforesaid.

And so remains £40 9s. 4d.

---

* The tenement in question was probably given to the convent, on his daughter's profession as a nun at Dertford.

Farm of the *Demesne Land* with Lands in BEXLEY and
SWANSCOMBE.

And also £26 18s. 4d., of the farm of divers parcels of land
and meadow of the demesne *occupied* and *reserved to the use
of the monastery aforesaid*, viz: with 100s., of the farm of
one hundred acres of land yearly, lying in Stoneham-field
and Herken-feldes, which is at the rate of 12d., an acre;
25s., of the farm of thirty acres of land lying in Goldocke-
feld rated at 10d. per acre; £4. is of a piece of one hundred and sixty acres of pasture lying and existing in
Hethcrofts, Broomcrofts, and Shippowcroft, rated at 6d.
the acre; £8. of the farm of fourscore acres of pasture
lying in the field called Farthinglese, Ducklinghope,
Meloorlese and Broomdehope; £6 13s. 4d. of the farm of
forty acres of meadow lying in Hedgemede and Fresh-
mede, with 40s. from the farm of twenty-four acres of
marsh land near the same, rated at 20d. per acre
yearly; . . . . and £16. for the farm of certain lands in
Bexley, and Swanscombe in the county of Kent.

Of the Acknowledgements of the Prioress of this Monastery.

Sum total there £42 18s. 4d.—Besides £365 13s. 0½d, of
the *Incomings* and *Profits* of the lordships, manors, lands,
tenements aforesaid; *viz*: with £69 14s. 9d. of the clear
Outgoings from lands and tenements in Dertford, Wilmington, Sutton-at-Hone, Crayford, Bexley, North-cray,
and Southfleet, in the county of Kent. £255 10s. 0½d.,
clear Outgoings from manors, lands, and tenements
with their appurtenances, in the counties of Kent,
Dorset, Wilts, Surrey, Suffolk, Norfolk and Wales.
And with £40 9s. 3d. of clear Outgoings from divers
tenements within the city of London.

And if the whole are conjoined £408 12s. 4½d.

FROM WHICH DEDUCT——£6 13s. 4d., for the fee of Robert Dymmoch, chief *Seneschall* [Steward] of this monastery; and allow £8. for the fee of Martin Sidley, *Supervisor* of all the Manors, Lands, and Tenements of the said monastery; and allow £11., with 60s., for the fee of Thomas Sidley, *Auditor*; and allow for the fee of John Sidnam, *Under-seneschal* of the lands and possessions of the said monastery: and allow £15., yearly *paid for the sustentation of Three Friars* [Custodians,] for the celebration of Divine Service *in the monastery aforesaid according to the ancient concession of the founder*; and allow 112s. 8d., given *in monies twice a week* for the sustentation of *thirteen poor persons* according to ancient custom of the said monastery. And also allow £6 10d., yearly, given certain weeks to *five poor persons*, to wit, in weekly sums of 6s. from lands given by William Millet for this use in Swanscombe and Bexley.

And so remayneth clear...... £380 9s. 0¼d.
The tenths are .... 38 10s. 0¾d.

E. NEVYLL

Per me THOMAS HATCLYFFE.
Per me ROBERT CRANEWELL.*

1534. The prioress and convent of Dertford by Indenture under their common seal, dated September 1st, anno 26 Henry VIII. let to George Tasser, of Dartford, their manor of Bignors, their two water-mills called the wheat mill, and malt mill, and several other premises to the manor appertaining, in Dertford, at the rent of twelve pounds per annum for twenty-one years.†

---

* Valor. Eccles. i. 114.---120. From the inaccuracy of the totals in the preceding Abstract, it is evident the copyist of the original record must have mistaken several of the amounts.

† Hasted. i. 222.

1535. Agnes Parker, widow, and second wife of William Parker of Dertford, innholder, by will dated 27th of August, bequeaths to the friars of the abbey three shillings, and to Mother Bolton a frock.* The latter was evidently a nun of this House.

The general Visitation of Monasteries having disclosed dreadful vices and crimes perpetrated by monks and nuns in their seclusion, and excited public hatred against them, the members of those religious communities endeavoured to interest the laity in the stability of their several Houses, by granting them beneficial leases of many of their estates, hoping thereby to weather the storm.

The prioress and convent of Dertford grant a lease of their capital messuage of Stoneham with the farm buildings and certain parcels of land thereunto belonging, to Robert Dove their husbandman.†

1536. Thomas Auditor, alias Barnard, gives by will dated 15th of April, 27 Hen. VIII. to Alice his wife, Elizabeth and Margaret his daughters, and Robert Dove and Dorothy his wife, daughter of the testator, all such land, parcel of the possessions of the

---

* Reg. Test. Episc. Roffen. ix f 154   Besides Agnes Parker's benefaction to Mother Bolton, and the friars in the abbey, she gave to every priest saying mass and dyridge for her soul 8d., and to every clerk 6d. ; to the College of Cobham 6s. 8d, ; "to the Almes-House at Dertford two payer of coarse sheets, etc. ; to George Cromer 20s. sterling;" she also wills, "that an honest priest shall sing within the church of Dertford by the space of one whole year complete for her soul and all christian souls, £6 8s." See also p. 27.

† Hasted, ii. 316, octavo edit.

priory "which he holds by lease granted by the lady prioress and convent of Derford."*

1537. September 4th. Joan Fane, prioress, and her convent by indenture under their common seal let to ferme for seventeen years to Robert Meriel of Swanscombe, husbandman, at the yearly rent of ten pounds, all that, their farm called Ingress, with all houses, buildings, pastures, marshes, etc. belonging thereto, in Swanscomb, late in the tenure of Robert Grove, fermer there, and all their cliffs called Down-Cliffs, together

---

* Thomas Auditor resided in Spital street, adjacent to the manor-house of Aleyns. His will contains the following *Items.* "I give for my burial in the body of the church of Dertford 6s. 8d. ; I will and bequeath all that terme of yeares which I have yet to come of and in an acre of land holden and had in exchange of the ladie prioress of Dertford near Gilhaugh, in Overy; with two messuages, late Richard Pinden's, to those who are and shall be owners in possession and reversion. Item, I give and bequeath to Robert Dove and Dorothy his wife aforesaid, five quarters of Barley; to Robert Dove my godson, son of the above Robert and Dorothy, 20s.; to Vincent Dove, another son of the said Robert 10s.; and I will Sir John Buckley or some other honest secular priest diligently sing or say mass and other divine service, and to help ye quere in the said parishe church of Dertford to pray for my soul and all christen souls by the space of half a year, taking for his salary and wages by all the time five marks to be paid him quarterly; to Margaret my youngest daughter two tenements and a garden called Gilhaugh, lately purchased of John Skogen; to my daughter Elizabeth, all such lands as I have by indenture of my ladie prioress and convent of Dertford, after the decease of my wife; to Robert Darby of Dertford, and the heirs of his body, the croft called Dallingcroft, containing four acres, paying therefrom three shillings yearly to buy peasons, to be distributed to poor people the first week in Lent; my leasehold, plate, ready mony and stock, to Alice my wife, etc." Reg. Test. ix. f. 227.

with liberty to dig chalk there to the amount of one acre in length and breadth.*

1538. The intended suppression of all the remaining monasteries in England, being clearly manifested by the passing of an Act of Parliament in May this year, granting to the king all Religious Houses that should hereafter be surrendered or suppressed. Joan Fane and twenty-three nuns surrendered their house and all its revenues into the hands of the king's commissioners, and for this compliance received the following pensions :

To Joane Fane, late prioress there, one hundred marks, or £66 13s. 6d. per annum.
„ Agnes Roper,† six pounds per annum.
„ Elizabeth Cressenore,‡ five pounds, six shillings and eight pence per annum.
„ Beatrice Marchal,¶ one hundred shillings, per annum.
„ Catherine Cloffyld, one hundred shillings, per annum.
„ Margarit Cooke,‖ one hundred shillings, per annum.
„ Alice Davie, one hundred shillings, per annum.
„ Anne Lego, one hundred shillings, per annum.
„ Elizabeth White, one hundred shillings, per annum.
„ Mary Bentham, one hundred shillings, per annum.
„ Dorothy Sydley,** one hundred shillings, per annum.
„ Margerie Warren, one hundred shillings, per annum.
„ Maud Frior, one hundred shillings, per annum.

---

* Hasted i. p. 263. folio edit.

† John Roper, her relative was capital seneschal of Colwynston.

‡ The lady formerly prioress.

¶ A family named Marshall held Nethercourt farm near Riversham, Hast. i. 707.

‖ A Dartford family, heretofore benefactors to the monastery.

** Probably a daughter of William Sydley, of Scadbury, in Southfleet.

To Elizabeth Exmewe,* one hundred shillings per annum.

„ Margaret Oakley, one hundred shillings per annum.

„ Ann Bowson, one hundred shillings per annum.

„ Mary Blower,† four pounds per annum.

„ Mary Kytson, four pounds per annum.

„ Elizabeth Seygood, forty shillings per annum.

„ Eleyn Bosteck,‡ forty shillings per annum.

„ Elenor Wood,¶ forty shillings per annum.

„ Alice Grenesmith, forty shillings per annum.

„ Katherine Garrett, forty shillings per annum.

„ Mary Stoney, fifty three shillings and four-pence per annum.

Thus closed this religious House which had existed for one hundred and eighty two years, as a never failing source of relief to the poorest individuals of the neighbourhood, and oft-times an asylum for the widow, the orphan, and broken-hearted female in the upper classes of society. It had long been renowned as the principal *Seminary for the Education of the female Nobility and Gentry in the County;* and the nuns devoted themselves so entirely to that object, combined with the service of their Redeemer, that even slander breathed not an injurious whisper when spies where sent from the court to get up charges against the religious. The surrender was solely effected by the will of the king, whose power was evidently unlimited over the royal foundation at Dart-

---

* John Exmew gave a tenement in London ; p. 153.

† One John Blower, (perhaps her brother,) was chantry priest of Stampit, in Dertford, a few years previously, p. 70.

‡ The Bostecks were a Dartford family some of whom remained till the eighteenth century.

¶ See more of this lady ; p. 141.

ford. They were called White Nuns,* from the colour
of their hood and tunic, which nevertheless was formed
of coarse grey cloth, and they wore a white wimple.
At the Dissolution they were prohibited wearing this costume, and sent abroad clad in the dress of a lay person.†

---

* Weever, Funeral Monuments.

† Perhaps the annexed extract of a letter from the writer to a
friend, giving an account of a visit to the Benedictine Nunnery at
Hammersmith, may somewhat illustrate the manners of Religious
Houses.

        "Dear Sir,

"You are well aware that for many years I have been particularly
desirous of obtaining a view of the arrangement of a British Convent. This object has been at last effected through the interest of
the Rev. Mr. V——— of Kensington with the confessor of the nunnery at Hammersmith.   Having obtained the recommendation of
that gentleman, Mrs. D——— (whose presence, by the bye, was a
sort of pledge of the uprightness of my intentions towards the
ladies) and myself, on Sunday, June 29, 1817, proceeded to that
place for the purpose of seeing the confessor. We arrived just as
the sisters were commencing *Complines*, and understanding that the
service was public, entered the Chapel, and were much surprized
and delighted by the sound of female voices engaged in the loud
harmonious chaunt, at intervals accompanied by the swelling notes
of the organ. The conviction of being in the immediate presence of
professed nuns, engaged in the solemn exercises of devotion, gave
me an indescribable pleasure, while the impossibility of seeing them,
cast a sort of mysterious veil over the recluses themselves. At the
close of the service we waited upon the priest, who received us in
the parlour of the convent, and inquired into the motives of our
visit. Being satisfied on that head, he stepped aside, and surprized us
with the view of a nun, apparently about thirty-five, arrayed in the
costume of the Order, but without her veil, seated in a chair behind
him, adding at the same moment, 'That lady can give you much
better information than I can.'   She received us with the utmost
politeness and good-humour, immediately commenced a conversation

Those of them who had relatives naturally sought an

---

by repeating the questions of the confessor, and, with a bewitching archness which ladies know how to assume, playfully attempted to convince us that we ought not to pry into conventual matters. On my still pressing her for some information relative to their mode of living, and the regulations of the house, she pertly replied, ' But my dear Sir, such things can in no way concern you; besides (added she, after a moment's pause) a correct knowledge of these particulars can only be obtained from the Rule, which is to be had of the superior alone.' I observed, the Rule of the Order had been published by Dugdale and several other writers long ago, and therefore was no secret; that the object of my visit was simply to learn if any alteration had taken place in the regulation of monastic establishments, and if the ancient spirit subsisted in full vigour. She however, denied that the Rule had become publicly known, intimated that they had their secrets as well as freemasons, and assured me that it could only be had of the superior, not purchased like a sixpenny pamphlet. On pressing her to procure a copy, she left us for a few moments, probably to consult the abbess; for when she returned, she evidently evaded every question connected with the domestic concerns of the community. Willing, however, to indulge us as far as possible, she led us into the Refectory, a large oblong room, ascended by a low flight of stairs:—here we found the cloth laid ready for dinner, which was just coming upon table, and were further gratified by the entrance of two aged nuns in full costume, who severally replied to our salutations by a slight inclination of the head. Our conductress pointed out the different places of the nuns and boarders by the napkins on the table, which latter ran along the sides of the room; and further informed us, that as 'spiritual reading' was continued during the whole time of meals, absolute silence was enjoined; and if any lady wanted a little more bread, beer, or other article, they motioned their attendants, who supplied them without the exchange of a word. The high table at which the superior alone sat, crossed the upper end of the room; and a small desk for the reader, separated two long tables on the southern side of the apartment. Several portraits of nuns decorated the wall, but if we were told who they represented, their names are now forgotten. From this room

M

asylum in the bosom of their own family or amongst their

---

we proceeded into the Chapel, were taken into the gallery, and shewn
the places which the sisters occupied in their devotions.   To the
best of my recollection, the floor is level, and the back seats are
without any elevation   The front of the gallery is filled by the
scholars, and a low rail separates them from the devotees.   Our
kind friend informed us, that as the Catholic worship consisted
of a *continual* series of prayer and praise, the leading portion was
performed by the nuns in rotation; two of whom standing or
kneeling on either side of a low desk, alternately relieved each other.
The singing and chaunting are exquisite, several of the ladies having
most excellent voices.   The organ is played by one of the sisters, and
placed so as to face them in their devotions; by which means a sort
of recess is formed, which entirely excludes them from the gaze of
strangers though they themselves obtain a fine view of the altar.   A
beautiful picture of a saint eminent for piety decorated the walls of
this part of the chapel; and in the windows are paintings of St. Bene-
dict and his sister; to the latter our conductress particularly called
our attention, as she observed, '*That Saint was the foundress of our
Order.*'   Whenever we came opposite the altar, our nun instantly
fell prostrate, and remained in that position for several moments,
even in the midst of conversation, though she resumed the subject
the instant she rose from the ground.   From the Chapel we proceeded to the sitting room of the nuns, a large apartment on the
ground floor at the back of the house, which commands a view of
the garden.   Here we were shown an engraving of the French convent where this society had been originally settled, and remained until
driven thence by the storms of the French Revolution.   The building
apparently consisted of three sides of a quadrangle, but the church
or chapel was not particularly distinguishable.   Near the engraving
was a fine portrait of the foundress.   On the walls of the sitting
room were also small *memorials* written by the nuns in memory of
their deceased sisters, chiefly descriptive of their character and virtues; they were framed and glazed.   We then visited the burying-
ground, originally a portion of the garden, near the end of the chapel,
and remarked several inscriptions on the grave-stones for priests,

friends and being released from their religious obligations

.

---

abbesses and nuns, who were alike distinguished by the epithets of
'Reverend,' and 'Right Reverend,' notwithstanding the difference
of sex. The sisters are placed with their feet to the east, but the
priests have their heads towards the altar. Only one of the stones
was erect, the others laid flat on the turf; all of them were ornamented with a cross. On the east side of the cemetery stood an
ancient wood-cross, on which was originally represented in coloured
straw, in twenty-four oval compartments, 'The Passion of our blessed
Lord.' The figures are now, however, decayed by its exposure
to the weather, and the foot of the cross itself has repeatedly
rotted away, and been afresh fastened in the ground by the gardener.
The nun informed us that it was originally brought from Rome to
their convent in France, and on their removal hither, having no
room sufficiently lofty to admit of its standing upright, they placed
it within these consecrated limits. Whilst on this spot, our communicative recluse observed, 'I have been in this house fourteen
years, here shall remain while I live; and (pointing to the earth)
when I die, shall be buried in this ground.' Mrs. D——— asked her
if she had not a desire to go out sometimes; without a moment's
hesitation she replied, 'No, never—not a wish:—why should we? We
have every comfort here that we desire.' Mrs. D———, however, could
not help suspecting the accuracy of this statement, as it was impossible to avoid remarking the pleasure she evidently felt in an opportunity of conversing with one of an opposite sex, and the desire she
manifested to render herself pleasing.* Indeed, she afterwards
acknowledged she had only conversed with two gentlemen since her
profession. On our return, happening to express myself warmly in
favour of monastic institutions, she turned suddenly round and
said, 'Then, my dear Sir, I am surprised at your not becoming a
monk.' I remarked that there were no religious orders among Protestants; if there were, it is not probable that I should have had sufficient

---

* Mrs. D. has since often said, "as I followed them, I observed she clung to my
husband's arm with the greatest delight, fondly pressed herself to his side, and looked
so kindly in his face that I felt convinced she was in this particular a very hypocrite."

probably some of the younger married, while the elder

---

self-denial to have subjected myself to the Rules.—'Oh then,' replied she, 'you are more fond of the theory than the practice.' As we proceeded through the chapel, she again fell prostrate before the altar and passed a few moments in mental devotion; and on our leaving that edifice, asked us how we should like to leave our warm beds at midnight, go into that cold chapel for two hours, and then return shivering to bed. The bare idea produced an involuntary shudder from both of us. At that moment we were opposite a side door, when pointing to it, she observed, 'Through that doorway fourteen years ago I entered this house—I shall never step over the threshhold again.' By this time, perhaps the silent conviction that we should soon part to see each other no more for ever, had depressed all of us; the conversation, however, again rallied, and she told us that the sisters only visited the chapel three times in the night—that the superior had power to relax, but not to increase, the austerity of the Rule; and that the present community consisted of fourteen nuns, and seventy scholars. On her being asked in what way the convent was supported, and whether endowed or not, she politely declined giving an answer. An apology being tendered for any improper questions, which might have been inadvertently asked, she replied that she should have considered several of them improper had they not been put by a stranger evidently desirous of eliciting information: further apologies were offered, and feelingly accepted —the lady adding 'I've lost my dinner—never mind—I am amply repaid if I have contributed to your gratification!' On parting, our recluse affectionately squeezed my hand, and in a low tone with much apparent pathos, said 'God Almighty bless you,' then instantly assuming a look of the utmost indifference, stepped away across the front garden, without exhibiting the least concern, while we entered the street, lost in rumination on the inexplicable character who had just quitted us: her manners, talents, and disposition, being well calculated to render any man, on whom she might have bestowed her hand, supremely blessed; while here, those charms bloomed unknown, and perished unregarded.

> "I remain, dear Sir,
>
> "Yours, etc. ————."

were compelled to eke out their days on their miserable pensions. Of all the twenty-three professed sisters at Dartford, I have only been able to obtain a glimpse of Elizabeth Wood or Woodford, who in 1540 again obtained an asylum at St. Ursula, although I have taken some pains to examine the Parish Registers in this town and neighbourhood, if peradventure, some evidence of their funerals might appear.*

The situation of the several conventual buildings may be tolerably well ascertained from the present remains, disfigured as they are by the alteration of ages. The building was quadrangular, one of the principal entrances still exists in the pile, which once constituted the eastern front of the monastery. A north east view of this building was drawn anno 1739, and engraved for Grose's antiquities, from which it appears that there was then an embattled tower over the gateway, ornamented with octagon pedestals, which once supported the statues of St. Mary and St. Margaret, and that an embattled parapet ran along the whole eastern front.† On the south but near to the western side of the quadrangle was another entrance, doubtless ornamented somewhat like the former, which led from the side of the hill into the great road to London, possibly the refectory, kitchen, etc., may have stood in this part, as well as the apartments allotted for the

---

* *Vide. p,* 41. Dartford Parish Register did not commence till Jan. 5th, 1568, nearly thirty years after the Dissolution of the monastery; when most of the nuns may reasonably be supposed to be dead.

† This tower was taken down by Mr W. Sears the present tenant about 1828, one of the pedestals is standing in front of the house.

residence of the friars, who superintended the celebration of divine service.* The church of the convent was
situated on the northern side of the monastery, and
from its height and magnitude, sheltered the rest of the
edifice from the cold blasts issuing from the marshes.
A faint idea of this structure may be gathered from
a representation of the model borne in the hand of the
founder, on an ancient seal, attached to a deed in the
archives of the Leather Seller's Company in London;
it is there represented as consisting of a nave, choir
and short transepts, intersected with a low tower surmounted with a spire.† There was a "chapel of our
lady" within the walls, wherein was a tomb for dame
Catherine Berkeley, and before the image of the virgin
hung a lamp, remembered in the will of John Joyner
of Dartford, A.D. 1478.‡ Weever, who seems to have
received his information from oral testimony, states

---

* The store house of the brethren is expressly stated to have stood
opposite to the pasture of the prioress on the south side the abbey
lane. *Terrier, temp. Hen. VII.* Arundell MSS. No. 61, f. 47.

† There is a rough drawing of this seal in Coles MSS. vol. xlv. 389.
It is full of figures—in the middle compartments St. Mary and St. Margaret standing under a double or divided canopy of Spiral work, both
crowned, one holding a globe on her knee, the other praying; in two
niches under canopies on either side of them, is first, a person crowned,
holding a book in his right hand, a cross in his left; the second figure is
a bishop, mitred, holding a crosier; below, in an arch is a man in armour
on his knees, (the founder,) holding a model of the church; and on
the ground a coronet. There is the following legend around the seal
𝔖. 𝕮𝖆𝖚𝖘𝖆𝖓𝖎' 𝖕𝖗𝖎𝖔𝖗𝖎𝖘𝖘𝖊 𝖊𝖙 𝕮𝖔𝖓𝖇𝖊𝖓𝖙𝖚𝖘 𝔐𝖔𝖓𝖆𝖘𝖙𝖊𝖗𝖎𝖏 𝖉𝖊 𝔅𝖊𝖗𝖙𝖋𝖔𝖗𝖉.

‡ Reg. Test. Episc. Roffen iii. 244. *vide p.* 132.

"that lady Elizabeth Cressenor witnessed" *i.e.* informed a visitor, (apparently the writer himself,) "that in the said church, lay buried the lady Bridget, daughter to king Edward the IV., dame Joane, daughter to the lord Scrope of Bolton, and dame Margaret, daughter of the lord Beaumont, both prioresses of that place."* The preceding annals also shew, that, besides the religious inmates, other persons of respectability in the neighbourhood were interred therein, or in the cemetery adjacent to the priory church.† The cloisters were situated on the south side of the church, probably enclosing a small quadrangle, the south west corner of which ran nearly up to the great gate. There was a small chapel attached to the infirmary.

Part of the south wall of the tower still exists in Mr. Sears' garden, and from indications which appeared therein, upon a careful inspection in April, 1841, the present writer concluded, that the choir or chancel was about fourteen yards long, and divided from a nave of the same length (at least)‡ by a tower, the northern side of which, was only fifteen feet in breadth. The principal entrance on the south side, by a doorway ornamented by receding mouldings, is still apparent; the opening is about six feet wide, and three yards above the tower. Farther westward was a smaller door perhaps used for private purposes. The site has long

---

* Funeral Monuments.

† Richard Fagg, buried in the cemetery of the monastery, 1450; Richard Bolton, buried in the priory church, A.D. 1456; some of the Rotheleys, and several others.

‡ The unbroken surface of the wall clearly indicates the nave of that length, but I suspect it extended to the boundary of the garden.

been a garden and consequently affords no traces of the
breadth of the edifice, although it is not impossible the
foundations might be traced by digging.

Some years ago, the late occupier dug up some of the
ornamented tiles of the church floor in his garden, and
Mr. Brames, the former lessee, found near the same
place a triangular piece of glass with the figure of a
friar apparently cut thereon with a diamond, which more
than thirty years past hung up in his premises, but has
since disappeared.*

All the outer garden walls have been evidently rebuilt
or repaired with the *materials* of the *Priory Church*; many
portions of broken columns, sculptures, mouldings and
ornaments are visible in every part. Capitals of double
and single columns of early Norman architecture—zig-
zag,—hatched,—and billet mouldings, interspersed in
ample profusion,—convince the most casual spectator,
that the *Chapel of the* ancient *Palace* had been *retained* for
the use of the convent, and, perhaps with some necessary
additions, constituted the Priory Church, until the final
dissolution of the community.

There is no evidence to shew, whether the edifice
remained as an *oratory* to the Tudor palace, or at what
period it was doomed to destruction.

No Cartulary of this monastery is known.

The *priory church* seems to have resembled that of the *Commandery* of
St. John's, Sutton at Hone, with the exception of the tower.

* Information of L. P. Staff, Esq. the grandson of that gentleman.
Mr. Brames on digging a bath at the spring in the priory gardens,
circa 1800, discovered a great quantity of horns, supposed to have

DARTFORD PRIORY AND CLOISTER, WITH CHURCH, TEMP. HEN. VIII.

Among the papers in the Augmentation Office, is the following survey of the possessions while they remained in the crown, in the time of Henry VIII.

COMPUT' MINISTRORUM DOMINI REGIS. *temp. Hen. VIII.*

Rot. 84 Augment. Office, com. Kanc'.

PRIORATUS DE DERTFORD.

		£	s.	d.
Dertford - -	Redd' lib' ten' in Heth Stret -	o	5	3
	Redd' lib' ten' in Heth St' -	o	19	6
	Redd' al' lib' ten' - -	1	o	5¼
Loffyld in Dertford	Redd' lib' ten' - - -	o	14	3
Wylmynton -	Redd' lib' ten' - - -	o	11	7½
Dertford - -	Redd' mobil' - - -	o	2	2
	Redd' ten' ad vol' -	41	o	2¼
Loffeld - -	Redd' et' firm - -	4	2	9
Bygnore et al' -	Firma maner' etc. -	12	o	o
Dertford - -	Firma prati - -	9	o	o
Stoneham - -	Firma maner -	20	14	o
Wilmyngton -	Redd' ten' ad vol' -	6	4	10
North Cray -	Firma terr' - - -	2	16	o
Gyldon-hill -	Terr' et ten' - -	4	o	o
Southflete - -	Redd' terr' - - -	o	7	4
Bexeley - -	Firma de la Tylehouse, etc. -	2	6	8
Norton Bavent -	Redd' assis' - -	1	18	8
	et 2 lib' piperis			
Norton Bavent -	Redd' cust' tenent -	14	10	11½
Emwell Wood -	Pastur' - - -	1	13	4
Norton Bavent -	Mess' mol' etc. - -	3	10	10
	Firma ten' etc. - -	2	o	9½
	Firma terr' - - -	o	15	o

been thrown there from the slaughter house of the priory. The priory gardens are designated in ancient and modern leases as the *Great Orchard,*—the *Wax Orchard,*—the *Pigeon-house-close* and the *Little or Pear Orchard.*

Rolleston and Madeston }	Firma terr' -	-	-	1	0	0
Billey -	- Maner	-	-	4	0	0
Norton Bavent -	Maner	-	-	20	16	0
	Rector' -	-	-	12	16	0
Fyfield -	- Maner -	-	-	20	0	0
	COM SURR.				
Whytely -	- Rector' -	-	-	6	2	6
Pytfold -	- Red' custum'	-	-	2	9	3
Hatchem Barnes -	Maner -	-	-	25	0	0
	COM SUFF.				
Bavent Combes -	Maner -	-	-	8	0	0
	COM. NORF.				
Thorphall -	- Maner -	-	-	13	7	3
Massyngham Magna	Maner -	-	-	6	13	4
Shipborne -	- Redd' assiz -	-	-	6	7	10
	Firma Maner -	-	-	13	6	8
	COM. CANC'.				
Rey -	- Prat' voc' Bavent	-	0	2	8
Finsbury et Cowling	Firma ten' -	-	-	2	0	0
Crockenhyll	- Maner -	-	-	4	4	0
Pettescourt	- Firma ten' -	-	-	12	0	0
*Ingryce** -	- Firma placeæ	-	-	10	0	0
Howmayth	- Marisc' -	-	-	1	6	8
Batons -	- Firma ten' -	-	-	2	0	0
	COM. GLAM.				
Colwynston	- Redd et Firm'	-	-	21	2	5½
Borowe Castel	- Maner -	-	-	4	6	8
	COM. KANC.				
Dertford, etc.	- Perquis' cur'	-	-	1	10	0
	Terr' d'n'cles	-	-	33	7	7
London -	- Firma ten' etc. -	-	50	12	0

* Ingress, near Greenhithe.

Although King Henry the Eighth immediately after the Dissolution, announced his intention of converting the priory at Dartford into a Residence for himself and his successors, and retained the land in the immediate vicinity in his own hands for that purpose, he nevertheless granted sundry portions of its endowments to the following individuals.

A certain tenement called *le Crown* or the King's Inn, in the High Street, Dartford, known for ages as the principal hostel in that town, to John Thomson.

Another tenement in the same town to Matthew White; and a lease of the manor of Bignors, to William Vaughan.*

In the thirty-fourth year of Henry VIII, the farm or manor of Ingress in Swanscomb, together with the Ferry at Greenhithe, part of the possessions of this Religious House, were demised for twenty-one years, at the rent of 33s. 4d., and the further yearly advance of 6s. 8d., to John Bere of Dartford.† Two years later the *Tylehall*, with other lands in Bexley, Cray, Wilmington, etc. were granted to Hugh Coke, and his heirs, to hold of the king in capite, and by military service.‡

About the same time, the king granted [inter alia] to Sir Ralf Vane, (brother to the late prioress,) and Anthony Tresham, Esq. the manor of Shipborn and its appurtenances, lately belonging to the priory at Dart-

---

* Hasted's MSS. in Brit. Mus. The gateway of the Crown Hostel is perfect, and great part of the edifice remains; the western side has been rebuilt, and the gallery, which commonly ran round the court yard of ancient inns, removed. Mr. Dove is lessee.

† Hasted's Kent. i. 263. ‡ Addit. MSS. No. 6366. Brit. Mus.

ford. Sir Ralph, notwithstanding he stood so high in
royal favor, in the reign of Edward VI., was accused
of being an accomplice in the treason of the Duke of
Somerset, and hanged on Tower Hill; he left no issue—
thus serving as an additional illustration of the inevi-
table misfortunes which were then observed to befall
the grantee of church lands.* The whole of the male

---

* Spelman's History of Sacrilege, shews, that the "Curse of God"
seemed to affix itself upon the families of all directly or indirectly
concerned in the spoliation of Religious Houses. Henry VIII., and
all his posterity perished in the same generation, and the crown
passed into another family. All *those instrumental* in effecting the
destruction of monasteries, suffered by violence, or died in disgrace
and poverty. The same "Curse" also followed the *Families enriched*
by acquisition of *their lands;* many of the different members came to
an untimely end, and at the period of Spelman's writing, *nearly* the
whole of their posterity had *failed* in the *direct* line, and the property
had passed to *collateral branches* or into *other* families. Even *in our own
day,* when an ancient chapel, *which stood in this neighbourhood,* long
desecrated, was pulled down, and the tiles carried away to pave a
stable, the common people remarked, that "*there was always something or
other the matter with the horses.*"—Near Dartford an individual broke up
some stone coffins, paved his cowhouse therewith, and was observed
never to prosper *afterwards.* Some say A CURSE SEEMS STILL TO REST
UPON *possessors of* ANCIENT CHURCH ESTATES. A late writer has remarked
that "when a stream of water, or some apparent convenient locality
"has induced some Speculator or Artisan to erect his Factory on
"*Church Land* and substitute the noisy rattle of machinery for the
"Holy Worship of God formerly offered in the Sanctuary of an
"adjoining monastery—it is no wonder the Curse of sacrilegious
"Profanation invariably attaches itself to his pursuits; and though he
"may attain opulence, some *accident* or *calamity* frequently closes his
"career of cupidity—His purse-proud family are often visited by the
"Judgment of God, with direful maladies,—*spurned by the ancient*

issue of the three sons of the above John Bere also perished in the next generation, and a female carried the estate into another family.

"*gentry* upon whom they fain would *intrude* themselves—and too "commonly, the next generation witnesses their descendants fallen "into their original poverty and insignificance." *Hall, On Avarice and Pride. p. 70.*

Gainsayers may call this SUPERSTITION, and adduce the noble family of Bedford in confutation. But be it remembered, that only forty-five years after the grant of the rich abbeys of Wooburn and Tavistock, the two eldest sons of the second earl had died, and the honours and estates passed to the third. Forty years later, Edward, the third earl, died without issue, when the same honours and estates passed to a cousin. The last duke died without issue.

It would be inviduous and indecorous to name *existing* families, which might verify the preceding remarks. But if the reader only considers how often ancient church property in his own immediate neighbourhood has changed hands, and apparently brought misfortune upon its owners, he will find believers in this doctrine, can adduce forcible arguments in its support.

THE KING'S HOUSE OR PALACE.

King Henry the eighth as before stated, retained the buildings, garden, orchard, etc., of the late dissolved priory in his own hands, converting them into a Residence for himself and his successors, and granted the office of keeper thereof, to Sir Richard Longe.*

1539. Upon the approaching marriage of king Henry, with the lady Anne of Cleves, it was determined that that lady should rest one night at Rochester, and another at the King's House at Dartford, upon her journey from Deal to London. For this purpose, " Edward Lloyd, "yeoman of the wardrobe, and John Askewe groome of "the same, and a smith that was with them were directed "to set up too beds of the kingis, one at Dartford, and an "oder at Rochester, and to make redy for the Queenes "grace by the space of xxx days, the yeoman at ijs. the "day, the grome at xxd. and the smithe at xijd. the day, "as appeareth by a bil with the lord chamberlain's hand. "p. xx. dies."†

The lady Anne, on her journey to the coast, was met on the 11th of December, near Gravelines, by Lord Lisle, deputy of Calais, and conducted to that fortress under a guard of honour. About a mile distant from the place, she was received by the earl of Southampton great admiral of England, who was apparelled in a coat of velvet, cut on cloth of gold and fastened with four hundred large trefoil clasps of gold, in the fashion of a belt, he also wore a golden chain from which was

---

* Hasted's MS. in Brit. Mus.

† Introduction to Nicholas's Privy Purse Expences of Hen. VIII.

suspended a whistle of gold set with precious stones. She landed at Deal about 5 o'Clock on the afternoon of St. John's day, and afterwards set out for Dover attended by the duke and duchess of Suffolk, the bishop of Chichester, and numerous knights and esquires of the county of Kent. Similar honours awaited her on the road, until she arrived on the 1st of January, 1540, at the bishop's palace at Rochester. There the king with eight gentlemen of his privy chamber in "marble coats" (coats perhaps of a stone colour) came *incognito* to Rochester, and suddenly introduced himself to her presence. He is described as somewhat astonished at the sight of the lady, her person so little corresponding with the ideas he had derived of it from Holbein's portrait. She received him on her knees, and he had, at least on this occasion the gallantry, humanity, or policy, to conceal his disappointment and aversion, "he gently raised her" says the venerable old chronicler, "kissed her, and all that "afternoon communed and devysed with her, that night "supped with her, and the next day he departed to "Greenwich, and she came to Dartford."*

1540, Jan. 2nd. She slept that night in the royal

---

* Stowe says he complained of his disappointment the same evening. He said to the lord admiral 'How like you this woman? Do you think her so personable, fair, and beautiful as report has been made to me of her? I pray you tell me true.' The admiral rejoined 'I take her not for faire but to be of a brown complexion.' 'Alas!' said the king 'whom shall men trust? I promise you I see nothing in her as has been shewn me in pictures or report, and am ashamed men should have praised her as they have done, and I love her not.' *Annales, 578.*

bed, prepared for her at the palace,* where her retinue also lodged, and on the morrow, the 3rd of January, proceeded to Blackheath, where, near the foot of Shooter's hill, she was received by the king and a pompous array of noblemen, knights, gentlemen and citizens and thence went to Greenwich.

Her marriage to the king at eight o'clock in the morning of Twelfth-day, her subsequent divorce and retirement are facts well known.†

1548. Thomas lord Seymour was appointed keeper of the late dissolved priory and its estates in Dartford on the accession of Edward the sixth ;‡ but that monarch

---

* There is the following curious Memorandum in the Bexley Register, by Benjamin Huntington, *Vicar* (who was buried Jan. 10. 1706) "Sandrell Ebbs, wife of John Collyer of Blackfen, in Bexley was born "in Stanham, in Dartford parish about Allhollan tyde, the lady Ann "of Cleves then lying at Dartford House, which was 1539. This lady "in January following was marrid to king Henry VIII. The said "Saundrell had a daughter named Elizabeth, by her said husband, "baptised in Bexley church, October 10th, 1596, which daughter the "4th of November, 1605, the day of this note writing, was nine years old "complete; so that her mother was very little of fifty-six years old at "her byrthe."

† King Henry cohabited six months with the lady Anne of Cleves, but actually practised no discourtesy towards her; her consent to a divorce was produced by the offer of £3000 per annum, and on the 24th of July, 1540, a bill was passed to annul the marriage, (Stat. 32 Hen. VIII. c. 25.) On the 8th of August following, the king wedded lady Catherine Howard.

‡ The late keeper, Sir Richard Longe, died the previous year his fee or wages was eight-pence per day, and half an acre of wood for firing, to be delivered there to that officer by the king's wood-reeves, and there only (i.e. in the king's house) to be used and expended. *MS. in Augmental. Office.*

in the second year of his reign in consideration of the surrendry of lands in Surrey, granted to the lady Anne of Cleves, the repudiated wife of Henry VIII, sundry premises in Dartford, lately belonging to the Priory, there late in the occupation of Sir Richard Longe, knight, and the amount of £30 7s. 7d. reserved as a rent for the same; and also the manor of Dartford with its appurtenances, belonging to the late priory; a certain tenement in Overy, late in the tenure of Thomas Maythin; "his park called Washmede in Dartford," in tenure of Robert Dove; the site of the late monastery or priory of Dartford, together with the houses, buildings, gardens, and orchards, belonging to the said priory, with all waters, fisheries, wears, courtleet, views of frank-pledge, liberties, warren, etc., with other premises therein mentioned to the late priory belonging to him in Dart-ford, to hold for the term of her natural life, or so long as she should reside within the realm, at the yearly rent of £18 16s. 1½d.; and the king covenanted to save her harmless of all outgoings except the yearly fee of twenty shillings to the bailiff of the manor, and eight-pence a day to Sir Thomas Seymour, Knt. (Admiral lord Seymour,) as for his office of keeper of his chief messuage at Dartford, amounting to £12 8s. 4d. per annum.*

The lady Anne immediately entered upon the prem-ises, continued to occupy them during the whole of this reign, and was living therein 3 & 4 Philip and Mary, A.D. 1556, as appears from some memorandums in the

---

* Inrollments in the Augmentation Office.

Loosely Manuscripts, wherein it is stated that in the
months of January and February of that year, she
requested Sir Thomas Cawarden to provide certain necessary articles for her house at the Blackfriars, London,
"before her officers at her howse a Dartforth, for that,
"her grace at that tyme lacked money for the furniture
"of the same, and promised payment agayne of the same
"unto the seid S͏ʳ. Tho͏ᵃ."* This money it appears Sir
Thomas did not receive and therefore applied to the
crown for payment.

1557. The lady Anne of Cleves died possessed of
these premises on the 15th of July [4 Phil. et Mar.]
when they reverted to the crown;† and on September
the 8th, the following year, they were granted by that
queen to the Friars Preachers at King's Langley in
Hertfordshire, whose house she had lately re-estab-
lished.‡ Upon the final dissolution of all the new Religious communities in the first year of queen Elizabeth,
they again escheated to the crown, when that sovereign kept Dartford in her own hands and retained
the late priory as a mansion for herself.¶   And here

* "Money demand owinge to Sir Thomas Cawarden, Knight, as
well for sondry provisions as divers other fresh acats [purchases]
and . . . ., provided and bowght at the request of the Lady of
Cleves' Grace, to be laide into the Black frers before her Grace's
cominge thither; and the remaynent taken by Michael D . . . . ly,
Clerke of her Grace's kechen, the vi of Januarie." *Loosely Manuscripts,*
p. 11. edit. by A. J. Kempe, esq.

† Stowe's Annales. p. 631. n. 62.

‡ Pat. 3 et 4 Phil. et Mar. p . .   Pat. 5 et 6 Phil. et Mar. p. 3. m . . Dat.
Sep. 8. Pro situ prioratus de Dertford. Dorman saith " Queen Mary
restored the nuns at Dartford," but the assertion is not justified by any
record.

¶ That Queen Elizabeth maintained an Establishment at this palace

in 1551, on July 17th she slept on going to visit lord
Cobham; and again in her progresses into Kent, anno
1573, when she had been entertained by that nobleman
at the same place, on her return "she slept at her own
"House at Dartford, and then returned to her palace at
"Greenwich."*

*Erection of Smelting Mills and Furnaces at the Queen's
House at Dartford. A. D. 1577.*

After the return of Sir Martin Forbisher from his
second voyage† for the discovery of a north west
passage to Cathay, etc. in November, 1577, with his
ships laden with a quantity of mineral ore [ewar],
assays and experiments of its nature were first made in
two small furnaces erected at the queen's storehouse on
Tower-Hill by John Baptista Agnello, Jonas Schutz, and
Robert Denam. But when the two latter had reported

---

although she did not reside here, is evident by the following entry in
the Dartford Parish Register. "CHRISTENINGS, A.D. 1562. The 11th
"Januarie Xtned Susan Byrde, daugh to Thomas Byrde, yeoman
"sv'it'r to the queen's Ma'tie w'thin the office of her pastrye, and son in
"law to G. Edgcot."

* Nichols's Progresses of Queen Elizabeth. i. 73. Ibid. 350.

† Only £875 was subscribed for the first voyage, and it appears to
have been totally unsuccessful by Forbisher's observation "so by this
voyage was lost and spent of the sum of £875, the sum of £830, which
God restore."

The subscription to the second voyage amounted to £5180, and the
three ships employed were the Michael, Gabriel, and Ayde.—The
alluring object held out to the subscribers were Mines of Gold in
Cathay; for they took out three gold-fynars, and a number of miners
with apparatus.—The subscribers assumed the name of the Company
of Cathay.

favourably thereof, an agreement was made by the Company of Cathay who had subscribed the funds for the expedition with the lord Treasurer for certain of the premises of the queen's house at Dartford for erecting thereon mills and furnaces on a large scale.* The operations of smelting and refining were for some time carried on very spiritedly, and besides the ore brought to the Tower, 140 tons were landed at Bristol from the ships Ayde and Gabriel and from thence taken to Dartford. These works seem to have occupied the refiners until the return of Sir Martin from his third and principal mining voyage† the following year A.D. 1578, when he brought home 1296 tons of ore which also was deposited at Dartford. From the quantity of lead and other additaments purchased to assist the smelting, it would appear that their method of proceeding was, by first adding the metals to the ore.

Soon after the third voyage, disputes arose among the subscribers, and auditors were employed to examine into the Company's assets; these reported that there were 1300 tons of ore remaining at Dartford valued at

---

* As an extensive building was necessary for these erections, perhaps the ancient priory church was selected; if so it is easy to account for its entire ruin and demolition.

ʃ † The third voyage was undertaken upon a larger scale, consisting of the ships Ayde, Michael, Gabriel, and Judith, belonging to the Company, and nine other ships hired for the voyage. The men were hired for six months from May, but the time of their sailing and return does not appear. The expedition comprehended a large number of miners' implements. The expences of the three voyages amounted to £20,345. of which the Queen advanced £4000. *Papers in the Exchequer containing the Account of Michael Lok, Treasurer to the Company of Cathay, with Forbisher's autograph explanations.*

£13 6s. 8d. per ton, amounting to £17,333 6s. 8d. As
no further information can be collected respecting this
ore, it may be presumed that it did not turn out so
valuable, because it is immediately after said "that the
same like ewar may be obtained at £6. per ton, whereas
this cost the Company £16.

Captain Forbisher was charged with having taken
out four ships without the knowledge of the Company
on his own venture, but at much cost to them, and that
he brought home two of them laden with ore; this ore
was deposited in the Queen's House at Dartford and
agreed to be considered of in equity.

These disputes evidently led to the suspension of the
works at Dartford, and eventually the ore was sold to
discharge the incumbrances of the Company.

At the latter end of the reign of queen Elizabeth, or
the commencement of that of her successor James I. the
manor, site and land lately belonging to the dissolved
priory of Dartford, were granted to Sir Edward Darcy,
during the term of his natural life; who hereupon made
the mansion his residence, and gave it the name of
Dartford Place. By that name it was long known, but for
upwards of a century past it has recovered its ancient
designation of "The Priory."

That Sir Edward and his family were living here very
early in the seventeenth century, is shewn by the following entries of the marriage of two of his daughters in the
parish Register,

"William Bate, esquire, of the p'ishe of West Lathes, in the
county of York, and Eliz. Darcy, dau. of Sir Edward Darcy, knight,

were married the xxij of May, by a licence from my lord's grace of Canterburie."

" Thomas Carewe of Stone, gent. and Ffrancys Darcy, the dau. of Sir Edward Darcy knight, were married the xxiij of Januarie, by a licence at the Arches in Powles."

In 1606, James I, granted " the manor of Dartford, alias Temple Dartford," (by mistake described as parcel of the priory or monastery of Dartford); the site and mansion of the said late priory, and all the lands in Dartford and Wilmington belonging thereto; and all other the king's lands and possessions in those parishes, among other premises to Robert Cecil, earl of Salisbury, in exchange for the house and manor of Theobald's, in Hertfordshire, to hold of the king as of his manor of East Greenwich, by fealty only, in free and common soccage, and not in chief, nor by knights service; yielding and paying to the king, his heirs and successors for the manor of Temples, £20 14s. 5d.; and for the manor, site and lands late belonging to Dartford Priory *during the life of* Sir Edward Darcy, knight, *nothing*; and after his decease, forty nine pounds and two and twenty pence halfpenny. This exchange was confirmed by act of parliament.

In 1612, by a deed, inrolled in the king's bench, dated April 24th, 10 James I, the earl of Salisbury and Sir William Cecil, knight, his son and heir apparent, conveyed these estates to Sir Robert Darcy, knight, (the eldest son of the above Sir Edward) and his heirs. Sir Edward Darcy at this period was in the seventieth year of his age, and surviving the transaction only a few months, died at Dartford Place, and was buried in a vault among his ancestors in the church of St. Botolph, Aldgate, London.

Sir Robert Darcy who thus became possessed of Dartford Priory and the manor of Temples, married Grace,
daughter and coheir of Alexander Reddish, co. Lancaster,
esq., by whom he had one son, to whom, these estates
eventually descended, together with another at Newhall
in Derbyshire.*

I have met with no document in either the public or
parish archives, relative to any act of Sir Robert Darcy
while resident at Dartford. He appears to have died
before 1631, for in that year the name of "—— Darcy"
appears among the landed proprietors in the parochial
assessments.†

Four years later, Edward Darcy, esq., his only son and
heir, inhabited *Dartford-House* and succeeded to the
family estates. His name first appears in a church
rate granted in May, 1635.‡ He was twice married;

---

* Hasted i. 217. He was descended from Thomas lord Darcy,
beheaded 30 Hen. VIII. who left issue by Dousabella, daughter of Sir
Richard Tempest, of Ribesdale, knight, three sons and one daughter;
George the *eldest* son, was restored to the title of lord Darcy, in 4 and 5
Philip and Mary; his line is now extinct. Arthur, the *second* son was
knighted, and dying April 3rd in the third year of queen Elizabeth, left
by Maria, daughter and heir to Sir Nicholas Carewe, of Beddington,
seven sons; of whom Henry the eldest, ended in a daughter; Thomas,
the *second* son, left issue Conyers Darcy, who was restored to the *Barony
of Darcy*; and the *third* Sir Edward Darcy, knight of the privy chamber
to Queen Elizabeth, married Elizabeth, daughter of Thomas Astley, of
Writtle, co Essex, esq.; by whom he had fifteen children; Sir Robert
the eldest son acquired Dartford, as above mentioned. Sir Edward died
October 28th, 1612, and his son Sir Robert, caused him to be buried in
St. Botolph's, Aldgate, among his ancestors, according to his desire.
Strype's Stowe's Survey of London, i. 361.

† Poor Rate Books. ‡ Churchwarden's Accounts, sub an.

first to Elizabeth, daughter of Richard Evelyn, of Surrey, esquire, by whom he had no issue; secondly to lady Elizabeth, daughter of Philip Stanhope, first earl of Chesterfield, by whom he left three daughters, his coheirs—Katherine, who married Sir Erasmus Phillips, of Picton Castle, Pembrokeshire, bart.; Dorothy, who married Sir. . . . Rokesby; and Elizabeth, married first to Thomas Milward of Derbyshire, esq. and secondly to. . . . Barnes.*

Mr. Edward Darcy resided chiefly at the *Place-House* until the raging of the civil war, and his name is found in many of the Parochial Rates and Books for upwards of forty years. He separated Temple-farm from the rest of his estates, and sold it to a person named Priestley. His lady survived him, and seems to have resided at Dartford Place until 1680, when she was assessed at an estimated rental of £23 per annum. In 1681, John Jackson occupied *The Place* and farm and was assessed at £50 per Annum. In 1683, Lady Darcy's assessment was reduced to £7 per annum. Lady Darcy is presumed to have died that year, since in September, 1683, the same property was assessed on *Madam Elizabeth Darcy* her daughter. In 1688, *the Place* and farm was in the occupation of Philip Bassock.†

By deed dated May 27th, 1699, dame Catherine Phillips, dame Dorothy Rokesby, and Thomas Milward esq., son of the above mentioned Elizabeth, conveyed these manors and premises to Thomas Gouge, esq. of London. He left three sons, Thomas, Nicholas, and

---

* Hasted i. 217.   † Assessments, sub ann.

Edward; they were all possessed of it in succession, the estate being of knight's service.   They all died bachelors; the youngest by his will devised it to his nephew, Robert Mynors Gouge of Hertfordshire, esq., He bequeathed it to Mary, his widow; she married Charles Morgan, esq., from whom it descended to the present possessor.*

Ever since the time of Lady Darcy, *Dartford Place* has been appropriated to the occupiers of the Priory farm for a residence.   As early as 1693, it was tenanted by William Hill, a farmer, who then rented the Place farm and Close heath, and the whole assessed at £65 per annum.†   The buildings have undergone such alterations as the necessities or caprice of the several occupiers have suggested, yet the greater portion of the present remains are those of the priory, built of brick about the time of king Henry VII.   At the commencement of the present century, they consisted of a large Gate-house with a south wing adjoining to it,‡ but about 1824, some of the materials being

---

* Ex orig. penès C. Morgan, Bar. *v.* Manor.   † Parish Books, sub an.

‡ John Thorpe, of Bexley, esq. communicated the following account of the existing remains of this monastery in a letter to Grose dated Nov. 9th, 1771: "Saturday last, I went and took a "particular view of the ruins of Dartford Nunnery, and found that "what remains of it is only a fine gateway, and some contiguous "buildings used as a farm-house.   The Gateway is now a stable for "the farmer's horses and over it is a large room, serving, I suppose "for a hay-loft.   The site of the abbey was where the farmer's garden "and stack-yard now are, and must have been a vast pile of build- "ing, from the great number of foundations of cross walls, drains "etc. which have been discovered.   There were, and are to this "day, two broad roads or avenues leading to the gate; the eastward

decayed, the tower over the gateway, with the battlements were taken down by Mr. William Sears the present tenant, and a plain straight roof continued over the building.* One of the staircases are formed of solid blocks of timber, and bids fair to outlast the walls themselves. The priory must originally have been very extensive, since vast foundations have been discovered around the whole precincts.

" flanked by the old stone wall on the right hand, from the street called
" Waterside, was the principal avenue from the town to the abbey. The
" other to the west leads up the hill into the great London road ; the
" large hilly field to the right is to this day called the King's field. . . .
" . . . . On the north-east side were the large gardens, encompassed
" with the ancient stone wall still entire and more than half a mile round,
" inclosing a piece of ground of twelve acres, now and for a long time,
" rented by gardeners to supply the London markets, and famous for
" producing the best artichokes in England."—They were occupied by
Mr. Peter Brames, a *market-gardener*, many years, and are still rented by
his daughter Mrs. Hall.

* Information of Mr. William Sears. In a previous page the date of
1828 has been inserted by mistake.—The pedestals which formerly supported the statues of St. Mary and St. Margaret, were taken down, when
an iron conductor was placed on the tower to prevent accidents by lightning. *Vide Grose's Antiquities.*

THE HERMIT OF DARTFORD.

" AGED the sires, who dwelled such cells within
   Head-shaking sages, prone to moralize,
And him disciple who made there his inn ;
      Their cheeks were hollow, slender was their size,
      And ever on the ground they bent their eyes ;
One book they had, the book of holy lore ;
      Against the wall a cross stood leaning-wise,
A table small, a skull and cross-bones bore ;
      And bosky ivy hid the bell above the door.
                        Fosbrooke's Economy of Monastic Life.

A.D. 1235. The accidents which oftentimes occurred
to passengers at the ford of the Darent induced one of
those devout solitary persons called Hermits to construct
a cell at that spot, as early as the reign of Henry the
third,* whereby he might be at hand to assist persons in
danger, and collect such alms as the charitable might feel
induced to bestow.†

In the time of Edward II., and perhaps long before,
there was a *passage* or *ferry* over the Darent, the steward
of the manor providing boats for the purpose of

---

* Rot. Pat. 20 Hen. III p. 11. A Hermit was noticed here at the
time of the marriage of Isabel the king's sister to the emperor of Germany
—perhaps attracted hither by the concourse of persons who attended that
ceremony.

† Excepting the occasional alms of the faithful, the Hermit derived
his sole subsistance from the esculents which he cultivated with his own
hands in his garden ; yet he cheerfully welcomed the weary or benighted
traveller to partake of his scanty fare, and the shelter of his roof.
Hermits exhibited an austere piety ; frequently got the whole psalter by
heart, and recited it every day. In their dreamy hallucinations they
were believed to hold converse with the spiritual world ; and their
affected holiness of life was thought to confer upon them the power of
healing diseases and working miracles. *Fosbrooke's British Monachism,*
503. Doubtless many were lazy hypocritical vagabonds, but they must
have been very demure.

transit, and accounting to the lord for the profits among the rents thereof.   In the inquisition taken after the death of Edward of Woodstock, earl of Kent, among the *Accounts of the ferme of the Royalty of Dertford,* the "Rent of the passage of the Darent" is stated at thirteen shillings and four-pence per annum.*

From the above period, a succession of recluses seem to have occupied the station, and by their holy ascetic life and unwearied exertions in the cause of humanity succeeded in extracting from the benevolent, sufficient funds to construct a bridge for the use of foot passengers.   This was effected about the time of Henry IV.† At the foot of the bridge the hermit solicited arms of the passengers for its repair, as well as for their own support and the relief of wayfarers.   The bridge though narrow, steep, and inconvenient,‡ continued to exist until the middle of the last century.

In 1415. (3 Hen. V.) Henry lord Scrope left by will a bequest of 13s. 4d. to the hermit of Dertford.¶

The hermitage appears to have stood immediately contiguous to the foot of the bridge and to have had a small chapel attached dedicated to St. Katherine.‖ The earliest name of the hermit which appears in the Bishop's Registers at Rochester is that of John Sodeman, who under the title of "Hermit of the chapel of "the blessed virgin and martyr, St. Katherine of Dert-"ford, for the reformation of the poor," obtained letters

* Esch. 3 Edw. III. No. 58.

† Dr. Latham's MS. notes to Hasted's Kent. i. 214. The pilgrims to Canterbury probably greatly assisted in the undertaking.

‡ The bridge was similar to that now at Eynsford (1842).

¶ Rymer's Fœdra. ix. 275.   ‖ Regist Spiritual. f. 135.

of Indulgence from the bishop of the diocese, dated June 1st, 1438.*

On the 20th December, 1509, John Colebrant, a single man, came before John, bishop of Rochester, in the parish church of Bromley, after the ordination of some priests, and there taking upon him the habit of a hermit,† after the accustomed form, made profession "to live to "the honour of God, according to the rule of St. Paul the "hermit, in the hermitage of the town of Dertford, "erected in honour of St. Katherine the virgin."‡

The last profession of a hermit which appears in the Register relative to this hermitage was made by Walter Combes, 5th December, 1518, before the Bishop in the palace at Rochester, during the celebration of mass, in this form, "I Walter Cowmbe, layeman, promyse and "professe here in the p'sence of God and his saynts, and "before you my lord John bushop of Rochestre, that "henfforth everwhiles my naturall lyff shall endure, will "live chaste of my body, in voluntary poverte, and "under obedience of you my seid ordinary in the chapel "of St. Katherine in Dertford, or in some other chapel or "hermytage ordeyned for a hermit: so help me God and "holidem."¶

---

* Act Cur. Consist. f. 135.

† The hermit's dress was a long gown with a hood covering the whole body and having arm-holes; a tunic, and rosary; beard very long, dress often ragged, and wearing a rope for à girdle.

‡ Episc' Cur. Mun. f. 53.

¶ Ibid. f. 78 By a clerical error the town's name is written *Debtford* in one part of the entry in this Record, although the mistake is obvious both from the context and the name of the chapel, as well as by the preceding extracts.

No further notice of a hermit, a hermitage, or chapel of St. Katherine at Dartford, occurs in any Record which I have seen. That they had ceased to exist before 1535, is clearly shewn by their being unnoticed in the general Ecclesiastical valuation taken that year.

———

The collection of Pontage or toll for the repair of the bridge was vested in William Stockmede in the first year of Henry VIII., in right of a messuage in Overy for which he paid a quit rent of twenty pence per annum.*

THE TRINITY HOSPITAL OR ALMS-HOUSE.

A.D. 1452.   King Henry VI., in the thirty-first year of his reign granted licence to John Bamberge, William Rothele, Roger Jones, and Thomas Boost, or the survivor of them, to found here an Hospital or Alms-House in honour of the Holy Trinity,† for five poor persons, that they might every day pray for the

———

* Rentale de Dertford [Temples]. Addit. MSS. Brit. Mus. No. 5493.

† Hospitali de Dertford in agro Cantiana. — *(Licentia Regis Henrici Sexti pro Fundacione ejusdem.)*

Rex, etc. Sciatis, quod ad laudem, gloriam, et honorem sanctæ et individuæ Trinitatis, in cujus honore ecclesia parochialis de Dertford in com. Kanc. dedicata existit, de gratia nostra speciali, et ex certa scientia nostra concessimus, et pro nobis et heredibus et successoribus nostris, quantum in nobis est, licentiam dedimus Johanni Bamberg, Willielmi Rothele, Rogero Jonet, et Thomæ Boost, quod ipse sue ille, vel illi eorum qui supervixerit vel supervixerint in honore præfatæ S. Trinitatis, quandam domum elemosynarium diversorum mansorum, de perpetuo vicario ecclesiæ prædictæ, et

health of the king's soul, and that of his beloved consort the queen, while living, and for their souls after
they have left this light, and for the souls of their
progenitors, and all the faithful departed this life; and
also do such deeds of mercy [misericordiæ] and piety
as the aforesaid John Bambergh, William Rothele,
etc., or all or any of the survivors shall ordain: the
said hospital to be called The Trinity Alms-House of
the new foundation. The vicar, churchwardens, and
their successors to be a body corporate, in name and
thing, and in all future times to be Master of the
House aforesaid, and as such, be capable of acquiring
lands, and tenements, and holding the same to themselves and their successors: and that by the name of
Master of the Alms-House of the Holy Trinity in

---

custodibus bonorum catallorum, et ornamentorum ecclesiæ illus, ac
quinque pauperibus debilibus in eadem domo de tempore in tempus per eosdem vicariam et custodes et successores suos imperpetuum sustentandis et inveniendis, in prædictâ villâ de Dertford, pro
salubri statu nostro et charissimæ consortis nostræ, reginæ, quoad
vixerimus ac pro animabus nostris cum ab hac luce migraverimus
et animabus progenitorum nostrorum, et omnium fidelium defuncto-
rum singulis diebus oraturis; necnon ad aliam misericordiæ, et
pietatis opera faciendis, supportandis, et sustentandis, juxta ordina-
tionem prædictorum Johannis Bamburgh, Willielmi Rothele, etc.
seu eorum illius, vel illorum qui supervixerit inde faciendam, vo-
candum sive nuncupandam, *the Trinitees Almes-House in Dertford*
de novo fundare erigere unire, et stabililire possint et posset. Et
quod iidem vicarius et custodes et successores sui perpetuis futuris
temporibus, sint magister domus prædictæ, ac unum corpus in
futurum incorporatum in re et nomine; ac personas habiles et in
lege capaces ad perquirendum terras, tenementa, et alias possessiones quascunque, et de dono aliorum recipiendas et habendas
sibi et successoribus suis in feodo et perpetuitate imperpetuum: et
quod per nomen magistrorum Domus Elemosinariæ S. Trinitatis de

Dertford, they should plead, or be impleaded, prosecute or defend in suits of law in the courts, whether temporal or spiritual: and that there should be a Common Seal for affirming the business transactions of the House aforesaid.

Licence is also granted to the said John Bambergh, William Rothele, etc., or all, or any of the survivors, to acquire by gift or otherwise, lands, tenements, rents, reversions, or other possessions, in mortmain, to the value of Twenty pounds per annum, beyond reprises, which should be held by the said Master, for the support of the said five poor persons, as well as other acts of charity, according to the direction of John Bambergh, etc., in form aforesaid according to the tenor of the licence.

Dertford implacitare; necnon prosequi et defendere in quibuscunque curiis coram quibuscunque judicibus, tam spiritualibus, quám temporalibus, omnimodas actiones reales, personales, et mixtus, sectas, querelas, et demandas, motas seu movendas, pro ipsis vel contra ipsos in curiis supradictis: et quod habeant commune sigillum pro negotiis Domus prædictæ deservituram.

Concessimus etiam, ac præfatis Johanni Bamburgh, Willielmo Rothele, etc, et illi vel illis eorum qui supervixerit vel supervixerint, licentiam dedimus, quod ipsi vel ipse terras, tenementa, redditus, reversiones, et alias possessiones quascunque, ad valorum $xx^{ti.}$ per annum, ultra reprises, quæ nobis, non tenentur in capite per servicium militare, dare possint et assignare hujusmodi magistris domus prædictæ, cum sic fundata, erecta, unita, et stabilitæ fuerit; habendas sibi et successoribus suis, ad sustentandum et supportandum tam hujusmodi quinque pauperes, quám prædicta imperpetuum: ac eisdem magistris, quod ipsi eadem terras, tenementa, redditus, et alias possessiones à præfatis Johanne Bamburgh, etc. aut illo vel illis eorum qui supervixerit vel supervixerint, enenda sibi et successoribus suis imperpetuum, et prædictum est,

This Alms-house was partly erected on the eastern bank of the Darent, between the Hermitage and the river, and partly over the stream, upon piers standing therein.* The edifice originally consisted of a rather spacious room or hall, where strangers were received, or the inmates met to partake of their common meals, and some smaller apartments intended for dormitories or cells. But there was no chapel or oratory attached, the brethren being directed to perform their daily devotions in the adjoining parish church, to which this hospital was considered an appendage, and for which they had a desk or stall erected, known in after times as the *Great Freretory*.† The surviving founders together with the vicar and churchwardens (as a corporate body), exercised the office of perpetual *Master* or *Governor*, and, under their direction, the alms-men, (besides attending their prescribed religious duties,) were required to perform various active works of charity, *i.e.* relieving and assisting strangers and wayfarers, as the Hermit-of-the-Bridge had been heretofore accustomed, but whose services were found too limited and inadequate, since the number of persons who now

---

recipere et habere possint, sibi et successoribus suis prædictis in formâ prædictâ, tenore presentium, licentiam similiter dedimus specialem, etc. In cujus. etc.   T. rege apud Westm. xx. die Junii.   *Pat.* 31 *Hen. VI. p.* 2. *m.* 1.   *Caley's Dugdale.* vii. 721.

* See subsequent quotations from Vestry Books, A.D. 1650, and 1754 ; the extracts distinctly specify the locality.

† Thomas Chapelyn, by will dat. 10 July, 1552, (34 Hen. VIII.) directs his "body to be buried in the church of Dertford, near to the great Freretree there," and at the day of his burial divine song be performed by three priests, and that three masses be said for his soul and all christian souls.   Reg. Test. ix. 402.

flocked on pilgrimage to the shrine of St. Thomas of Canterbury had so vastly increased.*

The parties entrusted with this Foundation evidently failed in procuring funds for its endowment, since there is no further reference to any lands, rents, or tenements, in connection with the Trinity Hospital or Alms-house in Dartford to be found in public or private records. It is nevertheless probable that policy induced the founders, at first, to place therein the five poor persons proposed, in hope that the duties in which they were seen continually engaged, combined with their *utter destitution* might stimulate wealthy passers-by to foster the infant institution. No benefactor of note, however appeared, and the donations of the neighbourhood were only found adequate to fulfil

---

* These pilgrimages professedly undertaken by each individual pilgrim in penitence and contrition for sin, were performed *barefoot*, but alas! degenerated into holiday excursions. Parties generally met together at some appointed rendezvous and journeyed in companies of both sexes, and as the roads were lonely as well as dangerous, some of the pilgrims would frequently hire wandering minstrels to beguile the wearisomeness of the way, by singing: and too often the wanton song was preferred to the psalm. Others would have bagpipes or different musical instruments, so that through every town they passed, what with their piping and singing, and the barking of dogs which ran out after them, the procession made more noise than if the king and all his clarions journeyed that way   The practice of engaging these pipers was defended upon the necessity of endeavouring to solace the unfortunate pilgrim who wounded his foot against a flint or stone, by striking up a stave to attract his attention from the anguish thereof. Edward the Third and his mother performed the Canterbury Pilgrimage in Lent. *Ang. Sacr.* i. 368. The which season seems to have been generally selected by individuals for the purpose.

the *minor* object of the foundation,* that of affording the *destitute temporary relief*, and a *lodging for the night;* yet so long as the *catholic religion* prevailed, that priesthood never failed to impress upon the faithful, living or dying, the absolute necessity of performing works of kindness, mercy, and benevolence towards their distressed brethren.† But after the change of religion, the clergy of the *new faith* no longer representing relief of the poor "meritorious," active charity rapidly declined; and the long reign of Elizabeth only produces one recorded instance of a fresh supply of necessaries bestowed upon this institution—the Donation of Jerome Warren, a surgeon at Dartford,—who, by Will dated Dec. 3rd, 1507, gave "to the Alms-house "standing on Dartford bridge for the lodging of poor "people, three mattresses, three pair of sheets, and three "shred coverlets."‡

In after ages, when compulsory provision was made for these objects by poor rates, the parish officers of Dartford converted the Alms-house into habitations for widows, or other feeble and destitute parishioners. Hence it became needful to provide the separate tene-

---

* Under the head "Dartford Hospital" Willis states that in 1553, there remained an annual payment of £8 6s. 8d. chargeable upon the revenues of that House, then vested in the crown. This memorandum Tanner attaches to the Trinity Hospital, but as there were no estates belonging to this institution at the dissolution of Hospitals and Chantries, the Record evidently refers to the Priory of Dartford.

† Vide, Wills of parishioners in the Registry at Rochester, Vols. viii. and ix. passim.—1535. Agnes Parker, "I will to the Alms-house of Dartford, two payer of coarse sheets, etc." Ib. ix. f. 176.

‡ Parish Records, No. 16. *Landale's Abstract of Charities.* 22.

ments with chimneys,* and other requisite appendages, the costs of which appear among the church-wardens' annual disbursements.

The "Houses on the bridge" as they are invariably stiled in the subsequent Parish Accounts, continued to be occupied in a similar way until the year 1754, when the projected improvements on the road having

---

* From some of the following items in the Churchwarden's Books it may be presumed that there was no chimney in the original hospital, and, that in ancient times a fire was made against a *Reredose*, and that the smoke escaped from a *Louver* in the roof.

1643.   Paid to John Needle for making the chimney in the Bridge house, 16s.; a load of bricks . . ; sand to chimney, 3s.; carriage to ditto 1s. 6d.   Total . . . . . .

1645.   Paid for making a chimney in the Bridge-house, 15s.

   Paid for six spikes for the Bridge-house, 1s.

1649.   Paid John Belloway for stuff for curbs for two wells, at the Bridge-house, and workmanship, £1 7s. 7d. p. 35.

   Paid for a journey to London, about the bridge at Dartford. . . s.

1660.   Paid Thomas Taylor for one day's work in the water, about the repair of the Bridge-house, 2s. p. 75.

Tradition relates that when king James II. returned from Feversham to London, Dec. 13th, 1688, the river had so overflowed its banks, that as he could not reach the bridge, one of the townsmen carried him over on his back, and the women spread their aprons for him to walk upon.

The Churchwardens' Books also contain the following entries:—

1696.   Oct. 6.   Paid the ringers when the King (William III.) came through the town, 10s.

   Paid for six pounds of candles which were set upon the church wall and bridge, to light the king through the river, 2s. 6d.

   Paid for six links to light him down the hill, 1s. 6d.

——   Nov. 15.   Paid when the king went through the town from Flanders, 10s.

   Paid for lights and candles to light the king down the hill and through the river. . . s.

rendered the rebuilding and widening of the bridge absolutely necessary, the parishioners assembled in vestry determined, that the parish houses then standing thereon, being in a ruinous condition, should be taken down, and Mr. Sloane the builder, be allowed to make use of the stone piers the said building stood upon for that purpose.* The last lingering remains of the Trinity Alms-house were demolished in the autumn of that year.

———

The bridge was a second time widened, and altered into its present form, in 1792, and several houses on Short Hill set back to improve the road.†

———————————————————

* 1754. At a vestry holden Aug. 13th. Agreed that on the enlargement of Dartford bridge soon about to take place, the houses now inhabited by widows Chapel and Ridsell, on the said bridge as a poor house, be taken down with the out-houses adjoining, for the ornament and advantage of the said bridge—the houses being in a ruinous and bad condition; and the materials of the said houses to be applied as the parishioners may hereafter think proper. *Vestry Book*, 201.

1754. Sept. 25. "The vestry agreed to petition the bishop of Rochester to grant a faculty that a quantity of ground not exceeding seven superficial yards be taken off the south side of the lower church yard to render the passage from the bridge now about to be built, more commodious. This faculty was granted 25th Sept. 1754, and the bridge widened accordingly; but in Sept. 1755, the parishioners complained to the bishop that the agents to the contractors for building the bridge had taken away the strong wall built with flints and coped with stone, which bounded the south side of the church yard, and used the old materials in and about the works of the bridge. *Vestry Book*, p. 208.

† Information of Mr. Brand, the Vestry Clerk.

THE LEPER'S HOSPITAL.

This Hospital stood on the site of the present Spital
Houses, near the middle of the Hill on the entrance
of Dartford from London, in conformity with the ancient
practice of building those Houses without towns or
cities; the disease being considered loathsome and infec-
tious.*

Tanner, on the authority of some ancient wills in
the Prerogative Office, says, this hospital for lepers

---

* The leprosy of the middle ages, is supposed to have originated in
persons living so much on fish and salt provision. *Joinville* asserts that
the whole army of St. Louis, in the Crusade A D. 1250, from living
during Lent only, upon *Eel-pouts* (a glutinous fish which fed upon the
dead bodies of the Saracens, slain by the French and thrown into the
Nile,) became infected by a leprosy, which dried up the flesh on their
legs to the bone, caused their skins to become as dark as tanned
leather, or like an old boot that has long lain behind a coffer, and
generated such a sore complaint in the mouth, that the gums rotted and
caused a most stinking breath. Very few escaped death who were thus
attacked, and it was invariably fatal when accompanied with bleeding
at the nose. *Memoirs*. 159. *Hafod*. 1807.——Lepers were separated from
society by a particular Religious Office—their *Costume* was a mantle and
beaver hat. In early times they were allowed to go to the churches, and
on market days, to the markets, with a clap-dish and cup to collect alms
for their maintenance, but their sickness and loathsome appearance
giving great disgust, many withheld their charity, and they were
afterwards restrained from begging at large, and permitted to send a
proctor, who thus collected the voluntary offerings of the people.
Phillip's Shrewsb. 116. The disease is supposed to have disappeared
through the use of tea and linen next the skin, *Fosbroke, Encycl. Antiq.*
i. 414.

existed before 1330, and was dedicated to St. Mary Magdalen.*

If this account be correct, it is clear there is some mistake in the inscription on the front of the present edifice, which states it as "A VERY ANCIENT CHARITY "BEGUN AND ENTIRELY CONTINUED FOR SEVERAL GENER- "ATIONS BY THE HORSMANS OF HORSMAN'S-PLACE, IN "THIS PARISH," there having been only one person of that name, Thomas Horsman, who inherited that estate by the marriage of Margaret, only daughter and heir of Thomas Shardelowes, in the reign of Henry V. circa, 1420; and re-built the mansion in Lowfield-street. This Thomas Horsman died without issue about 1493, when his widow possessed the property in her own right, and at her decease left it to her kinsman Thomas Brune.

There can be no doubt that the foundation may be ascribed to some of the ancient owners of this estate, (for its whole endowment consisted of lands appendant thereunto, and the edifice itself was held of the priory of St. John of Jerusalem by the same tenure, a quit rent, as Horsman's Place,) and were invariably connected therewith; nor does the name of any other benefactors

---

* Notitia. His authorities are Lib. Test. i *f.* 2.; and the Will of William Quoyf, A.D. 1491. Ibid. v. *f.* 261. Perhaps instead of the Prerogative Office, Canterbury, a reference to the *Registry of Rochester* would have been more correct—If so, his first quotation refers to John Oakhurst of Dartford, who, by will, dat. 15th Oct. 1440, gave to the Hospital of the Leperous in that place, twelve-pence. *Regist. Test. Ibid.* This date would *agree* with the inscription on the present Spital Houses which ascribes the Foundation to the *Horsman's*, whereas the former would point to Thomas de Luda.

appear. Subsequent events, however, shew that although lands were allotted for the perpetual maintenance of the hospital, the founder procured no *charter* for its settlement from the crown, nor executed any *special conveyance* to the Prior or his brethren. Hence, instead of existing as an independent community, the *Horsmans, Brunes,* and their successors in *the estate* of Horsman's place, continued *sole patrons* of the institution, appointed the officers, and managed the estates.

The establishment consisted of a Prior, and certain lay brethren charged with the superintendence of the Lepers admitted into the hospital.*

In the reign of Henry the Seventh, part of its endowment was called "the old Spittal land" and lay "in *Highfield,* on the south side of the king's highway as you go from Dartford towards Crayford, and south-west towards Bexley. There were lands also pertaining to the hospital of the leperous, in *Bronyllsland,* near the former; and certain "meadows in the Saltmarsh, called *Cokkenshote,*" adjoining others vested in the lady prioress of Dartford.† The hospital was held of Temples manor, and paid twelve pence annually Quit Rent to the prior of St. John of Jerusalem.‡ The ancient estates constitute the endowment of the present Spital-House.

---

* Rentale, etc. Dom. Eliz. Cressener, Prioressæ de Dertford. f. 39.

† Ibid. f. 45a. f. 45b. f. 39a. See also Rot. 32. Hen. VIII. B.M.

‡ R'd. of the Hospital or Governor of the Hospital of the Leperous called *le Spittal house* in Dertford, viz., for the Capital messuage where the seyd leperous inhabit and dwell, 12d. Rental of Temples Dartford, No. I. 1 Hen. VIII. Similar entries occur in other Rentals, preserved in the same volume until 28 Hen. VIII. 1536.

In 1541, John Byer or Beer purchased the mansion and estates of Horsman's Place, and with it were transferred the *patronage, etc.* of the Leper's Hospital and lands, as an appanage thereunto. That the institution was then regarded as a *private Charity* is evident from its not being entered in the Roll taken pursuant to the Act passed 37 Hen. VIII. A.D. 1545, for valuing and surrendering all Colleges, Hospitals, etc., and remaining unnoticed in the subsequent Roll, 1 Edward, VI., when hungry courtiers were so rapacious after confiscations. By slow gradations the disease of leprosy had greatly abated, although it had not entirely disappeared among the common people, and therefore to prevent the contagion spreading, Lepers were not compelled by the Act to leave their domicile like the monastics on the suppression of Religious Houses.* Beer, however, remarking the alteration that was taking place in the habits and condition of the neighbourhood, finding the hospital thus fallen into his hands, REFOUNDED the same "for poor, impotent, diseased, and lame people."

---

* By the Act 1 Edw. VI. c. 3. § 19. "All leperous and bed-red "creatures whatsoever, may at their own libertie be allowed to continue "in such houses appointed for leperous or bed-red people, and shall not "be compelled to repair into other countries or places appointed by "this Act." And it was "made lawful for leperous and bed-red persons "to appoint proctors, for each House not more than two, to gather alms "of all such inhabitants who were within four miles of the said "houses." This permission was speedily abused. Sturdy *beggars* went about with a clap-dish, and pretending they were Proctors to a Spital House terrified people into contribution: so *Proctors* were put down by Act 39 Eliz. c. 4. and adjudged rogues and vagabonds. Vide Article *Leprosy*, Appendix.

THE SPITAL HOUSES.

It is uncertain at what precise period John Beer
attempted to change the objects of the ancient charity,
but it is probable that the revolution was effected
gradually as the diseased were removed by death. The
parish Register contains an entry as early as June,
1568, of the burial of "John Parker, one of the
Spittle House" without specifying any particulars of
the individual. From that silence, however, he may
be presumed a member of Beer's New foundation,
and thus afford a glimpse of its having originated
soon after the commencement of the reign of Queen
Elizabeth.

By will dated 4th April, 1572, John Beer, esq.
directed that his "Poor-Hospital or Spital-house of our
"saviour Jesus Christ, with all the lands to the same,
"whereof" he "was Founder, should continue and be
"employed for and to the poor, impotent, sick, diseased,
"and lame people, then to inhabit and enjoy the same
"to the best use they can, and in as ample manner and
"form as they have had and enjoyed the same at any
"time heretofore... And the ruler and governor of the
"said Poor-hospital and Spital-house, and all such
"sick, diseased, lame, and decrepid people, as shall
"be from time to time received and admitted into
"the said house, shall be *nominated, chosen, admitted,*
"and *appointed* by the said Henry Beer, my son, and
"such other" his, the testator's "heirs male, and heirs
"general coming of testator's body lawfully begotten;
"and by such *other* as thereafter should *have, enjoy,*

"and *inhabit* in his manor or mansion-house called
"HORSMANS, if the laws of this realm will permit or
"suffer; otherwise, the said Poor-house, or Hospital,
"with the lands to the same, to remain to his son
"Henry, and his heirs, as here limited and appointed."
The will does not specify the lands, nor provide for
repairs.*

From this and the subsequent extract it is evident
the hospital then consisted of a single mansion :—that
the inmates were lodged in the several apartments, and
were regulated by a person bearing the title of governor
instead of prior.

1635. Sixty years afterwards a lawsuit arose between
the churchwardens of Dartford and the Twisletons,
then heirs and proprietors of the late John Beer's estate,
respecting this and the Alms-house charity in Lowfield-
street instituted by that gentleman, when the court of
Chancery appointed Sir Anthony Weldon, knt., and
Richard Champneis, esq., arbitrators, to settle the same,
who accordingly ordered

First. The Spital-houses and lands in the complainants' (the churchwarden's) bill mentioned, should remain and continue for ever,
to the use and relief of the poor only of the parish of Dartford,
and that John Twisleton the elder, should give information, as

---

* Certainly the lands appropriated to the support of the ancient
hospital were then well known, but Beer, like the preceding founder, in
his anxiety to preserve the patronage and government to his descendants, endangered the stability of the hospital, by neglecting to execute
some public instrument of endowment,—thereby rendering the lands
perpetually liable to become merged in some crafty owner of the
Horsman estate. And subsequent events shew this would have speedily
occurred had not the parish officers by a suit in Chancery, compelled his
descendant to furnish the annexed specification.

near as he could, of the quantity of acres belonging thereunto, unto the churchwardens of Dartford.

That the said John Twisleton the elder, his heirs and assigns, and the *owners* and *proprietors* of Horseman's Place, should have the election and nomination of those who shall from time to time dwell in the Spital houses, or Alms houses in Low-field Street, or receive pensions out of the land belonging thereunto.

That the churchwardens shall set down the names of six poor people, out of which Mr. Twisleton, his heirs, or *the owners* of Horsman's Place,* when any vacancy in the Spital house occurs, shall cause it to be filled in six months, otherwise the election to fall to the churchwardens of Dartford; or in case Mr. Twisleton, his heirs, or the owner, or proprietor dwelling in Horsemans' Place did for six months after such vacancy neglect or refuse to nominate, then the churchwardens to nominate such poor of Dartford, without the lett or hindrance of the said John Twisleton, his heirs and assigns as aforesaid.

That in case of vacancy when there is no *owner* or *proprietor inhabiting Horsman's Place*, then the churchwardens *shall appoint* such *poor, aged, lame, or impotent persons*, as have been *ancient inhabitants of Dartford*, of good reputation.

That the churchwardens for the time being, with the privity of the said John Twisleton, his heirs, and successors, should for ever thereafter make leases and let to farm to the best value, the barn and lands belonging unto the Spital-house, and out of the

---

* In 1831, Mr. Storey's *right* to "appoint the Indwellers of the Spital Houses, and to be a consenting party to the leases of the Spital lands, "*as the owner and occupier of Horsman's Place*," being questioned by the parish officers, Mr. S. took the *opinion* of Mr. Knight, of the Chancery bar, on the subject, which being decidedly *in favor of his claim*, his Solicitor duly announced the same to Messrs. David James and J. Snowden, the Churchwardens, and, according to the above Award, the claim has ever since been admitted.

rents and profits, pay and discharge all former rents, quit-rents, and other dues from the said premises, and repair and maintain the said House and edifices thereunto belonging. But if any arrears of rent, whether quit-rent or other rent-charge, should be behind during the time it formerly was enjoyed by a Spital-man, then such arrears to be paid out of the profits of the land belonging thereunto.

That the churchwardens for the time being, once in every year, when they pass their accounts to the parishioners at a public meeting, pass an account also to Mr Twisleton, his heirs and assigns, if present, and unto the said parishioners, of all the rents and profits they have received of the said tenement.

That at the charge of the said Churchwardens, the Spital House be divided into two small tenements, and as many of the poor of the quality aforesaid, be in them placed, as the rents, revenues and profit of the premises may conveniently maintain.

For the maintenance of this Award, a bond of £100 was required from Mr. Twisleton, which was lodged in the Vestry Room of Dartford Church; it is dated 20th January, 1635.

In pursuance of this decree, the following "*Particular of the Lands belonging to the Spital House in Dartford*," was given, and entered in the Churchwardens' books.

IMPRIMIS. *The Spittle-House*, the *barn*, the *orchard* or *croft* adjoining.

2. *Two Closes of arable land*, containing by estimation, nine acres, lying together on the south side of the highway leading from Dartford to Crayford, in the tenure of Thomas Smart.

3. *One Close of arable land* lying upon Dartford-heath, con-

taining by estimation, one acre, in tenure of the same Thomas.

4. *One Close of arable land* lying toward the way next which leadeth unto a farm called Joyces, by the Fresh-marsh, containing one acre and a half in tenure of John Shott.

5. *One Close of arable land* lying in Dartford Salt-marsh, in tenure of the said John Shott ; one half acre thereof lying in the hither end of the said marsh toward the lady Darcie's land, last toward Bugden's land, next toward Tilden's land north, and upon land in the tenure of Henry Staple south ; one other half acre thereof lyeth in the hither end of the said marsh toward the common sewer north, towards the land of Mr. Throgmorton south, and next toward the land of Sir Henry Appleton, knt. ; lastly, the other half acre thereof lieth on the hither end of the said marsh toward the land of the said Mr. Throckmorton north, toward the land of the lady Darcie south, toward the land of Mr. John Walter, and toward the land belonging to a fancie of Mr. Twisleton's, in Wilmington, west.*

The Churchwardens' books intimate that from this period, the parish officers undertook the management of the Spital revenues; and in 1646, granted a lease of the ten acres of land on the Crayford road, and the Close at the back of the hospital, to Iacanimshawe Staple, of Dartford, widow.† for twelve years; this

---

* It is much to be regretted that the ancient and curious Vestry and Churchwardens' Book containing this document is now (1842) missing from the parish archives. Fortunately, at the commencement of the author's researches into the parish antiquities, Mr. G. Payne, then churchwarden, permitted him to copy the most interesting memoranda, which have therefore been preserved, and are used in the present work.   † Parish Records, No. 19.

lease she surrendered in 1657 to Robert Van Ransborough, a brewer, in Dartford.*

---

* Icanimshawe Staple occupied a tenement on the north side of Spital-street called the Blue Anchor, or One Bird in Hand or Two in Bush.—In 1676 part of the Hospital endowment called "the Spital lands" described as one acre joining the Spital house westward, and nine acres adjoining the Crayford road, were leased to Thomas and Richard Fielder, father and son, of Stanham; and in 1697 the vicar and churchwardens granted them on lease to Thomas Waller for twenty-one years at £10 a year. In 1776 the close and lands were in the occupation of Mrs. Sarah Glover at a rental of £17 per annum; but at a public meeting held for that purpose 14th June, 1787, these three pieces of land, were then with consent of Richard Leigh, Esq. (the owner of the estates heretofore belonging to Horsman's Place,) by the vicar and churchwarden let to Richard Sanham, on lease for twenty-one years, at the yearly rent of £24 15s. In 1814 the land adjoining the Crayford road was leased to John Morley for twenty-one years, at £30 per ann. for the two first years, and £40 for the last nineteen, subject to covenants on the part of the lessee to build thereon and plant the land with fruit trees. The public house then called the Wellington, together with a cottage and other buildings were erected on part of the land, and were long occupied by the said John Morley: but the public-house was assigned for the remainder of the term, with consent of the churchwardens, to Mr. Wheelhouse This lease expired Michaelmas, 1841, when the whole Wellington estate was re-let by tender to Mr. William Pittock for twenty-one years at the annual rent of £116, payable quarterly. *Parish Records. Nos* 80. 92. 101. *Landale.* 42---45. *Churchwardens' Account Book.*

The piece of land behind the Alms-houses was in 1809 leased to William Dockery for twenty-one years at £7 8s. per annum. In 1826 the National School was erected on part of the last mentioned land, in consequence of which a new lease was granted to Mr. Richard Tippetts the then occupier of the remainder of the land, for twenty-one years, from Michaelmas, 1825, at £6 per annum; and a lease was granted of the site of the School, etc., to the Rev. George Heberden, vicar, David James, and Thomas Broadley

In 1660 John Twisleton, Esq., in consideration of eight pounds in cash paid to him by John Darker and other Feoffees of estates given to the use of the Dartford poor, and of their relinquishing and releasing to him one acre of land called the Poors' Acre, situated on the south side of Heath lane, bordering on Dartford Heath, (given by his grandfather John Beer to the Spital House,) conveyed to the above-named trustees John Darker, and others, the remaining part of the Loam-Pit field;* directing *one third* of the yearly issue to be applied to the same use as the said Poors' Acre was limited, viz. to the Alms House in Spital street,— and the other *two thirds* to be distributed yearly to such poor of the parish as the feoffees and churchwardens shall name on Easter Monday in vestry.†

Fooks, as trustees, for sixty years, from Michaelmas, 1826, at £5 per annum. The field is in the occupation of Mr. George Cooke. *Book of Benefactions. MS.* 180. *Leases in Parish Archives. Churchwardens' Accounts —Easter,* A.D. 1842.

* In ancient times when most of the houses in Dartford were constructed of timber frame-work and covered with plaster, the inhabitants were allowed the valuable privilege of digging loam in the Loam-pits freely. One acre had been given to the parish for this purpose as early as 1344, by Richard Sone of Dartford, and another by John Beer, 1572, both of which the vicar and churchwardens, in 1638, let to Edward Kippis, carpenter, for a term of years at 10s. per ann, on condition of his digging and selling loam at 6d. a load : but in 1699, when the loam-pit field was let to William Johnson, at 40s yearly, liberty was allowed for any parishioner to dig loam so that he did no wilful damage. *Parish Records. Nos.* 34. 29. 131. 108. *Landale passim.*

† Mr. Twisleton's benefaction could not amount to an acre in the Loam-pit field; and lest some succeeding feoffees might question his title to the Poors' Acre, the feoffees by another Indenture covenanted that if at any time the Poors' Acre was taken away from the

In 1704, the Hospital being completely decayed and ruinous, it was re-built by its patron Mr. Twisleton, in its present form; and the following description, placed in front of the Edifice.

THIS HOSPITAL (A VERY ANCIENT CHARITY, BEGUN AND VOLUNTARILY CONTINUED FOR SEVERAL GENERATIONS BY THE HORSMAN'S OF HORSMAN'S PLACE, IN THIS PARISH, WAS BY THE LAST WILL AND TESTAMENT OF JOHN BYER, OF HORSMAN'S PLACE, ESQ., BEARING DATE THE 4TH APRIL, 1572,) FOUNDED BY THE NAME OF THE HOSPITAL OF OUR SAVIOUR, THE LORD JESUS CHRIST, IN DARTFORD, AND ENDOWED WITH LANDS FOR EVER, FOR THE USE OF THE POOR OF THE SAID PARISH, WHICH LANDS WERE ALSO TO MAINTAIN THE REPAIR OF THE BUILDINGS. BUT THE SAME BEING DECAYED AND RUINOUS, IN FURTHER CHARITY TO THE POOR, AND OUT OF A GRATEFUL REGARD TO THE MEMORY OF HIS PREDECESSORS AND ANCESTORS, OWNERS OF THE SAID ESTATE, JOHN TWISLETON, OF HORSMAN'S PLACE, ESQ., DID AT HIS OWN PROPER COST AND CHARGES NEW BUILT AND ENLARGED THIS HOSPITAL, IN THE YEAR OF OUR LORD, 1704.

John Twisleton, Esq., by his will, dated the 7th July, 1704, proved in the Prerogative Court of Canterbury, "desires his posterity, honestly and carefully from time to time, for ever thereafter, to repair the Spittal-house at Dartford, and all the fences, well, and house of office thereunto belonging; rebuilt by him, at his own charge, in the then present year of our Lord God, 1704, containing nine rooms, and as many

---

said John Twisleton, his heirs or assigns, the said trustees, or their successors should re-convey to him one acre of the above-mentioned Loam-pit piece —The same year, [1660] Mr. Twisleton took a lease of the Loam-pit field at 29s. a year for twenty-one years. In 1699 it was let to William Johnson, Victualler, for eleven years, at 40s. a year; George Swift, was lessee at the same rent in 1716; Edward Rawlings in 1776, at a rental of £5 6s. 3d. In 1794, Charles Hugget, (as trustee for Mr. Thomas Hall,) at £5 5s.; and the field is now in the occupation of Mr. Thomas Hodsoll, at a rental of £12. per annum. *Vide Book of Benefactions*, 175,—178. *Churchwardens' Account Book.*

P

outlets, to every room an outlet." And he thereby declared his whole estate in Kent, and Barley in Yorkshire, should be charged for repairs of the said Spittalhouse as aforesaid, for ever.

On the sale of Horsman's Place with other portions of the Twisleton estates by Williams and Smith, (circa 1770,) to Richard Leigh, Esq., the repairs and maintenance of the structure of the Spital Alms Houses were charged upon two pieces of land adjoining Brickhill wood near Dartford Heath,* which repairs Mr. Leigh has accordingly hitherto done, and in consequence, claimed the right of presentation; but since 1831, Mr. Storey, as the proprietor and occupier of Horsman's Place has exercised the right.

The present annual revenues of the Spital-Houses were thus specified in the Churchwardens' Accounts, Easter, 1842:

	£	s.	d.
For one year's rent of a field at the back of the Spital Houses, in the occupation of Richard Tippetts, Esq.	6	0	3
One year's rent of the site of the National School	5	0	0
Two-thirds† of the rent of the Loam-pits, let to Thomas Hodsoll at £12. per annum.	8	0	0
The late Wellington, or Rising Sun, estate, let on lease to William Pittock for 21 years	116	0	0
One year's rent for a piece of land next the Stone-Mason's yard held by Mr. Geo. Cooke from 1831, for twenty-one years	8	0	0
	£143	5	0

---

* Memorandum made in 1776, in the Book of Benefactions. p. 178.

† Only four pounds, the amount of one third of the Loam-pit rent

There are now nine widows inhabiting the Spital Houses, each of whom receives one pound per month, and nine sacks of coals per annum, and from the increased revenues, the churchwardens have been enabled during the last twelvemonth, to give an additional benefaction, of one pound to each of the inmates, which they hope further to increase, when all the present demands upon the charity have been paid.

Each house consists of one large room, together with a pantry, or wash-house, the whole are situated on the ground floor.

---

ought to be carried to this Account, and £5 5s. the rent of the Marsh lands (called the *Manor-way piece, Bald Holland Common piece*, and *Stony croft*,) now let to Mr. Thomas Parkhurst added thereto. This would make the income about £144 5s. per annum. Mr. Snowden, the present churchwarden, proposes to rectify these accounts if continued in office, and as the widow's incomes have so greatly increased, to exclude them from receiving the other parish charities, of which they have been heretofore accustomed to partake.—The Spital Marsh lands were in 1776, in the occupation of Mrs. Anne Pettet at £2 10s. per annum. The following year they were leased to Hussey Fleet for twenty-one years at the yearly rent of £5; in 1799, they were held by Richard Kirke for the same term at £10 10s.; but in 1824, Mr. Edward Rawlings obtained a lease of them at half that rental.

Richard Leigh, esq., of Hawley-house, on whom the repairs of the Spital-house devolved, was the last male descendant of one of the most ancient families in the kingdom, by its alliances connected with many of the highest nobility. Mr. Leigh was a man of superior attainments, and possessed a most extensive knowledge of the world, as well as of the local history of the neighbourhood. To him the author is indebted for some of the most valuable communications. Mr. Leigh married Miss Moon, but has left no issue. He died in Mount-street, London, Oct. 9th, 1841.

FOUR ALMS-HOUSES IN LOWFIELD-STREET.

Some time before his decease John Beer, (or Byer as his name is sometimes written,) who then inhabited Horsman's Place, erected four Alms-Houses next adjoining to his mansion or manor-house in Lowfield street, to each of which he allotted a garden, and ordained the said houses "to be employed and continue for ever, for "the dwelling of four poor, aged, lame, and impotent "people, *not able to labour for their living*, and such as shall "be of *good and godly behaviour*."

The nomination and appointment of these four persons, in common with those of the Spital House, by the said John Beer's last will and testament, (dated as aforesaid 4th April, 1572,) were vested in Henry Beer his son, his heirs and assigns, or such others as should own and inhabit Horsman's Place, and the testator directed that there "should be given to that use and behoof *"Twenty six shillings and eightpence,* "annually, that is to say, *quarterly, to every of them* *"Twenty-pence;"** which sums were made chargeable on certain lands and tenements named in the said will,† which were "to maintain and keep the said Alms-

---

* Equivalent to four times the value of money in the present day.

† The lands and tenements are thus recited in the testator's will: (1) *Four tenements* with four gardens, lying and being on the north and west sides of the great house, or curtilage; (2) a tenement with a garden or orchard in the tenure of John Terrett; (3) a tenement with a garden and orchard, in the tenure of Holland the cooper; (4) a tenement with a garden or orchard, in the tenure of John

"Houses with *sufficient reparations, as often as need shall* "*require.*"

Master; and (5) a corner tenement with a garden or orchard;— all being situated in *Lofeld-street*, next *Wood-street* (Heath-lane), leading to Dartford-heath. (6) A croft of land, with three yards of wood adjoining to the same, *where the Loam-pits and Sand-pits of late where made*, called *Bose-Croft*, otherwise the *Haske*, containing six acres of land and woods. (7) A parcel of land containing three yards, with two houses [built] by old William Parker* upon the same, lying to the north of the common Inn called *the Swan* (8) A parcel of land, containing one acre demy, or more or less, (lying in the cherry garden where is a hall there,† parcel of the revenues of the late Monastery of Dartford, lying within and next the lands of the late Chantry of Stampits,) now in the occupation and tenure of Sir George Blagg, knt. deceased, and of his assigns. (9) Also, all testator's part parcel of meadow, enclosed with another parcel of meadow, next *Hedge-mead*,‡ appertaining to *Rochester-Bridge*, together with (10) all his Quit-Rents and Services in Dartford aforesaid. (11) A parcel of land, containing four acres, called *Little Wirfield* ; (12) also an acre and a half of land lying in the land called *Stokkisherst*, in *Wilmington*, now in the tenure of Peter Smith ; (13) also a woodland called *Wetcroft-Spring*, containing three acres ; also (14) another parcel of land called *Watersgrove*, containing two acres demy, adjoining Wetcroft-Spring ; (15) also another acre of woodland, lying on the south side of the highway *opposite* Wetcroft-Spring ; (16) also a wood and woodland, containing by estimation twenty-three acres, called *Hooke and Fair-pit lands* : (16) also a yearly Rent-charge coming out of the lands of William Hoope—and now Thomas Dumee—all which premises last recited are lying in *Wilmington* aforesaid (19) Also after the decease of Barnard Pattinson, the tenement and garden to him bequeathed, together with all the lands, tenements, and hereditaments

---

* An extract from William Parker's will is given, p. 100.

† Coppyd, or Copt-Hall near Stampits at the back of the Priory. It was held by John Bere, A D. 1539 of Temples manor, at four shillings quit rent. Sir George Blagg, the subsequent proprietor, 1572, was a gentleman of the bedchamber to Henry VIII. he left a widow named Dorothy, and a daughter named Hester, afterwards maid of honor. *Gages Suffolk*, 52.

‡ Near Temperley's Wharf, Waterside.

The litigation which ensued between John Twisleton, of Broughton-Castle, co. Oxon, Esq., and the Rev. Thomas Cokshutt, (although the trial at Maidstone, A.D. 1757, established the right of the former to Horsman's Place, and the rest of the entailed estates,* lately belonging to John Twisleton, deceased,) involved the successful claimant in such heavy legal expences, that he found it necessary to mortgage the whole of the recovered property to Messrs. Williams and Smith, his attorneys, who conducted the suit.   And in 1768, Thomas Twisleton, his son, afterwards tenth Baron Say and Sele, conveyed Horsman's Place, together with the whole of his estates in Dartford, to the same gentlemen.

By a memorandum made in the Book of Benefactions A.D. 1776, the four Alms-Houses were then repaired and maintained by the above-named Thomas Williams and Thomas Smith, out of that part of Mr. Twisleton's estates purchased by them.   The payment of twenty-eight shillings per annum, or three shillings and six-pence half-yearly, to each inmate of the Alms-houses, as well as the reparation of their several dwellings, was ultimately settled upon the house and offices held by those gentlemen in the High-street, Dartford.†

---

whatsoever belonging to the said Joan Beer, at the time of his decease, and not otherwise by deed or grant assigned, or by this his last will and testament given or bequeathed.

* John Twisleton the last descendant of Byer, died in 1757, without issue, leaving his estates by will to his nephew, Thomas Cockshot. All those entailed were claimed and recovered by John Twisleton of Broughton Castle, a distant relation and the next heir male.

† The premises then consisted of two tenements ascended by several steps; the western, nearest Hithe-street, was inhabited by

The premises eventually became the sole property of Mr. Thomas Williams, who having granted a long lease to John, his nephew and successor, settled it upon his great-nephews, John Williams, jun., and his brother Thomas. About 1800, John Williams, sen. rebuilt the house;--but his sons [circa 1806,] sold their reversionary and life-interest therein, to John Hills,* a victualler in Dartford,

Smith, and the other by Williams J. Tinsley, a bricklayer, was commissioned to new-front them; the parish surveyors pronounced the building insecure, and Mr. Williams retired to his seat at Horton-Kirby, (now Mrs. Muggridge's,) and never slept in it more. John Williams his nephew succeeded him in his practice about 1789, *(Vide Court Rolls of Dartford Priory.)* He had two sons, John and Thomas, upon whom their great-uncle settled many of his Dartford estates.— Both acquired expensive habits, and during their father's life time, sold their reversionary and life-interests in the property. John having run through the whole, poisoned himself at the Wheatsheaf,† a public house adjoining the Town Hall, about 1808; Thomas retired into the country, and is since dead. That house continued to be occupied as an attorney's office for many years, and in 1840 was advertised for sale by the heirs of the late Thomas Walker. The particulars then published, describe it as a leasehold dwelling house, let to John Hayward, esq, on lease for the remainder of a term of forty-six years wanting a day from Michaelmas, 1823, at a rental of £205 per annum The premises are stated to be held by the lessor, for the term of the lease, at a yearly rent of £30, subject to an annual quit-rent of six shillings to the manor of Dartford Rectory, and also to the charge of *repairing, maintaining and supporting* of Four Alms-Houses in Lowfield-street, Dartford, and to the payment half-yearly, of 3s. 4d., to each of the poor in-dwellers therein, at Michaelmas and Christmas.

* John Hills kept the Eight Bells:—was originally a post-boy so much addicted to cards that it is said having once lost all his money he proposed gambling for his clothes, and in the hilarity of the moment exclaimed 'now I am stark-naked Jack.' The soubriquet adhered

† Is this another instance of the *usual misfortune* attendant in every age on the owners of ancient church lands? *See page* 172.

who bequeathed the premises to Sarah, daughter of Abraham Nettlefold, his son-in-law, now wife of Mr. Weaver. *Mr. Nettlefold's agent pays 14s., half-yearly, as settled by Mr. Williams, and repairs the Alms-houses.*

The mode of appointment of the in-dwellers of these Alms-houses, was by the Chancery arbitrators, (A.D. 1635,) directed to be precisely similar to that of the Spital Houses, namely, at every vacancy, the churchwardens were to set down the names of six poor persons possessing the required qualifications,—out of this list, the owner or proprietor dwelling in Horsman's Place, shall select one, and if he omits or declines the selection for six months, the churchwardens are to nominate without let or hindrance.

---

to him ever afterwards. Subsequently marrying Mrs. Nettlefold, the landlady of the above house (1791), and diligently attending to business, he acquired considerable property in the town and neighbourhood; and there is an entry in the Court-Rolls of the Manor of Dartford Rectory, which speaks much for his good humour under unpleasant circumstances. It is therein recorded that while sitting as a juror in the Court-Leet A.D. 1794, he was PRESENTED "for keeping false measures, to wit, pewter pots;"—and the charge proved by producing the pots in court. His compeers fined him three guineas—adjudged the measures forfeited, and ordered them to be rendered unfit for use by their own officer. What proves he acquiesced in the decision, is, that he signed the verdict against himself in the Minutes of the court. Numerous stories are rife concerning his gambling tricks; people tell how he seated his opponents beneath a large mirror, overlooked their hands and contrived to cheat them out of their property. Certainly in those days, much gambling was notoriously carried on in the back rooms of public houses in Dartford, and losers almost always invariably accused winners of unfair practices—At his death, Feb. 1816, he bequeathed his property chiefly among his wife's children by a former husband.

THE GRAMMAR SCHOOL.

In 1576 (19 Eliz.) William Vaughan, of Erith, esq., yeoman of the queen's chamber,* Edward Gwyn, mercer, of the city of London, and William Death, gent. then lord of the manor of Charles, in Dartford, conveyed a messuage or tenement with a *garden* and backside, in the High street, Dartford,† heretofore their joint inheritance to Thomas Ashley, and twenty-seven other persons, in trust, to let it for the best rent, and after deducting the expenses for repairs, quit-rent and other just allowances, to apply the remaining rent towards the supporting of an honest sufficient and learned man in grammar, for teaching, instructing, and eruditing the children of the town of Dartford aforesaid, in the knowledge of grammar.‡

---

* William Vaughan was a gentleman of the wardrobe to Henry VIII. who in 1536, obtained a grant of the manor of Bignors. *Fee Farm Rolls.* He was buried at Dartford 8th May, 1580. *Par. Reg.*

† The situation of the messuage, garden, and premises, are thus described in the instrument "abbutting towards the east to a tenement "and garden of Robert Heath, gent. (*now Mr. Fleet's*); to the High-street "on the north; to a tenement and garden of Robert Rowed, known by "the name of the Red Lion, (*now the Post Boys,*) to the west; and to the "lands of Anthony Poulter towards the south (now also *appertaining to* "*the same hostelry*).

‡ The trust-deed of 1660 provides for the continuance of this charity, that when only four trustees are left, they shall convey the premises and tenements to two others, who within twenty-eight days shall re-convey and settle the same upon sixteen other persons of the parish of Dartford, nominated by the four surviving feoffees, and the vicar and churchwardens of Dartford, upon trust, and so to be continued from time to time for ever. *Book of Benefact.* 228.

This School immediately after its establishment was appointed to be held in the room or loft above the Corn Market-house* then standing on the south side of the High street, Dartford, and seems to have been continued therein beyond the middle of the following century,† but amidst the confusion which followed the civil wars the feoffees so violated their trust, that after the re-establishment of order under Charles II, it was deemed necessary to appoint commissioners to investigate this Charity. Their deed dat. 5th July, 1678, set forth that Edward James of the town of Dartford had wrongfully possessed himself of the loft or room over the Corn Market-house, heretofore the school-room, and up to that time pertinaciously detained it ;‡—and also that Lydia Twisleton, widow,¶ under a pretended lease, held and occupied the messuage in the High-street, the rent of which should be applied to the maintenance of the Free Grammar-school.—To remedy these malversions the commissioners, by virtue of their powers, adjudged the lease void, directed the premises to be let for the best rent, and the same to be applied for the benefit of the charity ; and they furthermore

---

* From this direction, and the fact of the Corn Market-house belonging to the trustees, there can be no doubt that they built it at the foundation of the school, on the site of the market-cross.

† William Stanley temp. Jac. I. gave by will, £5 "to repair the school-howse and markett-howse at Dartford." *Reg. Test.* xiv. 250.

‡ Edward Barnard was assessed at 5s. for it, 1675. *Overseer's Accts.*

¶ Probably a poor relation placed therein by the influence of the Twisletons of Horsman's Place : in 1667 the overseers paid her a weekly allowance for keeping Mason's child. She died about 1687, for the following year goody Holmes was paid 4s. weekly for keeping her two children. *Overseer's Accounts*

ordered the school loft to be restored to the surviving feoffees, and directed it to be employed thereafter as a School, and for no other purpose whatsoever.*

How long the trustees continued the Grammar-school in the restored loft, does not clearly appear; its scanty revenue eventually did not enable the trustees to procure a master of competent erudition to instruct the pupils in grammar learning. They were therefore induced to place the alumni of the foundation under the master of a private seminary in the town, who instructed them in the school attached to his own residence with his other scholars. The ancient school-room consequently became unoccupied—was let to private individuals as a storehouse, and in the next century (1730,) leased to Mr. Durrant a miller, and afterward occupied by Henry Wooden, and John Pettit.†

It is clear that the majority of individuals who successively assumed the office of *schoolmaster* in Dartford after the removal of the Grammar-school from the Market-house, and until the middle of the following century, were men of inferior literary attainments, and that the feoffees either considered all of them *incapable* of giving the sound instruction demanded by the rules of the institution,—or from the scanty number of applicants *inferred* that the townsmen considered it *unnecessary* to educate their children in *classical literature* then *solely professed* to be taught by the master. Hence for upwards of fifty years (although perhaps not in strict succession,) the trus-

* *Book of Benefactions.* 255. James however held it two years longer, and in Oct. 1680, it was assessed to him at £3., per annum.

† Vestry and Parochial Assessment Books, sub anno.

tees did not think it necessary to appoint any master to the office.—The savings from the rents were allowed to accumulate and invested in the South Sea Annuities to the amount of £700 Stock.

At length, in 1765, James Sanham received the appointment of master with a *limited* number of scholars on the foundation;* like his last predecessors, he held it in connection with a private school. The annual revenues then consisted of the rental of the house in the High-street, (the original endowment,) the rent of the market-loft; the rent-charge of 40*s*. per annum, issuing out of the farm called Hammonds, at Halsted;† and the interest of the South Sea Annuities.

---

* Limited to six *only!* whereas the founders instituted the school for all the children in the town who would *accept education* thereof

† Near the commencement of the seventeenth century John Beare by will, gave to the master of Dartford Grammar School 40*s*., yearly, charged on fifteen acres of land belonging to a farm called Hammonds, in Halsted, Kent, to teach two boys of Swanscomb parish for ever. A decree of Commissioners for Charitable Uses dated 1609, states that the tenement of Hammonds came into possession of Thomas Walker, esq., who for two years before the date of the decree did not pay the 40*s*., to the schoolmaster although regularly demanded: the said commissioners decreed that Walker should forthwith pay to John Cottesford the schoolmaster the £4., owing, and that he and his heirs, or the possessors of the tenement of Hammonds, should ever hereafter pay the rent half-yearly, in equal moieties at lady-day and michaelmas, to the school-master at Dartford so long as there should be any grammar teaching there: and that whenever the rent is due and left unpaid the said schoolmaster should have liberty to distrain on the land and tenement, and hold the distress until full payment is made. *Par. Rec. No.* 102. *Land.* 29. This payment was continued by the successive proprietors down to lord Vere, and received by Mr. Sanham from his lordship's steward from 1766 to 1783. Lord Vere sold the estate to Mr. William Brookes, and in 1814 they were purchased by Mr. Pemell; but the rent charge was never paid after Mr. Sanham's time.

But at this period the increased trade, and traffic through the town had rendered the frequent blockade of the High-street occasioned by the Market-house and shambles a perfect nuisance, to induce the feoffees of the school to consent to its removal, John Calcraft of Ingress park, esq., offered to settle on the institution a rent-charge of similar amount to the rental of the market-loft ; the offer being accepted, the said gentleman granted a perpetual rent-charge of £6. 15s., payable out of Black-dale farm in the parish of Darenth.* In the

---

* The indenture dated March 20th, 9 Geo. III. 1769, between John Calcraft, of Ingress, esq , on the first part ; Charles Morgan, of Treago, co. Hereford, esq., and Mary his wife, on the second ; John Garrett, John Pettit, Mark Fielder, Benjamin Pettit, Edward Stigger, Thomas Smith, William Quelch, the elder, William Quelch, the younger, Thomas Williams, John Budgen, James Lawford, George Hards, Thomas Brandon, Robert Robins, and Richard Reeves, (feoffees of the Grammar school,) all of Dartford, on the third part ; after reciting—That the feoffees or trustees, were seized and possessed of a certain room or loft over the Corn Market-house, which was formerly used and employed for a schoolmaster to teach and instruct the boys of the said town, reputed to be the school-house for that purpose—That the said Charles Morgan, and Mary his wife, in right of the said Mary, are entitled to the said Corn Market-house aforesaid, the room or loft of which was heretofore used as the school-house,* and also to the building adjoining thereto, which hath been used and occupied as the butcher's shambles in the said town—That the said Corn Market-house, and the room or loft over the same, are grown very old and ruinous, and by reason of the great thoroughfare are great obstructions to pas-

---

* The Market-house consisted of a long room supported on pillars, the edifice itself belonged to the feoffees—The tolls of the market beneath, to the lord of the manor. Mr. Williams, the steward, drew up the above instrument, and this may account for its strong colouring in favour of Mr. Morgan's rights.

year 1769, the house and buildings given by W. Vaughan etc. in the High-street being very old and ruinous, the feoffees took them down, and with the produce of the said £700 built a new house, which was afterwards known as the Wheat-sheaf, erected a *new Market-house* on a part of the garden at the back thereof, and a pent-house for the butcher's shambles along the west side of the premises to the cage. They also allotted the space beneath the Market-house and the premises

---

sengers passing and re-passing—That the said feoffees are possessed of certain premises near the High-street, on part whereof a convenient Market-house and shambles may be erected in lieu of the old one, by which means the estate of the feoffees may be greatly benefited—That the said John Calcraft, in order to forward the removal of the old building, hath made a voluntary offer to the feoffees, to grant to them and their successors a clear annuity or yearly rent-charge, out of lands hereinafter mentioned, of £6 15s., in lieu of the room over the Corn Market-house, and of and for so much ground belonging to the said feoffees near the High-street, as shall be sufficient to erect a *new Market-house*, and shambles upon, which said rent-charge, being more than the value of the said loft and ground, the said feoffees have as far as in them lies, agreed to accept—That the inhabitants of the said town and neighbourhood encouraged by the generous offer of the said John Calcraft, have requested the said Charles Morgan, and Mary his wife, to consent to the removal of the old Corn Market-house and shambles, and proposed in lieu thereof, to build and erect by subscription, a new Corn Market-house and shambles on the said ground to be assigned for that purpose: to which request and proposal the said Charles Morgan and Mary his wife, have assented—And whereas, the ground whereon the said Market-house and shambles has been agreed to be built has been set out and assigned, and is to contain the several dimensions herein set forth, that is to say, the ground from the High-street intended for a way to the said market and shambles, contains in front from east to

which extended from the street nearly to the southern
extremity of the Market-house, for the site of the market,
and a passage thereunto; which Market, they intended
should be ever thereafter held on the premises.   The
tolls of the market heretofore held in the High street

---

west, 13 feet, more or less; and from east to west on the north
end thereof, 12 feet or thereabouts; and on the west side thereof,
from the said High-street southward, 47 feet, or thereabouts; and
the ground assigned for the said Market-house and shambles, and
for a convenient way and passage to the same, contains from the
end of such way or passage in the High-street, upon a break eastward, 21 feet or thereabouts; and from thence southward, on the
said east side next the premises of John Pettit, esq., 45 feet, or
thereabouts; and in the rear or back part thereof, next the lands of
William Hollingworth from south to north to the ground on which
the said cage or stocks are intended to be built by the inhabitants
of the parish of Dartford, 82 feet or thereabouts—the plan whereof
is more particularly delineated in the margin [of the deed itself].
THIS INDENTURE WITNESSETH that in pursuance and performance
of the agreements and covenants between the said Charles Morgan
and Mary his wife, and the said feoffees, that the old Corn Market-
house, shambles, etc., shall be removed, the said Charles Morgan
and Mary his wife, their heirs and assigns, shall for ever henceforth
have and peaceably enjoy the aforesaid ground so assigned, in as
full and ample manner as they enjoyed the said old Market-house:
and the sum of ten shillings of lawful money of Great Britain having been well and truly paid in hand to the said John Calcraft, by
John Garratt and the rest of the feoffees before the execution of
these presents,—John Calcraft, for this, and divers other considerations, hath granted and confirmed one Annuity or Rent-charge of
£6 15s., issuing and payable out of a messuage, barn, stable,
backside, garden, or orchard, situate in the parish of Darenth, or
Sutton-at-Hone, co. Kent, formerly in tenure of George Middleton,
afterwards of William Lane the younger, then of Thomas Under-
hill, now of George Cooper, or his under-tenants, to receive the said
annuity or rent-charge to the use of the said John Garrett and the

belonged to the lord of the manor, and on its removal
to a new site were secured to him by a special clause
in the indenture. The instrument also states that to
induce Charles Morgan, esq., and Mary his wife to
consent to the removal of the old Market and shambles
from the High-street, the inhabitants of the town

---

other feoffees, free from all expenses, at the two several feasts of
Michaelmas and the Annunciation, upon special trust, for supporting
and maintaining one sober and sufficiently learned man in grammar, for
teaching, instructing and eruditing of children in the town of Dartford
in knowledge of grammar, according to the pious and charitable intent
of William Vaughan, formerly of Erith, one of the grooms of the
chamber to queen Elizabeth, Edward Green [Gwyn], heretofore citizen
and grocer [mercer], of London, and William Death, formerly of
Dartford aforesaid, gentleman, expressed and set down in a deed of
feoffment made and executed to Thomas Apsley and twenty-seven other
persons, bearing date 24th March, 18 Eliz.: And upon this further trust
and confidence reposed in them—that so often as the said feoffees by
death or removal out of the parish of Dartford are reduced to the
number of ten or under, then they shall convey the rent-charge unto two
or more honest and able persons of Dartford and their heirs, upon
condition that the said two or more persons, within twenty-eight days,
shall convey the said rent-charge to twenty or more persons of Dartford
nominated and appointed by the said surviving feoffees and by the
vicar and churchwardens of the parish of Dartford for the time being,
upon trust aforesaid—And this to be continued from time to time
for ever, as often as death or removal of the feoffees reduce them to
ten or under—the annuity or rent-charge to be employed to such
uses as before appointed. And whenever the annuity or rent-charge
is behind for twenty-one days over the said feasts, although no
demand has been made, the feoffees are empowered to enter, distrain, and impound, until all arrears and costs are satisfied. And
the Indenture further witnesseth that in consideration of five shillings
paid by the said Charles Morgan and Mary his wife, the feoffees
do, as much as in them lies, covenant that they shall from hence-

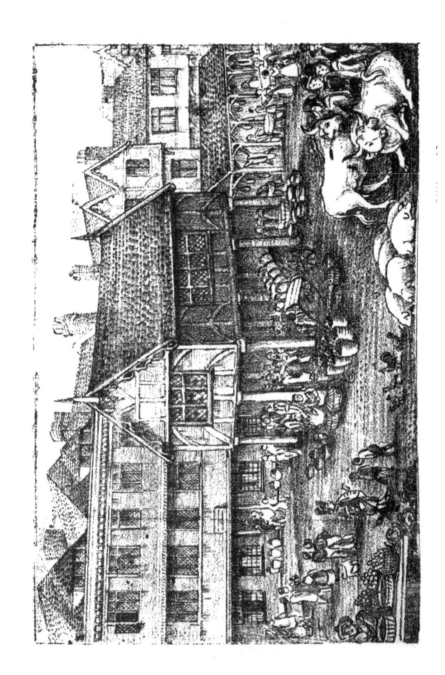

proposed to erect a *new Market-house* and *shambles* by subscription†—and that the feoffees covenanted to secure to the said gentleman and his lady, their heirs and assigns, thenceforward for ever, the peaceful enjoyment of all the assigned ground for the market and buildings erected thereon, in as full and ample manner as they had held the old Market-house, without let, molestation, claim, or demand.

---

forth enter upon and hold all that the aforesaid ground described and delineated in the margin of this deed, for the purpose of holding the corn-market and butcher's-market thereon, and erecting a Market-house and shambles, and use and exercise all the several powers and authorities which were vested in them as owners of the old Market-house, and without let, interruption, eviction, ejection, molestation or demand whatsoever of them the said feoffees, or any person claiming through them :* PROVIDED that the feoffees shall at all times be at liberty to build and erect one or more rooms over the said Market-house if they think fit for the benefit of the trust,—for which considerations the said Charles Morgan and Mary his wife consent that the old Market-house and shambles be taken down and removed out of the High-street, and such part of the materials as be fit, be used in the construction of the new Market-house and shambles as aforesaid—Signed and sealed by John Calcraft, Charles Morgan and Mary his wife, and all the trustees— *Indorsed :* Mutual agreement for removing the old Market-house and shambles in Dartford and erecting new ones, and Mr. Calcraft's grant of an annuity of £6 15s. in lieu of the School-loft over the old Market. *Ex orig. penes Aug. Morgan, cl.*

† Mr. Bell who is now (1842) upwards of ninety-four years of age and in full possession of his faculties, remembers well the old Market-house and shambles standing in the High-street, and all the particulars of its removal. He says there was *no subscription* raised for the erection of the new Market-house.

---

* This clause however, is only intended to secure the tolls and stallage in perpetuity to C. Morgan and wife ; for the feoffees being only trustees, could not convey the freehold. [In corroboration hereof, see a deed quoted respecting the Loam-pit field. *Note on page* 208.] If by any erections the market and premises are improved, the charity ought to derive a proportionate advantage, otherwise how can "the Estate of the said feoffees be *greatly benefited ?*" by the establishment of the market on that site, as stated in the above instrument, p. 222.

Q

In 1801 Richard Kirk, then tenant new fronted and
repaired the house in the High-street, called the Wheat-
sheaf,* and in consideration thereof obtained a renewal of
his lease for twenty-one years at the old rental.

On March 24th, 1819, the Commissioners appointed to
investigate Charities for the Education of the Poor,
sat at Dartford to enquire respecting this Grammar-
school.   Their Report stated that the Rev. John
Bradley was master ; that there ought to be EIGHT
boys instructed on the foundation, but the number is
incomplete† :—that the scholars were nominated at a

---

* *Book of Benefactions,* 257. Andrew Beckett in 1786 obtained a lease
of twenty-one years at £28 per ann. ; in 1795 the lease was assigned to
Richard Kirk, who enclosed the premises with gates. Kirk failed, and
his lease eventually passed to T. Caldecot, esq., but he was succeeded in
the Wheatsheaf by Clark, Peters, Mrs. Pitt, (who changed the sign to
the White Hart), Wetherell, and W. L Pearce ; the latter relinquished
the licence. When Mr. Pearce was first appointed clerk of the market
about 1815, he found it nearly deserted ; with much difficulty he persuaded some tradesmen from London to bring their goods down ; they
succeeded, and he enclosed the huckster's stalls for their use.   In 1841,
the Rev. Augustus Morgan, who, in right of his manor, claims the toll,
took down the sheds and REBUILT handsome and commodious shops upon
their site.

† Mr. Bradley told the Commissioners that the reason why the
school was not filled up was, that people who could afford to pay did
not like to send their sons to a charitable foundation ;—that others
did not like the expense of the books, and classical instruction would
be of no use to the children of such parents.   On being asked
whether he had any of the free boys who learned latin ? he said it
was not absolutely necessary for the boys to learn latin, and that he
had three or four boys who were only taught English reading,
writing, and arithmetic. The drift of the Commissioners' interrogatories
indicated they thought that the *tone* of the education ought not to

meeting of trustees, and if approved the master is bound
to receive them. The Commissioners add, that the school
was originally held in a room above the Corn Market-
house which was pulled down many years ago, but that
when a new Market-house was erected in another
situation, a room over it, now called the Town Hall, was
reserved for the use of the school, if at any time it should
be required; that at present the school is held more
commodiously in the house of the master, and the room
is let with the messuage in the High street which is
adjoining to the Market-house.

The Commissioners were informed that the rent-
charge given by John Beare on Hammonds farm had
not been paid since 1783;* and also that the Rev.
Henry Draper by will dated 8th Sept., 1691, gave to
Henry Wooden and Leonard Ansell, their heirs and

---

have been *lowered*, and if somewhat popularised, its classical advantages
fostered with the Trustees' unabated vigilance.

* When Mr. Bradley was appointed master, he went over to Halsted
to enquire, but could not find any farm of the name of Hammonds. In
1819, the Commissioners appointed to investigate Charities for Education, obtained a statement from Mr. Pemell, that he purchased the
manor of Halsted, a freehold estate called Widmores, and Clarke's
farm, the former containing 153acr. 2r., the latter about 7 acres; and
that in the printed particulars, the four lots, or some part of them was
specified as subject to a payment of £1 16s. but payment had not been
demanded for forty years. Mr. P., added, that he had sold fifty acres of
the estate, and was unable to learn what part was called Hammonds.—
The Commissioners in their Report say they are not supplied with
sufficient evidence to connect the annuity of £1 16s. mentioned in the
bill of sale with the 40s. bequeathed by John Beare, but they suspect the
difference may be accounted for by supposing 4s. to be deducted for the
land-tax.—The rent-charge is therefore lost.

assigns, an annuity of 20s. charged on twenty-four acres of land in Chislehurst, Foots-cray, and North-Cray, for the use and behoof of the schoolmaster of the Free-School at Dartford, with power of distraint; this annuity was never received, and Mr. Bradley informed the commissioners that Thomas Caldecot, esq., was heir-at-law of Henry Wooden the surviving trustee.*

---

* Mr. Caldecot in a letter to Mr. Carlisle, dat. April 6th, 1819, replying to an application of the Commissioners said "I am heir-at-law to Henry Wooden, stated to be the surviving trustee of the will of Henry Draper, 1691 ; but I never heard of the co-trustee of the testator, nor of the trust, from any of my family or other person, until informed by Mr. Bradley a few years since. I then told that gentleman he would save himself some hundreds of pounds, as well as years of trouble, if instead of prosecuting that claim he invested a sum in the public funds that would produce 20s. per annum for the use of the school. That nevertheless I would take the trouble of enquiring into the matter. From my attorney Mr. Williams, I learned that the property supposed to be charged, had come into the hands of Mr. Coventry of North-Cray, but that he had no means of ascertaining the specific lands without much troublesome investigation. I however wrote to Mr. Coventry, making the claim, and offered in any way he wished, to verify the documents on which the claim was founded. I received an answer from Mr. Jones a respectable solicitor of Salisbury-square and Foots-cray, saying that Mr. Coventry was a stranger to the claim, and that if pursued, *process might be served upon him* as acting for Mr. Coventry. Mr. Bradley, whom I made acquainted with this, said, he would speak to his friend Mr. Hart of the Chancery bar—I told him I would save him the trouble, and Mr. Hart, as I expected, reported that I had given good advice. And so the matter has rested." The commissioners add, no further steps were taken, nor considering the length of time since the date of the will, and the difficulty of ascertaining the precise lands on which the rent was charged, we do not think payment can be obtained by any course of proceeding, without more trouble and expense than the bequest warrants. *Appendix to Second Report of Commiss. on Education of the Poor,* 193.

There are now ten boys on the foundation, and their books are paid for by the feoffment;—the education of each boy is estimated at £5 per annum.*

The present income is thus stated—

	£	s.	d.
Rent of House, etc. in High-street, let on lease to John Hayward, esq., for 12 years . . .	55	0	0
Rent-charge on Calcraft's Estate	6	15	0
Dividend on £350, three per cent. consols . .	10	10	0
	£72	5	0

NAMES OF THE MASTERS:

John Cottesford,† 1609.
James Sanham,‡ appointed 1765, resigned 1783.
Rev. William Wiseman,¶ appointed 1784.
John Bradley,‖ appointed 1791; died 1824.
John James Barton,** appointed 1827; resigned 1833.
Thomas Barton, appointed same year, present mast.

---

* Information of Mr. Brand, one of the feoffees.

† Decree of Commissioners for Charitable Uses. p. 220.

‡ Held the school in a large house in the High-street, opposite the new Market-place, formerly inhabited by the family of Death.

¶ Mr. Wiseman resided in Horsman's Place, Lowfield-street.

‖ This gentleman purchased and rebuilt the ancient mansion in Overy-street, heretofore the residence of John Morley, the *donor* of the *Church Houses* adjacent The mansion for upwards of a century afterwards was inhabited by the family of Rogers. It formed three sides of a quadrangle, was open towards the river, and the upper story overhung the street. The hall or parlour stood at the south end of the mansion. The gateway, together with a portion of the tenement is still in tolerable preservation. *Vide* p. 24, *ante.*

** Mr. Barton resigned his situation and retired to Hall Place, Bexley, soon after his eldest son entered upon that distinguished

A quit-rent of two shillings and sixpence half-penny,

---

seminary, where he continued to reside, so long as his advanced age and health would permit. Few persons have experienced more vicissitudes, or have been witnesses of more important and exciting events than this gentleman, during the earlier portion of his existence. He was born in the year 1762, at Garstang, in Lancashire. His father was a substantial yeoman, and his son John, like his brothers was brought up to agricultural pursuits. When he had attained his seventeenth year, a relation dying, left him a considerable sum of money, on condition that it should be invested in the French funds, and the interest applied to defray the expenses of his education at the English college at Douay. These conditions were accepted, and Mr. Barton became an inmate of this celebrated academy—He pursued his studies with considerable success, acquiring together with some Greek, a sound knowledge of the Latin and French languages, as well as of such branches of Natural Philosophy as were at that time taught in the college. Here he remained until his education was completed. Subsequently to this, he appears to have resided alternately in Lisle and Paris, until the Revolution broke out ;—war being declared in 1793 between France and England, the funds on which he had hitherto depended for the means of support were confiscated, and he obtained for some time a precarious livelihood from the liberality of friends, being preserved from the inconvenience of personal restraint, from having acquired such a perfect French accent, that the authorities did not discover his English origin. At the end of September 1792, Lisle was besieged by the Austrians, and Mr. Barton accompanied to Paris the officer charged with the despatches to government, announcing the bombardment He remained in Paris until the execution of Marie Antoinette, when he returned to the seat of war, and was present at the battle of Fleurus. In a skirmish of cavalry which took place near Charleroi, a few days before the battle, he was fortunate enough to make a prize of a fine black German charger, which was galloping wildly about the fields, his rider having been killed or disabled. The young Frenchmen of those days were very ambitious of being able to ride a l'Anglaise, and some young men of Lisle, knowing Mr. Barton to be a good and fearless horseman, proposed that he

is annually payable from the premises in the High

---

should avail himself of the present opportunity to accompany them in their rides, and receive payment for the lessons thus given. To this he readily consented, having no other means of existence, and this arrangement continued for some time, until he received an appointment under the French government* as Inspector of assignats

---

* In Oct. 1789, the French National Assembly upon the plea of preventing a dreaded national bankruptcy, not only resumed the estates given by their forefathers to the church; but confiscated the domains of their sovereign, thus reducing *both to yearly salaries.* But, when they attempted to render these robberies available for the exigencies of the state, sufficient purchasers were not to be found who could pay ready money. The municipality of Paris therefore subscribed for a large amount of this church property, with the view of selling it hereafter and paying the receipts into the public exchequer. The other municipalities in the kingdom followed the example. These bodies were as coinless as private individuals, yet having the land and some credit, they were enabled to circulate Municipal Billets or Bank notes. The government took these notes, and passed them over to the public creditors, such notes being to be redeemed at some future undefined date, until which time, they were to bear four per cent. interest. Such was the birth of the memorable Assignats! *Life of Geo. III Pict. Hist. of Eng.* ii. 444. *Where there is a representation of these Notes.*

The interest was soon discontinued, notwithstanding which, they for some time maintained their value on a par with the metallic currency. In June 1790, a fresh issue of eight hundred millions of francs was made. The partizans of the expatriated princes considering that the ruin of the French republican government would be effected by the loss of credit attendant upon the destruction of their financial system, devised a large forgery of these securities, vainly imagining the nation would then demand the recall of the Capet family, and facilitate *their own re-instatement* in the good things they had lost. With this view, they entered into a contract with a stationer in St. Paul's Church Yard, who employed Mr. Finch, to make the paper at Dartford, and superintend putting them in the line of the French army, then advancing into Germany. This dangerous undertaking, as before stated, had well nigh proved fatal to Mr. Finch, from the activity and intelligence of the inspector. The moulds of the forged Assignats remained in the paper mills at Dartford, until they were closed, after the failure of Mr. Towgood, and were finally sold by auction by Mr. Hubbard, in 1832. Although after the discovery of the forgery, the Assignats fell eight or nine per cent. and Brissot in his place in the Legislature of his country had declared "their fall had rendered nugatory every plan of finance which could be devised,"—yet, (notwithstanding in some instances, they would only pass for a fifteenth part of their legal value,) they extended their ramifications among all classes: swelled the holders of National property, and enlisted a large and influential body by INTEREST, on the side of the Revolution. *Thiers.* i. 204. *Allison's Europe,* i. 219.

street, Dartford, to the manor of Dartford Rectory.*

at Delft; Holland forming at that period a portion of the French dominions. He remained in Holland from 1795 to 1799, residing in the principal towns as the government might require, and occasionally following up even into the heart of Germany the importations of forged assignats with which the continent through the policy of the English government, was at this time inundated. In 1799, seeing no prospect of any termination to the war, he resigned his situation of Inspector, and took up his residence in the neighbourhood of Calais, from whence, after many years absence, in which he had lost the idiom of his native tongue and had been nearly forgotten by his kindred, he escaped with several English detenus, in an open boat to Dover, where he landed without money, with no other property than the clothes he wore, and a quantity of lace which he had concealed in his hat, and with difficulty succeeded in making himself understood on his journey to the metropolis. Strange to say, by his subsequent settlement at Dartford, the self-acknow-ledged *forger* (Mr. John Finch, vide p. 307.) of the spurious paper and its once anxious *detector*, the ci-devant employé, in the decline of their days, resided within a few doors of each other, and oft times convivially spent their evenings together, where the writer has often heard the former detail with great unction, the narrow escape he once had from the latter, whilst accompanying a convoy of several chests full of the base money through the Black Forest, where the chase becoming too hot, they were eventually buried. To add still more to the coincidences, the immediately previous occupant (Mills) of the apartment at Bromley,† in this county, wherein Mr. Barton

"The measure of his days being full,"

breathed his last, was an apprentice in the very printing office in London where the forged assignats were printed, and *he too*, had actually been engaged in the dishonest and discreditable work.—Mr. B. died March 31st, 1842, in the 81st year of his age, and was buried at Bromley, Kent.

* *Court Rolls of the Manor.*

† The present writer occupied the house for many years, but had then let it and left Bromley.

This Grammar-school has produced the industrious and talented GEORGE MOIR BUSSEY, author of the Pictorial History of France, and a number of other useful and valuable literary works, and I believe the present editor of the Kendal Mercury.

———

This School endowed for the sole use of the inhabitants of Dartford, is such an invaluable acquisition that it ought to be guarded with the utmost vigilance. Unlike a National School, its high branches of education were never intended for the multitude,* but to facilitate the aspirations of *every* Dartford youth who should manifest a desire for erudition and be unable to attain it through poverty. At the time of its foundation, education in greek and latin generally procured an easy admission to the university, the legal and medical professions, or the management of mercantile pursuits; for the bulk of the younger sons of the gentry associated poverty with book-learning, and held both in contempt. They had not yet been taught to regard the church, medicine, and law, as their own peculiar inheritance. The changes of time have indeed rendered Grammar-school education of less value, without there is instruction in other branches of science. Yet as a recent act, 4 Victoriæ c. 77, has enabled trustees to extend the system of learning, and thus superadd a good English education to the classics, the feoffees of this Grammar-school will deserve the severest reprehension if they

---

* Grammar-schools were chiefly established in the reign of queen Elizabeth, from the lack of means of instruction (deeply felt throughout the country) after the suppression of the monasteries.

suffer its highest and most valuable branches to fall into disuetude.*   Granted, that to the sons of the poor trades-men generally, a knowledge of greek or latin may be superseded by more homely but useful knowledge,† yet at intervals, poor, and perhaps *then despised* individuals will arise, who shall shed a lustre on their native town, to whom these opportunities will be incalculable.   Gentle-men-feoffees—rather than suffer the education to be *lowered,* ought to cherish in their pristine purity these advantages, and render the mode of admission easy.—Let a testimonial of ability and desire of the candidate for the higher branches of education, be a certain passport to one of the upper forms in the school.—With most of the feoffees I have the honour of a personal acquaintance, and from a knowledge of their excellent character, feel satis-fied they need only see an improvement pointed out, to induce them to adopt it.

---

* Section 3, enacts that nothing but the insufficiency of revenue of the Grammar-school shall authorise trustees to *dispense* with latin and greek, or treat such instruction otherwise than as *the principal object* of the foundation ; nor dispense with the qualification in a master.   Section 5, enacts that the course of instruction prescribed shall maintain the character of the school as nearly analagous to that contemplated by the founder.   Sect. 7, subjects all Grammar-schools to the ordinary ; masters not to teach without licence, etc., and Sect. 15, appoints the bishop of the diocese Visitor where there is no other, and authorizes him to appoint Regulations.   *Stat.* 4. *Vic. c.* 77.

† The utilitarian, matter-of-fact, plodding ideas of the men of the present day—devoted as they alone are to the sordid miserable notions of money-getting—in accordance with the "spirit of the times" are endeavouring in some instances to merge and metamor-phose those alas ! too rare institutions yclept "Grammar Schools,"

The children are admitted at seven years of age and may remain until fourteen.

---

endowed by their future-providing ancestors for the higher education of the generations destined to supersede them, into the time-serving miserable abortions, "National Schools,"—a wretched mean of superficial education, which holds in the scale about the same paltry level, as the comparison between the gigantic architectural elevations of the old cathedral edifices with the pretty pigmy Paris-plaster churches of the present era.

"Our fathers built for eternity, we, ephemera-like, for an hour!"

Yet the present generation egotistically and complacently plumes itself upon its immense superiority and knowledge; and in utter contempt for all previous attainments, exclaims, "the Schoolmaster is abroad." And *all abroad* he certainly is; for how few can place their hand upon their brow, and to *themselves* conscientiously confess that *there* "is store of learned lore." A great abuse in Grammar Schools is the appointment of the feoffees. Wealth is unfortunately generally the test of fitness for office in this kingdom; ignorance is too often unhappily its accompaniment; and parties are appointed to the direction of these institutions who conceive, and reiterate "in season and out of season," that "the three R's—Reading, 'Riting, and 'Rithmetic," are amply sufficient for a boy to make his way through the world. Such is not the meaning of a "Grammar-school:" it has a nobler rendering than such a narrow-minded translation. The *intentions* of a founder of a charity ought to be respected.

Can men be fit for feoffees of a Grammar-school who know not the monetary value of a latin-dictionary, and think half-a-dozen shillings an outrageous price?—imagining in their superlative wisdom that *grammar* can be taught without books. In mercy, and pity, and charity, it is inferred, the parties are not aware of the wide distinction between a Grammar-school and a National-school—between the high and lofty education taught in the one and the mongrel tuition in the other.

Nor ought the feoffees to be so forgetful of the noble duties intrusted to their care, by endeavouring to further their political ends, in striving to strengthen and procure election-hustings influence through the trust deposited in their hands; and in accordance with such

Fifty pounds per aunum is paid the master for the
instruction of the boys, and ten pounds in addition, is
allowed to find them books. The remaining annual
income of the school is stated to be kept as a reserve
fund, but I am unable to learn what is the present
amount in the treasurer's hands.

NAMES OF THE FEOFFEES APPOINTED 1836* :

Edward Cresy.	James Hards.
Thomas Broadley Fooks.	James Charles Hurst.
William Brand.	Richard Tippetts.
Thomas Housson Sears.	John Callow.
Rev. Francis Bazett Grant.	John Tasker.
John Willding.	Charles Hussey Fleet.
John Landale.	John Hall.
Thomas Devereux Cavell.	William Philcox.
Joseph Jardine.	James Barrell.
William Sears.	John Hayward.

subversive mean motives, narrow in many instances the splendid benefits
their ancestors wisely (and fortunately unacquainted with such selfish
conceits) founded and endowed for the rising generation.

The Grammar Schools of this country are celebrated for the able men
they have sent forth; but who has heard of any benefit conferred on
any one individual by the new-fangled party-purpose-serving National
Schools?

* The instrument of appointment is imperfect ;—certain names were
inserted therein, without the assent of some parties in whom the right
of appointment vested, and very properly, they refused to affix their
signature.

THE CHARITY AND NATIONAL SCHOOL.

No plainer truth appears,
Our most important are our earliest years;
The Mind, impressible and soft, with ease
Imbibes and copies what she hears and sees,
And through life's labyrinth holds fast the clew
That education gives her, false or true.
Cowper's Progress of Error.

This Institution originated in a bequest of the Rev. Charles Chambers, vicar of Dartford, A.D. 1745, of £25, given to the vicar and churchwardens, to apply the interest in procuring a yearly Sermon to be preached in recommendation of a New Charity School in this parish, to be established and maintained by a voluntary subscription of the parishioners, and he directed that after each sermon the churchwardens should stand with plates at the church doors, to receive the alms of the congregation after the manner of the charity schools in London.   And to begin and encourage such subscription, he directed his executor to pay £25 in his name.*

The first attempt at establishing a School of this kind in Dartford, was made in December, 1748, when the minister and churchwardens employed the money collected after a sermon, in putting to school as many poor children as it would afford, selected at their discretion.†

The school was afterwards held in the vestry, and a regular master appointed; in 1751 a chimney was

---

* *Book of Benefactions*, 79. One of the earliest country Charity Schools was established in the writer's native town, Bicester, in Oxfordshire, A.D. 1721.   † *Vestry Book*, sub anno.

ordered to be built therein, and the school cieled and repaired.*

In 1771 John Randall bequeathed £100 to the minister, churchwardens, and overseers, in trust, to be put out to interest, for schooling and clothing as many poor boys as the interest would admit.†

Mary Pettit by will dated 27th February 1795, gave to the vicar of Dartford, and other trustees, £1,000 three per cent. reduced, to pay the interest and annual dividend to the charity school of Dartford.‡

In 1778 Catherine Tasker bequeathed £50 for promoting and encouraging this charity.¶

This income with the addition of further sums raised by Annual Subscriptions and the Collections at church, (to the amount of upwards of £100,‖) is applied to the

---

* *Vestry Book, sub an.* It acquired hence the name of the School.

† Randall's legacy, with the addition of £8., per cent. interest, and a further sum of £324, for other charitable uses, was invested in pursuance of an order of Chancery of 26th Feb. 1777, in the purchase of £495 2s. 7d., three per cents. in the name of the Accountant General. The portion applicable to the purposes of this school is £123 17s. 7d. and produces a dividend of £3 14s per annum.

‡ The interest and annual dividend to the charity school produces a dividend of £30 , a year. Miss Pettit, died in July, 1801.

¶ The testatrix died in 1802, and the legacy was invested in the purchase of £64 14s. 7d., three per cent. consols, in the name of the vicar and trustees of the school, and produces £2 1s. 6d. per ann. The whole of the dividends abovementioned make together the annual income of £36 10s. 9d. *Report of Commissioners on Education of the Poor. Appendix.*

‖ The Subscriptions (1841) were £80 6s., Collections £28 12s. 5d. How easily institutions of this kind may be converted into instruments of petty annoyance and personal ill-will by professedly charitable, but crafty, designing, and overbearing individuals, has

support of a school for boys and girls, which at a Resolution passed at a public meeting, held 5th January,

---

been often manifested, and in this instance most glaringly. For several
years the writer was a subscriber to this school, but he had the *misfortune (?)* successfully to obstruct a pet project of certain parties : viz:
the wicked attempt to pull down the Church-houses in Overy-street ; and
afterwards had the *impudence (!)* to defend himself against an outrageous
attack engendered in ignorance and perpetuated by intolerance—*(vide p.*
16, *ante.)* an attack which he regarded with utter indifference, and pro-
found contempt. The next year the treasurer who *himself* collected the
subscriptions, *never called upon the writer,* and cancelled his name from the
list, that he might have no voice in the management of the school. The
same principle of exclusion is still adopted by the whole of the same
party in Dartford, who rightly imagine that a man habituated by a long
career to literary investigations would never degrade himself to become a
sycophantic tool.* A somewhat similar measure was pursued towards
the late Robert Pocock at Gravesend.—Pocock had written a History of
that place ; and inserted therein the translation of the charter granted by
king Charles I., anno. 1632, which so offended the mean-spirited cabal
that then (1797) governed the destinies of the town, that it was moved at
a burgmote by a clever but overbearing jurat, (whose name is forborne
to be mentioned, as the worthy still lives) that Pocock, as a punishment,
should be deprived of their printing and support. This was carried ;
and so bitter and uncompromising was the hostility of those dogmatic
rulers, that in a few years he became a ruined man. Mr. Pocock died at
his son's residence, Lowfield-street, Dartford, October 26th, 1830, and
was interred in his old friend Mr. Denne's church yard, at Wilmington.
Requiescat in pace. Mr. Pocock projected a History of Dartford, but did
nothing beyond collecting a few manuscript memoranda, which afterwards perished in the butter shops.

---

* Not that the clique thought the writer was a "*destructive*" or a
leveller, for they knew he had long acted under the auspices of public
authorities in supporting valuable time-hoary institutions and preventing
their perversion from the founder's design.

1816, was united with the Sunday School,* and ordered to be conducted on Dr. Bell's system. *Every scholar admitted, to pay 2d. weekly, except the charity boys.*†

The present schools were erected on the Spital land in 1826, a lease of 60 years having been granted by the feoffees for that purpose, at a ground rent of £5 per an.

There are now, (1842,) about 120 boys and 80 girls receiving instruction in the schools; of whom 20 boys are annually clothed at an expense of £20 yearly.

A salary of £60 per annum is paid to the Master, and of £40 to the Mistress.

No Master with the slightest pretensions to erudition has ever filled the situation, nor has it produced a single scholar who has in the least distinguished himself.

---

* The Church Sunday School in this parish originated in the benevolence of two individuals, Mr. Storey, a market gardener, and Mr. Emery, a linen-draper, who for a considerable time conducted it at their sole expense, and to induce parents to send their children regularly, they gave to each child in attendance one half-quartern loaf every Sunday. The school was held in the vestry of the church, but the donation was discontinued after it was taken up by the more influential persons in the parish. *Information by Mr. Storey.* The *policy* of this donation was obvious—for the Wesleyan Methodists, and the congregation of Zion Chapel had already established Sunday Schools in Dartford, which were become very popular and flourishing.

† The vestry-meeting also resolved, that the clothing of each boy should be confined to a coat, shoes, and cap for twelve boys;— that all the boys admitted (except the twelve charity boys) should each pay two-pence per week; and that the vicar and churchwardens should be allowed to apply out of the discretionary donations to the parish not directed to any special purpose, any sum of money not exceeding £35 annually, towards the better support of the school, and in aid of the subscriptions and donations. *Vestry Book.*

ASSIZES; HOUSE OF CORRECTION; ETC.

A prison appears to have existed in Dartford coeval with the commencement of the reign of the House of Tudor, perhaps earlier, and in the time of queen Elizabeth the Assizes were held in the town, at the undermentioned periods.

1559. 2 Eliz. In the third week in lent. *Judge*, Serjeant Reginald Chomley.—*Attorney-general*, Gerrard.—*Sheriff*, Nicholas Crispe, of Whitstable, esq.

The same officers, etc., attended 1st July at Maidstone.

1560. 3 Eliz. In the third week in lent. *Judge*, Serjeant Philip Chomley.—*Attorney-general*, Gerrard.—*Sheriff*, Warham St. Ledger, of Ulcomb, esq.

1563. 5 Eliz. Monday, in the fifth week in lent. *Judge of the queen's Bench*, Justice Southcote.—*Attorney-general*, Gerrard.—*Sheriff*, Thomas Walsingham, of Scadbury, in Chislehurst, esq.

1564. 7 Eliz. *Queen's Bench.* The same judges.—*Sheriff*, Sir Thomas Kempe, of Olantigh, in Wye, knt. Monday in the fourth week in lent.

1567. 10 Eliz. *Queen's Bench.* Justice Southcote; Queen's serjeant, Wray.—*Sheriff*, William Crowmer, of Tunstal, esq. Monday, eighth of March.

1570. 13 Eliz. *Queen's Bench.* Justice Southcote; Serjeant Gawdy.—*Sheriff*, John Leonard, of Chevening, esq. Monday, the second week in lent.

1573. 16 Eliz. *Queen's Bench.* The same judges.—*Sheriff*, Thomas Willoughby, of Bore Place, in Chiddingstone, esq. Thursday, the second week in lent.

1579. 25 Eliz. *Queen's Bench.* The same judges.—*Sheriff*, Thomas Copinger, esq. Thursday, the second week in lent.

R

1597. 40 Eliz. *Queen's Bench.* Justice Gawdy; C.B. Justice Owen.—*Sheriff*, Thomas Kempe, of Olantigh, in Wye, esq. Monday, 20th February.

1602. 45 Eliz. *Queen's Bench.* Justice Gawdy; Queen's-serjeant Heale—*Sheriff*, Peter Marewood, of St. Stephens, esq. Monday, 21st February.

———

Criminals were hanged at the gravel-pit near the entrance of the Brent from Dartford, on the same spot whereon heretics were burned in the reign of queen Mary. In 1772, on digging for gravel, eight human skeletons were found lying contiguous to each other; probably they were the remains of malefactors.

THE HOUSE OF CORRECTION.

In 1611, the house in the High-street erected by William Vaughan in the reign of queen Elizabeth and given shortly after to the vicar and churchwardens for the use of the poor,* was granted by Richard Wallis the vicar, and the churchwardens of Dartford, to six justices of the peace, on lease for twenty-one years, to be by them used as an House of Correction.

1647. Fifteen years after the expiration of the above term, the house was again leased to eight justices of the peace for the same purpose for twenty-one years, beginning at Michaelmas, 1647, for five pounds a year, but the deed was not signed by the magistrates.

———

* This house then recently built, and in the occupation of Austyne Kenneworth, was in 1557, (11 Eliz.) given by William Vaughan, one of the founders of the Grammar School, in Dartford, for the use of the poor, and directed to be let for the best rent, and the proceeds thereof given to the poorest parishioners; and that the benefactor might not be

It seems to have been continued to be applied to the same purpose until some time after the commencement of the eighteenth century, when being found too small and incommodious, the Magistrates for the neighbourhood obtained a lease of a plot of ground in Lowfield-street for ninety-nine years, and built thereon A.D. 1720, a *new* House of Correction, provided with cells and every necessary convenience for a prison.

The writer has been able to procure little notice of this Bridewell* from the time of its erection until 1779

---

forgotton, the "Cedule" [instrument of benefaction,] was ordered to be publicly read in Dartford, before all the parishioners present, whenever the churchwardens passed their accounts. *Parish Records.* No. 14, 104, 105. *Book of Benefactions.* 32. *Landale's Charities.* 61, 66.—The house is now in the occupation of Mr. Kempe, a butcher.

* Among Hasted's MSS. in the British Museum is a curious account of a young woman committed to this Bridewell March the 1st, 1759, by Thomas Jones of East-Wickham. She is described in the warrant of commitment to be of the age of nineteen or thereabouts, of a swarthy complexion, and 5ft. 3in. in height, her name unknown; but as one plainly coming within the meaning of the vagrant act. She remained within the same Bridewell till the Quarter Sessions of the County, when she appeared on the 25th of April following, made no defence and spoke but little except in answer to questions put to her by the court, and not then without much equivocation. By what can be gathered from the answers, she was born at Redbourn in Hertfordshire, in the great house called Bayman's Hall; her father's name Aislabie, M.P. for Ripon in Yorkshire; that his christian name was Thomas, and his seat at Ripon, but she could not tell whether it had any name. That her mother's name was Aislabie, and she was the present wife of the above gentleman. That there were two daughters more, but she could tell nothing about them. That about five years ago she was married to an attorney, (or perhaps he only wrote attorney) at Redbourne, where her father had resided for five years. That her husband's name was Warriner; he died about half

when William Carr became keeper, and held the office for ten years, he was succeeded by his son who also filled it for about a similar term, when he became insolvent, and Thomas Okill received the appointment.

———————————————

a year ago leaving her with one child, which was sent for by her family out of compassion. The latter end of last year she went in the St. Alban's coach to Woodford to pay a visit to lady Asgill, whom she knew no otherwise than by sometimes casually meeting when visiting; she staid there three nights, and then went back to Redbourn—which time she afterwards said might be about Christmas. That she came into Kent with no other design than to ramble. She was some little time about Wickham when a young woman was drowned, and Mr. Chapman and Mr. Hodges came down to the ale-house where the drowned woman was laid, and she was staying. They (Hodges and Chapman) asked her several questions concerning herself, she refused to answer, on which they went to Mr. Jones, who on hearing from them what sort of person she was, sent for her—but when she came she would only say she was of a good family and had eloped on a love affair: and though many entreaties were used, and some threats, yet it was to no purpose, and she was committed to Bridewell as before stated. She moreover said that she knew the St. Quintain family very well, and had been at Scarborough. That her mother's name was Charlotta, and that she had never gone by any other name than Charlotta Warner, since she had been named— That her child was a boy about three years old, and she believed now might be in Yorkshire That she was not quite nineteen years old; and on being asked what profession her father was of, or whether he lived on his estate, she said he had some little matter, a trifle or so, which she spoke with much affectation, and that she had been wandering about, near half a year.—She was in person, much the same as Mr. Jones described her, she had a scar over her eyebrow in shape of a horse shoe; a remarkable fine hand and arm, and might be thought seven or eight years older that she said herself.

Annexed to this account is a letter from York, stating that on July 7th, 1756, a young woman came begging from Scampston, who told the people where she lodged that she was a gentlewoman who

1804. In the Gentleman's Magazine for May, is the following statement respecting this prison when visited by Mr. Neild:—

"DARTFORD BRIDEWELL."   Thomas Okill, keeper, salary—£70; *Fees.* felons, 13*s.* 4*d.*—misdemeanors, 6*s.* 8*d.* *Prisoners,* 7; allowance, three half quarter loaves each per week. *Court yard,* 40ft. by 22ft. *Infirmary,* 14ft. 7in. long by 11ft. 6in., white-washed four times a year. *Employ-ment,* picking oakum, at which the prisoners were at work, and they receive the whole of their earnings—none of them in irons. The keeper told me [Mr. Nield] he very seldom made use of any; the gaol clean, the prisoners healthy and cheerful; but in this prison divine service is never performed, in every other respect how different from that at Maidstone, though both are in the same county.

---

had eloped on a love affair. She said she was acquainted with Sir W. St. Quintain's family, and named their ages. Sir William hearing of it, took a ride with his son and a clergyman to her; she would not tell him who she was, though he offered to reconcile her to her family—She said she was a near relation to the Duke of Montague, and signed herself Clarissa Montague—she returned to Scarborough on the 13th or 14th of September, and continued there until she was brought to bed of a girl in December, 1756; Sir William sent his steward to her, but at last finding she was getting into debt, he caused it to be publicly reported that he knew nothing of her and believed her to be an imposter; she was thrown into Scarborough gaol for debt, where she lay some months—on 31st of July 1757, she went to Lady Neithrop's at Burton-upon-Humber, and all traces of her were lost   Hasted's MS. here breaks off abruptly,— but she seems to have been the same female who was committed to Dartford Bridewell, and been generally considered by the Magistrates, (who seem to have taken much interest in her case,) as an imposter.

Thomas Okill retained the governorship until his appointment to the situation of govenor of Maidstone bridewell, a period of about nine years; his son Robert succeeded him, and retained the office for about a similar period, when on the completion of the new Gaol at Maidstone the lease having expired, the prisoners were removed thither.

Mr. Fleet who then held the premises granted a lease to the late keeper for twenty-one years, and sold him all the materials of the cells, etc. which he immediately employed in other erections.* Mr. Okill converted the late Bridewell into private dwellings, and the principal part of the edifice is now known as the "King William." It is surmounted with a pediment in which is a stone inscribed with the names of the Magistrates under whose directions it was built, and the date of its erection.

---

* Information by Mr. Okill—At the period of the erection of the Bridewell, the owner of the site kept the Magpie, in Spital-street, nearly opposite the Methodist School. He mortgaged it either to Mr. Wooden, or Mr. Pettit, from whom it descended to Messrs. Fleet, the present proprietors.

MARKET AND FAIR.

There is little doubt that a Market existed in this town in the time of the Saxon kings, and that it was regularly continued from that period until the present day. We have direct historic testimony of its existance in the time of Henry III; and that Robert de Rydware, the bailiff of Queen Alianore, his consort rendered for this and other appurtenances of the royalty of the manor, the sum of thirty pounds yearly.* The farm of the royalty and market were granted with consent of parliament by King Edward II., to Edmund de Woodstock his half brother July 28th, in his fifteenth year, when he created him Earl of Kent; at his death the market was entered in the Inquisition Roll, as worth forty shillings per annum.† His son Edmund dying in his minority, the manor and royalties passed through John Plantagenet his brother, to Joan his sister, the fair maid of Kent, and wife of Sir Thomas Holand, knight; then to Thomas her son and heir, and descended through the successive lords of the manor to Margaret countess of Somerset and Richmond, the mother of Henry the Seventh.‡

---

* *Mag Rot.* 13 *Edw. II.* The market was included in the royalties of the manor, and had belonged to the Earl of St. Pol, a Norman lord, who mortgaged it to King Henry III , to enable him to undertake a pilgrimage to the holy land. *Pat. 6. Hen. III m* . . . .

† The Inquisition taken after Edmund de Woodstock's death, states the rents of the bailiwick of Dertford at £1 4s, the tolls 40s. and the views of Frankpledge and perquisites of court at £8 7s. 8d. *Esc.* 4 *Edw. III.* No. 58.

‡ Dugdale's Baronage, ii. 94. Hasted's Kent i. 214—217.

The Fair seems of later growth, and the profits thereof are first noticed in the Records of the court of Augmentation among the receipts issuing out of RICHMOND'S LANDS. It is however highly probable that it had existed long anterior to the reign of Henry VII, as the country around was usually supplied with commodities annually purchased at those marts.

20 Hen. VI. In 1442, John Sherborne gave by will to his son John, a messuage in Dartford with its appurtenances, upon condition of his erecting a cross in the market-place of Dartford of similar form to the market cross then standing in the market-place of Sevenoaks.*

This cross was defaced and perhaps partly demolished by the reformers in the reign of Edward VI.,† and being ruinous the founders of the Grammar-school took

---

* John Sherborne, de Dertford etc. Mess' cum pertinen' in Dertford Johanni filio etc., sub condicione etc., unam crucem secundum formam facture illius crucis in loco marcati de Sevenock, etc. *Reg' Test. episc' Roffen. i. f* 8. From the steps of this stone cross, [which stood nearly opposite the present Bank,] the friars of the various religious orders visiting Dartford, frequently preached to the assembled multitudes on market days, and were listened to with the most devout attention. Around the cross also the market people usually knelt and performed their devotions before they commenced their avocations of buying and selling. The practice of kneeling and praying before a crucifix in the open air, is extremely common in catholic countries, (the writer saw several women kneeling before one of cast-iron at Vendôme in France,) and in sea-port towns a crucifix is usually erected not far from the mouth of the harbour, where the wives and families of the fishermen may be frequently seen kneeling at its foot absorbed in the liveliest devotion.

† A market cross stood in nearly every Market-place in the kingdom, in catholic times.

it down and built a Corn Market house on its site, circa
1576, allotting the space beneath for a shelter to the
sacks of grain which had been heretofore pitched in the
open air around the cross, and the loft above for a
school-room.*   It may be presumed that about the

---

* It is evident the Market-house was ever considered an appurtenance
to the parish, and never belonged to the lord of the manor ; in the reign
of James I., William Stanley left £5 by will to repair it.   *Reg. Test
Episc' Roff.* xiv. 250.   After the loft ceased to be occupied as a school-
room, poor diseased persons were occasionally placed there for shelter.
In the Overseer's accounts 1644, March 10th, is an item "paid for a
sheet and stockings for a poor woman that died in the market-house
2s. 8d."   She was buried the next day and 1s. paid for carrying her to
the grave.   The body was probably sewed up in the sheet, and carried
for burial in the coffin which the churchwardens Thomas Fare and John
Round, had that year employed "John *the goiner*," to make at a cost of
five shillings, "to *stand by* to cartye poore people to the grave:"—at
those funerals, the body was taken out and deposited in the grave and
the coffin brought home again.—Notwithstanding the loft over the
market house was let as a store-room, possibly from 1675, downwards,
and the rent claimed by the feoffees of the grammar school, it was
evidently repaired by the parish, from the following entry in the vestry
book.   "1701. Sept. 24, ordered that the churchwardens do repair the
Market-house."—It was also customary for the market-house and tolls
of the market to be assessed to the relief of the poor as appears by the
following entries, "1675, Mr. Bennett assessed for market house 5s."
"1685, Henry Wooden ditto, and Brewhouse £30."   In 1689, the
tolls of the market were let to Henry Glover and Madame Bury,
and they were assessed at £20 per annum.   The following year
they were assessed to Henry Pierce at the same sum.   Pierce was
churchwarden 1694, and continued to hold the market till his death in
1705, when they were assessed to his widow.   In 1707, Henry Blackwell
and Edward Goldsmith held them ; but the following year they passed to
Mr. Strong, when they were assessed at £20 yearly.   In 1714, they were
estimated at £40, and continued thus to be held by his widow in 1723.
Assessment Books in the parish chest.

same time the shambles were erected over the stream of the Cranpit, which flowed open and exposed, on the south side of the High street to the Waterside. The market then being regarded as one of the principal marts for agricultural produce in the county.

There was also a *Fish-market,* on the west side of Lowfield-street, held on the narrow causeway; immediately contiguous to the One Bell Inn.*

1597, Oct. 17. Queen Elizabeth granted the Fair and Markets† together with certain parcels of Richmond's lands, on lease for twenty-one years to Edward Walsingham, esq., at a yearly rental. James I. granted the manor, its royalties and appurtenances, inter alia, to George and Thomas Whitmore of London, for ever, who conveyed them to Sir Thomas Walsingham of Scadbury, in Chislehurst.† That knight in the eleventh year of king James, demised Dartford and its royalties to Sir Robert Darcie, whose descendants sold them to the Gouges,‡ from whom they passed to the present proprietors.

---

* *Court Rolls of Dartford Manor, al's Dartford Priory.* George and Jervis Brooke, 1795, sold to John Tasker, brewer, two messuages, one called the Bell, and the other adjoining westwards, etc., also several tenements adjacent to the old *Fish-Market,* on the west of Lowfield-street, held by services to the lord, and a payment of 1s. 6d. quit rent, etc. No. 11. There was a fishery in Dartford creek belonging to the lord of the manor, and in the reign of queen Elizabeth, salmon were frequently caught in this river. Anciently boats came up the Cranpit stream along Hythe street to the Fish-market.

† The Wednesday cattle-market has been long discontinued, but the Saturday market is flourishing Both were held by prescription.

‡ Memorandums of prices of grain, etc. made by William Bampfield in Rider's Almanack of 1676, now in possession of W. L. Pearce.

1676. 5 Quarters of wheat sold at Dartford . . £7 10s. od.

The Market-house and shambles continued to exist in their original situation till 1769,* when having been long found most incommodious to the thoroughfare and trade of the town, pursuant to an arrangement with the feoffees of the Grammar-school, they were removed to their present situation; the farmers however continued to assemble in the High-street, as heretofore, but the

---

1676.—Six Quarters of wheat sold at Dartford . . . £8 11s. 0d.

    Dec. 5. Sold to Will. Yemans 8 beasts for . . . £29 0s. 0d.

1677.—Sold 6 Quarters of Wheat . . . . £9 0s 0d.

* Mr. Bell says the Market-house was somewhat of a gothic structure (Elizabethan), supported by pillars, and the space below generally filled with sacks of corn on market-days. Chained to one of the pillars was a bell-metal Winchester bushel provided by the lord for measuring the corn, inscribed in raised letters on the outside, THOMAS GOUGE, 1709. This bushel came into possession of the steward on the demolition of the market-house, and was given to W. L. Pearce by the late Mr. Walker, in whose possession it remains. The Shambles were a long shed open on both sides, nearly extending from the west end of the Corn Market-house to the end of Lowfield street. The Cranpit ran in an open channel beneath the butcher's stalls, and opposite the entrance of the Dartford printing-office was a dipping place. Immediately in front of the Corn Market-house stood the Stocks, which, when out of order, were repaired by the churchwardens. The Cage stood on the opposite side of the street on the present site of the tap-room to the Black Boy. The greater part of the inns were situated in this neighbourhood. The Crown or King's Inn fronted Lowfield, and extended to the Waterside; the "Hole" (old) "Bull," is now the Victoria Hotel; the ancient house at the corner of Lowfield-street, was a coach and waggon inn, long known as the King's Head: on the site of the writer's residence stood the Butcher's Arms; next door but one the Dolphin, and houses of public entertainment were scattered around in every direction. So large was the agricultural mart, that within memory, at most of the inns, market tables or ordinaries were provided, and usually well filled by farmers and others.

practice of selling corn by sample having ultimately
entirely superseded bringing it in sacks to market, the
space below the Market-house gradually became unoccupied ; and at the close of the last French war the Market-
place was nearly deserted by hucksters, butchers, etc.,
when Mr. William Lucas Pearce who rented the tolls,
with difficulty persuaded some tradesmen from London to
bring down their goods.   They succeeded, and he enclosed
the hucksters' stalls for their use.   One tradesman brought
another and the market so much increased, that Mr.
Pearce finding the space too small, accommodated them
with stalls in the High-street, which from its thoroughfare
every one seemed to prefer, insomuch that at last the new
market-place in the feoffees' yard became deserted ; and
the traders again took their station on the ancient site.*—
In 1841, the Rev. Augustus Morgan, took down the sheds
and erected tasty shops in the new Market-place, whether
these have sufficient attractions for traders, remains to be
seen.

---

* *Ex inform. Gul. L. Pearce.*   In November, 1842, in consequence of a
dispute with Mr. Hayward the steward of the manor, Mr. Pearce who,
up to that time had continued to collect the tolls of the fair and market
and convert them to his own use, seized upon the new market shops,
under the alledged plea of being still the lord's bailiff—no notice of
ejectment having been served upon him.   Mr. Pearce's defence has since
been published, wherein he alledges that more than *sixty* years having
elapsed since the removal of the market, the lord of the manor cannot
enforce any tollage from stalls in the High street, and that the market
therein has become free ; and that his (W. L. Pearce's) charges have only
been for the use of his stalls, in proportion to their length, etc. *County
Paper, Nov.* 19, 1842.   In 1839 the proprietors of the late Richardson's
theatre being deprived of their accustomed situation in Lowfield, during
the fair, moved to a meadow at the upper end of the same street, and
were followed by many of the itinerant traders, as well as the proprietors

An inspector has been long attached to this corn-market, as well as to those of Maidstone and Canterbury, (formerly the only towns in the county making returns of the quantity of corn sold, and specifying the price). This office has been rendered more efficient by Stat. 5 Vict. c. 14. § 9. which imposes a fine of twenty pounds upon every buyer neglecting to send a true statement of all grain weekly purchased by him, together with the price given, and the name of the seller.

The market-bell is seldom rung except on occasions of fire.

The general business-market commences about six o'clock in the evening.

---

of dancing and drinking booths. This division of the fair being not only a violation of the laws passed for its due regulation, but also a robbery of tollage and stallage from the lords—while, at the same time lessening the amount of business, and affording increased opportunities of licentiousness and crime—*calls loudly* for magisterial interference to restrict it within its legal limits, or place it under the strict surveillance of a vigilant police.

THE WESLEYAN METHODIST CHAPEL.

"Now you will prosper in the world!—I charge you in the Name of that God whose I am, and whom I serve, when you have the means To build a methodist chapel."

Prophetic injunction of a Local Preacher to the late J. Hall, esq., on leaving High Wycomb.

> These walls we to Thy honour raise,
> Long may they echo to Thy praise;
> And Thou descending fill the place,
> With choicest tokens of Thy grace.

Perhaps the pages of hagiography present few more striking incidents than those connected with the principal Founder of this chapel. His settlement in Dartford hinged upon the most precarious circumstances. He entered the town without pecuniary advantages, or any adventitious aid, excepting those resulting from high moral character, a good knowledge of business, and untiring assiduity. Attached to Wesleyan Methodism,* and with the above prophetic charge ever

---

* The earliest notice of any Methodists in Dartford is found in an old interleaved Ryder's Almanack abounding in memoranda of Dartford made by its successive owners during a long series of years. The entry is written by Edward Banfield thus "1758, May 9th. A watch night." There is a tradition that the celebrated John Wesley preached in Dartford sometime after the middle of the last century, in the room now occupied by Mrs. Quait as a pawnbroker's shop, but then licenced as a meeting-house or chapel, and in tenure of Mr. William Hall, a linen draper. It appears, however, from the poor-rate assessment books, that Mr. Hall did not occupy the premises before 1778, and moreover, was an Independent. Both John and Charles Wesley, and also Mr. Whitfield often officiated at the neighbouring church of Bexley in the early part of their career, and there are the following entries connected with them in the Register of that parish, which were transcribed and forwarded me by my honoured friend Frederick Holbrooke, of Parkhurst, esq.

"1739, Anne Mason, Mary Start, Hannah Start, all baptized by Mr. Whitfield, the 12th of August."

tingling in his ears and stimulating to activity, his ear-

"1739, June 17th, Ebenezar Blackwall, an anabaptist, baptized by Mr. Whitfield."

"1742, March 27th, Ann Wood, an anabaptist, was baptized by Mr. Charles Wesley by immersion."

"1742, March 30, Sarah Barnes, an anabaptist, was baptized by Mr. Charles Wesley by immersion."

"1742, Edward Clark, a quaker, was baptized by Mr. Charles Wesley, the 7th of December."

"1739, June 10th, Collected at a Communion on Whit-sunday, Mr. Whitfield preached, £2 16s. 6d."

"1739, June 17th, Collected on Trinity Sunday, £2 2s. 0d., Mr. Whitfield preached."

"Mr. Ingham preached in Bexley church, August 14th, 1737."

"Mr. Wesley, September 11th, 1737, "Salvation unto God."

"Mr. Wesley, November 13th, 1737."

Mr. Whitfield preached frequently in the church at Bexley, and administered the Sacrament. The vicar of Bexley, Mr. Piers, was much attached to him, but was compelled at last by his diocesan, to deny him the use of the pulpit. But the vicar went no further than the letter of the injunction, he employed Whitfield in the desk and at the altar, when he could no longer admit him to the pulpit. "Read prayers and assisted in administering the Sacrament at Bexley church,—many came from far and expected to hear me." The pulpit being denied me, "I preached in the afternoon in Justice D's [Delamotte's] yard, [at Blendon Hall] to about three hundred people, and in the evening at Blackheath to upwards of twenty

SOUTH SIDE OF BEXLEY CHURCH.

liest connections were formed with professors of that

---

thousand, on these words :—"And they cast him out." I recommended to the people the example of the blind beggar, and reminded them to prepare for a gathering storm." *Whitfield's Journal.*

A few days before this expulsion from the pulpit at Bexley, he had introduced Mr. Wesley at Blackheath. *Life and times of Whitfield, by Philip. p. 93. 8vo. Lon. 1837.*

"Friday, Feb. 3rd, 1838, I came to Mr. Delamotte's at Blendon." *Wesley's Journal, p. 35.*

Mr. Piers became vicar of Bexley, on the death of Robert Huntington, A.D. 1737. His acquaintance with Charles and John Wesley originated in their visits to the Delamotte family at Blendon hall, who regularly attended Bexley church on the Lord's day. Mr. Piers introduced the Wesleys to the Rev. Vincent Perronett, the pious vicar of Shoreham, who became one of the most valued and faithful of their friends.—Mr. Piers was present at the first Methodist conference, (1744), which was held in London, he also published a very faithful sermon, which he addressed to the clergy at Sevenoaks, in 1742. *Information of the Rev. Tho. Harding.*

In Nov. 1729, John Wesley fellow of Lincoln college, Oxon ; Charles Wesley, student of Christ-church, —— Morgan, commoner of Christ-church, and Kirkman, of Merton, began to spend some evenings together every week, in chiefly reading the Greek Testament, and from their regularity of life were nick-named METHODISTS, by a young gentleman of Christ-church. In 1732 their numbers were increased by Mr. Ingham, of Queen's ; Mr Broughton, of Exeter ; Mr. Clayton, of Brazen-nose ; Mr. James Hervey and George Whitfield.—In 1735, the two Wesleys, with Mr. Ingham, and a Mr. Charles Delamotte, the son of Mr. Delamotte of Blendon hall, Bexley, undertook the mission of Georgia : and embarked at Gravesend Oct. 21st. Charles Wesley returned to England, Dec. 1736 ; John, Feb. 1738 ;—and in 1737 Charles Wesley frequently officiated at Bexley church—John Wesley, by his preaching soon after his return from Georgia in the London churches, attracted vast crowds ; but becoming gradually excluded from all the churches, preached in Moorfields. In May 1738, by the advice of Peter Böhler, the Wesleys formed about forty or fifty of their personal friends into a So-

faith; and most zealously he laboured, in conjunction with Mr. Brame* and his family, to introduce public

---

ciety for reading and prayers, and they met in Fetter lane, in connexion with the Moravians: similar societies were formed the next year at Bristol, Bath, and wherever their labours were successful. In Nov. 1739, John Wesley preached at the Foundry, Moorfields; and in December following, formed his disciples into the first society, under his own pastoral care, or as he terms it "*The first of the United Societies,*"—yet he did not break off his connexion with the Moravian church till June 1740. In May, 1739, Thomas Maxfield had been converted by John Wesley's preaching, at Bristol, who came to London, and was appointed to assist at the society in London. Maxfield began to preach to the people, and John Wesley, by the advice of his mother, permitted him to continue the practice in private houses and other subordinate places of worship. Soon after came Thomas Westall, and Thomas Richards, and thus began the employment of lay-preachers without episcopal ordination. Maxfield was subsequently ordained by one of the Irish prelates.

The Wesleys commenced their ministrations by travelling from place to place, and when they admitted laymen, every one was required to be a travelling preacher. They divided the country into Circuits, and to each appointed two or three regular Itinerants who visited towns, villages and hamlets in succession. They were removed every year, and the first Annual Conference to regulate the itinerancy was held in London (as before stated) in 1744. It was only attended by six persons, five of whom were clergymen—and among this number was Mr. Piers, the vicar of Bexley. The Wesleyans erected their first chapel at Bristol.

Mr. Perronet the vicar of Shoreham, was almost invariably visited by John Wesley whenever he was in difficulty or trouble, and regarded by him as an able and judicious counsellor in seasons of perplexity. Mr. P. died May 9th, 1785, in the 92 year of his age. His two sons became travelling preachers. *Wesley's Journal. passim. Centenary of Methodism. ibid.*

* Mr. Peter Brames became resident in Dartford, 1789. *Poor Rate Book, sub. ann.* Methodist preaching commenced in one of his rooms in the ancient manor-house of Charles, circa 1790. *Ex inform.*

preaching by the Methodists.* The friendly feelings of Mr. Wellard, Mr. Hall, Mr. Charles Pearce, and other "religious professors" of that day, originally induced them to propose sinking the peculiar tenets of "free grace" and "free will;" and combine their united efforts to erect an edifice wherein they might spiritually worship the Most High, untramelled by liturgic forms—in which ministers of Lady Huntington's Connection, and Wesleyan preachers, might alternately

---

L. P. Staff. armig. The name of John Hall first appears in the Lowfield Assessment, made May 9th, 1791. He married Miss Sarah Stainton Brames, 17th Dec. the same year *(Par. Reg.)*, and opened the first Methodist chapel a little more than two years afterwards.

* Itinerant preaching did not originate with the Methodists; they only revived an ancient practice. When christianity was first planted in Britain, the priests lived in a collegiate manner within the precincts of the cathedral, and the bishop sent them as itinerants, to preach and perform the offices of devotion in the churches of the district. *Kennett's Paroch. Antiq.* i. 107. In later times, when secular clergy were settled in every parish to supply the spiritual wants of the parishioners, the catholic priest often felt his functions invaded by some straggling bald-headed friar, who clad in a thread-bare serge frock, girt round his loins with a piece of rope, would barefoot mount the cold stone steps of the church-yard or market-cross, and there in a torrent of rude impassioned eloquence expatiate on the joys of heaven, or torment of the damned, lashing the vicious follies of the age, (not even sparing the dronish sleek curé,) and calling sinners to repentance. It was no wonder the hearers trembled, and contrasting the friar's zeal and fervor, accompanied with such manifestations of superior piety, with the luke-warmness of the priest, were induced to select him for their confessor—as is previously shewn was the case in several instances in Dartford. Nor is it wonderful that these advantages combined with the loss of emolument made them thoroughly hated by the parochial clergy. Similar effects followed the religious excitements of the last century.—In vain contempt or ridicule was poured upon the shabby itinerant Methodist

officiate every Sunday. The abandonment of the plan led Mr. Hall to convert two cottages on his premises at the corner of the Priory-lane, Waterside, into a chapel, which was opened on New-year's day, 1794; but although furnished with a gallery, in four years time, it became too small for the accommodation of the usual congregation. The new edifice was therefore erected in 1798, at a cost of £700, upon some premises adjoining the manor of CHARLES, which the Trustees obtained upon a lease of fifty years.—Eighteen years afterwards, the congregation had so much increased that another enlargement was found necessary.* This was effected in 1819, at a further expense of £736. 15s.

————————————————— ——————————— ————————— ——————— ————

preacher as with hymn-book and bible in hand he mounted his chair by the way-side, in towns and villages, and there twanged out the dissonant stave, and then, oft-times in uncouth language, cried aloud "warning sinners to flee from the wrath to come." The man was seen to be in earnest, his ardour riveted attention—many received the word—multitudes reviled; but eventually it was found these apparently wretched instruments produced such a revolution in religious opinions that nothing yet has been able to withstand.

The founders of the Wesleyan sect determined their preachers should not eat the bread of idleness. They, not unfrequently travelled from village to village, preaching as many as from twelve to sixteen sermons a week—rarely less than nine, independent of their supervision of class-meetings, love-feasts, prayer-meetings, and all the et-cetera labour, John Wesley thought it advisable to maintain. Yet much marvelle is it, these preachers find opportunities to make considerable progress in general literature, write books and acquire languages. Their general commerce with mankind also enables them to become good counsellors to any of their flock in moments of trouble and perplexity.

* From a survey of the congregation, censorious persons asserted that several of the most respectable hearers were induced to attend chapel from a desire to partake of Mr. Hall's business-favours.

(towards which, Mr. David James gave £160,) and the chapel assumed its present form.*

The enlarged edifice is a paralellogram 48ft. 9. long, and 28ft. 3. wide, within the walls, terminated by a semicircular orchestra or organ loft, to which the pulpit is attached. The chapel is commodiously furnished with pews, and surrounded with galleries; it is estimated as capable of containing 450 hearers. On either side the organ is a circular window, tastily filled with stained glass, which produces a pleasing effect, and though plain, the structure internally, assumes a handsome appearance.

Beneath the communion table is a brass plate thus inscribed,

MARY, wife of the REV. CHARLES GREENLY, she was a member of the Methodist Society forty years, and died in the faith of the Lord, April . . . 1827.†

The Organ is a fine toned instrument, built by Green, at a cost of upwards of one hundred pounds; it was originally the property of a lady at Hammersmith. The

---

* W. L. Pearce says, his father and Mr. Hall became joint securities for the debt upon the chapel, and his mother had to pay £300 on that account after she became a widow. In May, 1835, the debt mounted to £800. Mr. Hall held a bill for £280, on which was due twelve and a half years' interest, amounting to £175; to reduce the debt the Methodist Loan-Society gave £160, which was paid over to Mr. Hall, and all demands for his unliquidated pew-rents accruing during the same period relinquished, upon which Mr. H. gave up the remainder of his claim. *Vide, Funeral Sermon by R. Rymer.* 43. .

† Mrs. Greenly was buried the 10th of the same month; she was wife of the resident preacher; she entered Dartford in ill-health, and never recovered. Until Mr. Avery introduced the popish practice of kneeling at the sacrament, the plate remained uncovered.

society purchased it for £50, in May, 1821, and added
thereto a set of pedal pipes and a swell, at an additional
expense of £60 and upwards, making the cost altogether amount to £112. The money was raised by
subscription. The choir, when complete, is very effective; Mr. Hall's bass and Mrs. Alder's treble are much
admired.

The organ was opened with an Oratorio, consisting
of a Selection of Sacred Music, in May, 1820.* Mr. J. C.
Nightingale of the Foundling Hospital, presiding at the
organ, Miss Williams and other eminent vocalists assisting the choir.

———

The chapel was first united to the Deptford district,
and divine service oftentimes conducted by the local
preachers† until about 1820, when it was annexed to

———

* It was intended by annual Oratorios to clear off certain debts
incurred through the organ, but the second year proving profitless no
other was ever attempted.

† James Bulpit and James Tagg, were two of the earliest preachers;
the former was a native of Poole, in Dorsetshire, afterwards a missionary
in Newfoundland ; then a travelling preacher. They were succeeded by
a Mr. M'Allum, who resided at the entrance of the chapel yard, (now the
Smith's Arms) ; Mr. Churton, and Joseph Sutcliffe, the grammarian and
Biblical commentator Messrs. Kersworth and Gibbons, were also
travelling preachers, who supplied the Dartford pulpit, as did Messrs.
Reynolds, Rowe, Thomas Wood, and many others of whom no recollection survives, inasmuch as the officers of this chapel keep neither Registers nor Church Books. Possibly this paucity of documents arises from
the Wesleyan scheme of "paternal" (despotic) government.* Their
Societies are never assembled in a body at a church-meeting, wherein each
individual member may openly *discuss* and *vote* upon every measure affecting

———

* Russia and Austria call theirs, PATERNAL GOVERNMENTS.

the Gravesend circuit, and one of the travelling preachers
became resident.

PREACHERS RESIDENT IN DARTFORD.

1820		—— Arbuthnot		
1823	24	Alexander Strachen.	He established the Dartford Branch Missionary Society.
1825	26 27	Charles Greenly.*	
1827	28	William Stokes.	
1830	31	William D. Goy.	Missionary, West Indies.
1832	33	Stephen Kay.†	Missionary, South Africa.
1833		Benjamin Firth.	
1833	34	Samuel Leigh.‡	Missionary, New Zealand.
1834	35 36	Richard Rymer.¶	
1837	38 39	John G. Avery.‖	
1839	40	Benjamin Johns.**	
1841	42	James Osborn.††	
1842		W. B. Dennis.	

---

the community, but all their concerns are managed by a few *leaders*, who
settle every thing without any reference to the Society at large. And if
individuals complain, Conference *stifle* enquiry by advising them to
"quietly withdraw themselves," and "not to agitate or disturb the peace
of the Societies" *Min of* XCII. *Conference. p.* 152. 155 Or should any
person dispute the mode of exercising the discipline of the connexion, the
class-leader is directed to report him to the preacher, who is advised to
exclude him, *quietly,* by *withholding his* quarterly society-ticket, and erasing
his name from the class-book. *Ibid.* 153.

* He became a local preacher at eighteen ; in 1793, was appointed to
a circuit and died at the age of 69. A D. 1835 *Min of Conference*

† His "Travels in Caffraria" is an excellent publication.

‡ Author of several useful Tracts.

¶ Mr. Hall's funeral Sermon is admirable for its pulpit eloquence.

‖ "Twenty Good Reasons (?) why I am a Wesleyan Methodist" by xx.

** A most able, faithful, zealous, and eloquent pastor.

†† A memoir of this family appeared in the Methodist Mag. 1841.

The superintendent of the Circuit usually resides at Gravesend. The gentleman filling that office is the Rev. George Scott. There are thirteen local preachers, who assist those appointed by the Conference in the exercise of their pulpit ministrations at the different chapels in the district. Four of these, viz. William Green,* J. Kingshott, Edward Hall, and J. Kingshott, junior, are resident at Dartford.

The Societies in connexion with this chapel, are a "Benevolent Society," for visiting the sick and offering temporary relief; and an "Auxiliary Wesleyan Mission-ary Society" which has been established many years.

There is also a Library of general literature, contain-ing about 500 volumes; a "Sunday School;" and a "Day School" upon the plan of the British and Foreign School society.

The present trustees of this chapel are

JOHN HALL.
EDWARD HALL.
WILLIAM LUCAS PEARCE.
LUKE HOOK.
WILLIAM HART.

Mr. Osborn's whole soul was in the ministry; his deep insight into the human mind, and originality of thought, rendered him a most impressive preacher. His manners were gentlemanly, without the slightest affect-ation: yet with some he was not popular.—He too strongly insisted upon the discharge of every moral obligation. Like his predecessor Mr. Johns, he boldly maintained that those professors who affected liberality, and left their debts unpaid, committed robbery upon their creditors—a doctrine too true, to be at any time palatable.

* Mr. Green by his own industry has acquired much literary and practical knowledge; and by the townspeople is universally considered a man of unimpeachable probity.

THE WESLEYAN SUNDAY AND DAY SCHOOL.

A Sunday school in connection with the first Methodist chapel was endeavoured to be established by
Messrs. Hall and Donkin, but, from some unknown
cause relinquished, and nothing further attempted until
the year 1813, when the habitual desecration of the
sabbath-day, spent by so many children of the poorer
classes in idleness and mischief,* induced several

---

* Those only who are old enough to remember the former state of our
villages and country towns, can adequately judge of the striking effects
produced, by the novel scheme of Sunday schools upon the poorer
classes. In remote hamlets, even if there were services in the parochial
church twice a day, no villager ever thought of attending more than the
morning prayers, and the afternoon was spent in "cricket," "football," or
other rural sports; while the female or more aged inhabitants usually
assembled to look on—indulged in a sauntering walk, or betook themselves to the village alehouse. In the towns, every court and alley
poured forth its densely crowded inmates into its adjoining lane, where,
arrayed in tawdry finery, or clothed in rags, the youthful or the aged
female spent the live-long afternoon, intermingled with the other sex,

members of the Wesleyan body to attempt effecting an alteration by the introduction of a Sunday school in Dartford.   A strong effort was therefore made by Mr. Hook, Mr. Pearce, and others, to accomplish this object.   The advice of some influential individuals was

---

listening to ribald jests, or playing coarse pranks upon each other.   They seldom or never thought of entering a Place of Worship: and as it was next to impossible for an individual of a more respectable class even to pass the end of their lanes without being insulted, few or none had the hardihood to venture among them on that day.   Left to themselves, they therefore formed a distinct community ; and nursed in ignorance and vice, they stimulated each other to an inveterate hatred of all who seemed in better circumstances.   *Vide MS. Notes in Hist. of Bicester.*

It was a similar horrible appearance which the population of the lanes in Gloucester presented on his passing or repassing to worship on the Sabbath day, which led the benevolent Raikes to devise the experiment of a Sunday school, and invite these wretched outcasts to avail themselves of its anticipated benefits.   The novelty of the bold scheme awakened their curiosity to a consideration of its advantages : and the circumstance of individuals of the more respectable classes volunteering to become their gratuitous teachers appeared to elevate them so much in the scale of society that multitudes rushed at once to the institution, and the lanes became suddenly deserted.   Even grown persons partook of this desire for learning ; and at Bicester in Oxfordshire, young men and young women actually presented themselves at the doors, and were admitted scholars, A D. 1804

These doings were speedily noised abroad, and the Dissenters becoming alive to the mighty influence which the system must eventually exercise over the rising generation, at once countenanced it with all their might, and laboured to direct its operations.   But secure in their rights and immunities, the clergy of the Established-church looked coldly on, until their diminished hearers evinced the tide had set in favour of education.   Even at Oxford, where the advantages of literature were well known, the instruction of the poorer classes was deemed too ignoble for gentlemen who aspired to

taken, an "Address to the Humane and Benevolent"
was issued stating "that the religious body of people
"called Methodists in the town in their wish to pro-
"mote the glory of God, and best interests of the rising
"generation, had determined to establish a Sunday
"school wherein as many poor children as their parents
"might choose to entrust to their care, should be
"INSTRUCTED FREE OF EVERY EXPENSE to themselves
"or their relations, for which purpose they solicited
"subscriptions to procure books, and hire a place of
"accommodation for holding the school." This Address
dated January 11th, 1813, produced an immediate
subscription of £22 1s. ;* a school was opened January 21st, and fourteen scholars admitted, and the following Sunday, January 24th, twenty-three others,†

---

the high honours of the hierarchy, and more than three or four years
elapsed before it was clearly seen that unless they bestirred themselves
their craft was in danger. And when, at last they awoke from their
lethargy, and became active, the people attributed it to jealousy of the
Dissenters and not anxiety for their welfare.

Leaving to others, to state as matters of history, how the high-
churchmen and clergy of the day, by threats of withdrawing parochial
relief, and exclusion from the benefits of local charities, sought to compel
the unfortunate poor to remove their children from the Dissenter's
school to their own ; the writer will only express his satisfaction that the
advantages of Sunday schools are now become so strikingly apparent, as
to refute the objections of all gainsayers. Consequently a host of patrons
both in and out of the church has arisen. Public Meetings have been
held, at which eloquent advocates have pleaded most successfully in
their behalf.

* *Original Address.* Subscribers. J. Banks, £2. J. Stringer, £2.
Robert Warren, £2. John Wood, £2. John Hall, £5 5s. 0d. Luke
Hook, £1. William L. Pearce, £1. John Hall, junior, 15s. W. Hart,
£1. R. Clarke, 10s. R. Watson, £1. Mrs. Brames, 3s. etc.

† *Teacher's Book.*

the age of the eldest not exceeding fourteen years. A conviction of the advantages of this school speedily became apparent, that in a few months the Teacher's Book exhibited the names of between two and three hundred scholars, including a statement of their ages, and description of their parents. The first Sermon in aid of the School was preached by Mr. Toase, missionary to the French prisoners, 28th November, 1813.

On its first establishment the business of the school sustained such interruption from riotous and mischievous persons that the conductors found it necessary to place the institution under magisterial protection, and opposition immediately ceased.*

---

* The magistrates enquired into the mode of conducting the School, Mr. W. L. Pearce answered that they usually commenced its duties by prayer and praise, and were frequently interrupted by assemblages of riotous persons, who often broke the windows and otherwise annoyed and interrupted them. The magistrates commended their exertions, and assured them of protection.

[This Mr. Pearce was an acknowledged young man of talent, (the second son of Mr. Charles Pearce a most respectable tradesman in the town, the original lessor of the ground whereon the present Methodist Chapel is built, and one of the founders of that society in this place,) who had for many years, devoted himself to furthering its interests in Dartford. His own statement of his final expulsion from that connection is appended, as a disgraceful and wanton exercise of despotic power ever exercised by a preacher over a prostrate congregation. Mr. P. and two or three others, in desire of knowledge had been induced to join a lodge of Free-Masons. Of course this step was represented to the Superintendent of the District. One Saturday night, at the close of a Leader's meeting, Mr. Wood called the offenders before him, angrily told them he had been privately informed they had become Free-Masons, and been initiated into their mysteries by the practice of secret and improper rites, and therefore unless they would immediately promise never more

In 1814, a School-room was erected at a cost of One hundred pounds, upon some ground at the north end of Bell's-row, granted on lease by the late Mr. Hall for ninety-nine years to Robert Warren and others, for that purpose; and in September following, Thomas Dove, afterwards distinguished as the superintendant of the Wesleyan African Missions, was admitted as a scholar.*

to attend their meetings again, he would expel them the Methodist Society. Pearce somewhat warmed at this unexpected address immediately replied "Never attend my lodge any more?—Why it is more than I dare promise—I, that am a Master therein—No! sooner than do it I will cut your concern altogether." No further notice was then taken of the ebullition—and the next day (Sunday,) Mr. Wood asked Mr. Pearce to visit a dying man in Lowfield street, as he had urgent business another way. Pearce did so; gave him the viaticum: the man died; and he thought things would go on as before. Herein he was mistaken. Alas! he had forgotten the priesthood had been considered in every age vindictive and unforgiving.—Monday night was a prayer-meeting; and Pearce being a Leader was called upon to officiate. While giving out a hymn he was greatly surprised to see the superintendant take up his hat, stalk down the chapel, and retire. The following day, Pearce received an angry letter from Mr. Wood expressing his surprise at his assurance to attempt to lead a prayer-meeting when HE had expelled him the Society. A correspondence followed, in which Pearce alledged that as Mr. Wood had thought proper to select him as HIS SUBSTITUTE to perform the last offices for the dying man, surely he must be fit to lead a prayer-meeting. Nothing however, would mollify the preacher; most inflexibly he persisted in his determination, and though Mr. Pearce, continued some time longer in the school, he gradually became a backslider: and being not in Class, was finally removed by a Vote "That the School be under the entire management of members of Society."]

* "No 179. T Dove. 14 yrs. old.—Frying-pan street.—labourer's son.—Admitted July 10th, into 2d. class." *Teacher's Book.*

This school had also the honour of enumerating Gregory Page, amongst its scholars and teachers, now a popular travelling preacher among the Methodists.

In 1836 "the room in which the Wesleyan school "had hitherto assembled had been for some time past "inconveniently crowded, and many more children had "applied for admission than could be accommodated, "the services of gratituitous teachers had also been "tendered, and only the want of a larger room been "the barrier of usefulness." "Under these circumstances "the committee attempted to raise Funds for the erection "of a larger, and more commodious building, by applica- "tion to the inhabitants to obtain subscriptions for this "purpose." The committee were successful; an eligible plot was purchased and settled upon trustees.* The building is 40 feet by 27 within, and 12 in height, with a moveable partition,† to form distinct schools for boys and girls.‡ The whole was completed in 1837 at an expense of £670.¶

---

* The Halls subscribed liberally, and the trustees re-conveyed the old School-room again to that family.

† John Callow and James Sanham sent in tenders according to specifications. Sanham's tender was £295, Callow's, £395. Some alterations were made, and the contractors sent in fresh Estimates. Sanham's second tender was £320, Callow's £348 The job was finally offered to Callow at £330, which he accepted. No. II. *M S. Account of many Families, Individuals, and Transactions, in Dartford, and its Vicinity, written by divers hands, towards forming a History thereof.* Penes me.—The preacher's house has been built adjoining.

‡ A view of this edifice is given at the commencement of this article, said to be from pencil of the talented Miss Blount, and engraven at the expense of the Rev. J. G. Avery.

¶ The three Miss Halls are generally considered the chief benefactors to this edifice; as well as to most of the Institutions in connection with the Wesleyan Chapel.

REV. THOMAS DOVE.

Thomas Dove the present superintendent of the African Missions of the Wesleyan society, was the son of a labourer, in Overy-street. When quite young, he entered the Methodist Sunday-school; at an early period was admitted a teacher, and devoted much of his energy to the institution. He was apprenticed to Messrs. Taylor and Co., Calico-printers at Crayford. By his marriage with the daughter of Mr. Charles Pearce, he obtained some property, and commenced business as a Grocer at Eaton, in Buckinghamshire. There he became a local preacher among the Methodists. Desiring the office of a missionary, he was sent by Dr. Lander, to the station of Sierra Leone, the grave of so many Europeans. Fortunately his own health withstood the deleterious effects of the climate; yet he had the misfortune to witness his wife falling a victim thereunto. His industry surmounted the difficulty of acquiring the language of the country; and in his intercourse with the natives, his dexterous management of certain negociations between the African chiefs and British authorities, so won upon their confidence that he obtained many valuable presents, and amongst others is said to have been a grant of six hundred acres of land in the island of St. Mary's, at the mouth of the river Gambia, abounding in rosewood timber, which he is reported to have cut down, and then presented the estate to the Wesleyan Missionary Society. Mr. Dove in 1842 returned to England for a short period for the benefit of his health, but purposes to reimbark and resume his African station,

THE DISSENTERS.

In the Dartford parish Register 1726 is the following entry "Thomas Andrews, a Dissenting Teacher buried, June 13th." No further notice of this individual appears in any document I have seen, it is doubtful therefore, whether there was any regular dissenting congregation in the town, or an attempt made to introduce any other public service than that of the church of England, before Mr. William Hall, commenced business as a linen-draper in Dartford. This occurred in the year 1778, when he succeeded John Bedwell. Mr. Hall appears to have been an Independent; and about two years after his residence in this place, to have fitted up a large room at the back of his premises, (now used as a pawnbroker's shop in the occupation of Mrs. Quaits), as a "Meeting-House." It continued to be occupied as such during the whole of Mr. Hall's time, a period of seven years. The worship was often interrupted by disorderly and riotous persons, and at one time upwards of twelve young men were taken before the magistrates at Greenwich for destroying the seats, etc. and heavily fined.* Mr. John Wesley is said to have once preached there; but the majority of the preachers were evidently Independents or Calvinists. In 1788, Mr. Hall ceased to occupy the premises, and they were no longer used for the purposes of divine worship.†

From this period till the erection of Zion chapel, there was no place of worship in Dartford for the Calvinists.

---

* Information of Mr. Massinger, one of the offenders.

† In a poor rate made 28th Feb. that year, they are described as "the late Meeting House," and assessed at only £6 per ann., and entirely omitted in the rate made in June following.

ZION CHAPEL.

This chapel chiefly owes its origin to the zealous exertions of Mr. John Wellard, a native of Eynsford, near Farningham, who about 1777 settled at Dartford as a paper-maker. Influenced by the eloquent preaching of Mr. Richard Cecil, then assistant to the Rev. Mr. Simons, vicar of St. Pauls Cray, he became so much attached to the doctrines and ministrations of those gentlemen, that he took the whole of his family to that village church for some years; at length feeling the inconvenience of journeying six miles every Sunday, he listened to the suggestions of a friend and endeavoured to establish an evangelical ministry in Dartford, although such ministry might not be in connection with the Church of England. Two young men, students in the college of the late Countess of Huntington at Cheshunt, were known to this friend, and having arranged for an alternate supply of their labours, Mr. Wellard opened his house for preaching. Opposition followed, but hearers becoming numerous, and as his biographer asserts "the Lord in his providence having "blessed him in his basket and his store, granted the "desire of his heart in making him the humble instru- "ment of introducing the gospel into the town,(?) Mr. "Wellard therefore seriously contemplated building a "house for God."*—A suitable site near Spital-street

* Mr. Hall the engineer, proposed joining Mr. Wellard in the erection of a chapel, and that it should be supplied with preachers by the Wesleyan and Lady Huntington's connection alternately. As Mr. W. then knew little of the difference of the doctrines, he

was found and with very "little aid from his friends he
"erected a chapel thereon.* In this undertaking how-
"ever, he nearly spent his little all, and some con-
"sidered him imprudent; but Mr. W. was a man of
"strong faith, and believed what he lent to the Lord
"would be repaid with interest." The chapel was
opened on Whit-Tuesday in 1794, by the Rev. J.
Nicholson, tutor of Cheshunt-College:—the cause prospered, a congregation was raised, and a church formed.
The first resident minister was the Rev. G. Waring;
he was succeeded by the Rev. J. Miskin. In a few
years the chapel was found too small, and under Mr.
Hawthorn the third pastor, (a student from the same
seminary,) it was found absolutely necessary to enlarge
it. Towards this work Mr. W. again stood forth most
prominently;† but some of the congregation having
hinted that as the edifice stood vested in Mr. Wellard,
some of his family might hereafter claim it as their
own, and dispossess the church, he demised it to trustees at a pepper-corn during his life, and then charged
it with a payment of ten pounds per annum afterwards
to his family, so long as the lease should remain unex-

---

consulted Lady Ann Erskine, then at the head of Lady Huntington's
sect, who advised him by no means to agree, as the preachers would be
perpetually contradicting each other. The result was Mr. Hall immediately converted two of his cottages into a chapel and opened it on
New-year's day following.

* The enlargement and repairs cost upward of £300, towards which
Mr. Hawthorn collected £70 among his friends at Birmingham.

† Mr. Nettlefold granted an underlease; a shed only was proposed to
be erected, and the congregation seated on forms, but unexpected contributions enabled him to furnish it with pews.

T

pired, on condition that the pulpit should be supplied by ministers of the late lady Huntington's connexion.

About 1805, some disagreement arose among the congregation, and many influential persons considering that Mr. Hawthorn had on sundry occasions acted most overbearingly, endeavoured to accomplish his removal. To prevent the trustees carrying this into effect, Mr. Hawthorn declared himself and church *Independents*, and in that character claimed the chapel. A law-suit followed, but notwithstanding Mr. Hawthorn was in possession, Mr. Wellard succeeded in establishing his right to the chapel, and Mr. Hawthorn was ejected. He preached his last sermon in *Z*ion chapel 24th April, 1818.*

The greater part of the congregation having followed their pastor, Mr. Clark the minister sent by Cheshunt College, began his labours under most discouraging circumstances. Possessing, however, independent property, considerable talents and very conciliating manners, he began to repair the breaches in his church, and bade fair to gather a large congregation, when failing health combined with other circumstances, in little more than two years effected his removal. And although his place was supplied by students from the same institution, the superior attractions of the new chapel in Lowfield-street and the popularity of its

---

* Mr. Wellard's biographer says that he (Mr. W.) was a most affectionate husband, kind father, and faithful friend :—that in the church of which he was founder, he was a prudent and laborious deacon, the support and advocate of his ministers, and servant of its members. That "although a dissenter" he nearly filled the whole of the parish offices, to the credit of himself and satisfaction of his neighbours. Thus he lived beloved, maintaining the noiseless tenor

preacher caused its hearers to dwindle away, that it was deemed advisable to close its doors, A.D. 1821. The edifice thus reverting into the hands of Mr. Wellard, was by him let to the Rev. Mr. Currie, vicar of Dartford for a National School, and continued to be thus employed until a New one was erected on Spital-Hill, when it was again shut up.

But in 1820, on the secession of many members from Mr. Harris's church in Lowfield on the affair of Mr. Thwaites,—the chapel was once more opened for public worship; and since that time, has been chiefly supplied by ministers of Lady Huntington's connexion. The congregation however, consider themselves Independents. The old lease has long expired, and the chapel is now held at a rental of twenty pounds per annum. The Rev. Mr. Paul, is minister.

---

of his way until the year 1814, when to his great mental anxiety, the unfortunate differences in his church ended in the separation of its minister and many of its members. About the same time he lost a son; and in 1825 he was bereaved of his wife, to whom he had been united nearly half a century. He, however, survived five years, and departed this life without a groan, Dec. 2nd, 1820. Mr. Harris preached his funeral sermon at the Independent chapel, Lowfield-street, to a crowded and attentive audience, from Philemon, i. 21. *Memoir by R. Penny. Home Mission. Mag.* xiii. 67.

INDEPENDENT CHAPEL.

This chapel owes its origin to the secession of Mr.
Hawthorn from the Countess of Huntington's connexion,
as before stated. On his ejection from *Zion Chapel*
he preached in a barn in Bullis Lane for upwards of
twelve months, during which time, his friends strenu-
ously exerted themselves to procure freehold premises
for the erection of a place of worship. Some land was
purchased for that purpose on West Hill, near the
turnpike, and considerable sums raised by the exertions
of Mr. Hawthorn, in the neighbourhood, and elsewhere.
Further consideration combined with the facility with
which the funds had been raised, induced them to
abandon West Hill, and to purchase other premises
of Mr. Okill, in Lowfield-street, as a more favourable
situation. The ground was cleared—the edifice rapidly

progressed—and the collections were speedily expended. The committee however, persevered in the completion of a handsome chapel, relying on their minister's assurance of being able to raise sufficient sums in time to meet every engagement. Confiding in his representations, the leading members of his congregation individually became responsible, and eventually severely suffered, Mr. H. raising little, or nothing. The chapel was opened in September, 1819, and tolerably well filled from its novelty, and by the preacher's talents; still it was saddled with a heavy mortgage;—the congregation were unable to collect little more than the preacher's salary, (£150 per annum,) and the current expenses. This accumulating debt in a few years alarmed the trustees, who delicately hinted that a temporary slight remission of a part of this annual payment would afford considerable relief to the embarrassed managing committee. To this appeal the preacher however, would not listen—alleging that the claims of a numerous rising family precluded acquiescence, and intimated that further mention of such a proposal would impel him to leave the congregation. In this dilemma, it was determined at a church meeting to raise the price of the sittings; and they ultimately amounted to nine-pence per week, for each person. Many of the hearers consisted of journeymen, or others in little better circumstances, and these individuals feeling themselves unable to afford the subscription, gradually withdrew—others followed their example,— the preacher observing that his congregation gradually declined, and feeling the impossibility of his income being continued, sent in his resignation, Jan.

31st, 1826, immediately after announcing from the pulpit that he had again joined Lady Huntington's connexion, adding "if any one asks the reason, my only reply is, because I choose it."

From Mr. Hawthorn's secession, 1825, until July 8th, 1827, the congregation remained without a pastor, when Mr. Harris was recommended by Mr. Thomas Wilson, the treasurer of the Dissenting College, at Highbury, to supply the vacant pulpit. His ministry proving acceptable, that gentleman settled amongst them, and soon after succeeded in removing some of the incumbrances on the chapel by the subscriptions of his friends. Those exertions were however, ultimately arrested by whispered allegations of inconsistency against some of the officers of the church.*

---

* A Mr. Thwaites, one of the deacons, was charged with having two wives. His own account of the fact is as follows:—"My late unhappy "wife left me to live in open adultery with Mr. Smith.* I commenced "an action, proved the adultery, and obtained damages of £100. The "money I left in the hands of my attorney—disdaining to touch a "farthing—desiring him to get me a divorce—which I expected would "enable me to marry again. He took me to his proctor, who, after "hearing my case, said, 'Sir, you must come into court with clean "hands,' my attorney replied, 'Mr. Thwaites character is invulnerable' "and so it was in this matter. After some months, the proctor searching "out my case more minutely,—and considering that the woman was still "living in adultery;—and that I had in open court proved the same, etc. "and that it was my full intention to marry again,—honourably informed "my attorney of the insufficiency of my present suit to accomplish those "ends, seeing it would only get a separation from bed and board, (and "that was already done by herself,) which, as he said, rather tended to "bind than to loose me, seeing that I could not for want of money,

---

* Smith was a coachman on the Dover Road. He was subsequently imprisoned for debt. After he abandoned Mrs. Thwaites, she married again.

Inquiry naturally following accusation, many of the members considering their deacon, scripturably justifiable, warmly defended his conduct. Divisions followed — the congregation separated, and after some

---

"prosecute my suit to get an Act of Parliament. [For in such a divorce, the party must find two sufficient sureties, under a bond of £200, not to marry in this country till he gets an Act of Parliament.]*

"My friend laid the matter before me, and seeing me much hurt on the "occasion, said, another and more effectual plan was suggested, by which "I might live in the holy estate of matrimony, without offending the "laws of God or man. A case was laid before an eminent special "pleader, by whose direction I acted, though it was very difficult and "expensive" In Mr Thwaites' published "DEFENCE, Addressed to the Church," from (which the above has been extracted) those directions are not stated ;—but the result was, with the sanction of his pastor, Mr. Hawthorn, he publicly married another lady (Miss Barnes) and pleaded in justification the Mosaic law, whereby a man was permitted to put away his wife by reason of adultery and marry another.+ But however satisfactory these scriptural arguments might have been to the mind of himself or his friends, they added not an iota to the legality of his new connexion.

It may, however, serve to caution others against meddling with

---

* In the early periods of English law, a divorce could be had only by mutual consent. John De Camoys transferred his wife [Temp. Edw. 1] to William Paynell (Dug. i 433) Until the 44 Eliz. a divorce could be had in the Ecclesiastical Court, *a vinculo matrimonii,* [from the bonds of marriage itself] ; but now only *a mensa et thoro,* [from bed and board] ; but the parties cannot contract another marriage, not even for adultery or cruelty.

"The cost of proceedings in a Suit for adultery in the Ecclesiastical Court, if unopposed is at present (1843) about £150 ; but this does not enable an injured and guiltless party to marry again without obtaining an Act of Parliament also, the cost of which is about £500 in addition. To all save the very opulent classes therefore adultery is virtually speaking, no ground for divorce in England." *Leg. Tim.*

+ Mr. Thwaites remarks, "How oppressive is the law to a poor man! Our blessed Lord says I am allowed to put away a woman who commits adultery, and marry another. MATT. xix. 9 By His word DEUT. xxiv. 45. JEREMIAH iii. 1 I am forbidden to take an adulterous woman home again lest the land be defiled. On what foundation then stands the charge of Mr. H. against my having two wives? Unless he has the blasphemy to charge the Son of God with sin." (Vide Evan. Mag 1826, p. 444.—466.) Then addressing the Church he adds:—"As wise men judge ye what I say! I request nothing at your hands, but strict impartial justice. The Lord give you understanding on all things."

acts of impropriety had been committed, the seceeders once more opened *Zion Chapel*, as a place of public worship, A.D. 1829.

The members attached to Mr. Harris's ministry, on March 12th, 1832, called upon that gentleman to become their settled pastor, and on April the 10th, following, he was publicly ordained over the church and congregation.

DESCRIPTION OF THE CHAPEL.

The structure as before stated is a handsome elevation, inscribed in front "Independent Chapel," together with the date of its erection, A.D. 1819. The chapel is forty-seven and a half feet long, and thirty feet broad, but a part of the interior is enclosed for a vestry. It is commodiously furnished with pews, and has a gallery running around the end and sides. The pulpit is circular, and in addition to its windows, is lighted and ornamented by a handsome lanthorn in the centre of the roof. The chapel is considered capable of accommodating five hundred worshippers; the congregation which stately attend, may be estimated at about three hundred persons. Since the

---

such matters, to state that the unfortunate result of this was, that Mr. Thwaites, who had lived for several years in good repute at Dartford,—had a young family by his last lady, and was a deacon of the Independent church,—was thereby removed from his office ; and the stigma thus inflicted upon his unfortunate wife and unoffending children, so preyed upon his mind, that aberration of intellect followed: and in about twelvemonths afterwards he died in confinement His widow and young family were thus thrown into a state of destitution,—from which we are happy to hear she was relieved by a marriage with Mr. Jennings, of Staplehurst.

passing of the Act, enabling the dissenters to be married according to their own forms, this chapel has been licenced for that purpose.

There is a Sunday School* connected with this chapel, consisting of about 150 Scholars. It was originally established at *Zion* Chapel, but removed with the congregation upon the erection of the present edifice.

---

* To the young persons of the Dissenting Congregation, and the elder scholars of this Sunday School, Mr. Joseph Robins addressed his "Reasons for Dissenting from the Church of England." A well-written pamphlet on the subject, embodying the chief arguments of De Laune, Dr. Calamy, Towgood, Robinson, Scales, James, and other luminaries in the hemisphere of protestant Dissent. In the following year, [1843.] Mr Robins again entered the field of polemical controversy and published, "A Letter to the Rev. F. B. Grant, Vicar of Dartford, on his avowing himself an admirer of, and an advocate for the principles of Dr. Pusey of Oxford;" principles which Mr. R. shewed to be "diametrically opposed to those contained in the Holy Scriptures, which are the only written Revelation of God to man." Mr. Robins is a member of this church, and clearly the most able champion of Dissent in the town. He is also said to be author of several well-written articles on other subjects. We believe he is a native of Barking, in Essex, and on his marriage with Miss C. Loweth, settled in Dartford.

Mr. Richard Penny an active advocate for Sunday schools, was also long connected with this chapel. In 1823, he published "An Account of the Ordination of the Rev. Evan Watkin Harris over the Congregation in Lowfield-street chapel;" and in 1825, "A Letter to the Inhabitants of Dartford on the projected Ship Canal. Mr. P. was the author of some other works, and an esteemed contributor to several periodicals. He was an attentive and judicious chronicler of passing events and traditionary anecdotes; and the present writer acknowledges himself indebted to him for many reminiscences concerning the town and neighbourhood.

TEMPLES MANOR.

This manor was anciently called the manor of Dartford Temples, from having been the property of the Knights Templars* in early times, and [seems to have] included the whole of the lands from Temple-Hill on the north-east side of the town, down to the river Thames, together with the whole of the Waterside; and also from the Cranpit on the south side of High street round the corner of Lowfield street, to the road leading to Messrs. Fleets' brewery; and (with the exception of the premises between the said road and the House of Correction included in the Manor of Dartford Rectory,) the east side of that street; together with the west side from the Alms houses to Heath lane.

The following slight notices of some of the grants to this brotherhood in this parish, are presumed to be all that are now recoverable, and indicate the period when they obtained possession of their several estates.

King Henry II. gave the Knights Templars one carucate of land in Dartford, which one Gilbert rented A.D. 1185, at twelve marcs. Nicholas, son of Nicholas Twitham soon after the reign of King John, gave fifteen shillings rent to them in this parish.

---

* The order of Knights Templars was one of those grotesque confederacies of military monks which grew out of the Crusaders. Its founders were nine of the followers of Godfrey de Bouillon, who soon after the conquest of Jerusalem, united themselves by a vow to defend the holy city, and its devout writers from the outrages of the Paynim. Their zeal rapidly attracted imitators, and many of the christian warriors having joined their company, King Baldwin II. granted them a residence contiguous to the Temple, whence the name by which they were afterwards known.

A.D. 1221. In the Sixth Henry III. William, prior of Rochester, granted to Alan Martel, master of the Temple, half an acre of land in Dartford, lying by the stream which flowed down from the mill belonging to that brotherhood.*

The importance in subsequent ages attached to Dartford Temples, generates a suspicion that there was a Preceptory projected, or in actual existence at Temple Farm, but involved in the ruin of that order. The writer has heard old men say, large foundations have been there discovered.

A.D. 1308. In the reign of Edward II. the wealth and power of the Knights Templars throughout Christendom, conjointly with the arrogance which riches naturally induce, having excited a general envy and enmity towards them throughout the European nations, the fraternity were accused of the most atrocious crimes, their persons seized and imprisoned, and their estates sequestrated. The king in his fifth year, (A.D. 1311,) granted the custody of their lands and tenements in Dartford, to Robert de Kendale, to hold them during his pleasure, accounting for the profits thereof at his Exchequer.† Their order was suppressed by Pope Clement V. in a general council held at Vienna, A.D. 1312, when he bestowed their riches on the Hospitallers, which, as far as concerned their English Estates was confirmed by Edward II, November 28th, 1323, although they were not given up until the following year.

---

* Reg. Roff. p. 368.   Rymer iii, 288.

† Rymer iii, 482.

KNIGHTS HOSPITALLERS.

This Brotherhood were already in possession of a considerable estate in Dartford, having obtained lands soon after their establishment in England. One of their earliest benefactors, appears to have been Robert Basing, who in the reign of King John, gave his manors of Dertfelde Sutton, and Halgel, to them, and shortly after, King John, or his son Henry III, gave them the lands of Robert Bacun, one of the Norman Proprietors whose lands had been confiscated, as specified in a roll of the 6 John, entitled *De terris Normanorum*, of five pounds value in Dartford. A list of other benefactors also appeared, whose names and benefactions are registered in the Cartulary.

Although henceforward the whole of these estates were attached to the Commandry of St. John's at Sutton-at-Hone, and conjointly constituted one of the chief endowments of that foundation, the name of Temples remained paramount. It was however customary for the religious of every order to grant portions of their estates to individuals for certain numbers of years, accordingly in the 14 Edward II, Thomas Archer, then prior of St. John's, granted in farm to one of the family at Cobham, a term in the manor of Dartford, the interest in which descended down to John, son and heir of Henry de Cobham, about 17 Edward III, who obtained a charter of free warren within his demesne lands, within his manor of Dartford. Hasted, however, remarks, that he was not possessed of any land here in fee, but that the whole manor continued parcel of the possessions of these Knights, until their dissolution, A.D. 1540.

From a curious manuscript still remaining in the British Museum, formerly belonging to Mr. Hasted, it appears that the Hospitallers of St. John's Sutton-at-Hone, in right of their manor of Temples Dartford,*

---

* *Rentale de Dertford cum Sutton-at-Hone renovatum* xx *die Marcii, anno primo Henricii* VIII. *tempore venerabilis fratris Domine, Thomi Docwra prioris Hospitalis S. Johannis Jer'l'm in Anglia.*

ADDIT. MSS. 9493. [TRANSLATION.]

The prioress of Dartford for the manor of Bignors, or Portbrugge, a quit rent of 10s.

The same prioress for certain Briers, formerly Gregory de Rokesley's, afterwards Galfred Wykeham's, 22d.

The same prioress for lands and tenements at Gildenhill, and for Fyndlare's tenement, per annum to the feast of St. Michael Archangel, 11s. 10½d.

The same prioress for other lands at Gildenhill, formerly Robert Flambards, 16d.

The same prioress for land, formerly Stephen at Gildenhill, 11s. 9¾d.

The same prioress for land in Soceden, formerly John Goverode's, (Grovereste's,) 16d.

The same prioress for half an acre of wood in Bammeswode formerly Robert Brixce's, near the wood of the said prioress, and renders per ann. 1s. 2d.

The same prioress for Foxcroftes above the Briers of Dartford, 8d.

The same prioress for land and tenements of Richard Martin, as paid by an ancient rental, 4s. 2d.

The same prioress for land in Bullhede, in Dartford,   s.   d.

Robert Blagge, for divers lands and tenements, [belonging to Horseman's Place,] formerly Thomas Shardelowes, afterwards Margaret Horseman's (his daughter,) per annum, 6s. 8d. from which 5s. only is paid, and no more, (but from what part of the said lands

exercised seignorial rights over the manor of Bignors,

---

and tenements the deduction is made, the jury are ignorant,) together with suit of court,—5s. per annum.

The Governor of the Hospital of the Leperous, called le Spyttel-house in Dertford, viz. : for the Capital messuage there, where the seyd leperous inhabit and dwell, 12d.

Margery Cotyer, for le Hythe, or le Wharf, and the Wallshangeth, pertaining to the Bridge of Rochester, formerly in tenure of John Freningham, for rent per annum, 3s. 8d.

William Croke, for a tenement formerly Richard Sand's, near Stampit, formerly of the land of Arthur Ormesley, and afterwards in the tenure of the chaplain of the said Chantry, per annum, 2s.

Walter Goedmaii per ann. 4s. 2d. to the feast aforesaid, with suit of court,   s.   d.

Let to farm, viz. : six acres in Stonyland formerly John Waryn's, per ann. 16d.

The same for Parymande's tenements viz. : five and a half acres in Paryfield ; two acres in Assenbangth ; two acres in Cockslond ; two acres in Southlond ; five acres in Burrymannes-croft ; one and a half in le Brook ; one and a half in Eldeland ; one in Seldecroft ; one rod in Northfelde ; and one and a half in Bammewode ; and one acre in Cnildred ; and one formerly in tenure of William Cole, at 3s. o½d. per annum.

Richard Sale for a certain messuage formerly Ralph Small's and afterwards Walter Hamgold's lying in Upstrete, between the garden of John Bride on the east, and John Knollis, formerly Hugh Roper's, afterwards the Guild of the Blessed Mary, on the west, and the King's highway on the south, 12d. per annum.

Sir John Willshire, Knt. for a part of a messuage at le Hoke, formerly John Stonybele's (Stanhill's) afterwards Reginald Moge's, and formerly John Hoke's, sen. at Stonyhill, and afterwards Nicholas Lokke's, of Fotestrawe (Footscray,) at the feast aforesaid, 1d.

John Lambe for a former crofte land, containing two acres, called Daviesland formerly William at Hokes, afterward Thomas Gardiner's, per ann. at the feast aforesaid 6d.

The same John for a certain other croft inclosed, called Claycroft in Stoneyhill formerly John Goldwyn's, afterwards Paul Umfrey's ; per ann. at the feast aforesaid, 12d.

Horsman's Place, the Spital, sundry of the chantry

The same for lands called Bacons' land formerly William at Hoke's afterward Thomas Gardiner's per ann. at the feast of St. Michael, the Archangel, 6½d.

John Hart for four cottages in High street, now claimed by the said John Hart and Richard Hervey, 2s. per ann.*

William Heynes for lands at Lampytt, (probably Loam pits) formerly Richard Burleton's, and before William Goodman's, per rental, 2½d.

Henry Lane and Robert Blake for lands at Loampitt aforesaid, formerly Richard Sand's and before William Goodman's for rent, 3d.

Edward White for a cottage in Lowfield, formerly Thomas Plomar's, the which cottage William Goodman held and new-built with another house, and owes, 4d.

Isabel Payne for the farm of a garden, formerly John Christmas' afterwards William Goodman's,   s.   d.

John Edwards, now Constance his widow's and Richard his son's for his tenement formerly Thomas Drewbody's and opposite the messuage of John Coldwyn, in close, 20d.

John Morley, for a cottage formerly John Merkedale's, 4d.

William Stockmede for a messuage with pontage in Overy, formerly John Portbrege's lying opposite Charlesler, formerly in tenure of William Gilbert per ann. 20d.

The same, for a messuage called Shethers, formerly John Punchon's, afterwards John Goodrode's, afterwards Nicholas Gardener's, lying between the former messuage of John Baker against the south and Walter Ayle against the north, and formerly in tenure of Robert Stockmede per ann. 3d.

The aforesaid William, for another messuage and appurts. formerly Richard Gardener's, &c 4d.

Richard Golding in right of his wife . . . . . . of John Knight for a certain cottage, 4d.

William Joanys for a messuage and garden lying in the High-street near Fernyngham style, between the land of Thomas Cotyer on the east and south, and another way on the west, and the said Fernyngham style on the north, per ann. 20d.

---

* Standing between the Cranpit and the Dartford Printing Office

endowments and lands, belonging to private individuals,

The heirs of William Lakyn of London, mercer, for three cottages with their appurtenances lying in Lowfield, near the mansion of the said William Lakyn on the north, per ann. 4s. 7d.

The same for a messuage with appurtenances which William Adams inhabited, and lying in Lowfield aforesaid, to the three cottages aforesaid, 6d.

John Copyng for a garden with appurtenances, adjoining Overy street in Dertford, between the lands of John Edward, 4d.

Sum of rents in Dertford, 66s. 1½d.

The above quit rents appear in an inquisition taken at Dartford, on Monday before the feast of the Decollation of St. John the Baptist, in the first year of King Henry 8th, after the conquest of England, before John Colepepper, William Hersyw, Thomas Lodelow, John Urban, John Cressynor,* John Martyn† and Thomas Appleton, by virtue of letters Patent of the lord the king, dated the 16th July, Anno . . . . . of all in this part directed to superintend the care of walls, ditches, gutters, sewers, bridges, highways, weirs, flood-gates, trenches, etc, in the marshes of Dertford, and to inquire of divers articles contained in the said letters patent on the sacramental oath of Robert Coup, John Woolokstone, John Bodeman, Richard at Gildenhill, Robert Bole, John Osborne, William Colyn, and William Alfield, who say on their oath aforesaid, that the prior of the Hospital of St. John, of Jerusalem, in England holds in the manor of Dertford, fifty-two acres pertaining to the manor of Sutton, of which William Davis is farmer of the said prior there. And the same prior of St. John's holds forty-six acres of meadow in the marshes of his manor of Temple Dertford, of which William Cave is farmer.

The Bishop of Rochester holds in the marsh, seven acres.

The tenants of the manor of Clayndon, six and a half acres.

The heirs of Richard, lord Poyning, hold four acres pertaining to the manor of Rokesley.

John Loffyke, holds there seventeen acres, pertaining to his manor of Littlebroke

Item, the aforesaid jury say that divers persons hold the residue

* Probably father or brother of the Prioress.   † Then living at the corner of Lowfield-st.

paid the quit rents specified in the Rental given in the Note for the same.

The prior and brotherhood, 20th May, 28 Henry VIII., demised this manor to Nicholas Statham, citizen of London, for 65 years,* at the yearly rent of £27 16s. 8d. His widow, Elizabeth, carried her interest in the term to Sir Maurice Denys, her second husband, who became receiver general of the crown for the revenues of the Knights of St. John of Jerusalem. And three years after, A.D. 1543, Sir Maurice so managed as to procure a grant of the entire buildings at the late Commandry of St. Johns, at Sutton-at-Hone, by knight's service, which he held together with the lease of the estates in Dartford, heretofore known as the manor of Temples.†

---

of the same marshes, and that all and singular the tenants in the said lands in the marshes of Dertford, have of old, common pasture, from the feast of the Exaltation of Holy Cross, until the first day of March, for all their own proper animals, and beyond this, no others have common pasture there. And that all and singular, the tenants in the marshes aforesaid, have a common fishery at certain times in the year at Bigpole —and the said jurors say, that all and singular the tenants of land in the said marshes defend and save by walls and other means the marshes there. And there is a certain ditch called Throwedicke, or a long gutter called le Thowe. And that by the same tenants of land and messuages, the walls, ditches, gutters, and highways of old were repaired, and the same tenants are free from the accustomed advesture for payments of the products of wild fowl, found among the reeds throughout the whole marsh aforesaid.

* Collection of Rentals, and Bailiff's Accounts of the manor of Sutton-at-Hone, and Temples Dartford. Addit. MSS. 5493. B.M.

† Hasted's Kent. i. p. 122. folio edit.

The edifice of the church of the commandry at Sutton-at-Hone, he converted into a residence for himself, and

upon his death, in the 5th Elizabeth, A.D. 1562, the manor and mansion became the property of Lady Elizabeth Denys, his widow.

In the 19 Eliz. the interest in the term was vested in Francis Rogers, of Overy-street, Dartford, who on the surrendry of the twenty-five years lease unexpired, had a lease of twenty-one years granted to him at the yearly rent of £20 7s. 9d., and £10, fine. In 1581, there being sixteen years of this term subsisting, the queen renewed the lease to the said Francis Rogers,

---

* John Rogers the first of this family, settled at Dartford in the reign of Henry VIII., and is recognised as the holder of a Dove-house in Overy-street. (*Addit.* MS. 5535) He enriched himself by purchase of confiscated estates of the church, he also held lands in Up-street, A.D. 1556, and with Francis his son, was appointed a feoffee of the Grammar School by the founders ; he died soon afterwards. Francis Rogers, who acquired the lease of Temples manor, occupied the mansion in Overy-street, heretofore the residence of John Morley, and was one of the most influential persons in the parish. In 1608, he, with Charles Brooke, claimed the vicarage of Cobham, and in 1603, occupied the parsonage of Dartford, then valued at £160 per ann. He departed this life Sept. 1610,

Robert, and Henry [Thomas], his sons, for three lives successively, on payment of a fine of one year's rent.

Subsequently becoming vested in the crown, James I. in the 4th year of his reign, granted it to the Earl of Salisbury, in exchange for Theobald's and other lands. Since which it has remained under the same ownership with the manor and priory of Dartford, and belongs to Sir C. Morgan before mentioned. The name only, is now retained in a farm to which no house is attached.

---

and was buried by the vestry door, the 4th of the same month.* He left two sons, Robert, and Thomas; and two daughters, Tomson and Frances, the latter married to Arthur Bostock. Robert Rogers settled at Sundrush, and in 1622, pursuant to his father's intention, vested a house opposite Dartford church in trustees for the benefit of the poor of the parish. Robert died about 1658, leaving Thomas, an only son. Thomas, the second son of the above Francis Rogers, resided in Dartford, in his late father's house in Overy-street. In 1635, he lent the parish £20 to purchase materials for employing the poor, which employment, incurring a loss, was discontinued the same year. At his death in 1637, he gave 20s. to the church, and 20s. yearly, to the poor, to be paid by his heirs so long as they were quietly permitted to occupy the parish house adjoining their dwelling. Francis, his widow, was buried 8th February, 1645. Thomas their son, was a magistrate in Dartford, A.D. 1640; and by will, dated 2nd Dec. 1666, gave 10s. a year additional, to the poor of Dartford, on condition the same house be continued to his sons, Robert and George, their heirs and assigns, and their land of Dowlingcroft be discharged from the payment of 3s. yearly towards buying a bushel of peas to be given to the poor, pursuant to Thos. Auditor's will. Landale says the family remained in possession till 1728. Their house in Overy-street was partly rebuilt by the late Mr. Bradley, vide p. 241.

---

* Ellen his widow was buried 27th Nov. 1611. She was sister to Mrs Ann Death, and grand-daughter of Christopher Lamb, gent.

HORSMAN'S PLACE.

Horsman's Place was a mansion of some note in the parish, situated southward of the High-street, in Low-field, near the small stream called the Cranford.

The estate in the 14th Edward II. was owned by one Thomas de Luda, between whom and Thomas, Abbot of Lesnes, there was a composition touching the passage of a current of water here.* It afterwards passed into the family of Shardelow, one of whom Thomas de Shardelow, possessed it about the beginning of the reign of Henry V., and on his death left it to his daughter Margaret, who carried it in marriage to Thomas Horsman. That gentleman probably rebuilt the mansion, and called it after his own name, which it has ever since retained. He died in the beginning of the reign of king Henry VI., leaving no issue, when Margaret his widow held it in her own right of the manor of Temple Dartford, by the payment of a quit rent of 6s. 8d. per annum, 9 Henry VI. She died in the nineteenth year of that reign, and bequeathed it to her kinsman, Thomas Brune, alias Brown, whose daughter and sole heir, Katherine, carried it in mar-

---

* Thomas de Luda, the owner of this estate temp. Edw. II. made a composition with Thomas, abbot of Lesnes, to allow him to bring a current of water from the Cranpit through his lands to supply his house which stood on the site of Horsman's Place. *Philipot.* 128. When Bugden Hall was erected, permission was also obtained to bring a similar current from the same stream to that house; both flowed through the black ditches, and afterwards ran down Lowfield-street. In 1713, Mr. Twisleton endeavoured by planking to divert its course, but the vestry directed the Surveyors to remove the obstructions. *Parish Books sub ann.*

riage to Robert Blagge, or Blague, one of the barons
to the court of Exchequer, who left a son, by her named
Barnaby Blagge, he conveyed it by sale to John Byer,
Henry VIII.*

John Beer, or Byer had been some years previous
to his purchase of Horsman's Place settled at Dartford,
and appears to have occupied, or at least held, a tenement in the Market place, about the middle of the
reign of Henry VIII. on the site of one, lately
rebuilt by the writer for a Printing Office. Byer's
tenement immediately after fell to decay, and the site
became the cart-way leading to the mansion or head
tenement of John Martin,† situate at the corner of
Lowfield, one of the principal inhabitants of Dartford.
Bere also occupied divers lands belonging to the different religious orders, and was much esteemed by
many of the inhabitants, one of whom, Thomas
Heathcote of Dartford, by will dated 10th April 1572
bequeathed Master Bere a legacy of 6s. 8d.‡ By the
marriage of his first wife having acquired much property, he availed him of the cheap offers of land made
at the dissolution of the monasteries, and purchased

* Notes to Hasted, by *Dr. Latham.*

† John Martyn, the kyng's justic' for John le Bere, w'ch holdeth
c'tayn part of a mesuage sometyme of John le Berr, now called the cart-
way of the said John Martyn in his hede tenem't, w'ch certayn part
lyeth betw'x the tenem't of the said John M'tayn, on the sowthe, and the
messuage of the same John, and a messuage of John Bodemay, clarke, on
the west, and the kynge's strete on the northe, and a messuage of the
Chantry of our ladye, on the est, and owes per ann iis. iiid. *Rental of
Manor of Temples Dartford, temp. Henry VIII. f. 6.*

‡ Reg. Test. apud Roff. ix. f. 75.

valuable portions of those lately belonging to the priory
of Dartford.*   In 1541, as before stated, he bought
Horsman's Place of Barnaby Blagge, the year after the
suppression of the Knights of St. John, of whom it was
held by a trifling quit rent.   In 1551, he rebuilt the
mansion and gate house, and on the latter, he inscribed
his initials, and the time of its erection.   He re-modelled
the ancient Spital house, founded four Alms Houses in
Lowfield, and endowed both institutions out of certain
lands belonging to him, by his last will and testament in
1572.   His manor, or mansion called Horsman's or
Brune's Place, he devised to his eldest son Henry, in tail
general, with remainder to his second son Nicholas.

John Beer's first wife was Alice, daughter and heir
of William Nysell, of Wrotham ; his second, Joan, or
Johanna Egglefield, by whom he left two sons and two
daughters.†   Ann one of the latter, became the wife of

---

* 34 Henry VIII. the king granted him a lease of Greenhithe-Ferry,
late parcel of Dartford priory, for 21 years, at a rental of 33s. per ann.
and a further yearly advance of 6s. 8d.   *Hasted* i. 263.

† *Harl. MS. No. 757. f.* 134.   In an Inquisition taken at West Greenwich, 25th May, 15 Eliz. 1572, on death of John Beer, it is stated, that he
died, leaving issue, by Johanna Egglefield, his second wife, Henry, his
eldest son and heir, 40 years of age, married to Ann Hewlett, and
Nicholas.   That he died possessed of the manor of Horsman's or
Browne's Place, of the value of £10 per ann., and of lands and rents in
Dartford and Wilmington, held of Henry Appleton, gent. for 2d. per ann.
Also of a capital messuage called Bodmins, value £6 ; of a messuage and
lands in Wilmington, and 20s. rents held of Sir Thomas Kempe, of the
manor of Grandisons ; also of certain lands in Merton.—Possibly, Joan,
the wife of Beer, might be one of the family of Egglefield, who married
Elizabeth, daughter and heir of G. Killingworth of Extable house.

Christopher Twisleton of Barley, co. York, Dorothy died unmarried. Henry Beer, his eldest son, survived his father two years, and leaving no issue was succeeded by Nicholas.

John and Clement, the grandsons of the last mentioned Nicholas, dying without heirs, Edward Beer, their uncle, inherited Horsman's Place, with the other estates, but did not enjoy them long; and also dying without issue, March 14th, 1627, bequeathed them to his cousin John Twisleton, grandson of Christopher, by his Aunt Ann, daughter of John Beer. Between this John Twisleton, and the churchwardens of Dartford, a law-suit arose touching the nomination and election of persons to the Spital and Alms-houses founded by Beer, which after continuing some years, was settled in 1625, by commissioners appointed by the court of Chancery. His son and successor of the same name, had four wives; by the third of whom, Elizabeth, eldest daughter and co-heir of James, viscount Say and Sele, who died in 1762, he left an only daughter, first the wife of George Twisleton, of Wormesly in Yorkshire, and secondly of Robert Mignon. John Twisleton died in 1682, having bequeathed this manor and seat to his nephew, John, eldest son of his younger brother Philip.

This John who usually resided at Horsman's Place, in 1704 rebuilt the Spital house, and throughout a long life appears to have taken much interest in the welfare of Dartford. In his last will he desires his posterity honestly and carefully, and for ever thereafter to repair the Spital house which he had rebuilt at Dartford, and declared his whole estates in Kent and

Barley, in Yorkshire, chargeable thereunto for ever. Mr.
Twisleton died July 28th, 1721, aged seventy-two, having
devised his estates to his nephew, John Twisleton, in tail
male, and after divers intermediate remainders to Fiennes
Twisleton, son of Cecil Morgan, esq., by her first husband,
George Twisleton, above mentioned.

John Twisleton, the nephew and devisee before mentioned possessed this estate, and died 1757, without issue,
leaving his estates in Kent, by his will to his Nephew,
Thomas Cockshutt, of Kigworth, in Leicestershire, clerk.
But it being discovered that Horsman's Place, and other
parts of the estates had not been barred, John Twisleton,
of Broughton, esq., laid claim to them. The issue was
tried at Maidstone, in 1758, when he was adjudged to
be entitled to Horsman's Place. He died possessed of it
in 1763, leaving three sons, the eldest of whom being
killed in Germany the same year, his brothers became
entitled to it, as heirs in gavelkind, and on a partition
made of their father's estates, this at Dartford fell to the
share of the second son, Thomas, a colonel in the guards,
afterwards Lord Say and Sele, who in 1768, conveyed
Horsman's Place with the rest of the estates in Dartford,
to Thomas Williams, and Thomas-Smith,* who sold it to
Richard Leigh, esq., serjeant at law. Richard Leigh died
possessed of the same in 1772, leaving by Elizabeth

* The estates which comprehended a great number of the houses and
a considerable portion of the lands in Dartford, were first mortgaged to
Williams and Smith, and afterwards sold to those parties. This estate
they broke up, and sold in separate portions at a great profit. The sons
of both the parties were very unfortunate.

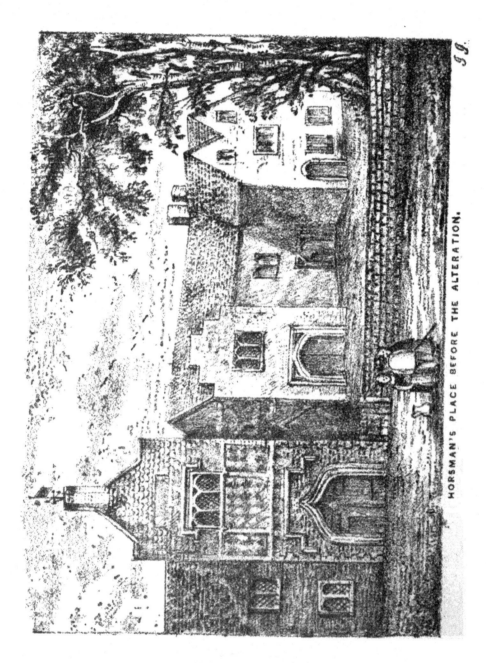

HORSMAN'S PLACE BEFORE THE ALTERATION.

his wife, daughter of Prosper Brown of Horsman's Place, Dartford,* one son Richard, and a daughter Elizabeth. He died intestate, and was succeeded in the inheritance of this mansion, by his son Richard Leigh, esq., before mentioned.

The house having been long out of repair, in the summer of 1782, Mr. Leigh let it with the garden adjoining, to Mr. James Storey,† a market-gardener, who a few years afterwards obtained permission to pull down the old mansion and rebuild a modern dwelling of smaller proportions.‡

---

* John Twisleton who died without issue in 1657, appears to have been the last gentleman of that family inhabiting Horsman's Place; and in the litigation which followed between the claimants, it is not improbable that it stood empty for several years. It was at length occupied by Prosper Brown, esq., whose daughter Elizabeth, married Serjeant Leigh. Prosper Brown died September 20th, 1739, aged 56; his widow subsequently married George Breton, (brother of Sir William Breton, privy purse to George II. formerly an officer in his majesty's army,) and resident here in 1769 Mr. Breton died in 1780, and she left Horsman's Place the same year. Mrs. Breton survived till February 28th, 1785, and was buried in the abbey church, Bath. *Information of R. Leigh, esq*

† Mr. Storey was originally an artillery driver, who came to Dartford while the camp existed on Dartford heath. Being a very industrious man, he was employed and patronised by several gentlemen in the town, and commenced business in the garden opposite Horsman's Place.

‡ The ancient mansion remained unoccupied, and was advertised to be sold or let. It was ultimately taken by Mr. Storey, in 1784, chiefly for the sake of the land, and although then unmarried, he resided therein upwards of a twelvemonth, when he let it to the Rev. William Wiseman, master of the Grammar-School. Mr. Storey eventually returned thither again, but (as above-stated) finding the premises much too large, and

Mr. Leigh sold this estate to Thomas Caldecot, esq., of Dartford, who conveyed the same to Mr. James Storey, the present proprietor.*

---

greatly dilapidated, he obtained Mr. Leigh's consent to replace the house with one of smaller dimensions better adapted for his business.

* Mr. Storey says that a long gallery ran along the whole front of the mansion, into which the several apartments opened ; and that the walls of this gallery were hung with a vast number of portraits of the Bere and Twisleton families, which had been left there, when the house was sold to Mr. Leigh. That these pictures, greatly injured by time, being considered valueless, were given to him by Mr. Leigh, and that he repeatedly offered them to picture dealers in London, without being able to find a purchaser. At last he obtained an offer of 40s, for the whole collection, which he refused, but after keeping them some time longer, found himself unable to obtain a higher price.

Mr. Cresy says the principal front of the ancient mansion faced the west, and was originally approached by an avenue of lime trees from Short-Hill, near the Spital-house, and that some of the stumps remained until Mr. Storey's time.—The cellars still remain under Mr. Storey's house. A large court in front, nearly extended across the present street, rendering the road narrow and inconvenient ; but on rebuilding the house, Mr Storey set back his walls in a line with the street. Hasted says on the gateway, entering the court, were the initials of the founder, J. B. [John Beer] and the date 1551.

Harris states that a record of this family appeared on an oaken beam, to the following effect, SOLI DEO HONOR ET GLORIA JHON BEER, IN THE YER OF OUR LOYD MCCCCCXXXVIII. On the pulling down of the Gatehouse, a part of the materials, with some of the letters of the inscription, were purchased by an inhabitant of Horton Kirby, and affixed on the walls of his house, where they are still to be seen. This is probably the correct date.

MANOR OF CHARLES.

This manor took its name from an ancient family, resident in the parish, one of whom was Edward Charles, an admiral or captain of the fleet from the Thames' mouth northward, in the 34 Edward I. He retained possession until the beginning of the reign of Richard II., when Nicholas, son of Sir John Brembre, became the proprietor, who, rendering himself obnoxious, by his attachment to the unwarrantable measures adopted by that monarch, was attainted and forfeited his life and estate 10 Ric. II. It afterwards was the property of John de Cockham, and by him alienated to John Mitchel.* Soon after the king granted this manor to Adam Bamme, esq. of London, goldsmith, who was twice lord-mayor of that city, in the 14th and 20th of that reign. One of his descendants sold it to William Rothele, whose son Roger died possessed of it 11 Edward IV. In the beginning of King Edward the Sixth's reign, it became the property of William Death, gent., principal of Staples Inn, and ancestor of the D'aeths of Knowlton, in this county. This gentleman built a new manor-house in the High-street, Dartford, which was, henceforward, the residence of himself and his successors in the manor, so long as they lived in the parish.†

His grandson, Thomas Death or D'aeth‡ in the time of king James I. conveyed it by sale to Francis Gold-

---

* Harl. MS. 774. f. 244.　　　　† Hasted. i. 163.

‡ He married Ellen, the sister of Mrs. Rogers, of Overy-street.

smith, esq., of Marshall's Court, Crayford, who afterwards sold it to Edmund Tooke, gent., fourth son of George Tooke, esq., of Bere-court, Dover, who made the new mansion at Dartford, his chief residence.

This Edmund had issue a son of the same name, and a daughter. Edmund Tooke died, without issue, about 1766, upon which, the manor descended to his sister's daughter, Anna Margaretta Edwards, and her husband Francis Edwards, esq., became in her right proprietor. By her, he had one daughter, and on his death, March 19th, 1765, it came into the possession of Gerard Ann Edwards, esq., the natural son and devisee of her daughter above-mentioned. He married lady Jane Noel, second daughter of Baptist, earl of Gainsborough, and died Nov. 1774, leaving his lady and an infant son surviving.* In 1805, the court rolls of Dartford Rectory of which manor it was held, specify the heirs of Gerard Noel Edwards as the holder, and also of the manor house in the street of Dartford; but in the rentals of 1806 and 1822, Thomas Bailey is stated to be owner thereof, and Thomas Bradley of the messuage in the High street, which is described, "as lately taken down and re-built." Since then, the manor has become the property of John Illedge, esq. The manor pays 8s. 4d. quit rent to Dartford Rectory.†

The greater part of the land of this manor was let as a market garden to John Arnold in 1695; Prince Dumright succeeded him,‡ and died May 13th, 1731.

---

* Hasted. i. 163.   † Dartford Rectory Court Rolls.

‡ Assessment Books. sub ann.

THE MANOR HOUSE OF CHARLES, HIGH-STREET, ERECTED TEMP. EDW. VI.

The Sherrins obtained it near the middle of the last century, together with a lease of the priory garden. On the death of John Sherrin the younger, the leases* were sold to Mr. Peter Brames,† and during his occu-

---

* John Sherrin died in March, 1789, at the age of 34, leaving an orphan son and daughter; by will constituting John Hards and William Brand, executors and trustees for his children. The trustees advertised the property for sale: and a stranger entered the auction room wearing a blue apron, and habited in the usual costume of a working gardener. He bid for the lease and stock of the Charles-garden. It was knocked down to him for £700. He was requested to walk into another room, and agreeably to the conditions of sale, to pay down a deposit, and give security for the completion of the purchase. He gave his name "Peter Brames, of Chatham," then frankly added that he had come without money, but thought he could give satisfactory references. Only one of the trustees being present, that trustee hesitated in perplexity—and the sale remained for a short time suspended. At last it was determined to proceed—and the stranger not only bought this, but also the lease and stock of the Priory garden. *Ex. inform. W. Brand.* Peter Brames brought up his children industriously; died Feb. 10th, 1812, and was buried in the upper church yard: his wife survived till 1820, and died at the advanced age of 84; Matthew Brames, the eldest son, died two years before his father. He had three other sons, John, Peter, and Abraham; and four daughters, Judith, the wife of Leonard Staff; Sarah Stainton, married to John Hall; Mary, to Bryan Donkin; and Hannah, to John Nolloth.

† Peter Brames was descended from the Braems, opulent merchants in Flanders. Jacob Braems one of the family, settled at Dover, and the house he built for his residence, eventually became the custom-house of that town. His descendant, Sir Arnold Braems, of Bridge, near Canterbury, in 1638, purchased the manor of Patrixbourne, and on the site of the ancient Court-lodge built a magnificent mansion; was M.P. for Dover, 1660, and died the next year; but the expense of the mansion so impoverished the estate, that Walter his grandson, sold it to John Taylor, esq., who pulled down the greatest part of it. Their arms were—sable, on a chief, argent,

pation the freehold was purchased by Mr. Matthew
Stainton,* who left the same by will to his neice, Sarah,
the wife of John Hall.†

---

a demi-lion rampant, gules.—This Peter, who purchased the lease the
manor of Charles, was the son of John Brames, the grandson of Sir
Arnold. *Ex origin. penes L. P. Staff. armig.*

* Matthew Stainton, esq. was a retired merchant at Isleworth, and
brother-in-law to Mr. Peter Brames, who is said to have advanced the
purchase-money for lease, stock, etc., subsequently bought this estate of
the Noel family, and left it by will to Sarah, Mr. Brame's second
daughter. He gave £4,000 each to Judith, and her sister.

† John Hall, to whom this garden devolved in right of his wife, was
the son of a millwright at Whitchurch, Hampshire, and being brought
up to the same trade, came about the age of twenty, A.D. 1785 or 1787, to
Dartford, in quest of employment. Disappointed or dissatisfied, he left
the town without having accomplished his object, and proceeded to
Hawley, where standing on the bridge with one corner of his leather
apron tucked up, clad in a working mechanic's costume, as he watched
the men repairing the mill, hands being scarce, was asked if he wanted a
job. At first he answered in the negative, but was ultimately persuaded
to take employment. For some time he worked for Mr. Burdett, but
trade slackened, and he was discharged. He was again leaving the town,
with his tools in a bag slung over his shoulder, when he called to bid
Mr Finch, the paper-maker farewell, that gentleman said "its a pity we
should lose so clever a fellow," adding, that "he thought himself and the
rest of the mill-owners on the stream could contrive to find him employment," and promised to speak to Mr. Budgen and others if he would
remain at Dartford. Mr. Hall did so, took a small shop and yard in
Lowfield, in the Spring of 1791; and in May following, was assessed for
the first time to the Poor's-rate. *Inform. J. Hall, et J. Finch, armig. Parish
Books, sub ann.* He soon after removed to the Waterside, and settled on
premises heretofore part of the demesne of Dartford priory. Mr. Hall,
seems to have married the year he commenced business, since the birth
of his eldest son occurs in Oct. 1792. *Par. Regist.* Mr. Hall's acquaintance with the Brames arose out of their religious connexions—both were

Notwithstanding William Death, gent. built a new manor-house, he left the old mansion standing in the garden for his domestics. It has undergone many alterations, but still continues to subsist, though little of its ancient character remains. It was inhabited by Mr. Brames, and his family; and Mr. Staff of Gravesend was born here.

There was formerly a footpath across this garden which passed by the house, but was stopped up when Mr. Hall built the row of cottages called Hall Place.

—————

Anciently, there was a Court Baron held for this manor, to which about 42s. is payable as quit rents.

—————

Methodists. For twenty-four years Mr Hall superadded the profession of a market-gardener to his other profitable avocations; and during a long life was generally prosperous in his undertakings. His wealth, however, could not secure him against the infirmities of nature, for in addition to the common casualties of life, some of his family were afflicted with the most dreadful of all human calamities,—and his own end was melancholy.—For years he had suffered from calculus in the bladder, and having heard of the successful results of Lithrotrity* in foreign climes, was induced to submit to the operation. The relief which then followed, influenced him to submit to another operation by baron Heurteloup, under which he sank amidst the most excruciating pangs. His dying injunctions were to be buried as privately as possible.

—————

* Nearly a similar practice existed among the ancient Egyptians. *Alpinus lib.* iii. *cap.* 13.

THE MANOR OF PORTBRUGGE, OR BICKNORS,

WITH THE

GUNPOWDER AND PAPER MILLS.

This manor was so denominated from its contiguity to the bridge, thrown over the river or port of Dartford, and the ancient family of the name of Bicknore, the last of whom, John de Bicknore, died in the reign of Edward III.—when it was given to the prioress and convent,* by whom it was held of the manor of Temples, at a quit rent of 10s. per annum.

After the death of William Vaughan, in 1580, the mansion and mills came into the hands of Sir John Spilman, queen Elizabeth's jeweller, who on the site thereof, erected a paper mill, usually said to be the first of that kind constructed in England, for making writing paper; and in 1558, he obtained a licence for ten years, for the sole gathering of all rags, etc., necessary for making such paper,† and continued the manufacture thereof at this mill, until his death, in November, 1626. Sir John had two wives, Elizabeth, daughter of Nicholas Mengel, who died 1607, by whom he

---

* Vide page 111. The further account of the lease of this manor, and mill, by the prioress and convent is given p. 155, together with the grant of the lease to William Vaughan, p. 171.

† The Doquet of Licence, is dated February 31st, and is "for the gatheringe of alle maner of linnen raggs, scrolles, or scrappes of p'chment, pease of lymes, leather shredds, and clippings of cardes, and oulder fishinge nettes and necessarie for the making of all or anie sort or sorts of white wrighting paper, and forbidding all other p'sons for the making of paper, for the space of ten yeres next" Harl. MS. 2296. 16.

seems to have had no issue,* and Lady Katherine, by whom he had three sons and one daughter.† Lady Spilman was living in 1644, but seems to have died shortly afterwards.

The paper mill was carried on by John Spilman, esq., his eldest son, until that gentleman's decease in 1641;‡ but whether he was succeeded herein by George his son, is perhaps somewhat doubtful. George Spilman married about 1658, and died December 11th, 1679, but the family seems to have fallen to decay,¶ and to have been succeeded as paper-makers by Mr. Blackwell, (traditionally said to have been

---

* She has a handsome monument in the chancel, at Dartford.

† *Par. Reg. sub. ann.* Robert his son was buried 1611; John, 1611; Frederick, 26th May, 1618; Katherine, his daughter became the wife of Christopher Estcott, esq., who was buried by his wife at Dartford, March 28th, 1696.

‡ Widow Spilman, probably John Spilman's wife, was living in Lowfield, 1666, and assessed to the plague at £2. *Assessment Book.*

The names of the following members of this family occur in the Dartford Registers. John Spilman, buried 25th March, 1662. Elizabeth, bapt. 1647; Thomas, buried 17th November, 1675; probably children of John Spilman, esq., who died 1641.—The children of George Spilman and Jane his wife, were Elizabeth, buried 1689; John, baptized 1661: Edward Spilman, born 1684, buried 1690.—The children of Edward, and Sarah his wife, were Sarah, baptized 1684; John, 1691; Mary, buried 1690. There was also an Elizabeth, daughter of John Spilman, baptized December 4th, 1691.

¶ The overseers' disbursements for April, 1689, contain repeated payments of 1s. 6d. a week, to goody Spilman, (evidently Edward's widow,) living at the Waterside till Oct. 1690; she was then ill, had 2s. 6d. allowed her, and goody Banks was paid 1s. a week, for nursing her.—From 1694 to 1696, John Spilman's wife was in the receipt of 2s. per week; she probably died in August that year, since there are several subsequent entries of articles of apparel bought for her boy and girls. The boy was finally apprenticed by the parish.

an apprentice* to the Spilmans,) who was in possession thereof about 1686. The name of Richard Archer his successor, occurs in the parish books from 1702, to 1739, when he failed in business.†

The mill then remained unoccupied for many years, and became extremely dilapidated, when about 1732, they were taken by Messrs. Pike and Edsall, who converted them into a gunpowder manufactory.‡

On the death of Mr. Pike, Mr. Edsall became solely possessed thereof, and was succeeded by his son Mr. Thomas Edsall, who in 1778 becoming bankrupt, the business was sold by his assignees to Messrs. Pigou and Andrews; and the manor of Bignors with all the buildings, were subsequently purchased by Mr. Pigou.—Mr. Wilks was afterwards admitted partner. The business is now carried on to a great extent, by Messrs. Pigous' and Wilks.¶ The lime trees planted by Sir John Spilman, are destroyed.

PAPER MILL.

Towards the latter end of the seventeenth century, another paper mill was erected upon the same stream, a little below the former. Tradition has not preserved

---

* George Gill, who established the paper mills at Boxley, was also apprenticed to the Spilman's, or to Mr. Blackwall. He was the son of Thomas Gill of Dartford, who died Sept. 1667. *Geneal. of Gyll.* 9.

† *Vestry Book. sub ann.*

‡ The first explosion at these mills occurred March 22nd, 1745.

¶ In October, 1818, upon digging for the foundation of a powder magazine, near Dartford, the workmen discovered three ancient spear heads, the umbo of a shield, a brass ring of about three inches in diameter, and a few beads, formed of a yellow composition,—the spear heads were greatly corroded, the length of one was sixteen

the name of the first proprietors,* but in 1698 it was in possession of John Quelch,† and assessed at £40 per annum for relief of the poor. Mr. Archer is said to have subsequently purchased and held it several years, when he sold it to Mr. William Quelch, for £2,000. Mr. Quelch continued to exercise the business of a paper maker, till 1750. He died A.D. 1775 at the advanced age of ninety-six. Having some years previously formed two separate mills thereof, he left one of them together with the mill-house by will, to William his son, and the other to Eleanor, his daughter, the wife of John Terry.‡ William Quelch rebuilt the mill-house about 1756, at a cost of £500, beside the old oak and chesnut timbers which were worked up again.¶ He departed this life, May, 1797, when he left the house and business to John Finch, his godson, and other property to William, his brother.‖ During Mr. Finch's minority the house was taken by Mr. Andrews, the partner of Mr. Pigou, who at that time

---

inches, another fourteen, and the third, only five and a half. There was also a smaller weapon, about three inches long, having apparently a hook attached.

* The company of White-paper makers were in possession, 1694, and Mr. Elys, 1700. *Assessment Book, sub ann.*

† The ancestor of Mr. Quelch is believed to have been a German paper-maker who came over with Sir John Spilman.

‡ Mr. Terry was originally journeyman to Mr. Quelch.

¶ Mr Quelch, sen. was apprenticed to Mr. Blackwell, at Spilman's mill, and after it became dilapidated, the workmen at the lower mill would frequently tear off portions of the woodwork, and send them swimming down the stream. *Information of Mr. Finch.*

‖ He left the tenement called the Isle of Dogs' (now Mr. Cullane's) and the capital messuage, he had recently rebuilt, held of the manor of Dartford, by a quit rent of 6d. per ann., and the payment of 2d.

kept much company, and it was here, that on the night of November the 27th, 1779, the apparition of lord Littleton is said to have appeared to Mr. Andrews, upon the night he died.*

---

for a relief, to William Finch. No. 51 *Court Rolls*. Scandal accused Mr. Quelch of paternity. Mr. Finch's mother was a very handsome woman. John Finch her husband was a butcher in High street.

* Mr. Andrews was in youth the fellow rake of lord Littleton, who never would allow of a future life. They often discussed the subject, and at last lord Littleton told Andrews, that if he died first he would come and inform him. On the night above stated, Andrew's house was full of company, and he expected lord Littleton, whom he had left in his usual health to join them the next day, which was Sunday. Andrews feeling himself much indisposed on the Saturday evening, retired early to bed, and requested Mrs. Pigou to do the honors of the supper table. When in bed he fell into a feverish sleep, but was waked between the hours of eleven and twelve by somebody opening his curtains. It was lord Littleton, in a night gown and cap, and Andrews immediately recognized him. He also plainly spoke to him, telling him "all was over." Lord Littleton had often made Andrews the subject of horse play, and Andrews thinking the annoyance renewed, picked up his slippers, and threw them at lord Littleton's head. The figure retreated towards a dressing room, which had no ingress or egress, except through the bedchamber. The door was locked on the outside, yet no lord Littleton was to be found. At this, Andrews was astonished but not alarmed, supposing him to be playing a trick. He therefore rang for his servant, and asked if lord Littleton was come, the man said "No." Convinced however he was somewhere in the house, Andrews in his anger, ordered no bed to be given him,—saying, he might go to an inn, or sleep in the stables. Andrews went to sleep; the next morning, Mrs. Pigou went to town early, and on her arrival at nine o'clock, heard that lord Littleton had died the very night he was supposed to have been seen. She sent an express to Andrews, at Dartford with the news, who upon hearing it, swooned away, and to use his own expression, "was not his own man again for three years."

Mr. Andrews told Finch, that it was the Walnut-tree room where

In 1790, or 1791, Mr. Finch was employed by a gentleman in St. Paul's church-yard, to manufacture at this mill, the paper upon which the forged Assignats were printed, and afterwards undertook to deliver them to certain consignees for circulation in France. The narrow escape he once had while accompanying a convoy, and the burial of the assignats* in the Black forest, oftentimes formed the subject of conversation in his latter days. Entering upon his property while young, Mr. Finch became very gay, and eventually failed in business, about 1793; so that he sold his mill to Mrs. Budgen, the daughter of Mr. Terry, and sister of the before-mentioned William Quelch, about 1795, or 1796. Mr. Budgen, now the proprietor of both paper mills, united with them the profession of a leather cutter, died at the age of seventy-three, A.D. 1809, and the mill descended to John, his son, who became insolvent; he died in 1820, aged forty-four, and was buried near his father, in the upper church-yard, Dartford. The mill was afterwards occupied by Mr. Towgood, who introduced some new and valuable machinery. The whole however was sold by auction, when Mr. Towgood, removed to Hertfordshire. The premises were subsequently taken of Messrs. Pigous' and Wilks who had become the owners, by the Societé des Mines et Fonderies de Zinc de la vielle Montagne, in Belgium, and were for some time successively carried on by M. M. Chapman, Kinnaird,

---

lord Littleton appeared to him. The walnut-tree has been since cut down, but the room still exists at the back of the house, adjoining the mill, and the writer has repeatedly been therein.

* Vide p. 232.

Kavanagh,* De Stains, and Corniquet.   The business was eventually relinquished and the machinery sold.   The premises are now, (1843,) in the occupation of Mr. John Applegath, as a silk and calico printer.

CORN AND FLOUR MILLS.

In the reign of Edward the Confessor, there were two mills belonging to the crown, one of these seems to have stood immediately adjoining the town, and the other on the site of the present powder mills.   At the compilation of Domesday Book, the tenants of the hundred affirmed that Osward the sheriff, had let one of these mills to Alestan, portreve of London, (probably Bignors) and that Heltus, the king's steward, then held them with certain lands and meadows annexed.†

King Henry I. granted the tithe of his mills in Dartford, to the church at Rochester.‡

COLYER'S MILL.

King John in the seventeenth year of his reign granted this mill and land then of one hundred shillings

---

* Mr. Kavanagh was the author of the "Reign of Lockrin," an epic poem, written in the Spencerian stanza, said by several reviews to be a most able work. His removal from the Zinc Works at this place, was conducted with the utmost violence, and for nearly a fortnight, he sustained a siege, and defended the Zinc Mills with the utmost pertinacity, against a party of ruffians brought down from London to take forcible possession. An account of the proceedings, under the title of "Romance of the nineteenth century," formed the most interesting subject in the daily papers of the time. Mr. Kavanagh after being dispossessed of the premises, returned to France, with promise of compensation from the French Company, but we believe obtained none — M. de Stains, his successor, was a French officer, and a clever writer.

† Domesday Book.   ‡ Textus Roffensis, 35.

value per annum, which had been held by Aschard de Audenham, to Michael de Wallensi, valet to Philip de Langberg, and by writ tested at Rochester 27th October, 1217, directed the sheriff of the county to give him seizin.*

In 1253, it is stated to belong to the bishop, and still to be of the same yearly value; but at the time of the endowment of Dartford vicarage,† A.D. 1299, it appears to have passed from the see, and to be known as Orchard's Mill; the road leading to it is described to be on the north side the vicarage.‡

The names of the several owners does not appear in any public record until the seventeenth century,¶ when it was the property of John Twisleton, esq.; but for nearly a century it has belonged to a family of the name of Colyer.

HARDS' AND HILL'S MILLS.

The mill in the occupation of Hards' and Hill's stands just over the bridge, upon an artificial channel of the Darenth, evidently flowing from the ancient bed of the river below the silk mills, in nearly a straight line to Dartford bridge.

The cutting of the stream seems to have been effected about the fifteenth century. In the time of

---

* Rot. Claus. 17 John.   † Reg. Roff. 294.   ‡ Ib. 305.

¶ The parish assessment books state that it was in the occupation of Mr. Brown, 1691, and assessed at £30 per annum. Mrs. Ruth Brown seems to have been succeeded by Richard, William, and Nicholas Sewell. In 1756, it was in possession of Ruth Sewell, widow, and assessed at £25, but in 1783, Nathaniel Randall was occupier, and assessed at £105; it was in this gentleman's possession, 1797. It is now, 1843, in the occupation of Henry Colyer.

Henry VII., a fulling mill stood on the site of the present corn mill, which was the property of Henry Bamme. The adjoining field still retains the name of the Tenters, from the frames having stood thereon for stretching cloth.*

About the close of the reign of Henry VII., the mill was occupied by William Longe, fuller,† who resided in the High-street, and was continued in the same business until the conversion of the bread-corn, and malt mill, into a paper manufactory, when it seems to have been re-built, and applied to its present purpose.

In 1689, Henry Hornsby appears to have been assessed for this mill at £30; and in 1715, Thomas Durrant held it as a corn mill.‡

In 1749, the mill was let to John Loader, who died in 1753, and was succeeded by a son of the same name, who died 1787, and left it to his brother William, to whom Mr. Fonnereau granted a lease, on condition of his rebuilding it, which he did at a cost of £2,000. William Loader died November, 1810, at the age of seventy, leaving his mill to James, the son of John Hards,¶ his nephew.

---

* Arundell MS. 61, f. 130.   † Addit. MS 5535.

‡ Vestry Book sub ann.

¶ John Hards married Mary, daughter of John Loader, the lessee of the corn mill. He was renowned throughout the neighbourhood for his strength and courage, and numerous and interesting are the stories still current of his contests with, and hair breadth escapes from the highwaymen that infested all the roads of the district. His business, that of a seedsman, often compelling him to return home late in the evening. In 1788, driving late down Bexley-heath Hill, he was assailed by three foot pads, one of whom attempted to seize the bridle of his horse, when Mr. H. lent forward in his chaise, and shot the man. The villains fired at him

Mr. James Hards obtained the appointment of miller to George IV. and died February, 1817.* Rokeby his son, admitted Mr. Hills, as a partner.

---

but the spirited animal dashing forward, safely carried him to the Bear, at Crayford, where he told what he had done. The landlord supposing him romancing, took no further steps that evening, but next morning the man was found with a dreadful wound in his throat, weltering in his blood, at a short distance, whither he had been dragged by his comrades, who, supposing him dead, had taken his money from his pockets, and his silver buckles from his shoes. When discovered, the man was nearly insensible, but upon being taken to the Roebuck, Crayford, and the wound sewed up, he was found to be one James Smith, a native of that village He lingered a few days and died, having confessed himself one of those who stopped Squire Templar, of Crayford, brother-in-law of Judge Buller, and robbed him of his gold watch only a few days before. At that time it was almost impossible for anyone after dark, to pass from Dartford to Crayford without being robbed at Shoulder-of-Mutton Pond, (now Mr. Bayley's,) on White Hill Bottom, or if they proceeded onwards, to escape the highwaymen of Bexley Heath.

In 1794, his resolute demeanor saved Dartford from pillage and massacre, threatened by a detachment of Irish recruits, who had arrived in a high state of mutiny, and immediately picked a quarrel with the inhabitants; but Mr. H. arming the town's people, so overawed them, that, notwithstanding they had committed the grossest outrages all along the line of their march, their officers were enabled to resume their command, and conduct them peaceably out of the town towards their destination,—that of reinforcing the army of the Duke of York, in Holland.

* There is an admirable likeness of Mr. James Hards, painted by one of his daughters—On August 6th, 1830, the premises were put up for sale, and from the particulars, we learn, they were held on lease, granted in 1795, at a rental of £75 17s. per ann , and that the machinery drives four pairs of stones. That the premises comprised a convenient dwelling house, large garden, stabling for six horses, etc.

PHŒNIX MILLS.

The first mill which stood on the site of the present superb edifice, was erected by one John Brown, as a brassil mill for the slitting iron bars, rods, nails, etc.,* soon after the death of king Charles I. ;† but the iron mills were in the hands of Mr. Nicholas Tooke, the brother of Edmund, lord of the manor of Charles, in 1656, when he only paid an assessment to the poor rate for them of twenty shillings per annum. Mr. Nicholas Tooke, was buried December 26th, 1672,‡ and in the Parish Register is characterised as "a man well disposed to give to the poor." In 1687, he was succeeded by Mr. Charles Manning, a gentleman chiefly remarkable for the zeal he manifested in the improvements in the interior of the fabric of the Parish Church, having at his own expense, renewed the pavement within the altar rails, and restored the altar piece. Mr. Manning died 1719. His successors were Henry and Charles, his sons.¶ In 1740, they were in possession of Samuel Melchor, esq., a gentleman who resided in a handsome house, erected by Mr. Robinson, in what is now Dockery's garden. He held

---

* Hasted says, that the first Slitting-mill for the cutting iron bars, into rods, for converting that metal to different uses, was first set up on this stream in the year, 1595, by one Godfrey Box, of Liege.

† John Brown resided in Dartford, 1677, and was assessed at £50 per annum. His widow was living 1686, and paid 23s. 9d. upon an assessment of £45.

‡ Alice his widow died September, same year. *Par. Regist.*

¶ Henry died 1725, but his brother Charles was then in possession; and 15th Sept that year, made an agreement with the Vicar to pay £3 tithe, for the mill. *Vest. Book.*

them nineteen years.* In 1768, John Randall was occupier, and assessed at £400, but relinquished them in
1770, to Jukes Coulson, esq.† He carried on the iron
mills for nine years, when an action being brought
against him by the occupiers of the corn mills, for pen-
ning up the water so as to impede their working, threw
them up to Deacon and Co. They were then converted
to Saw Mills, and occupied by Messrs. Byers and Co.‡
till 1790, when Workman, Brummell, and Co., erected a
cotton mill thereon, six or seven stories in height. In
this mill they usually employed upwards of four hundred boys. After existing about five years, the mill
was accidentally destroyed by fire the first Sunday in
1795, and was lying in ruins when Hasted wrote his
history.

The following year, Mr. Matthias Wilks accidentally
passing through the town, observing the eligibility of
the premises, took a long lease, and thereon erected
the present edifice, A.D. 1797, at a cost of £80,000,
which he named the Phœnix Mills,¶ for the purpose of

---

* Mr. Melchor died about 1786, and devised his property to Martyn
Fonnereau, esq. *Court Rolls.*

† *Assessment Books,* sub. ann. When Coulson left them, the Assessment was reduced from £400 to £275.

‡ Byers and Co., lived in Spital street, 1789 and 1790, they afterwards
removed to the Waterside.

¶ Mr. Wilks was originally a share-holder in a slave ship, and
subsequently a privateer: whilst in the latter capacity, hearing
there was a ship loaded with dollars in an enemy's port, he dashed
in and captured it, notwithstanding they opened their batteries
right and left. He was afterwards a broker in the tea trade and
failed. About 1805 or 1806, on the establishment of a bank in
Dartford, he set up another at the Phœnix mills, principally for
the payment of his workmen. Upon his notes, was an engraving

making oil and grinding corn.* In 1804, he employed the celebrated engineers, Bolton and Watts, to construct a steam-engine, for the manufacture of oil, which he continued to work until 1824; when he employed Mr. Hall of Dartford, to construct one of superior power for the manufacture of oil and mustard. Some years after, the oil and mustard mills were let to Messrs. Wardle and Co., who failed herein, when they were again worked by Mr. Wilks, until about 1830, when they were taken by Messrs. Saunders and Harrison.

---

of the oil-mills. Soon after the commencement of the peninsular war, he obtained the contract for supplying the navy with biscuit, and carried on the whole process of manufacture upon these premises: the ovens stood on the site of the cement mills. The firm was opened in the name of Wilks and Brown, but, after the death of the latter, was known as that of Wilks and Bush; and eventually passed to Bowman, Garford, and Company.

Mr. Wilks was three times married; first to Miss Brown, the sister of his partner, Mr. Brown; after that gentleman's decease, he married his widow, and lastly a Miss Pace.

* In 1801, the vestry having sanctioned an Order of the magistrates, allowing Mr. Hall to turn the stream of the Cranpit into his premises for the use of a water-wheel, the scheme was opposed by Mr. Matthias Wilks, who offered to pay the parish £100, if the officers of the parish would assign a good right to the whole water flowing down the water-side, for ever, from six o'clock in the evening, till six o'clock in the morning, every day in the year. Mr. Hall offering, at the same time, if the parish would assign him the whole of the water now running down the street from six o'clock in the morning, till six o'clock in the evening, in like manner as to Mr. Wilks, then, at his own charge, to amend and make good the present road under the direction of the Surveyors of the highways. Hereupon a conveyance was directed to be made to these parties. *Vestry Book.* It does not, however, appear that Mr. Wilks obtained possession of the water—probably from the inability of the officers to convey in perpetuity.

PHŒNIX WHARF, DARTFORD.

Mr. Wilks died in 1841, leaving the Phœnix-mills to his son Joseph Brown Wilks,* the present lessee.

---

* By will dated 14th Dec. 1838, Matthias Wilks of Easton Neston park, Northamptonshire, gives to his wife his furniture, pictures, wines, plate, glass, horses, carriage, etc.

He gives to his executors Samuel White Sweet, Edward Richard Adams, and Ericus Robinson, whom he also constitutes trustees, all his personal property, freehold, copyhold and leasehold estates at Dartford, or London, UPON TRUST which (with the exception of his leasehold mills, machinery, etc.) they are directed to convert into money and invest in funded securities for the use of his wife for her life, and for any children born of her, or in ventre sa mère, and to pay her the sum of £800 a year in half-yearly payments during her life, independent of any husband with whom she may contract matrimony, so that she may not alienate, charge, or mortgage, the same, and after her decease in case she leaves any child or children born within a reasonable time of his death, a sufficient sum to be allowed for their education and maintenance, and the remainder to be invested in the same securities, until they attain the age of 21, or in the event of such child or children being female, until married.

He gives to his daughter Mrs. Jane Albert, of Baker-street, Middlesex, out of the same proceeds the sum of £700 per annum, which he empowers her at her decease to settle upon her husband for his life.

He gives £300 to Kitty Wood, of Bexley heath.

£200 to Mary Anne Brown.

£100 to his daughter-in-law the wife of Joseph Brown Wilks.

£100 to Hugh Lewis Albert, his son-in-law.

£500 to Maria Senior, his neice.

£500 to Jane Cassandra Featherstonehaugh

£100 to William, son of Joseph Wilks, his nephew; besides sundry legacies to his servants.

He also directs his trustees to discharge the reserved rents, and all outgoings of his flour, oil, mustard, and cement mills, at Dartford, and if they see fit empowers to repair, insure, or mortgage the same.

Should his wife survive until the expiration of his lease of the said mills, then he gives her one third of the machinery, fixtures, and utensils.

In August, 1841, these mills were offered for sale, and
were thus described in the particulars :—

The OIL AND MUSTARD MILLS are worked by a forty-
horse engine. The Oil mill contains thirty-six presses,
one hydraulic press, four pairs of edge stones, and four
pairs of rollers ; and will crush about six hundred quarters
of linseed per week. The Mustard mill contains nine
stampers, one pair of edge stones, and one pair of rollers,
with all proper machinery to manufacture mustard. There
are cisterns to hold 350 tons of oil. All the shafts and
wheels are iron.

In the FLOUR MILL, is a twenty-horse steam engine,
and thirteen pairs of stones, with all proper machinery,
which will grind about 650 quarters of wheat per week.

The Phœnix Mills are said to be never flooded, and

After the death of his wife, without issue, as aforesaid, he gives his
flour, oil, mustard, and cement mills, to his said executors upon trust to
pay the rents and proceeds to his son Joseph Brown Wilks, and after his
decease, to his (testator's) grandson Matthias Buckworth Wilks, his heirs
and assigns absolutely.

By a codicil annexed to his will dated, Sibton house, near Hithe,
Kent, 17th August, 1840, after specifying certain pictures therein named,
to avoid disputes, he gives to his wife his and her portraits, and a
painting of the woodman by himself ; to his son Joseph, the portraits of
his brother Robert, himself and wife ; to his daughter Jane Albert, a
portrait of herself and her husband.

He revokes his bequest of £300 to Kitty Wood of Bexley heath, and
substitutes the following for those named in his will :—

£100 to Mary Anne Brown instead of £200.

£200 to Maria Senior his niece instead of £500.

£100 to Jane Cassandra Featherstonehaugh instead of £500.

To his wife £400 per annum, instead of £700.

To his daughter, Jane Albert, he gives £500 per ann. for life instead of
£700.   *Proved 8th July* 1841, *in Prerog. offic. Cant.*

that the tide comes up to the mills. When the Creek now improving under an act of parliament is finished, vessels from 100 to 150 tons, will lay alongside the Wharfs.

Attached to this estate is a commodious WHARF, now used as a Coal wharf, with a large building formerly used as a cement mill-house, and machinery; an engine-house, with a twelve-horse steam engine. The use of them as Cement-mills being prohibited for 21 years. There are also three cement-kilns, each with four eyes and pent-houses.

The Corn, and Oil-mills, Residences, etc. are stated to be held under two leases of Martyn Fonnereau, esq. by Mr. Wilks, of which eleven years were unexpired at Lady-day, 1842, and under a reversionary lease granted in 1796, for a further term of twenty years from Lady-day 1852.

The oil mills are stated to be let on lease at £1,500 per annum; the corn mills as lately held by Messrs. Willding at £1,026 per ann.; and the wharf at £260 per ann. The whole premises are said to be held by Mr. Wilks at a ground-rent of £330 per annum, and produce a rental of £2,760 a year.

IRON WORKS.

This extensive establishment for the construction of steam engines, mill-work, etc., to which is attached a foundry of considerable magnitude, was erected by the late Mr. Hall, who removed to some premises on the spot in the autumn or winter of 1790 which he eventually purchased of Mr. Key.* Years of successful enterprise demanding an enlargement of his premises, Mr. Hall purchased some adjoining property of the heirs of Mrs. Mary Henley, and Mr. W. Mumford,† and built thereon his present factory; and here constructed an ingenious piece of mechanism, first turned by the wind and afterwards by the waters of the Cranpit,‡ thereby enabling him to execute certain portions of his mill-work, with accuracy and facility. This machine was ultimately superseded by a steam engine.

---

* *Assessment Book, sub ann.*

† The former is described as a messuage and tan yard, heretofore Fielder's; held of the manor of Dartford Priory at 1s. 4d. quit rent. *No. 27. Court Rolls.* The latter as two meadows, on a part of which is a messuage inhabited by Mr. Peete. *Ibid. No.* 12. The house was burnt down whilst under repair, and rebuilt by Mr. Hall.

‡ In 1801 Mr. Hall obtained an order of the justices to turn the water into his premises (p. 316.) but was thwarted by Mr. Wilks for some time. In 1804, Mr. Hall agreed to pay the surveyors £5, or repair the road, in consideration of their allowing him to use the water for his purposes, the inhabitants agreeing not to abstract the same. The following year Mr. H. covenanted to amend the dry road from the entrance of the water into his premises, to the discharge thereof, and to make an entailment on his estate through which it passed for ever, agreeably to the proposition of vestry, Sept 29th, 1804. *Vestry Book.* In the original proposal, it was stipulated that Mr. Hall, should be allowed to turn the water back into its accustomed channel, at pleasure.

Upon the death of Mr. Brames, his father-in-law, Mr. Hall succeeded to the business of a market-gardener. He shortly after took the paper-mills at St. Mary Cray, and upon Government relinquishing the gunpowder-manufacture at Feversham, purchased the premises, and appended an establishment of that description, to his other large concerns.

Mr. Hall subsequently parted with the paper-mill, at St. Mary Cray, and erected others on a more extensive plan on the Darent, at Horton-Kirby, which his business of an engineer enabled him to construct on the most improved principles, and thereby acquired for his paper a first rate celebrity.

Mr. Hall died in Holles street, Cavendish square, January 9th, 1836,* in the 72nd year of his age, leaving

---

* John Hall of Dartford, engineer and millwright, by will dated 29th Dec. 1835, gives his mansion-house in Spital street, Dartford, to Sarah Stanton, his wife, for life, together with his three houses on the north side of Spital-street, and one on the south side inhabited by Mr. Callow ; he gives her also all his furniture, wines, horses, carriage, &c. and empowers her to dispose of them as she pleases ; he also gives her all his interest in the priory garden, and in his remainder of the 21 years in the lease of the orchard behind his mansion-house.—The mansion and premises are described as mortgaged for £2,000, the payment of the annual interest is charged upon the residue of his estate, and directed to be paid by his executors.

To John Hall his eldest son, he gives his said mansion-house in Spital street, after the death of Sarah his wife, together with the three houses on the north side of the same street, and also that on the south side thereof ;—John his son to discharge the mortgage on the mansion and premises.

To John and Edward Hall, his sons, the factory, foundry, and all the buildings and premises connected with his business of an engineer, &c. at Dartford, (a moiety of which is vested in himself, and a moiety in John and Edward his sons ;) together with a piece of land containing about four acres, near the church.

his business as an engineer at Dartford to his sons,

He describes his business as a gunpowder manufacturer at Feversham and Davington, to be five-eighths vested in himself, and two-eighths in William his son; and enjoins the said William, to admit his son Peter Brames as a partner therein, from 1st of December last, and to have an eighth part of the said business; upon which condition he gives to his son William, all the furniture, wines, etc., in his mansion at Feversham. He gives to the said William and Peter Brames his sons, the premises, mills, mill-ponds, magazines, etc., at Feversham, which he bought of the Board of Ordnance, and also all those at Davington together with six houses at Feversham; he also gives them the magazines, etc., at Erith, and Tredegar, which he bought of the Duke of Beaufort, and Robert Wilks.—The premises at Feversham are described as subject to a mortgage of £4,000, the interest of which the said parties are directed to pay.—He also charges the business and premises with a payment of £85 a year to each of his daughters, Eliza, Maria, and Louisa, payable quarterly for their support, without any deduction, but should either of them alien, charge, or anticipate the same, then payment to such daughter shall cease.

His business as a paper-manufacturer at Horton Kirby, a moiety of which is his son Henry's, together with all his freehold and leasehold premises thereat, and upon which is a mortgage of £2,000, he charges with a payment of £250 per ann. to his son James, whom he commends to the care of his executors; and £85 a year to each of his daughters, Eliza, Maria, and Louisa, for their support, without any deduction, but should either of them alien, charge, or anticipate the same, then payment to such daughter shall cease.

He gives the residue of his estate, to Thomas Spalding, stationer; John Donkin of Blackfriars-road, engineer; Leonard Peter Staff of Gravesend, gentleman; and Sarah Stanton Hall, his wife, IN TRUST, that they shall sell to his sons John and Edward Hall, they choosing one valuer and his trustees another, all his moiety of the partnership estate, stock-in-trade, plant, utensils, book-debts, etc., of an engineer, etc., at Dartford; and to his sons William, and Peter Brames, if they will become the purchasers, his share of five-eighths of the partnership estate, stock-in-trade, plant, utensils, book-debts, etc., of a gunpowder manufacturer at Feversham and Daving-

John and Edward Hall, who have since made consider-

---

ton ; and to his son Henry, his moiety of the partnership estate, business, stock-in-trade, plant, utensils, book-debts, etc, of a paper-manufacturer at Horton Kirby ; and to take their several bonds, under a sufficient penalty, for payment of the same : the sum payable from his sons John and Edward Hall, to be paid by half-yearly instalments in seven years from the death of testator ; and from William and Peter Brames Hall, and from Henry Hall, by half-yearly instalments in ten years, the whole bearing interest at four per cent. per annum—to raise three several sums of £6,000, for each of his daughters, Eliza, Maria, and Louisa, which is to be invested in the public funds or securities in England or Wales, and the interest of the several sums paid to them half-yearly so long as each of them should live, and not to be subject to the debts or controul of any husband ; but their receipts only to be a sufficient discharge : if either of them should marry and leave children, their children to inherit the mother's property at the age of 21 : and in case of their marrying and leaving an husband surviving and no children, the husband to enjoy the annuity during life ; but in case either of his daughters should die unmarried, then half of the said £6,000, should fall into the residue of his estate, and the remainder be disposable by will of each said daughter. In case two or more of his daughters should die unmarried and intestate, the legacy to fall into the residue of his estate.*

The executors are also out of the said residue to invest the sum of £7,000 in the same securities, and to pay the interest to his daughter Sarah, the wife of John Day, during her life ; with similar provisions in case she should marry again, and leave any children survivors, with his other daughters ; but in case she should die leaving no children, then one third of the principal sum of £7,000, shall fall into the residue of his estate.

He gives to his brother Edward Hall the sum of £500 ; to each of his children John, Edward and Charlotte, 19 guineas each ; to William Hart and Richard Clarke, his clerks, £50 each.

To Mary Gosling his sister, an annuity of £20 a year.

He also charges the payment of the interest of the mortgage of £2,000 on his mansion in Spital street, on the remainder of his estate ;

---

* Hence it becomes the interest of the brothers to prevent their sisters from marrying.

able additions to the buildings,)* and dividing the remainder of his property among his family.

THE BANKS.

The first Bank in Dartford was established by Mr. William Budgen, about 1805, or 1806, a Currier and Leather-cutter, originally from Chatham, he married Mary, a first cousin of the same name, and with her acquired considerable property. She died in 1805, at the age of 51. Mr. Budgen died April 27th, 1826, having previously admitted as partner Mr. David James, a native of Wales, and an active clever young man.† Mr. James carried on the business of banker and currier, until December 1834, when he failed. Mr. Day from Rochester then commenced the business in the town, and abandoned it the following year. Near the same time another bank was started by Medley, Scott and Hayward, which has since been relinquished by all the parties. It is now carried on by Messrs. McRae and Co., of Gravesend. They do not issue their own notes.

---

and gives all the interest arising from the investment of the several remaining sums to his wife Sarah Stainton Hall, (called in the preceding part of the will Sarah Stanton Hall,) for her life, in lieu of dowry; and after her decease, directs that the principal shall be divided equally between his sons, John, Edward, William, Henry, Peter, and their heirs. Proved 21st July, 1836. *In Prerog. Office, Cant. Stowell.* 430.

* John Hall, the eldest son, married Hannah, the daughter of Mr. Powell, a cupper in Blackfriars, London ; by whom he has an only daughter of the same name.

† Mr. James was apprenticed to a shoemaker, and married in the principality. Mr. Brand was his first employer in Dartford, in Nov. 1793; and he was recommended to Mr. Budgen by Mr. Thomas Brandon.

THE BREWERIES.

There are now four Breweries in Dartford ; two of these are situated in Lowfield street, one* belonging to Messrs. Charles and William Fleet, and the other to John and William Tasker† ; a third near the High street, in the occupation of Mr. William Pittock ; and the other in the Waterside, recently erected by Mr. Miskin.

THE RIVER DARENT.

The Darent enters this parish a little above the Powder mills, and branches off into two streams, just below the Silk mills, which uniting their waters at Dartford bridge, becomes navigable for barges at the Phœnix wharf. Proceeding in a sinuous direction for about two miles, it receives the Cray into its channel, aad empties itself in the Thames. There was formerly a considerable *fishery* in this creek, which is noticed in the records of the manor and of the priory.

---

* The brewery was in the hands of John and Henry Wooden at the commencement of the last century ; near the middle it passed to John Pettet, and afterwards to Ann and Mary his daughters ; they were succeeded herein by Mr. Hussey Fleet, who left it to his sons, the present proprietors. The brewery was originally entered from the High street, and is held of Dartford Rectory, by a quit rent of two shillings per annum. *Court Rolls*, No. 22.

† The first William Tasker settled in Dartford about 1635. In 1656, he acquired some property in Lowfield street, and was assessed 2s. per annum. In 1670, he paid 3s. upon an assessment of rent and stock at £9 yearly value. *Parish Assessment books, sub. ann.* In 1685, William Tasker the younger held the parsonage of Dartford ; he died 10 May, 1732, leaving three sons.—John, the eldest, an attorney and steward of Dartford manor, died 1749.—Henry, the youngest was the occupier of the original brewery in Lowfield street. *Court Rolls of Dartford Priory, sub. ann.*

Even so late as the reign of King James I., the royal manor of Dartford received for the fishery six salmons yearly, of 40s. value, a kind of fish seldom found here; and the manor of Dartford priory received a rent of £3 for a fishery likewise here at the same time. No fishery, however, exists at this time, nor has for many years past. The fish at present caught are trout, dace, gudgeons, eels, and fine flounders. The fishery belongs to the Rev. Augustus Morgan, but no notice is taken of its being private property, every one fishing at his pleasure therein.

In the 18th Elizabeth an order was issued for the return of the several places in this county where there were any shipping, boats, or the like. That return states there were four quays or landing places on the Darent, at Dartford, and seven ships or boats—of which three were of three tons; one of six; two of ten; and one of fifteen. At that period there were fourteen persons who carried goods from Dartford to London by the Creek.

One of the quays or landing places belonged to the Wardens of Rochester bridge* from time immemorial; another formerly to Dartford priory;† a third

---

* John de Freningham or Farningham amortized his whole manor of Le Hithe to the wardens of Rochester Bridge, but only the wharf is now known. He constructed the first draw-bridge over the Darent to enable vessels to approach Dartford bridge.

† "The Priory or le Hegge wharf" originally included what was formerly known as Wilks and Colyer's (now Temperley's) wharf, and also that called the Town wharf. It was included among the tenements of the priory, which after the dissolution were acquired by the Beers, and descended to the Twisletons, and in 1658 was held of the manor of Dartford Priory by a quit rent of 30d. per annum. In ancient times, the prioress had granted to her tenants, which

was the Town wharf;* and a fourth private property,

---

then formed the bulk of the inhabitants of Dartford, permission to land goods on a certain portion of her wharf, this being continued after it came into lay hands, gradually grew into a right and passed unquestioned. To preserve some kind of order and control, the tenant of the principal adjoining wharf, (Temperley's) was by all parties admitted to exercise a superintendence over the Town wharf. Hence from 1681 to 1685, both the wharfs are stated to be held by Thomas Wakerell, who was assessed at £22. In 1688 the same superintendence became vested in John Warde, though he is only described in the parish books as "holding the Town wharf." In process of time a house was erected thereon for the wharfinger, and the tenant of "the Priory or le Hegge wharf," Charles Gregory and his wife, occupied it from 1756 to 1790. The Court rolls of the manor in 1790, state that a moiety of this messuage and wharf in Hithe street, still held of the manor of Dartford priory, was devised by Thomas Smith to his brother George Smith and his heirs, and that George Smith devised them to his sister Elizabeth Knoll of Offham, who appeared by her attorney, paid relief, quit rent, etc. These she again alienated in 1792 to Thomas Williams of Horton Kirby, who previously held the other moiety by purchase from Lord Say and Sele in conjunction with the above named Thomas Smith* in 1758, as part of the Twisleton estates. *Court Rolls.* The whole thus becoming vested in him, descended to his nephew the late John Williams, who sold that portion of the wharf which had formerly remained in the prioresses own occupation (and been heretofore claimed as private property) to Mr. Colyer, then in partnership with Mr. William Wilks, as Coal merchants.

* For years few of the inhabitants of Dartford except the wharfingers had kept trading vessels to London, and the "Town wharf" lay waste and nearly fell into desuetude, which Mr. Williams observing, partly by the *right of superintendence* formerly vested in the adjacent wharf, and partly by almost forgotten *dormant claims* derived through the successors of the prioress to the Twisletons, then usurped a right to the Town Wharf. His position as a lawyer and steward of the manor, induced acquiescence, especially as people were

---

* Mr. Smith, the partner of Mr. Williams, was buried at Offham.

now belonging to the Phœnix Mills, and let to Messrs. Hammond and Waller.

---

allowed to land and cart away their goods at pleasure without demand or interruption.   "About 1826 Messrs. Wilks and Colyer, coal merchants, "wanting a house and office, took it of the trust of the late Mr. Williams, "principally for the house which stood in front of the wharf, which "they wanted as an office and residence for their clerk. About the "same time Messrs. Leigh and Rawlins, brick makers took the wharf in "question as under-tenants of Wilks and Colyer, but then, and for three "or four years after, the inhabitants of the town had free access to "the wharf at all times. There was a person of the name of Knock, "a lighterman, who kept a sailing lug boat as a regular trader between "London and Dartford for the purpose of bringing down goods for the "tradesmen.   These goods were invariably landed and carted from the "wharf without any demand.   On January 9th, 1831, it was sold by "auction to Mr. John Willding.   Now a year or two previous, poor "Knock fell to decay and dropped his lug-boat, and with him dropped "the constant exercise of the right of the inhabitants of Dartford to "the freedom of the quay.   After the purchase, Mr. Willding announced "his intention to inclose it, a great outcry was raised against the "inclosure, but Mr. W. persisted in the erection of his fence and "locked up the premises.   The wharf was shortly after let to Mr. "Philcox, in whose occupation it remains.   Those whose business led "them on the water strongly protested against the procedure, unless "he left a passage or camp-shed whereby they could reach their craft, "but he refused, although it was said in consequence of the defective "title the completion of the purchase was made only upon a guarantee of "the Vendors.—The inclosure has rendered Dartford Creek only "accessible by a narrow inlet at the bottom of the waterside ; though "the navigation may be free, it is useless to the townspeople."—*Account of Dartford Town wharf, by R. Penny, Gravesend Journal, Nov.* 1838.

Formerly all decent persons were detered from passing down the Waterside by the rude and mischievous manners of the inhabitants, who were chiefly bargemen and others employed on the river.

THE CREEK.

The Creek, from its mouth to the public wharfs,* in its original circuitous route, was about three and a half miles in length, although those wharfs in a straight line from the same outlet, were not distant more than two, nor more than one and three quarters of a mile from the nearest point of the Thames. It was only navigable by barges of fifty tons burthen, and seldom except at spring tides could these come up to the wharfs with a full freight. At other times, especially at neap tides, it was usual for these barges then only laden with cargoes from twenty to forty tons, to anchor at Hibbert's wharf (a quarter of a mile below the Phœnix Mills) and for a considerable part of the goods to be brought to the wharfs in small vessels (punts) of ten or twelve tons each. The barges thus lightened, were then floated up as soon as a sufficient depth of water was obtained. At neap tides, and when a strong south west wind blew, the creek was at times unnavigable, and frequently small vessels were detained several days. To remedy these impediments and facilitate the navigation, a Ship Canal was projected in November, 1835,† which was warmly

* John de Freningham who gave the Hithe-wharf to Rochester Bridge, was sheriff of Kent in the reigns of Edw. II. and Edw. III.

† Mr. Penny says "the first idea of a Ship Canal suddenly flashed across the brain of Mr. Edward Hall, the projector, as he rode outside the coach to superintend some improvements in his father's gunpowder and brimstone works at Feversham; and that on his return to Dartford he arose early in the morning and ascending the heights in the neighbourhood of the Creek, saw the thing was perfectly practicable, and communicated the plan to his friends who

supported by the inhabitants of Dartford, but failed
through the strenuous opposition of Mr. Wilks the
proprietor of the Phœnix mills, (who considered the

entered heartily therein." *Letter to the Inhabitants of Dartford and Neighbourhood, on the proposed Ship Canal.* p. 16. [Dartford, 1835] See also
Verses on the same subject by a satirical rhymester, *Gravesend Journal.* *—
Mr. Hall then published "An Enquiry into the present state of Dartford
Creek with means proposed for its Improvement." This maiden performance being printed on Zinc was remarkably unfavourable for general
perusal, it was followed by a severe and caustic "Investigation" by Mr.
W. C. Fooks, which extremely annoyed the author Conjointly they
afford a complete view of the navigation.—The Ship Canal was proposed
to be effected by a capital of £65,000, to be raised in 2,600 Shares at £25
each.   From the Subscribers' Contract it appears 1,507 Shares were
taken ; and if the regular deposit of £2 per share was paid (?) a sum of
£3,014 was raised for preliminary proceedings.—Had this Canal been
completed, probably it would have led to the formation of new establishments on its banks and the material improvement of the trade of
Dartford.

* THE SHIP CANAL DARTFORD.   *From the Gravesend Journal.*

High on the coach one summer's
    day,
  When the sun was gaily shining ;
A man of Dartford took his way,
  Upon the roof reclining.

And drawing near his native town,
  He thought of her inland sta-
    tion ;
And idly wished as he hurried
    down,
  To change her situation.

"Ah! wert thou plac'd upon the
    shore,
  That's wash'd by yonder river,
Thy streets with streams of gold
    would pour,
  Like those of the Guadal-
    quiver."†

He thought it o'er and when
    arrived
  At his journey's destination ;
A Ship Canal he had contriv'd,
  And resolved its publication.

His friends consulted all declar'd
  Their fullest approbation,
And vow'd they were at once
    prepar'd
  With aid of rank and station.

A man of speech¶ said he'd pre-
    side
  At the first great public meet-
    ing ;
Another swore he might confide
  In him for a cordial greeting

The Parson told his readiness,
  To move any resolution,
But said not a word I must con-
    fess,
  Of the slightest contribution.

The Lawyer readily gave the plan,
  Professional skill and aid ;
But begged to know ere he began,
  How his services would be paid.

The man of Dartford warming
    quite,
  With th' welfare of town and
    friends,
Has only in his glowing sight,
  The advance of his own ends.

Thus sprang the project. Thus
    matur'd,
  The 'bandonment of the creek :
While the MODE pursued, so well
    ensur'd
  From loss, the projecting clique.

† A river in Spain, whose sluggish waters flow somewhat like metal in a state of fushion.
¶ Mr. Medley, a partner of Scott and Hayward, bankers.

tolls upon water carriage would materially deteriorate his property) and an embryo Dover Rail-road Company.*

In 1839 another plan was proposed for improving the navigation under the Commissioners of Sewers and others appointed by an act of parliament, by shortening the distance and deepening the old Creek, so as to admit vessels of 150 tons up to the wharfs.†   This

---

* Mr. Wilks consented to expend a sum not exceeding £500 to defeat the bill: but it was accomplished by the Dover Railway Company for £450, upon the principle of "no cure no pay!" *Ex. inform. T. B. Fooks, arm.* This Rail-road, projected by a Mr. Walter, was to run from the Greenwich viaduct through Dartford marshes towards Dover. The Canal would have offered an impediment—hence their opposition. In 1836 a searching examination took place in parliament as to the formation of this Company, and the manner in which subscriber's names had been obtained, which ended in the abandonment of the scheme; it appearing that individuals had been paid small sums to sign the Contract for a sufficient number of Shareholders to appear on its face, pursuant to an Order of the House of Commons.

† From a statement submitted to a public meeting held Sept. 5, 1839, it was intended to reduce the distance three-quarters of a mile in Dartford Creek, and half a mile in the Crayford; and also increase the depth three feet up to the Phœnix wharf. The estimated expense of the proposed New portion of the Creek was £3,058 11s.; for improving the present Creek £2,545 8s. 8d.; for the Crayford £1,565 10s. 2d.; making a total of £7,169 9s. 10d. This did not include the land, which would be about 17 acres, and would cost £1,020; obtaining the Act of Parliament and law expenses £1,000; engineers' charges £700; and various other sums which put together, amount to about £12,000, which it was intended to borrow on the tolls. The chairman then stated, that all parties were agreeable to 2d. a ton, and that the present trade was estimated at 75,000 tons a year which at 2d. per ton would only give £625 per ann.: this would only leave £25 yearly for expenses, a sum too small to induce people to lend money for the undertaking, they therefore must take 3d. by the Act.

they have partially accomplished under an Act 3 Victoria, c. lv. obtained for that purpose, by a new cutting which extends from a little below Hibbert's wharf to Great Moorden reach ; is 95 feet wide at top, and 30 at bottom.* It is purposed also to deepen the old channel three feet from the new cutting to the Phœnix mills.† At the highest spring tides there will be ten feet water. These tides last four or five days at every new and full moon. To effect these alterations, threepence a ton is allowed to be charged upon all goods, but the work at present (1843) is incomplete.‡

---

* The ship canal was proposed by Mr. Hall to have been 100ft wide at the water's surface, and 12ft. deep, so as to have admitted vessels from 300 to 400 tons.

† The marsh land through which the new cutting passed, appeared to be formed of the washing of the upland, and the river deposit, based upon a bed of peat.

‡ The Act 3 Victoriæ, ¶ 1, provides that the qualification of a commissioner, is a declaration that he is worth £1,000 after all his debts are paid ; ¶ 51, authorises them upon expending £1,000 on improving the navigation of the creek after the new line is certified to be completed to the Justices at Quarter Sessions, to levy 3d. per ton on all coals, timber and merchandize carried upon the navigation, and a further duty not exceeding 3d., on such vessels as shall carry any passengers, and a like duty for each and every time such vessels shall ply upon or navigate the said creek.

¶ 59, authorises the Commissioner to collect a reserve fund of £2,000, applicable to repairing and maintaining the navigation.

BALDWINS.

Baldwins is a seat and reputed manor situated at the south west corner of Dartford-Heath, at the extremity of the parish. It was antiently in the property of Sir John Baude, knight, descended from an honourable family, of whom it acquired the name of Baudiwins, and afterwards passed into the possession of the abbot and convent of Lesnes,* who held it with divers lands in the same parish of the manor of Temple, Dartford, by 2s. 5d. yearly rent, and suit of court. On the suppression of this abbey, 16 Henry VIII., (1524) the revenues were granted to Cardinal Wolsey, towards the endowment of Cardinal College, Oxford; on his disgrace, this, among the other estates of that College, were forfeited to the King, who, by letters patent, in the twenty-third year of his reign, granted it, by the name of the manor of Baudwyns, and other land and premises, thereunto belonging, in exchange for other lands to Eton College, near Windsor; to which establishment the inheritance of this seat and manor now belong.

The parish books of Dartford show the following gentlemen lessees or residents at Baldwins; Henry Elsing, esq.† 1641 to 1644; Mr. Loggins, 1685; Peter Wade, 1689; Mr. John Moseley, 1695, to 1714. In the middle of the last century, Sir Edward Hulse,

* The abbot of Lesnes possessed lands in Dartford as early as the reign of King John, among these, were some meadows opposite Horseman's place, in Lowfield-street.—Henry de Northwood temp. Edward II., gave also some messuages in Dartford to the same abbey.

† This gentleman's family seems to have been reduced to poverty during the civil wars, for we find in 1659, a Roger Elsing, accepting sixpence, part of a fine of nine shillings paid by Mr. Smith's man, for travelling on the Lord's day. *Overseer's Accounts. sub. ann.*

bart., first physician to his majesty, George II. was
lessee. He died April 10th, 1759, at the advanced age of
77, and was buried at Wilmington.* He was succeeded
in this estate, by Richard, his third son, who served the
office of sheriff for the county, 1768, and continued till his
death in the commission of the peace. About 1783, he
sold Baldwins to John Nisbit, esq., and retired to Blackheath. Nisbit resold it to Simon Frazier, a merchant of
London, who resided there 1790. Mr. Frazier was succeeded by Thomas Calvert, esq. a gentleman from India.
Mr. Calvert partly rebuilt the house about 1802; (the
front is in the Italian style, with a handsome recessed
portico, guarded by lofty Ionic columns which support
the entablature),† and thereby so much impoverished
himself, that he sold the estate in 1806, to Mr. Sparks,
who re-sold it in 1818 to Isaac Minet, esq. a gentleman
descended from a French refugee family who settled at
Dover.‡ Mr. Minet died at Baldwins, March, 1839, and
was buried at Westerham.¶

The reserved rent to Eton college is 4s. 8d. per annum.

---

* Sir Edward Hulse, practiced in London as a physician for many
years, with great reputation and success. He married Elizabeth,
daughter of Sir Richard Levitt, Knight, lord mayor in 1700, and had
issue by her, three sons; Edward who succeeded his father in title,
settled in Hampshire; Westrow, who died in 1746; and the above
Richard, who died 27th Oct., 1809, aged 78: Richard is buried beneath a
splendid monument in Wilmington church-yard.

† It was little more than a farm house previously.

‡ There was a monument in the middle aisle of St. Mary's church,
Dover, to this family; on which, are recorded the death of Isaac Minet,
merchant, who died April 8th, 1745. Mary his wife, died April 30th,
1738. Isaac Minet, junior, merchant, died October 31st, 1731. William
Minet, of London, merchant, died Jan. 18th, 1767.

¶ The grandfather of this family settled at Westerham. *Ex. inform.
Geo. Minet, armig.*

MANOR AND ROYALTY OF DARTFORD.

From a remote period this town was the property of the Saxon kings, and was regarded as part of the antient demesne of the crown of England. It is accordingly entered under that title in Domesday book.

(Translation.)

THE KING'S LAND, IN THE HALF OF SUTTON LATH, IN ACHESTANE, (AXTANE,) HUNDRED.

KING WILLIAM holds TARENTFORD for one Suling and a half; there is land of two carucates; and thirty-two villanes with ten borders, have fifty-three carucates. There are three servants and one mill; twenty-two acres of meadow; forty acres of pasture; eight small and three large dens of wood. There are two hithes or havens. In the time of king Edward the Confessor, it was worth sixty pounds, and as much, when Hamo, the sheriff, received it.

It is now rated by the English at sixty pounds; but the reve, a Frenchman born (p'posit' vero Francig'), who holds it to farm, says that it is worth no more than twenty pounds and ten pounds; yet he pays from this manor seventy pounds by weight, and one hundred and eleven shillings in pence, twenty in ore,* and seven pounds and twenty-six pence by tale. Besides these the sheriff pays one hundred shillings.

The tenants of the hundred affirm, that there are taken away from this, the King's manor, one meadow and one alder ground, and one mill, and twenty acres of land; and now so much meadow as belongs to ten acres of land; all which were in the occupation of King Edward as long as he lived. These were worth twenty shillings; but they say that Osward, then sheriff, let them to farm to Alestan, portreve of London, and now Heltus, the King's steward, and his grandson, hold them.

The above tenants likewise affirm, that Hageleit† is taken

---

* Ore was a nominal money among the Saxons—It is often mentioned in Domesday, as of the value of 20*d*. *Note by Hasted.*

† Hawley, in the parish of Sutton-at-Hone.

away from this manor; it was taxed at half a suling. The sheriff held the land; and when he quitted the shrievalty, it remained in the king's occupation; and so it remained after the death of King Edward; now Hugh de Port holds it, with fifty-four acres of land more. The whole of this, is worth fifty-one pounds. Of this same manor of the King, there are now taken away six acres of land, and a certain wood which the above-named Osward, the Sheriff, set without the manor to pledge, for forty shillings.

The bishop of Rochester holds the church of this manor, and it is worth sixty shillings. Besides this, there are now here three chapels.

———

In the reign of king Henry II., the sheriff of Kent accounted at the exchequer for the rent of DARTFORD MANOR then in the king's hands, as he did likewise in the first year of king John; soon after which it was granted to the earl of St. Pol, (St. Paul,) a nobleman of Normandy. In the third year of that reign, Hugh, earl of St. Pol, then going on pilgrimage to the Holy land, had the king's licence to mortgage his land at Dartford for three years.* King Henry III., in his fourteenth year, granted to John de Burgo, the manor of Dartford, which had been the earl of St. Paul's, and which was then held by Raymond de Burgo, the king's bailiff, till the king should by composition, or at his own pleasure, restore it to the earl's right heirs;† for when Normandy was seized by the king of France, many lands became vested in the crown by escheat, or seizure. Whilst England and Normandy were under the obedience of the king of England, the lands of the English and Normans were

———

* Rot. Pat. cod. an. m. 6.   † Rot. Claus. p. 2. m. 6.

common; that is, the English held lands in Normandy by hereditary right, and the Normans did the like in England; but when the countries were separated, each of the sovereigns seized the respective lands of each others subjects, and appended them to their crowns. The estates of the foreign proprietors thus escheating to the crown of England, were called Terræ Normanorum, and eventually granted to Englishmen under similar conditions.*

A.D. 1260, William de Fortibus, earl of Albermarle, died possessed of this manor, in the forty-fourth year of that reign, holding it of the king in capite.† It escheated to the crown on the death of his sons. King Henry III., in his forty-seventh year, restored it to Guy de Chastilian, earl of St. Paul, who held it for the remainder of his life, when having reverted to the crown, Edward I., in his ninth year granted it to queen Eleanor, his mother.‡ She died in the twentieth year of that reign, and her grandson Edward II., A.D. 1319, committed the custody of this place to Elias de Tyngewick, during pleasure, *in the same manner as Robert de Rydgware, the late bailiff, had the custody* of it, and for which *he paid thirty pounds yearly*, as for *the ferm of the royalty and market.*¶

The same king in his fifteenth year, by consent of parliament, granted to Edmund de Wodestock, his half brother, whom he at the same time created earl of Kent, among other estates of great value, the aforesaid ferm of the royalty and market still valued at thirty pounds, which was confirmed by Edward III.

---

* Madox's Excheq. 206.   † Esc. 44 H. iii. p. 1. No. 26.

‡ Pat. 9. Ed. I.   ¶ Mag. Rot. 13. Ed. II.

in the first year of his reign, and specified in the grant as held of him in capite, for half a knight's fee.

Three years afterwards, Edmund, earl of Kent, fell a victim to the machinations of queen Isabella and lord Mortimer, on the eve of St. Cuthbert ; and the inquisition taken after his death, specifies this estate to have then consisted of *rents of assize of the tenants of Dartford, Chesilhurst, Cransted, Coombe, Cobham, Stannel and Gilde; the passage of the Darent; tolls; views of Frankpledge; and perquisites of Court;* altogether of the value of thirty pounds.*

From this specific enumeration, it clearly appears that *no part of the lands* in Dartford were included in the manorial grant, but, that it *solely consisted of the seignorial rights.*

Edmund and John Plantagenet, his sons, successive earls of Kent, dying without issue,† Joan their sister

---

* Esc. 4. Ed. iii. No. 58.

† Edmund two years after his father's execution, died a minor. John became of age, and had livery of his lands, 25 Edw. III. He married Elizabeth, daughter of the marquis of Juliers, and died Dec. 27, following. His disconsolate widow, shortly after—in the bloom of youth and beauty—vowed chastity, and was solemnly *veiled a nun by the bishop of Winchester, at the convent of Waverley;*—but, afterwards, *repenting of having so precipitantly quitted the world,* she secretly withdrew from the monastery, and about eight years after, "before the sun-rising, upon Michaelmasday," A.D. 1360, was clandestinely *married* to Sir Eustace Dabrieschescourt, in a chapel of the mansion-house of Robert de Brome, a canon of the college of Wingham, by Sir John Ireland, a priest. Such a striking violation of ecclesiastical discipline, necessarily called forth condign punishment upon the culprits. The archbishop of Canterbury summoned them before him at his manor-house Maghfield, upon the seventh ides of April, and probably, had not their high rank and riches intervened, would

---

* Regist. Islip Archiep. Cantuar. 166. b.

usually styled the 'fair maid of Kent,' wife of Sir Thomas Holand, became their heir. She subsequently married Edward, the Black Prince, and died possessed of the estate, A.D. 1385;* as did her son by her first

* Esc. 9 Ric. ii. No. 54.

have instantly pronounced the marriage null and void. As it was, he enjoined for their penance, that, since their marriage was unlawfully solemnized in the church of Wingham, they should cause a priest to celebrate Divine Service daily in the chapel of Our Lady there, for the health of the souls of the said Sir Eustace and Elizabeth, and him, the said archbishop; that the priest should there, every day, say over the seven penitential psalms, with the litany, for them, and all faithful christians; and also *placebo and dirige* for all the faithful deceased. And also, that every morning, as soon as he had risen from his bed, he should say five paternosters and aves kneeling; stedfastly looking upon the wounds on the crucifix: and as many every night in the like way. Moreover, that they, the said Sir Eustace and Elizabeth, should find another priest to continually reside with one of them, to celebrate Divine Service for them, in the same manner as the priest at Wingham was to do, and in a similar manner, say the seven penitential psalms, liturgy, placebo and dirige. He likewise enjoined the said Elizabeth that *every day, during her whole life, she* should say the seven penitential psalms, and the fifteen gradual psalms, with the liturgy, placebo and dirige, together with the commendation of souls for the quick and the dead. And also, appointed the said Eustace and her, that the next day after any sexual embrace, they should competently relieve six poor people, and both of them, that day, abstain from some dish of flesh or fish, whereof they did most desire to eat.—And lastly, that the said Elizabeth should once, every year, go *barefoot* to visit the shrine of that glorious martyr, St. Thomas of Canterbury; and, once every week, during her life, take no other sustenance but bread and drink, and a mess of pottage; wearing no chemise— especially when her husband was absent. The lady endured this sentence of penance for fifty-one years, as she died at Bedhampton, June 6, 1411, and was buried at the Friars Minors at Winchester, in the tomb of John earl of Kent, her first husband. *Dug. Bar.* ii. 95. *Lond.* 1675.

husband Thomas Holand, earl of Kent, A.D. 1399,* still
holding it by capite, etc., as aforesaid. Thomas, created
duke of Surrey, and Edmund, earl of Kent, his two sons,
both died without issue, leaving their four sisters coheirs;
on the partition of the estates, the manor of Dartford, with
the rents of assize in Chesilhurst, were allotted to Joane
his fourth sister, duchess of York, who appears to have
died possessed thereof, leaving no issue, 12 Henry, VI.
It seems then to have devolved upon Margaret, her sister,
first the wife of John, earl of Somerset, and afterwards of
Thomas, duke of Clarence, who held it till his death, 30th
Dec., 1439 (18 Hen. IV.), John, earl of Somerset, her son
by her first husband, being her heir, then of the age of
thirty years.† Subsequently created duke of Somerset,
and dying without issue, 22 Hen. VI.,‡ the estate passed
to Edmund, marquis of Dorset, his brother and heir, who
was slain in the fatal battle of St. Albans, A.D. 1454,¶ and
afterwards to his eldest son, Henry, duke of Somerset,
who fighting for king Henry, was taken prisoner in the
battle of Hexham, in Northumberland, and beheaded in
the third year of Edward IV. Two years afterwards,
being attainted in parliament, all his possessions escheated
to the crown.

The manors of Dartford, Chesilhurst, etc., were
next granted to Richard Nevil, earl of Warwick, who
after many changes from one side to another, was
slain at the battle of Barnet, A.D. 1471, when his
estates were seized by authority of parliament, although,
subsequently, a great part of them were restored to

---

* Esc. 20 Ric. ii No. 30.

† Dug. Bar. ii. 197.   ‡ Ibid. ii. 123.   ¶ Ibid. 124.

his daughters, amongst which, were the manor of Dartford, with the rents of assize at Chislehurst, to Isabel, whose husband George, duke of Clarence, brother of Edward IV., became, in her right, possessed of them. Clarence soon falling under the king's displeasure, was drowned in a butt of malmsey wine, when the manor reverted by his attainder to the crown, and was granted to Thomas, lord Stanley, for life.

Both the daughters of Ann, the countess of Warwick, being dead,* in 1487, Henry VII. recalled that aged lady from her retirement in the north, where she was living in a mean and distressed condition ; and by a new act of parliament, annulled her husband's attainder, and restored to her all her possessions, with power to alien any part of them. Then, by his power, so influenced her, that, by a special feoffment, dated 13th December, the same year, and the levying of a fine, she granted the whole, consisting of one hundred and fourteen manors, to the king and his heirs male, amongst which, were those of Dartford and Wilmington, together with the rents of assize in Chislehurst.†

Notwithstanding this Conveyance, in consideration of lord Stanley's services, and his having married Margaret, countess of Richmond,‡ (the king's mother,) this estate continued in that nobleman's possession,

---

* Isabel the eldest, who married George, duke of Clarence, and died circ. 1476 ; Ann, married firstly, Edward, Prince of Wales, son of Henry VI. ; secondly, Richard, duke of Gloucester ; afterwards King Richard III., who is supposed to have poisoned her to marry Elizabeth, the daughter of Edward IV.

† Dugdale's Baronage, i. 306.

‡ His first wife was Eleanor, sister to Richard Nevil, the great earl of Warwick, the adherent of Edward IV. *Dug. Bar.* i. 303.

and he was advanced to the further dignity [1503] of earl of Derby. He died, in the nineteenth year of that reign,[*] leaving the lady Margaret, countess of Richmond, his second wife, surviving, who, by his will, peaceably enjoyed all the manors, lands, etc., assigned for her jointure, pursuant to an act of parliament passed 1 Hen. VII.[†] Amongst others, she possessed this manor and an estate at Wilmington, which, from that circumstance, are frequently called in the records of that time, "RICHMOND'S LANDS." She died, June 29th, 1509, (1 Hen. VIII.) and the reversion being vested in the crown, they remained therein, until the twenty-sixth of Elizabeth, when that queen for twenty-one years, demised the manors of Dartford, Cobham, Combe, and Chislehurst, with all her lands and tenements belonging to it, called "*Richmond's Lands*," the *two wharfs*, and the profits of the *markets* and *fairs;* (excepting to her and her heirs, all court leets, views of frankpledge and all belonging thereunto; advowsons; rents of assize of the free tenants; woods; underwoods; mines, and quarries,) at the yearly rent of £3 7s. with an injunction, that he should keep from time to time the court baron, court leet, and view of frankpledge, in the same manner they had been accustomed to be kept by the steward of the manor; and should collect and levy the rents, profits, and issues of the manor, and render an account and pay the same to the Receiver-general of the county of Kent. And she granted him, for keeping the said courts, a yearly fee of 20s., and for collecting the said rent, etc., 26s. 8d.

---

[*] Ibid. ii. 249. Holgrave, 19 Reg. Test. in Cur. Prerog. Abp. Cant.

[†] Collins's Peerage, 448, 450.

And further granted sufficient housebote, hedgebote, fierbote, ploughbote, and cartbote, growing on the premises, and there, only to be used; and also timber for the repair of the buildings thereby let, which the said Edmund Walsingham was bound to repair and maintain.*

In 1597, (40 Eliz.) Sir Thomas Walsingham had a further demise of these estates, still called "Richmond's lands;" for the same term of twenty-one years, under the like rents and covenants.

King James I., in the eighth year of his reign granted by letters patent to George and Thomas Whitmore, of London, their heirs and assigns, the Hundreds of Chadlington and Leighfield, in Kent, of thirty shillings yearly value, and also his manors of *Dartford, Cobham, Combe, and Chislehurst*, with all their rights, members, and appurtenances; and all his lordships, tenements, and hereditaments, in Dartford and Wilmington, with the *wharfs* in Dartford, and the issues and profits of the *fairs* and *markets* there, lately let to Edward Walsingham; and the profits of the courts of the Hundred, and of the said manor, late parcel of *Richmond's lands*, which were of the annual value of £6 5s. 10d.; to hold the same as of his manor of East Greenwich, by fealty only, in free and common socage, and not *in capite*, nor by knight's service.†

A.D. 1611, June 3rd. George and Thomas Whitmore conveyed the above Hundreds, manors, and premises, to Sir Thomas Walsingham, of Scadbury, Chislehurst; in as full and ample a manner as they themselves held the same.

---

* The lease is signed W. Burghley, and deposited in the Augmentation office.

† Deeds in the Rolls Chapel.

Sir Thomas Walsingham, in May, the eleventh year of king James, A.D. 1613, for £500, conveyed all these premises, excepting the manor of Chislehurst with all its appurtenances and courts in that parish, to Sir Robert Darcy, knt., the then owner of the lately dissolved priory, Dartford, in as full a manner as he held it himself.* This deed was afterwards enrolled in chancery.

From this period, the manorial history becomes *united* with that of the priory.

The great-grandchildren of Sir Robert Darcy, Dame Catherine Phillips, Dame Dorothy Rokesby, and Thomas Milward, esq., conveyed these premises by the name of *the manor of Dartford, alias Dartford Priory ;* to Thomas Gouge, esq., who died in 1707, leaving a widow and three sons, and a daughter married to a gentleman named Mynors, in Hertfordshire.†

Upon the death of the father, a dispute arose between the brothers, concerning the descent of these estates, which from the time of the conquest had been granted to hold in capite by knight's service. The two younger brothers, Nicholas, and Edward, insisted that a new socage tenure had been created by the act 4 Jac. I., and that the manor and lands ought to

---

* The estate was then valued as follows :—The two Hundreds, 30s. ; the fairs and markets, £20 ; the rents of assize in Dartford, 17s. 10d. ; in Cobham, £4 18s. 1d. ; in Combe, 24s. 10d. ; and for the fishery in the Creek, three salmons yearly, worth 40s.   Total £30 10s. 9½d.   From the wharfs not being mentioned, it is probable they had been sold to John Beer.   They are specified as the property of John Twisleton, in 1658, in the Court Rolls of the manor.   The Manor of Dartford still claims over Cobham and Combe.

† Vide Hasted, passim.

descend according to the custom of gavelkind, as other lands of socage tenure had usually done; and the elder brother on the contrary, insisting that a new tenure, created of late years, could not make the lands partake of gavelkind, which was gained by antient usage and custom. These disputes, however, subsided by the interposition of the mother, and Thomas the eldest brother, enjoyed these estates till his death, in 1731; when Nicholas, then becoming eldest brother, set up, and insisted upon the same right his brother Thomas had done before; and upon a trial in the King's Bench in Michaelmas term, 1734, the judges determined "That if lands were subject to gavelkind, nothing can alter the tenure, but an Act of Parliament expressly for that purpose; and, on the contrary, if not subject to the custom originally, there was nothing in the acts 4 Jac. I., or 12 Car. II., (the latter Act was to abolish the court of Wards and Liveries,) which, does expressly alter the course of descent of lands throughout England; and therefore, they did not apprehend that the tenure being turned into socage, would alter the course of descent here." It seems settled, that land held by military service is not subject to the above custom.* A verdict was consequently found for the plaintiff Nicholas, the eldest brother, who enjoyed all these estates till his death in 1755, he being then rector of Gilling, in Yorkshire, and prebendary of York and Lincoln.

He died unmarried, and by his will, devised sundry large sums to several public and parochial charities,

---

* Robinson's Gavelkind. 46. 51. 68. 92.

and these estates to his only surviving brother Edward, who likewise died unmarried, about two years afterwards; upon which, they, as well as others in Yorkshire and London, descended to his sister's son Robert Mynors, as heir at law, who took upon himself the name of Gouge, in pursuance of his uncle Nicholas's will, for which, an act passed 29 Geo. II.* He had, before this, become possessed of Temples manor in this parish, from the Priestleys, one of whom had former-married a descendant of the Darcys, and procured its separation. The estates, therefore, thus, again became united. Mr. Mynors died in 1765, without issue, and devised these manors to his widow Mary, who, afterwards, re-married with Charles Morgan, esq., of Herefordshire, who died possessed thereof in 1787, and was succeeded,† by his brother John, who, by will, dated 23rd June, 1789, devised his estates in succession to Charles John Van, and Thomas Van his nephews; and then, to Charles Gould the younger, in strict settlement. John Morgan died in 1792, when Sir Charles Gould, knt., took the surname and arms of Morgan, pursuant to the will of his wife's brother; and on the 15th of October, the same year, was created a baronet. Sir Charles died December, 1806, when he was succeeded by his eldest son.

Charles John Van, and Thomas Van, having died previous to 1799, without issue; Charles Gould the younger, thereupon became entitled to this estate; he

---

* An Act was passed 29 Geo. II. to enable Robert Mynors to take and use the surname of Nicholas Gouge deceased.

† Ex. origin. penés dom. Car. Morgan. bar.

afterwards assumed the surname of Morgan, and upon the death of his father, succeeded to his honours. He married Mary Magdalen, daughter of George Storey, esq., by whom he had several children.* She died 24th March, 1805; but the baronet himself still [1843] survives.

At a Court Baron held December 3rd, 1834, the Homage presented "that, since the last court held for this manor, Sir Charles Morgan, bart., late lord thereof, had granted and conveyed the same manor with all its rights, privileges, liberties, members and appurtenances, to the Rev. Augustus Morgan, his son, who in consequence had succeeded thereunto."

The Rev. Augustus Morgan is a younger son of Sir Charles, and chaplain in ordinary to Her Majesty, he married April 20th, 1837, Frances, second daughter of Rowley Lascelles, of Upper Grosvenor-street, esq.

ARMS OF MORGAN. 1st and 4th, Or, a griffin segreant, Sable, *Morgan*; 2nd and 3rd, Or, on a chevron between three roses, Azure, as many thistles of the field. *Gould*.

CREST. 1st, A rein-deer's head couped, Or, Gules. *Morgan*. 2nd, An eagle rising, proper, holding in the beak a pine-cone. *Gould*.

Hasted says, the Fee Farm rent now paid for the manor of Dartford is £49 1s. 10½d. to the crown, of which, the earl of Ilchester† was grantee in 1778.

---

* Kimpton enumerates three sons and as many daughters; the whole of whom, he says, are married. *Baronetage*.

† History of Kent. i. 248.

THE COURT LEET.

This court comprehends the whole of the parish of Dartford, except the bishop of Rochester's liberty, and that of Temples manor, together with all the parish of Wilmington.

At this court are annually chosen, the high constable of the hundred of Dartford and Wilmington, and four petty constables for the several liberties within the manor; and also an ale-conner, and a leather-sealer for the hundred.

A borsholder has, likewise, been then chosen for Temples liberty, which takes in the Waterside, or Hythe-street, in Dartford, and all the land from Temple hill, on the north-east side of the town, down to the river Thames. The tenants are all free tenants, holding by small quit rents, and subject to a relief of one-third part only of a year's quit rent, upon the death or alienation of every tenant.

The earliest roll of the COURT BARON and FRANK-PLEDGE which I have seen, is one of Lady Elizabeth Darcy's, alias Barnes, A.D. 1694, temp. Will. et Mar. written in latin, held before Henry Elwood, seneschal.

In the records of the Court Baron are entered all alienations in the manor, and the several fines paid to the lord thereon, the chief of which are: *e. g.*

1735. The manor of WEST-COMBE, in East Greenwich, alienated by the heirs of Sir Michael Biddulph, held of this manor at 9s. 2d. rent, whereof two reliefs are stated to be due, and the bailiff ordered to distrain.

There are also sundry lands in COBHAM,* near Round street, held also of this manor, by certain rents.

1777. The manor of WESTCOMBE, on the death of Sir Gregory Page, being devised by will to his great nephew Sir Gregory Page Turner, his attorney

---

* Both Cobham and Combe are called manors in the grant of James I.

attended, paid a relief of 3s. and all arrears of quit rent, when he was admitted tenant, and his fealty respited.

1805. The same also again occurred on Sir Gregory's death and the succession of his son.

At the VIEW OF FRANKPLEDGE, presentments of all sorts of local annoyances are made, and fines imposed upon the offenders. *e. g.*

1735. The jurors on oath, present, that Henry Blackwell, (a juror,) William Cronk, George Nokes, John Tadman, and others do wilfully receive and entertain in their several dwelling houses certain poor persons, and suffer them to remain and dwell for the space of one month, contrary to the form of the statute in that case made and provided : therefore, it is ordered, that they and every of them, do severally remove the said inmates from their dwelling houses, on, or before the 25th of December next, on penalty of twenty shillings to be paid by each of them.

1738. The common Stocks in Dartford, presented as ruinous and unsafe, and the churchwardens directed to repair them. The common pound was also presented, and the jury hope and desire the lord to repair and maintain the same.

1750. Whereas encroachments are made in the High-street by the proprietors of houses, building fronts under antient projections, and by erecting pent-houses, public notice to be given, that whosoever shall offend in like case, will be prosecuted by presentment in this court, and fined for the offence.

Robert Emery for laying carcases of dead horses near the Bull back-gate, to the great stench of the neighbourhood, amerced 6s.

Thomas Glover and James Crump for turning the blood of slaughtered beasts into the stream in Dartford, running from the Cranford to the Waterside, whereby the water is much polluted and soiled, amerced 5s.

Thomas Glover amerced 5s. for betraying the secrets of the jurors contrary to oath.

1756. James Newton and Francis Chapman, amerced 40s. for keeping ferrets, nets, and other engines for destroying game and fish.

The causeway next the King's Head Inn, leading up Lowfield, and the causeway opposite, adjoining to several houses in the fish market belonging to Mrs. Elizabeth Umphrey, being ruinous and out of repair—the owners or occupiers ordered to repair within one month, or be amerced 40*s.*

Robert Saxby amerced 40*s.* for suffering the soil of his lime-pits to run into the Cranford, and for every such future offence to forfeit to the lord of the manor, 5*s.*

Also the jurors on their oaths assert the lord of the manor has the sole right and royalty of the fishery in Dartford creek.

1762.   Thomas Glover amerced 40*s.* for killing calves in front of his shop in the High-street, and turning the blood into the Cranford.

John Archer fined 40*s.* for making his shop window project into the High-street, fifteen inches from the antient front, and ordered to remove it in six calendar months.

William Sears fined the same for suffering tippling and unlawful gaming in his house and nine-pin ground, on the Lord's day.

1763.   John Sherrin, fined 40*s.* for employing his servants to burn old asparagus on the Lord's day, 16th October, and for employing servants several times on the Lord's day, within this manor, to the evil example of others.

Thomas and Francis Twisleton, John Hards, and Elizabeth Quelch, ordered to repair the footpaths in front of their several houses in the Waterside, before 13th November, under penalty of 40*s.*

1768.   The parish of Wilmington ordered to repair their Stocks within two months under penalty of 20*s.*

1771.   John Shephard, tapster at the Bull Inn, fined 5*s.* for selling beer in a pot short of measure in deceit of the public, and the constable ordered to destroy the pot.

1785.   The stagnant water and soil on the west side of Lowfield-street desired to be taken away by the commissioners of the Dartford and Sevenoaks turnpike road, ordered to be removed under penalty of 40*s.*

STANHAM.

A little more than half a mile north-west-ward of the priory, lies the hamlet of Stanham, antiently called Stoneham; formerly part of the possessions of the priory of Dartford.

The principal mansion was used by the aged and sick nuns, as a place of occasional retirement, and the meadows and land around were occupied as a dairy farm for the use of the priory, but when their possessions became insecure, in the 25th Henry VIII., the prioress Elizabeth Cressener and her convent, let the capital messuage with the buildings thereon, and the several lands belonging thereunto for thirteen years, at the rent of £20 14s., to Robert Dove, their husbandman. After the suppression, the interest in the lease became vested in William Thynne, esq., who surrendered it up to the king, (37th Henry VIII.,) and had a further term of twenty-one years granted him, with the like rents and covenants.[*]

---

[*] Leases in Augmentat. Offic. Robert Dove of Dertford, by will dat. 18 Nov. 33 Hen. 8. bequeaths his soul to God, his body to be buried wherever Dorothy his wife pleaseth; he gives to Dorothy his wife three-score pounds of his goods and chattels; to Thomas and Vincent, his sons £20 a piece, to be delivered them at the age of 21; to Elizabeth and Margaret his daughters, £10 each, to be paid them at the age of 16; or if either of his sons or daughters die before they attain those years, then their legacies to be equally distributed among the survivors: if Dorothy his wife should marry before his children come to that age, then she shall deliver £20 to Bartholomew his brother, for the use of Thomas his son; and £20 to Sir Edward Parker, priest, for the use of his son Vincent; and £10 to Robert Mabrek, of Southwark, to the use of Elizabeth his daughter; and Dorothy his wife, to hold the £10 for Margaret his daughter.—"Item. I give to Robert Carter, my servant, 4 qrs. of

Queen Elizabeth in her eleventh year granted to Hugh Cartwright, her capital messuage, and a messuage called the Dayern house, in Stoneham; at the same yearly rent. This estate afterwards came into the possession of Mr. Smith, a merchant of London, and the two Mr. Bucks, of Norfolk; who about the middle of the last century, sold it to Mark Fielder, a linen draper of Dartford.* It was subsequently purchased by the late Mr. John Hall the celebrated engineer, by whom it was sold to Richard Berens, esq.†

STANHILL.

There is a farm and lands at the southern extremity of this parish, towards Birchwood corner, belonging to Mrs. Hodsoll and Mr. James Allen, bearing this name; which is said, to have antiently constituted a part of the manor of Stanhill, in Wilmington parish, heretofore belonging to the priory of St. Andrew, Rochester, and by Henry VIII., granted to the dean and chapter of Rochester. There has lately been a disputed right of road through this farm yard towards North-cray, but there is incontestible evidence it has not been publicly used within memory; and probably was originally only a private way leading through the woods. No carriage has passed for many years—The road is covered in with bushes; and tillers seven inches in diameter, are growing in the midst of the highway.

---

barley; and to all my men and married women, so that they remain with Dorothy my wife, and be good servants till Michaelmas, half a quarter of barley a piece :—I bequeath to the p'sh church of Dartford *one bible* of the greatest volume, etc." Prob. 13 April, A.D. 1542. *Reg. Test. epi. Roffen.* ix. 30.

* Hasted i. 225.   † Information of Mr. John Hall.

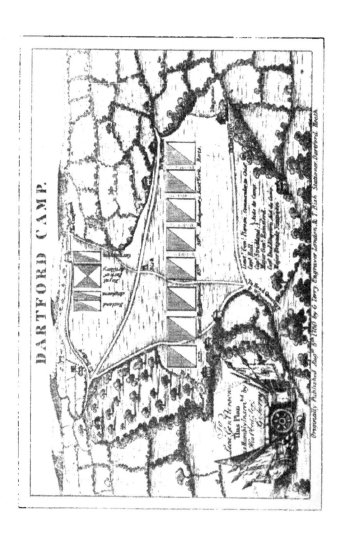

DARTFORD CAMP.

THE CAMP, DARTFORD HEATH, 1780.

From yonder Heath the lark no longer soars
The grasshopper ceases while the cannon roars—
Where sportive flocks once whiten'd o'er the ground,
Now bleaching huts are fixed our view to bound;
Where the furze phalanx could sweet herbage ward,
From prowling herds—now mounts the Captain's guard,
Or veterans wait till ovens here disgorge—
Or Sutler scores,—and here too glows the forge.
                    DARTFORD CAMP, 1780. *Mrs. Pott's Moonshine.*

In 1779 and 1780, the kingdom being threatened
with invasion by the French and Spaniards,* early in
the Spring of the latter year Camps were formed upon
Dartford-heath, and Cox-heath, in Kent; and on Warley-
common, in Essex. That at Dartford, seems to have
consisted chiefly of the 52nd, 59th, and 65th regiments
of the line; the North Hants; Northampton; Mont-
gomery; East-York; and Hertfordshire regiments of
militia; and a park of Artillery guarded by a portion
of the Rutland and Caernarvonshire militia. The troops
were under the command of lieutenant-general Pierson, as commander in chief, major-general Rainsford
and others. As usual, their military evolutions were

---

* This was strongly indicated by appearances.—In May, the French
marched down armies to the sea coasts of Brittany, and in June 1779, the
French fleet at Brest, joined the Spanish at Cadiz. Their combined fleet
amounted to between sixty and seventy line of battle ships, and directed
their course to the coast of Great Britain. In the middle of August, they
entered the British channel, and took the Ardent in sight of Portsmouth;
a sharp easterly wind drove them out; but they continued to range about
the mouth of the channel till the end of the month. When Sir Charles
Hardy was able to enter, they pursued him up to Plymouth,—and thus
ended the expedition. Never had so large a fleet been assembled on the
seas. *Annual Regist, p.* 12.

Y

the chief attraction of the neighbourhood.* In case of invasion it was designed these bodies of troops should act together; and "a grand public display" of the mode in which it was designed to effect the passage of the Thames at Gravesend, was made on July 27th, 1780.†

----

* Several of the officers took houses and apartments in the immediate neighbourhood of the heath for their families, and were visited by the daughters of Sir John Dyke, of Lullingstone Castle, Miss Mumford of Sutton-at-Hone, a Miss Buckley, the two Miss Struts, visitors to lady Mary Scott, of Blendon Hall, Miss Leigh of Hawley, and the Misses Catherina, and Ethelinda, daughters of Mr. Thorpe of Bexley, together with Dr. Munro, who frequently met and dined at the house of Capt. and Mrs. Mitton, and also with Colonel and Mrs. Greg, at the mess. The ladies consequently partook of the military mania, and are thus described dressed *en militaire*, while parading the Camp on Dartford-Heath, by Miss Ethelinda Margaretta Thorpe, afterwards Mrs. Potts.

> "Behold in epauleted scarlet BELLES advance,
> Like HEROINES painted in some old romance.—
> Who, thus accoutered may with due disdain,
> View the subaltern beauties of the plain :—
> By beaux protected, slowly march the groups
> In all the pomp of flounces, silks and hoops,
> By silken trains the wide parade is swept,
> In silken fetters rebel gauzes kept.
> Not only such are here—but those who blest
> By fortune's gifts—or if you will,—opprest ;
> May thank those graces education brought
> To deck in pleasing language many a thought.
> Perhaps but little differing if undressed,
> From those which harbour in a peasant's breast."—
> MOONSHINE ii. 216.

June 2nd. "By the riots in London, our Camp was deprived of three regiments, but with us remained the [earl of] Northampton, and one peeress." *Ibid.* 342.

Wednesday, 15th June, a duel was fought near Dartford-heath, between an officer in the Northampton militia and a gentleman of the law, the seconds interfered after the first shot.—*Morning Chronicle.*

† The newspapers announced that the troops were to receive His

Accordingly at day break that morning, the tents were
struck on Dartford heath, and the whole body consisting
of 8,000 troops were marched to Gravesend, and in three
divisions conveyed across the river backwards and for-
wards in less than eight hours, amidst an immense
assemblage of people who witnessed the proceedings.*
The troops then returned to Dartford-heath where they
arrived at about eleven o'clock at night.

Majesty at Dartford camp, before they marched to Gravesend; and it
was said, rooms had been prepared for the King and Queen at Tilbury
fort fronting the river, called the governor's ward, to see them cross the
Thames.   On Sunday evening, it was impossible to procure a bed either
at Gravesend or the adjacent villages, from the number of visitors.

* Pocock says, "three causeways were made for carriages to take them
down to low water mark; one above the town, the other at the town
stairs, [now the town pier,] and the third at the New Tavern; to each of
these, were ropes stretched across the river, and six barges affixed to
each, constructed with a moving platform in their stern so as to admit a
waggon with four or six horses to enter without unloading, and by means
of a hawser fixed in a block at her head, she soon proceeded to the Essex
shore, where unloading her cargo, she was let drop down by the side to
about thirty yards distance, where was a similar line of ropes to convey
her back across the river again.   The van of the army marching to New
Tavern, the centre to the town stairs, and the rear to the Hardway, west
end of the town."

On Wednesday, August 9th, appeared the following jeu d'esprit,
in a morning paper, burlesquing this "military display of crossing
the Thames, etc."   It began by stating "Last Saturday morning
lieutenant-general Pierson, lord Amherst, colonel St. Leger, earl
Fauconberg, the duke of Manchester, lord Le Despenser, general
Carpenter, with their military attendants, etc., held a grand review
of the troops at Dartford Camp, at which, after detailing their manual
exercise, platoon, grand and subdivision street and bush firing, says
—at half-past eleven the troops struck tents and the whole army
marched in four divisions off from the heath, with the artillery,

On Saturday evening, August 6th, a violent quarrel happened at Dartford Camp between a soldier of the 52nd regiment and one of the Northamptonshire militia, which occasioned a battle in front of the lines. Colonel Straubenzie of the 52nd endeavouring to quell the disturbance was exceeding ill treated; and it was with difficulty the two regiments were prevented making common cause with the combatants. One man had his ear cut off; another lost two fingers, and some had several very dangerous wounds, from swords, bayonets, etc.*

Notwithstanding the officers endeavoured to preserve strict discipline, the troops are said to have been

---

baggage, etc., the heavy ordnance being left at Camp, and proceeded thence to Gravesend, which they reached at half past three o'clock, and immediately warped over to the other side by a bridge of boats moored across the river, covered with a deal platform sufficient for 80 men abreast. They were 1 hour and 11 minutes passing amidst the greatest concourse of people ever assembled.—That batteries from Tilbury-fort fired as if with an intention of preventing their landing, when the grenadier light infantry marched up and took the fort.—At five, the troops being refreshed, re-crossed in the same order, and immediately set forward to Dartford-heath, where they arrived at a quarter past eight, pitched tents, and were dismissed with applause.

The nobility and gentry who attended, were afterwards entertained by a play called 'The Recruiting Serjeant,' performed by the officers and their ladies, in a large marquee; after which, the general entertained them with a supper, and some of the noble visitors did not leave the camp till Sunday noon."

A Gravesend correspondent on the 11th, thought proper to contradict all that is above stated to have passed relating to any troops being there on last Saturday from Dartford camp—though, he says, he does not disprove that the Camp was not reviewed by general Pierson, lord Amherst, etc., on the Saturday.

* Morning Chronicle.

guilty of much excess,* and committed several depredations.   They remained here until September, when to the
infinite regret of the belles of the neighbourhood, the
Camp broke up,† and, since then, Desolation has reigned
around.

The site of the long row of tents is still apparent (1844),
and clearly indicated by the turf-ruins, as the traveller
crosses from Heath-lane toward Baldwins.

---

* There were also many complaints of tradesmen, threatened to be
tossed in blankets, who had the impertinence to apply for their debts, or
sufficient temerity to seek the commanding officer's redress.

About the centre of the Heath, was a shop for supplying the troops
with stationery and small stores ; the Suttling house stood near Bowman's
lodge, and was kept by Mr. Powell, of the Granby, Dartford ; and the
Magazine was near the end of Heath lane.

† On the evening preceding the breaking up of the Camp, a select
party of the officers were invited to take a farewell supper with the ladies
of the neighbourhood : Miss Thorpe who was present, and very melancholy, says "they broke not the bread of cheerfulness—it was but the
ghost of gaiety ;—for what availed the attendance of beaux, to whom our
'GOOD NIGHT' might be for ever! and their morning salute accompanied
with the groan of [moving] forges—and—still more dismal sound—that
of departing regiments!"——*Moonshine*, ii. 334.

> Next Autumn, passing by the place,
> Described above, with its disgrace,
> We recognize a ragged set
> Of urchins creeping through the wet,
> Among turf-ruins and the rest
> We need not mention ; as 'tis guess'd,—
> There's one who seems to fill his basket
> With what ? 'twere worth our while to ask it.—
> Those ladies who on Camps attend,
> No doubt took all that they could rend,
> Nought they could forage can be left.—
> But on your patience to presume
> No more—they gather a mushroom.   *Ibid.* 22.

BOWMAN'S LODGE.

Here knights and damsels met in splendid show
Hailed the bright goddess of the silver bow,
And maids of Kent, expert in piercing hearts,
Supplied the archers with their eyes for darts;
From Love's artillery discharged their lances
And vanquish Cantia's heroes with their glances.—
Ye Virgin Sisters of chaste Dian's train
Have pity on the Archers ye have slain
For oh, what armour can secure be found
When arrows sharp as yours inflict the wound.

Lines by Miss Talbot.—MOONSHINE, 346.

On the borders of Dartford Heath is a house called Bowman's lodge, which obtained that appellation from having been taken by the Royal Society of Kentish Bowmen, instituted by Mr. J. E. Madox, [1785,] then resident at Mount Mascal,* in North Cray parish, where their first meetings were held. At the formation, eleven gentlemen only, enrolled their names, but in 1786, their numbers increased to thirty, and in the following year when their meetings were removed to Dartford Heath, and held every Saturday during the months of May, June, July and August, they numbered sixty-one; and when it was known to be patronized by His Royal Highness the Prince of Wales, the numbers increased to one hundred and twenty-three;† among

---

* The original members were J. E. Madox, Richard Leigh, Joseph Madox, Robert, Charles, and Felix Calvert, Thomas Latham, Rev. James Dadd, John Mumford, Robert Talbot, and Thomas Dalton.

† Among these were the following noblemen and gentlemen well known in the neighbourhood, Hussey Fleet, Thomas Waring, John Calcraft, Lord Eardley, N. Calvert, William Mumford, Simon Frazier, S. Frazier junior, John Randall, Robert Pott, George Norman, George Grote, William Whitmore, Major Rhode, Earl Darnley,

whom were some of the highest nobility. The Heath again became the favorite resort of youth and beauty, assembled to behold the splendid costume of the members, and witness their skill in archery, particularly on target days. In January 1789, His Royal Highness having been elected president, issued an order for the following uniform, to be worn by every member of the society —a grass green coat with buff linings, a buff waistcoat and breeches; black collar of uncut velvet in winter; tabby silk in summer, with yellow buttons according to pattern sent to NUTTINGS, 16, King-street, Covent Garden. By the established rules, a white dimity waistcoat and breeches might be worn at all meetings, but the uniform coat was indispensible, together with an R.K.B. button with a gold loop to a black round hat, and small black feather, without which no member was allowed to shoot,* besides being fined 7s. 6d.

Peter M. Andrews, Sir Henry Mann, bart , Sir P. Burrell, Captain M'Mahon, P. Honeywood, the Duke of Dorset, the Duke of Leeds, Viscount Lewisham, etc., etc.

* Captains and Lieutenants were to wear a gold or silver arrow embroidered on their collars. Clergymen, a uniform button of papier-maché. The number of ex-county members we limited to thirty-six. The qualification, a freehold of £10 a year, or a leasehold of £20, in co. Kent. No greater number than six were to shoot rubbers or games at the butts, and the same set not to shoot two rubbers together, if any others wished to occupy them; Seven to be the game; and .. games in three the rubber.—The large targets never to be shot at a less distance than sixty yards—and any member shooting games at the small target, fined. There were to be four targets every year; the 1st in May; another, to shoot for His Royal Highness's prize in June; 3rd the anniversary target July 15th; and 4th the Institution target, August 28th. The shooting

The society having been presented with two standards, one given by the Hon. H. Fitzroy, and the other by George Grote, esq.; standard bearers were appointed to attend every meeting of the society in full costume, with a cross belt of black leather and a swivel affixed, they also wore an epaulet of gold. Every target day and at the first meeting in each year, they were to carry the standards to and from the ground; all the members walking together in procession in full uniform.*

Every member on election, paid ten guineas, besides his annual subscription of £1 11s. 6d.; out of which he was allowed part of the expenses of his ordinary at every meeting; and in addition, he was to pay one guinea yearly, for his four largest dinners.

It would seem (that notwithstanding the ladies honored these meetings with their countenance and presence,) the greatest part of the society ungallantly professed celibacy; for in a splendidly bound manuscript book of their accounts is an entry, wherein each member engaged to pay a stipulated fine of £100 upon committing matrimony.

A Mr. Dickenson resided in the house, but the care of providing wines and other entertainment for the society, devolved upon a committee of members specially chosen for that purpose.

The house is traditionally said to have been the scene of many midnight revels and orgies. The mem-

---

to be at a distance of one hundred yards. *Rules of the Royal Kentish Bowmen.* 32mo. London, 1789.

* There were four standard bearers appointed; a treasurer, (R. Leigh, esq); an antiquarian [?]; and chaplain. *Ibid.*

bers previous to the breaking up of the society, fitted up an apartment, in which they frequently acted plays and other dramatic pieces, to which the inhabitants of the neighbourhood were invited by tickets—They also gave a grand ball on Shooter's hill, at which most of the gentry attended.*

Mrs. Potts states, that a large mirror once belonging to the Prince of Wales which had come from this house, was presented by lady Fermanaugh to the landlord of the Bull Inn, at Dartford.†

The house is now the residence of C. King, esq.

THE HEATH.

About three quarters of a mile south-westward from the town is Dartford heath, on which were formerly a great many pits and holes, some fifteen, others twenty fathom deep. At the mouth and thence downward they were narrow, like the tunnel of a chimney or the passage of a well, but at the bottom enlarged ; and some had several rooms or partitions, strongly vaulted and supported with pillars of chalk.

In the opinion of the neighbourhood, they were originally dug for chalk, both for the use of building and mending the land. Hasted, on the authority of Tacitus, thinks it most probable that some of them were used as secret hiding places by our Saxon ancestors, for their wives, children, and goods, in times of civil war or foreign invasion, as chalk alone is capable of admitting these excavations.‡

---

* The three daughters of Sir John Dyke, of Lullingstone Castle, Mrs. Thorpe and daughters, etc., were present. *Moonshine,* iii. 244.

† *Ibid.* 347.   ‡ *De moribus Germ.* 630.

It may however, be remarked, that some of these **holes** on the Heath reached to the chalk, and others no **farther** than the sand ; yet most of them are now stopped up, **and** thus accidents which heretofore occurred both to man **and** beast, are prevented.

The Heath consists of 329*a*. 3*r*. 9½*p*. and as the **lord** of the manor exercises a right of proprietorship over **it,** the tenants of the manor only are allowed to turn cattle thereon.

From an account of monies entered on the Court Rolls in 1811, it appears then to have been customary to **pay** 4*d*. a load for gravel, and 6*d*. a hundred for turf.

A.D. 1832.   In May, a special Court Baron was held for the purpose of granting to the Church-wardens of Dartford, for a certain number of years, ... acres of common waste land on Dartford-heath, in trust, for the employment of the poor, by the lord of the manor, and the major part, in numbers and value, of the persons having right of common on Dartford-heath.*

Pursuant to this grant, the church-wardens proceeded to enclose a plot of ground adjoining the east side of the Heath, upon Heath-lane, when on the remonstrances of Mr. Rawlins, the steward of Sir Charles Morgan, who announced the baronet's disapprobation, the plan was abandoned.

---

* Court Rolls. *sub ann.*

THE WATLING STREET.

The antient Roman road from Dover so called, enters this parish a little above the Brent, over which it passes a short distance before its junction with the present turn-pike road.* A few years since, it was carefully examined by that excellent antiquary A. J. Kemp, esq., F.S.A., assisted by the well known Messrs. Nichols, father and son; and the following statement is the result.—They found the crest of the agger to have been originally elevated about five feet above the surrounding waste, and to have been flanked on either side, by a foss and small bank, leaving an available road, eighteen feet in width between the margins of each ditch. The whole work was found to be about sixty feet in breadth. The road ran W.N.W to E.S.E. Their examination afforded no evidence of the mode nor materials of which it was constructed; it is highly probable that it preserved the same breadth throughout its whole distance.† The road originally ran nearly in a straight line from Rochester towards Shooter's hill, but in later times was diverted to Gravesend when that place became a station for shipping.

---

* Mr. Kempe in a letter addressed to me in Nov. 1833, says "I have some suspicion the true derivation of Watling-street is from the British *Wltra Llain*, converted familiarly into *Water-lain*, and corruptly into Watling; this would imply simply—the line of the highway. I am aware that there may be many suggestions at variance with this etymology; but whether right or wrong, it will not disturb the Watling way as it reposes in swelling majesty on Dartford Brent."

† Hollingshed says it was found 18ft. broad upon digging at Verulam. *Description of Britain.* 118.

Upon no better evidence than the discovery of a tomb which apparently belonged to a family inhabiting an adjacent Roman villa, modern antiquaries have usually affixed the station of Vagniacæ at Southfleet! Whereas it has been previously shown, by the extensive Roman cemetery discovered on East Hill, immediately contiguous to Dartford, (vide. p. 8.) there is much more reason to suppose that town to have had its origin in Roman times, both from its ichnography agreeing with the acknowledged form of Roman streets, which crossed each other at right angles,* as well as its antient history, clearly traceable to the period immediately subsequent to the Romans quitting Britain. Admitting this origin, the writer does not presume to appropriate the name of Vagniacæ, or Noviomagus to Dartford, although arguments, equally cogent, might be drawn from the distances of the Itineraries,† which place the one at Southfleet and the other at Crayford. 'Tis true the recent discoveries at Keston may have given antiquaries reason to presume that place the site of the Noviomagus of the Romans; but being present at those excavations, the writer knows Mr. Kempe was far from being confident *any* town had ever existed on the spot.

---

* Lowfield, and the Waterside cross the High street in that way; Darenth lane and Overy street run athwart the road nearly in a similar manner, at the entrance of the town.

† Richard of Cirencester, gives the distances thus, Iter. XV. from Vagniacæ to Noviomagus, XVIII. miles; from Noviomagus to London, XV. Dartford is precisely this distance from London, and if the antient Vagniacæ be Maidstone, it will be found to disagree very little with the miles given in the Itinerary. *Stukely It. Curios. p.* 135. Somner judges Noviomagus to have been at Crayford.

ANNALS OF DARTFORD.

A Roman Cemetery discovered upon East Hill near Dartford, A.D. 1792, in which have been subsequently found great numbers of urns, intermingled with stone and wood coffins; lachrymatories, etc., together with the square pits in which the bodies were burned.*—Cremation is believed to have ceased soon after the time of the Antonines, in consequence of the progress of Christianity. The cemetery must *then* have existed. The emperor Marcus Antoninus died A.D. 180.†

A.D. 328. Constantine the great, embraces christianity, when it becomes the leading religion throughout the empire.

Circ. 604. The Saxon king Ethelbert, said to have founded a seminary or nunnery, for noble virgins at Dartford.

Circ. 770. The Danes or North-men in a piratical excursion upon the coast, pursue their depredations up to Dartford, where they ravage the monastery, violate the nuns, murder Edgitha, the superioress, and destroy the establishment. The invaders defeated by Offa the same year.‡

1085. Three churches or chapels existent in Dartford.¶

1235. Isabella, sister of Henry III. married in Dartford church, by proxy, to Ferdinard II., emperor of Germany.‖

1330. Edward III. held a great tournament here on the Brent, in August, after his return from France, in the fourth year of his reign.

1382. [*Wat Tyler's Insurrection.*] In the reign of Richard II. the insolence of wealth, and the progress of knowledge, combined to make the common people throughout England feel

---

* *Ex. epistol. Johan Landale, armig.* In one of the coffins, probably that of an adherent to paganism, was found a coin of Constantine, apparently intended as a fee to Charon, the ferryman of the Styx.

† *Gibbon's Decline and Fall of the Roman Empire.* chap. iv.

‡ *Kentish Traditions, European Magazine,* lvi. 360. The Saxons and Danes are both of the same piratical origin, although they are not distinguished as a separate nation invading Britain before A D. 787.

¶ *Domesday Book.*   ‖ *Stow sub. ann.*

that they were little above slaves. Overburthened, and borne
to the earth with prædial services,* they felt the tax of *three
groats per head* imposed by parliament, (5 Ric. II.) upon
every person above the age of fifteen, as an impost almost
beyond endurance. And eventually, when it was rigour-

---

* It may serve as a specimen of these services to state, that in those
days there were few persons who worked for weekly wages ; but nearly
every family held a cottage and some small portion of land, from half an
acre and upwards, for which they were bound to pay a small rental and
perform certain specified services duly entered in the Court Roll. These
services consisted of ploughing the lord's land with one or more ploughs,
for a certain number of days ; sowing, harrowing, weeding, reaping, and
gathering in the lord's corn ; mowing, and (on days when summoned by
the bailiff,) the villane, his wife, servant, and whole family except the
shepherd, were required to assist in making the lord's hay and getting in
his harvest. The only remuneration allowed to the workman daily, was
a bundle or faggot of the grass, corn, wood, or furze, while cutting, for
the use of his household, on those days when the lord did not supply
them with food—but they were bound to find their own horses, ploughs,
harrows, waggons, and other agricultural implements. In like manner
they were also bound to make their lord's malt ; to thrash, and carry his
corn to market ; bring from thence to his mansion the goods purchased
for his household ; fell his trees ; cut his woods ; clean out his ditches ;
repair his hedges ; mend the highways ; gather his fruits ; and go a
nutting in his woods.—They supplied him with eggs and poultry ; were
required to grind their corn at the lord's mill, for which heavy toll was
exacted ; to bake their bread at the lord's oven, and pay in proportion.
None of them were allowed to breed up their sons to learning, lest they
should become priests, and the lord lose their services—neither were they
allowed to marry their daughters—nor sell a stallion, without leave of
their lord.—They were required to attend their lord's court, and therein
do suit and service—None of them were permitted to remove from the
land whereon they were born—and in many instances their persons and
goods were at the mercy of their lord who could dispose of them at
pleasure. *Hund. Rot. Paroch. Antiq.* ii. 120.

It is singular that although the clergy uniformly preached against the
sinfulness of holding christian men and women in slavery, they were the
last to grant them manumission ; consequently villanes existed on CHURCH
LANDS long after they had ceased to exist elsewhere. *Ibid.* 123.

The clergy said 'Slavery was the punishment of ORIGINAL SIN derived
from Adam !' *Hist. Episc. Attisod. Hist. de Fran. t.* xvii. 729.

ously exacted, the people openly resisted, in many places.* About a fortnight before Whitsuntide the collector came to Dartford, and entering the house of one Walter Tyler, then standing on the north side of the High-street,† demanded of his wife payment for herself, her husband, her servant, and her daughter. Against payment for the three first, she offered no objection, but insisted that her daughter was a child under the specified age. The lass, a comely, fine grown young woman, was standing by, during the altercation; when the collector turned, suddenly seized her, and attempted by the exposure of her person, to ascertain whether she exhibited symptoms of puberty—a practice frequently adopted in other places.‡ The mother and daughter screamed violently —the neighbours came running in—and the news was speedily carried to the father who was at work hard by, tyling a house. Immediately seizing his lathing hammer, reeking with perspiration, he ran home, and inflamed with rage asked the collector how he dared be so bold? High words followed, and irritated by an attempted blow, Tyler struck the collector so violently on the head with his hammer that his

---

* The tax was first collected with mildness, and proving unproductive the courtiers proposed to farm it. In an evil hour the king acceded, and Thomas de Bampton was sent down into Essex to enforce payment from defaulters. He opened his court at Brentwood, issued his summonses, and was instantly surrounded by the whole population of Fobbing, etc., who expelled him the town. Sir Robert Belknap attempted to repress these disorders in a court of Trailbaston; but this only led the infuriated populace to make the judge fly, and to murder both the jury, and lawyers. Victorious, they sallied forth into the country, despoiled sundry manors, dispatched letters into Kent, Suffolk, and Norfolk, advising the immediate rising of the inhabitants, and promising their assistance. *Stow's Annales* 284.

† Tradition affirms his residence stood on the site of the house now occupied by Mr. Robins, a corn-dealer. On pulling down the adjoining house in the autumn of 1834, an antient hammer was found, and exhibited to some curious persons as the instrument of Tyler's vengeance. Its form, however, was not older than the first Stuart.

‡ One John Leg of Fobbing, has obtained an imfamous immortality by the introduction of the indecency. *Hollingshed*, 434.

brains flew about.—The uproar filled the street—rumour
spread the transaction far and wide, and the population of
the surrounding district poured into the town by every avenue
anxious to defend the tyler, who had taken such summary
vengeance on an obnoxious officer. The ferment lasted all
day, and in a few hours the news reached Canterbury, where
multitudes were already assembled ; flushed with success in
having broken up a court of Trailbaston, which should have
sat in that town, to award punishment upon those who rescued
the bondman of Sir Simon Burley.* These hearing of the
transaction came flocking to Gravesend, and from thence into
Dartford wanting a leader. Thinking the spirited conduct of
Tyler pointed him out as a proper person, he was elected
Captain by acclamation, and in conformity with that character
immediately assembled the chief of the mob in council to
determine their future operations.

Resolved by an immediate attack upon the Government
to effect a beneficial alteration in the condition of the common people, the Dartford council first determined, that to
prevent the miscarriage of their project, by any foreign invasion during their absence ; those persons who dwelt within
twelve miles of the sea, should return to their several homes
and guard the coast. They then dispatched a party to free
John Ball, a seditious priest, from confinement at Maidstone,
constituted him their chaplain ; and partly excited by his fer-
vent addresses on the natural equality of all classes, and
partly by the smart of their own wrongs, they ranged themselves under Wat Tyler, Jack Straw, and other leaders, and
proceeded towards London, to effect the destruction of all

---

* Sir Simon Burley went to Gravesend with an armed force, and
claimed an industrious man living in that town for his bondman. A
villane by his residence of a year and a day in an incorporated town
acquired his freedom ; but Burley demanded 300 pounds of silver for
his manumission, and on his refusal he imprisoned him in Rochester
castle. *Stow sub. ann.*

vassalage, and the admission of the commonality to equal privileges with their lords.*

The banded rustics assembled on Blackheath, June 12th, then entered London, where, as may be expected, they were guilty of many excesses, but were at last persuaded to withdraw to Smithfield, to receive charters of manumission. The king, Richard II., met them there June 15th, entered into conversation with Wat Tyler, who as he was stating his grievances and pleading for the promised pardon with much gesticulation, Sir William Walworth the lord mayor of London, apprehending danger, treacherously stole behind him, and with a blow of the city mace nearly stunned him; turning his horse to rejoin his party, it stumbled, and he fell environed with the courtiers, who instantly slew him. Tyler, who seems to have been a brave, sagacious, but uneducated man, probably was less guarded against Walworth, who was the son of an emancipated native of Dartford, settled in London for the purposes of trade; and who mindful of his birthplace, had shortly before evinced his attachment by giving sixteen acres of land in Dartford towards the endowment of the priory.†

Neither Tyler nor his party had any historians who sympathised with their sufferings, consequently we entirely lose sight of his wife and family, but the probability is, that they remained at Dartford, and finally perished in indigence and obscurity.

The insurgents were no sooner dispersed than the new charters granted for their manumission, were annulled by proclamation, and the next parliament declared them void.‡

---

* That this was their sole object of rebellion, is shown by their anxiety to destroy court rolls, manorial evidences, and every mark of villanage.— They demanded the abolition of bondage, freedom to buy and sell in markets and fairs; and a certain sum, or yearly rent, to be paid for all services and produce. *Walsingham.*   † Vide p. 113.

‡ It is a fact that the laws of Slavery have never been repealed in this country. In 1526 a bill was brought into the house of lords for the manumission of bondmen, read three times in one day, and REJECTED. The slave trade has never been legally abolished, and the wretch who leads his wife into the market with a rope round her neck, and sells her has still the law on his side. *Pennie, Note to Varangian.* 429.

1382. January. Ann, daughter of the king of Bohemia, astonishes the townspeople, by riding through Dartford on a side-saddle, in her journey to London, as the affianced bride of Richard II. ; all ladies having heretofore rode astride, like men.

1387. Barley sold in the market at one shilling per quarter.

1391. So great a dearth of corn, that the common people make bread of fern-root, and in the fruit season almost live upon apples, nuts, &c. which gives them the flux; whereupon Adam Bamme, lord of the manor of Charles, in Dartford, and lord mayor of London, causes great quantities of corn to be imported, and sold at a moderate price.

1415. Henry V., returns to England with his royal and noble prisoners after the battle of Agincourt, and on the 25th Nov. passed through Dartford towards London, and the same day is met by the mayor, alderman and commonalty of London on Blackheath.

1416. May 7. The emperor Sigismond passes through Dartford and is met by the king at St. Thomas Watering; failing in negociating peace between England and France, he returned 16th August. Stowe says the emperor sent Henry III. three leopards, in token of his regal shield, which up to this time were the arms of the kings of England.*

1421. Feb. Henry V., and his queen Katherine, now declared heiress of France, pass through Dartford, on their way to London.

1451. Richard, duke of York, preferring a claim to the crown as heir to Lionel, duke of Clarence, was advised by his friends among the nobility who hated the duke of Somerset, to collect an army in Wales, which having done the latter end of that year,—on the 16th February, 1452, hearing that the king had collected another to oppose him, with which he was advancing towards that country, the duke by a well-directed countermarch pushed on towards London ; but

---

* *Stow sub ann.*

understanding he would not be admitted into the city; by a detour, he crossed the Thames at Kingston and proceeded to Dartford Brent, where he encamped.   Some of the lines thrown up on that occasion are still apparent on the south side, but much has been obliterated by digging for gravel. The king followed with his army; pitched his camp on Blackheath, and sent the bishops of Winchester, and Ely, together with the earls of Salisbury, and Warwick to propose terms of accommodation.   The duke not finding himself so strongly supported by the people as he expected, listened to the overture; concluded the agreement, and upon March 1st, yielded up himself to the king at Dartford, where contrary to promise, he still found the duke of Somerset in attendance as his chief minister.   After the interview the duke was sent forward to London, and some said would have been committed to prison, had there not been a rumour that his son the earl of March, was advancing upon London, with a strong force.*

1527.   July 8th.   Cardinal Wolsey leaves York house on his embassy to France, and enters Dartford with a retinue of nine hundred persons on horseback; among which were the earl of Derby, the bishop of London, Sir H. Gifford, and Sir Thomas More.   There were also two physicians, and a great number of gentlemen in velvet, with gold chains about their necks, who rode three a-breast, together with the cardinal's yeomen, followed by noblemen's and gentlemen's servants, the whole clad in a livery of orange tawney coats, with the cardinal's Hat and T. C. embroidered thereon.   In mock humility, he rode upon a mule, but beside him was a led horse superbly caparisoned; and before him were carried two great Crosses of silver; his two large Pillars of the same metal; his Cardinal's Hat on a cushion, and his embroidered cloak bag.   In this way he was escorted to Sir Richard Wilt-

---

* *Stow sub ann.*

shire's house at Stone place,* where he lodged for the night,
but the greater part of his retinue were compelled to return to
Dartford to procure entertainment at the different inns. On
the morrow they rejoined their master, and proceeded on the
road to Rochester, and so towards Dover. He returned
through the town in nearly the same state on the 8th of July
following, on his road to London.†

1553. Queen Mary's intention to marry Phillip king of
Spain being distasteful to many Englishmen, Sir Thomas
Wyat raises the county of Kent, and advancing toward London with six pieces of artillery and a large assemblage, is met
at Dartford by Sir Edward Hastings, and Sir Thomas Corn-
wallis, both privy councillors, to discover his intentions and
report the same to the queen. Here he was joined by Robert
Rudston, and Thomas Culpepper, both of this place, together
with one Thomas Fane, residing in the neighbourhood. On
the failure of the enterprise, Culpepper and Rudston were
imprisoned in the Tower of London ; and their names still
remain scratched, by their own hand, on their prison wall, as
a lasting memento of their fate, and the disasterous termination
of the insurrection.‡

---

* Probably Sir Richard Wingfield, son in law to the late proprietor
and builder of the mansion, Sir John Wiltshire. The gatehouse was
standing within memory, and several of the rooms, which are said to have
been handsomely finished with oak wainscot. Over the groined gateway,
and on a stone chimney piece were carved the arms of Sir Richard
Wingfield, who married Bridget the daughter of Sir John Wiltshire, who
died 28th Decem. 1526, and eventually inherited the estate. Sir John,
and dame Margaret his wife, were buried beneath an altar tomb in a
sepulchral chapel on the north side of Stone church. The site is now a
farm house occupied by Mr. Soloman.

† *Herbert*, 83. *Cavendish's life of Wolsey.* 87.

‡ *Bailey's History of the Tower.* i. 111. They were taken the 6th or
7th of February. By the side of the doorway leading to a cell on the
first floor of the White Tower, are these inscriptions:—"'HE THAT
ENDVRETH TO THE ENDE SHALL BE SAVID.' M. IO. R. RUDSTON,
DAR. KENT, ANNO. 1553.'" "'BE FAITHFUL UNTO DETH AND I WILL
GIVE THEE A CROWN OF LIFE.' T. FANE, 1553.'" And underneath the

1538. The priory dissolved, and the house retained as a mansion for the king and his successors.

1540. Jan. 2nd. The lady Ann of Cleves sleeps at Dartford palace, (late the priory,) on her way to London to be married to king Henry VIII. She was divorced in July following.

1549. Dartford palace settled upon the lady Ann of Cleves for her residence, by King Edward IV. She resided here occasionally for seven years.*

1555. The government of queen Mary having determined to suppress and punish heresy,† about the last day in June, Maurice, bishop of Rochester, passed sentence of condemnation on Nicholas Hall, a bricklayer, and Christopher Waid, a linen-weaver of Dartford for heretical pravity.

The articles exhibited against them, were :—

1. That they were Christian men, and professed the catholic determination of our holy mother the church.

2. That they which maintain or hold otherwise than our holy mother church doth, are hereticks.

3. That they hold and maintain that in the sacrament of the altar, under the form of bread and wine, is not the very body and blood of Christ ; and that the said very body and blood of Christ is truly in Heaven only, and not in the sacrament.

4. That they have been, and be amongst the people of that jurisdiction vehemently suspected upon the premises, and thereupon indicted, etc.

---

last, J. CULPEPER, OF DARFORD. All three were tried and condemned, but respited 18th March that year, and subsequently pardoned. Robert Rudston was the owner of Horton-Kirby castle and manor ; he bought Boughton-Monchensie of Sir Thos. Wyatt, and lived in the mansion in queen Elizabeth's days. *Hast.* i. 295. Thomas Culpeper was brother-in-law to Sir T. Wyatt, and was owner of Bedgbury, in Goudhurst. *Ib.* iii. 36. Thomas Fane married Elizabeth, daughter of Sir T. Culpeper, of Bedgbury, and possessed Scotgrove in the parish of Ash, and was a trustee of Cobham college. *Ibid.* ii. 266.—Walter Mantell, the owner of Monk's Horton and ancestor of J. H. Mantell, late curate of Dartford, (vide p. 103.) also joined in this insurrection and was attainted and executed. *Ibid.* iii. 319.   * *Losely MSS. by A. J. Kempe, esq.*

† Protestantism was not the result of the popular circulation of the bible ; it preceded every vernacular translation of the scriptures. The reformation sprang from within the church itself, for the bible was in latin.

To this they answer, as others commonly do, of like creed :

1st. Granting themselves "christian men, &c." save that Hall refused to call the catholic apostolic church, "his mother church" because he found not the word "mother" in scripture.

2. Touching the very body and blood of Christ under the form of bread and wine in substance, they would not grant, affirming the very body of Christ to be in heaven ; and the sacrament a token or remembrance of Christ's death ; Nicholas Hall adding, that, whereas he before held the sacrament only a token in remembrance of Christ's death, now, he said, there is neither token nor remembrance, because it is misused and clene turned away from Christ's institution. He also considered the Mass in the 4th article to be abominable ; and Christopher Waid, with the others say, that as they had confessed before, now they would not go from what they had said.

To the 5th article "for the people's suspicion" they made not any great account, not sticking to grant the same.

After the exhibition of the Articles and Answer, the accused received immediate sentence of condemnation, which was passed upon them by Maurice, bishop of Rochester, in the usual form.

Nicholas Hall was not burned at Rochester until the 19th day of July ; but Christopher Waid, was appointed to suffer at Dartford, July the 17th.

"Accordingly on the day appointed for his execution, betimes in the morning, there was carried out of Dartford in a cart, a stake, and therewith many bundles of reeds ; a load of birch faggots, with others, and a quantity of tall wood, to a place about a quarter of a mile out of the town called the Brimpth, unto a gravel pit thereby, the usual place of execution for felons. It being greatly bruited around that a condemned heretic would suffer there that day, great numbers of the country people resorted thither, and there tarried his coming. To this place also came divers fruiterers with horse-loads of cherries, and sold them. About ten of the clock cometh riding the sheriff, with a great many other gentlemen in his retinue appointed to assist him therein, and with them WAID riding pinioned, and by him one

MARGERY POLLEY (whom the sheriff was taking to be also burnt the same day at Tunbridge,) both singing of a psalm. This Margery as soon as she espied afar off the multitude gathered about the place where he should suffer, waiting his coming, she said to him very loud and cheerfully ' You may rejoice Waid to see such a company gathered to celebrate your marriage this day.'

" And so passing by the place which joined hard by the highway, they were carried straight down into the town, where she was kept, until the sheriff returned from Waid's execution.   Waid being ready, and stripped of his clothes at an inn, had brought unto him a fair long white shirt from his wife, which being put on, and he pinioned, was led up on foot again to the aforesaid place.   And coming straight to the stake he took it in his arms and embraced it, and kissing it set his back to it, standing in a pitch barrel brought from THE BEACON which stood hard by.   Then a smith brought a hoop of iron with two staples, and fixing it under his arms, made him fast to the stake.

" As soon as he was settled, with his hands and eyes lifted up towards heaven, he spake with a loud and cheerful voice the last verse of the eighty-sixth psalm, ' Shew me some token for good.'

" Near unto the stake was a little hill upon the top whereof, were pitched up four staves quadrangular-wise, with a covering round about, like a pulpit ; into this place, while Waid was thus praying, entered a friar, with a book in his hand ; whom when Waid espied, he cried earnestly to the people to take heed of the doctrine of the whore of Babylon, exhorting them to embrace the doctrine of the gospel preached in king Edward's days.   The sheriff repeatedly interrupted Waid while thus speaking to the people, saying ' be quiet Waid and die patiently.'   ' I am thank God quiet, master sheriff, and so I trust to die.'   All this while the friar stood still, looking over the coverlet as though he would have uttered somewhat : but Waid very mightily admonished the people to beware of false doctrine. When the friar perceived this, whether he were amazed, or could obtain no audience of the people, he withdrew himself out of the place immediately without speaking a word, and went away down into the town. Then the reeds being set about him, he pulled them to him and embraced them in his arms, always with his hands making a hole against his face, that his voice might be heard. His tormentors perceiving this, cast faggots at the same hole, which notwithstanding he endeavoured to put off in the best way he was able, his face being sadly hurt by a faggot cast thereat. Then fire being put unto him, he cried unto God often, 'Lord Jesus receive my soul;' without any sign of impatiency in the fire, till at length, after the fire was thoroughly kindled, he was heard by no man to speak, still holding up his hands over his head toward Heaven, even when he was dead and altogether roasted, as though they had been staid up with a prop standing under them.

"This sign did God show upon him whereby his very enemies might perceive that God had, according to his prayer, showed such a token unto him even to their shame and confusion. And this was the order of this goodly martyr's execution, this was his end whereby God seemed to confound and strike with the spirit of darkness the friar, that locust, which was risen to have spoken against him, and also no less wonderfully sustained those hands which he lifted up to him for comfort in his torment."

Spectatores præsentes Ricardus Fletcher, pater, nunc minister ecclesia Crambrooke, Ricardus Fletcher, filius minister ecclesia Kiensis.*

1558. The quartan ague rages violently in Dartford in harvest time: 17th November, this year, queen Mary died.

1559, 8th May. The English Service again performed in the churches.

---

* *Fox's Acts and Monuments*, with additions, iii. 44. Lond. 1682. On returning the sheriff carried Margery Polley to be burnt at Tunbridge.

1559, July 17th. Queen Elizabeth sleeps at her palace in Dartford on her visit to lord Cobham.

1572. That queen again slept here, and the next day returned to her palace at Greenwich.

1576. The Dartford grammar school founded by William Vaughan, Edward Gwyn, and William Death, and a school-room built over the market-house, newly erected on the site of the ruined market-cross built by John Sherbourne in the reign of Henry VI.

1607. May 10th, died lady Elizabeth, the wife of Sir John Spilman, in the 55th year of her age, and was buried in the chancel of Dartford church.*

---

* *Translation of the German inscription on her tomb.*

Here rests in Christ Jesus,
ELIZABETH, daughter of H. Nicholai Mengell, citizen and one of the council of the city of Nuremberg, formerly the wife of SIR JOHN SPILMAN, knight, who lived piously and in the fear of God with her husband 35 years, and at length happily fell asleep in the 55th year of her age, the 10th of May, 1607.

(Translation of the German portion of the trilingual verse.)

Gladly, dear wife, would I have given my life,
To deliver thee,
But since it could not be
This tomb shall make known the love I have for thee.

At Lindow on the } Sir John Spilman, knt. has caused this monument
lake of Constance. } to be erected in memory of his good and dear wife.

(On a small tablet at the base.)

On the 31st July, 1607, died her young companion Hans [Jock] Buoschor, at Lindow, on the lake of Constance.

Sir John Spilman apparently had no family by this lady, but about two years afterwards married a much younger woman, by whom he had four sons and one daughter. Sir John, was buried 8th November, 1626, his second wife, lady Katherine, was living at Dartford in July, 1644. John Spilman, esq. who succeeded his father, seems to have relinquished the business before 1641, as he then only paid an assessment of 2s. 5d. He was buried 7th March, 1641, and the family afterwards fell into poverty, see p. 305 and 53. Possibly they might have been injured by the civil wars which shortly afterwards followed.

The following Orders were made by the inhabitants of Dartford at a vestry, to which all those consented whose
names are underwritten, April 20th, 1629.*

Imprimis, It is agreed upon that wheneuer the officers
call a vestry the whole inhabitants shall make their gen'ral
appearance at it; and yf any of the said inhabitants hav just
cause to be absent, and do not make yt known to the vestry,
they are not to take offence yf they be reasonably punished
for the same.

Item. The publicque officers that shall yeerly be chosen
to doe service in their sev'll places in the towne shall have
all charges allowed, either for whipping of vagrants, or con-
veying of creeples, or other such charges as they shall be
put into by reason of their sev'all offices yerely allowed
them by the ou'eers of the poore for that yeare out of their
assessment.

Item. That the collector for the poore shall not take into
pens'on any new pen'con'r for a yerely or weekly pens'on,
without a vestry approving thereof.

Item. All the writings, deeds, and evidences, plate, vestments of the church, p'sh, and schoolehowse, and alle books
of account, be entered in a schedule, and kept in a chest or
trunk in the vestry locked up with three locks having three
keys; one to be kept by the minister of the parish, and the
other two by the churchwardens.

Signed,

John Twisleton.	Thomas Channes.	Isaac Thompson.
Thomas Pearceys.	Ralph Burrowes.	William × Markley
Robert Watts.	Thomas Barker.	*the mark of.*
William Smith.	Nicholas Tooke.	John Britt.
William Burrowes.	John Smith.	Thomas Andrews.
William King.	Charles Wardens.	Anthony Poulter.
Thomas Rogers.	John × Gibbons	John Clapsil.
Thomas Round.	*the mark of.*	Nicholas Holman.
Richard Mason.		

---

* Churchwardens and Vestry Book, No. 1.

1630. The parish feeling itself overburthened with poor, pass the following Resolution in vestry, 27th February.

Ordered, that every freeholder, and every lessee for a year or yeares, of any small and little tenements or cottages situate within this parish, who after midsummer day next, take in or let to farm, to any strangers not borne and breed up in the parish, any tenement or cottage, or any part of them, to inhabit and dwell therein, within one month after request made to them, shall give security to the church-wardens for the poor for the time being, to save the parish harmless of all charges that may thereby come upon it, by reason of the present, of future poverty of the person so received, or in case of refusal, the parishioners shall in every tax or assess-ment, tax or assess the offender double or treble the sum they are usually heretofore rated at. This Resolution is signed by seventeen persons.

11 August. Ordered, that henceforth none of the parish goods [long ladders, ropes and pullies, iron chains, leather buckets, etc.] be lent to any person, unless the borrower does pay a reasonable sum to the church-wardens for the use thereof, and restore them within three days of the lending, upon paine of forfeiting 3s. 4d. for the offence. The church-wardens shall carry the money so received to the parish account.

1631. 28th Feb. Whereas by the decease of Richard Streatley late p'ish clerke of the p'ish of Dartford the place and office is become vacant; We the said parishioners of the said parish, in vestry assembled doe elect, nominate, and appoint Thomas Harwood al's Taylor, to execute the said office of p'ish clerkeshippe and from henceforth to continue o'r p'ish clerke. In witness, etc. *Signed*, Richard Wallis, vicar of Dartford, John Twisleton, Thomas Rogers, Nicholas Tooke, and seventeen of the principal inhabitants.*

---

* Churchwardens and Vestry Book, No. 1. p. 17. This is the most valuable and interesting Record in the parish; I am indebted to Mr. G. Payne for allowing me to transcribe the principal items, when church-warden.

1633. Feb. 23rd. *Memorand.* According to the liberty granted, Stat. Eliz. 5. John Denne, vicar of Dartford, Kent, did licence Mistresse Elizabeth Rogers, the wife of Thomas Rogers the younger of Dartford, who then lay in child-bed, to eat flesh, as by law in case of such weakness is allowed.

1635. An assessment upon the inhabitants of Dartford of £29 9s. 10d. for removing his majesty's household.

1636. April 1st. A suit in chancery commenced by the churchwardens against John Twisleton the elder, and John Twisleton the younger, respecting the Spital House, which is finally settled by arbitration and a specification of its endowments. See p. 305.

1636. The parishes of Dartford and Wilmington, assessed at the sum of £54 14s. 1¼d. for Ship money,* of which £37 18s. 0½d. is collected in the former parish.

1637. The town of Dartford visited with the plague, and £29 8s. 2d. collected to relieve the poor sufferers.

1642. *Memorandum.* That the overseers of the poor having put into their accounts £1 1s. for horses and dinners in going to the Justices' monthly meetings, they are contented to lose the same if all ensuing overseers in time to come do the like and bear their own charges. *Churchwarden's book.* p. 33.

In July, this year, strong manifestations of public discontent appear respecting the administration of the government, and preparations for war are commenced between king Charles and his parliament. The men of Kent seem generally to have paid a cheerful obedience to the parliamentary Ordinances; but, it does not appear that the inhabitants of Dartford took any decided part in the conflict of opinions.

"Friday, 19th August. There met at Moor-Ditch some parliamentary troopers, every man furnished with armour and carbines, and some three hundred or thereabouts of dragooners all under the command of colonel Lamb; these marched all night and Saturday morning and rested not until they came to Dartford; when they baited for two or three

---

* The famous question which eventually gave rise to the civil war.

hours; and after that time were called together by sound of trumpet, and then advanced to Cobham Hall, the seat of the duke of Richmond, where it was reported there was a store of ammunition. Upon their reaching the Hall the lady through fear, sent out word the magazine should be given up, and the party thus getting easy possession loaded five waggons with the spoil which they sent to London; they also seized three Barbary horses valued at £200 each."*

1643. This year the parish provided a quantity of ammunition and constructed a magazine for its reception in the church, probably in the north chancel, heretofore known as the Virgin's chapel. The following items relative thereto appear in the churchwardens' books.

1643.	£	s.	d.
Item. Received of the Countryer's mony for fitting up a Rome for the powdir magazine in the churche	2	19	0
Cr.	£	s.	d.
Paid for two days' work for a bricklayer to fit the work in the chamber to lay the powder in, and covering the graves ...		5	0
Paid for four deal boards, and making the windows in the powdir roome and other workes in the churche		10	8
Paid for timbre to lay the powdir on, and workmen to set it up		18	0
Paid for two deal boards to mend the chamber, and for two deales to set between the walles and the powder		10	0
Paid to Thomas Round for bringing the powdir from London		5	0

Towards the latter end of this year John Denne† was sequestered from the vicarage, probably from the complaints of some of the parishioners affected with puritanism.

---

* *A perfect Diurnal of several passages in our late Journey into Kent*, from Aug. to Sep. 3, 1642. King's Pamphlets. small 4to. No. 72. art. 33.

† 1643. Paid for mending Mr. Denne's surplice 1s. 6d. *Ch. Ward. Acct.* Notwithstanding Mr. Denne's living was sequestrated he was living in Dartford, 1645, when he was charged £2 5s. 8d. for three weekly assessments, which John Clerk expected to get out of the sequestration money.

The rails surrounding the Communion table taken away, and the table itself removed into the body of the church; an hour glass (price 6d.,) provided for the pulpit, and the cross taken off the church. The churchwardens also accounted for 19s. 6d. given to poor persons, levied upon swearers, and drunkards.

In the spring of 1644 the Book of Common Prayer was discontinued to be used in the church, and extempore prayer substituted according to the Directory, pursuant to the Ordinance of parliament.

It appears the parishioners were unable to procure a competent vicar before July this year, when the celebrated puritanic divine, Vavassor Powell was appointed. See p. 86.

See p. 86.

1644. Item. Gave to a minister for preaching the 14 days in July by the chonsonk (consent) of the parish ... ... 10s. 0d.

Item. My charges and my horse for going into Essex about a minister to take the vickarage ... ... 3s. 6d.

The plague appears again in Dartford, and in consequence many houses are shut up. A seriousness pervades the whole town, and (as shown in the preceding article,) there is daily service in the church, and many persons having the sickness upon them attend, "yet amidst this danger, and while many of the bodies dying of the infection are carried for interment by the vicar's [Mr. Powell's] window, he is mercifully preserved."* Sixty-two burials are entered in the parish register.

The following sums were expended through this affliction.

	s.	d.
Item Paid for sev'ral thinges for the wisited houses (with the plague,) which John Darker had at sev'al times	2	0
Item Paid to William Dankes for thinges that goodman Blades had when he was wisited with the plague	8	0
Item Gave to the serchers, and laid out at other times for the wisited houses	3	4
Item Paid to Mr. Stapell, for 9 gallons of beer, at a penny per gallon, and 4s. beer, when the Spittal house was wisited ...	4	9

* Life of Vavassor Powell, passim.

Item   Paid to John Shott for mending of his carte, and the youse of his carte to carrye them that dide of the plague to the grave... 6 0

Until this period it was the general practice in Dartford and the neighbourhood, to inter poor persons without a coffin : the corpse being simply sewed up in canvas ; and the act of thus sewing it up and preparing it for the grave, is repeatedly described in the churchwarden's books as 'socking' [sacking] it.   But this year, probably from danger of contagion, a public coffin was provided to carry the corpse to the grave, which, when it was deposited therein, was brought back again, and reserved for the like purpose.*

Pade to John the giner (joiner), for a coffin to stand bye, to carye poure peple to the grave   ...   . 5s. 0d.

July 26th.   This summer a body of Kentish royalists six thousand strong, seized upon the magazine at Dartford, and carried off its contents.†

Pade for ringinge the bells when Sir William Waller routed Sir Ralf Hopton at Winchester   ...   . 5s. 0d.

The surplices, and other clerical paraphernalia sold.

Item, Pade for caryinge doune the surplusses and other parallel (apparel), to the waterside, and for a porter who furste carryd them to Dowgate, and then Ruygate markyt   ...   ... 1s. 0d.

---

* The practice of burying the dead without coffins was common in the middle ages   An antient illumination in a MS., "Office for Burial of the Dead" belonging to the late duke of Sussex, represents an interment in this way, as does an engraving of the burial of some friars in a monastery, in the "Pictorial History of England."   The practice continued in Oxfordshire till the close of the seventeenth century   A maternal relative, [Alice Wotton, temp Car I.] says "in her youth she often saw corpses wrapt up in old sacking, or the remnant of a blanket, and so laid in the grave ; and that the disgusting feelings generated in bystanders, on hearing stones and flints thrown upon the corpse led ultimately to its discontinuance, and the present English mode of burying in coffins." Abroad, to the present day they rarely use coffins ; and Ordericus Vitellus says William Conq. was buried in royal robes, without a coffin.

† *Mercurius Aulicus, 16th week.*   King's Pamphlets, 604, small 4to.

A bell rung at four o'clock in the morning, and the curfew at eight in the evening.

Item, Pade to Richard Hardon for hafe a yeare rinngen the 4 and 8 o'clock bell, due at owre ladye laste day paste ... 10s. 0d.

1645. June. A rising in Kent, and martial law proclaimed.

1647. Paid for a horse for John Ponte for to fetch a minister from London to preach of a fast day, Mr. Powell was gone to the seege of Okford ... ... 10s. 0d.

Paid Thomas Harwood for keeping the parish register* ... 8s. 0d.

Mr. John Round the churchwarden, on passing his accounts there were delivered up to his successor, a Bible, the book of Martyrs;† Jewel's Apoligie for the Church of England; two silver flaggons; two silver boats; two pewter flaggons; one carpet, the pulpit cloth and cushion; the evidences of parish lands and houses; two long ladders; two ropes and poles with iron chains, and twelve buckets. *Signed*, Edmund Tooke, Samuel Stonar, and others.

1648. In May, petitions being got up at Canterbury, praying the houses to treat with the king, occasion was taken by many of the royalists‡ to assemble great numbers of their party amounting to 6,000 horse, and 1,000 foot. They chose Edward Hales, esq. for their commander, and Sir Thomas Peyton, for their lieutenant general. Then, after threatening the parliament for some time at a distance, boldly advanced to New Cross, beyond Deptford, where they endeavoured to negociate with Sir Thomas Fairfax, whom the parliament had sent with four regiments of horse and three of infantry to suppress them. Negociation was refused, but peace and

---

* The entries made by these "Registers" if any were made, could be only private memoranda, for all the Parish Registers I have seen invariably present an hiatus from 1645, to the restoration of king Charles II.

† Fox's Book of Martyrs was part of the furniture of every parish church in the kingdom, until dishonestly taken away.

‡ *Bloody News from Kent.* The duke of Lenox, lord Colpepper, and others, headed the movement, and commenced operations by seizing upon the magazine at Sittingbourne.

pardon offered, provided they laid down arms and returned home.* The great body of the insurgents apparently accepted the conditions; retired to Dartford, twelve miles off, and left eight guns behind them. But his excellency determined upon putting down all resistance,† marched to Eltham, bivouaced in the fields all night, and the next day came to Crayford, and then followed the retreating army to Dartford, from whence, the general detached in pursuit major Husband, and with 300 horse and 100 infantry mounted behind them. They proceeded to Northfleet bridge which they found barricaded and fortified, with 600 men to defend it under major Child, a Kentish gentleman. Here Husband swam through the river, but narrowly escaped, the insurgents having thrown harrows into the water, which tore open the body of his horse so that its entrails literally dragged after him. Then bravely charging them, they fled with precipitancy through Gravesend towards Malling, spreading such wide alarm, that their pursuers could not discover a man left in the whole town of Gravesend, but only women and children. Fairfax hearing that 1,000 horse and foot had posted themselves at Maidstone, on Friday, June 2nd, he attacked the town, when Sir William Brockman advanced to its support with a large party, which increased its defenders to about 2,000 men. In this affair 200 of the Kentish men were slain, and 1,400 taken prisoners, which entirely broke their spirit in the royal cause, and dispersed the party.

---

* *Kingdom's Weekly Intelligencer*, from May 23rd, to May 30th, 1648.

† May 23rd, an imposter personating the prince of Wales, appeared in the neighbourhood of Sandwich. One Casimer Mathew, a butcher, took him to the Bull, in the town, where he drank freely. Here the old black clothes, not worth threepence, in which he at first appeared, were exchanged for a suit of crimson satin, with which he went to church on Sunday, the 3rd inst. One Thomas Richards, a tall man, being selected to carry the sword before him. The imposter was taken, and carried to London, where he owned himself the son of a poor Welchman, named Cornelias Evans, born at Marseilles, in France.

A*

1653.   A new Act passed for the celebration of matrimony directing public notice of every intended marriage to be given in the public market-place, on three successive market days, or in the parish church or chapel, by a registrar appointed under the Act.   The parties were then to appear before a justice of the peace, and declare their mutual acceptance of each other as man and wife, and the Justice was directed to pronounce the marriage valid.*   This constituted the whole ceremony.

The churchwarden's accounts indicate, from the paucity of charges during the suspension of the regal authority, that the parish paid only for the public celebration of the fifth of November, by ringing the bells at Dartford.

1654.   Paid to the ringers for two years' ringing on the 5th
        of November   ...   .   13s. 4d.

1660.   May 9th.   News arrived in Dartford that the king, Charles II., is proclaimed in London.

Tuesday, May 29th.   King Charles's restoration,—general rejoicing,—the king passes through the town from Cobham where he had slept ; the bells rung nearly the whole day, and the ringers receive a gratuity of 30s.—Several regiments of horse are stationed on Dartford-heath under general Monk, to await the king's coming, when they present an address to his majesty thus commencing "With such joys as flow "from reverence and love, we present ourselves before your sacred majesty, &c."†   This address was most favourably received, and the troops permitted to accompany the king to London.

The following expences were this year incurred by the parish.

P'd for taking down the frome of the old king's arms ...   3s. 10d.
P'd for cloth, fringe, and making, the pulpit cushion ...   18s. 10d.
P'd Thomas Gill for lining the pulpit cloth   ...   ...   6s. 10d.

---

* *Scobell's Collection of Acts.* 236.   This act seems to have formed the ground-work of the recent alteration in the Dissenter's Marriage Act.

† *Mercurius Publicus.* Newspapers, vol. i.

Sir Nicholas Crispe this year introduced the culture of Madder, (a root useful in dyeing reds or violets) into the parish of Dartford and the neighbourhood, which was allowed by competent judges, to be equal to any grown in the kingdom.*

1661. The liturgy restored, and two Books of Common Prayer purchased, price £1, for the use of the church.

[*Tradesmen's Tokens.*] The coin of the kings after the Conquest was chiefly of gold and silver, though often debased by alloy. The necessity of a smaller change compelled dealers and tradesmen to invent some token, as a medium for currency between themselves and their customers. Hence a diversity of these tokens, only current in their own neighbourhood. Under pretence of remedying this evil, but *really to enrich a favourite,* Charles I. granted a patent in 1626 to the Duchess Dowager of Richmond and Sir Francis Crane, knt., to coin farthing tokens. They soon made many thousand pound's worth ; and as a proof of the imposition practised on the public, it is sufficient to state that out of an ounce of copper which costs a penny, they made twenty-pence. Their patent was shortly after annulled, and all the tokens were left on the holders' hands, who sold them to the braziers at tenpence or a shilling the pound.

Then came the *public farthing token offices* in London. These gave one shilling in twenty to those who bought— the country was soon inundated with them—gold and silver vanished—but when they returned to the patentees, they disowned all that had not a double ring upon them, of which very few were found. This ruined the smaller tradesmen.

There was then such a scanty supply of small coin that tradesmen of most towns struck coins of the nominal value of half-pence and farthings for their own use in retail business, these coins upon the credit of the issuers obtained local circulation in the town and neighbourhood from their commencement in 1642, till put down by proclamation in 1672.†

---

* *Fuller's Worthies,* 57.   † *Hist. of Bicester,* 129.

The following Tokens were issued by inhabitants in Dartford.

Thomas Gill, of (a pair of scissors)—*Reverse,* Dartford, 1659, T^{G}A.

Nicholas Chambers, (arms)—*Reverse,* in Dartford, 1664, N^{C}M.

Isaac Manning, 1664, (arms)—*Reverse,* of Dartford in Kent, his farthing.

Henry Petroe, (sugar loaf)—*Reverse,* Dertford in Kent. H.P.

Thomas Smith, (a crown)—*Reverse,* Dertford in Kent, T^{S}M.

William Huish, (a cock)—*Reverse,* Dertford in Kent, W^{H}A.

Edward Rose, (a rose)—*Reverse,* Dertford in Kent, E^{R}M.

Henry Pierce, (a   ,)—Dertford in Kent, H.P.

Robert Capon, 1668, [arms]—Dartford in Kent, his halfpenny.

The following were issued in the neighbourhood.

John Child of Sutton-at-Hone, in Kent, (three wheat sheaves) his halfpenny.

William Chatwin (three birds) of Greenhithe in Kent.

——————

1662.   The parish Register discovered to have been kept in the most slovenly way, and John Ames employed to copy out all those entries of christenings, marriages, and burials, which can be recovered from 1640 to 1662, for which he is paid 14*s.*

1662.   This year was published the celebrated Annis Mirabilis, or record of the second year of Wonders, Prodigies, and Apparitions, seen at Dartford, and other places in Kent.

1666.   The plague rages again in September and October, and seventy-two funerals occur in Dartford.

P'd Abraham Pieters looking to the visited houses	...				5*s.*	0*d.*
P'd for a stone of beefe for the searchers	...	...	...		1*s.*	8*d.*
P'd in money, meat, provisions, meal for meshing, and for a coffin for John Anslowe	...	...	...	...	£1 2*s.*	7*d.*
P'd for digging a grave and searching Anslowe's child	...				2*s.*	6*d.*

A pest-house this year was provided for the diseased poor.

1666. In February the plague again began to show itself, the burials increased to seven in that month; there were eleven in March; in April only nine; but twelve in May. In June twenty-six; in July fifty-eight, among which was Thomas Harwood, the late registrar. In August the burials declined to twenty-five; in September to sixteen, and in October, to three. The disease may then be considered over, having carried off all the sickly and diseased persons. The average rate of mortality was between fifty and sixty burials for some years after.

1666. *Memorandum.* This year was collected in Dartford, five pounds for the poor who suffered in the fire of London.

Sir Edward Deering, bart. publishes a funeral sermon, preached by himself in Dartford church for Mrs. Elizabeth Deering, with some verses.

————

1667. Thomas Gill died in September, whilst serving the office of churchwarden with Edward James.

This gentleman was the son of John Gill of Sutton-at-Hone, by Ursula Langridge, his wife, (married in 1611,) both of whom were buried at Dartford, and grandson of John Gill of Sutton, who was buried there 6th April, 1624; a lineal descendant of John Gyll, lord of Wyddial, Herts, and patron of the church, in the sixteenth century. A branch of this family, (Robert Gill,*) also resided at Eltham, in Kent, and bore in the heraldic visitations, and armorial ensigns of the Gills of Herts. Thomas Gill settled at Dartford before the commencement of the civil war, and was first assessed in 1645. John,† his father, was buried here in 1646, and Ann his sister, died in 1667. From the circumstance of Thomas Gill being selected to serve the office of sidesman in Dartford during the ministry of Vavassor Powell in the eventful year 1647, so contrary to the usual routine of office, it may

* Son of George.　† Possibly a partizan in the civil wars.

be fairly inferred that he was purposely chosen to carry out the ecclesiastical and puritanic changes then in progress, to which he was favourable. In 1652, during the protectorate of Oliver Cromwell, he filled the office of overseer, and made several purchases in the vicinity. In 1655 the name of Alice his wife is conjointly mentioned with his own, in a deed reciting the purchase of two messuages, two barns, two gardens, two orchards, ten acres of land, and eighty-six of wood in Stone, and Darenth, which he had bought of William Johnson, and Alice his wife. In the overseer's accounts 1658, is a receipt for £1 18s., which Thomas Gill accounted for, levied upon persons travelling upon the Lord's day through his activity, whilst constable,* and given to poor people therein specified. Having prospered in business and become wealthy, in 1660 he was elected a trustee of the grammar school; in 1662 surveyor of the highways; and church-warden in 1667. The same year he purchased two parts of five acres in the salt-marshes, Dartford, for £41 sterling, which were sold by his son George Gill, and Susanna his wife in 1677. Death however, now closed his career, for he died in September following; and his widow Alice, (whom he married about 1646,) administered to his effects 1st October, 1667. He probably commenced business in Dartford near the time of his marriage, since we find him living in the High-street from 1647. The entry of his "marriage" as well as the "baptisms" of his children, were among the memoranda of the 'Register' [registrar] during the early part of the suspension of ecclesiastical authority, and consequently irrecoverable when John Ames was commissioned to make the re-entries in the Parish Register; Thomas Gill had by her, two sons and a daughter; Thomas, buried 4th October, 1664; Sarah, afterwards the wife of John Bency; and George

---

* Perhaps from religious scruples of desecrating the Sabbath. W. Crafter, esq., of the Ordnance office, Gravesend, has a token issued by this individual, the earliest I have seen.—*Obverse*, THOMAS GILL, of— (pair of scissors) *Reverse*, DARTFORD, 1659, ᴛᴳᴀ.

his heir. Alice, his wife, survived him, but left Dartford in 1668, and letters of administration were taken out to her effects, at Rochester, 18th January, 1672. George Gill his surviving son and heir, is believed to have been educated in the Dartford grammar school, and afterwards apprenticed to Thomas Harris, recognised in the parish books (1669,) as the successor to the Spilmans at the paper mills, Dartford. On the decay of the clothing trade around Maidstone, he purchased the fulling-mills at Boxley, and converted them into paper mills, where he long carried on a lucrative business; he left them to his son, William, who eventually sold them (in 1730) to Mr. James Whatman. They are now known as the Turkey mills, and have been long celebrated for producing the finest writing paper. George, and William Gill were buried on the north side of Maidstone church, beneath a monument surrounded with iron rails, thus inscribed "In memory of William Gill, esq., who died 10th August, "1754, aged 68 years, Son of George Gill, esq. of Dartford, "and Boxley, who died 28th January, 1726, and Susanna his "wife, who died 7th July, 1720, of the family of Gyll, of "Wyddial, Herts."

William son of the above, settled at Wyrardisbury-House, Bucks; which he inherited from Robert Prouse Hassel, esq. whose daughter and coheir he had married. A son of the same name, captain in the 2nd life guards, and equerry to his royal highness the duke of Sussex, married lady Harriet Flemyng, only child of Hamilton Flemyng, earl of Wigtoun: and to Gordon Willoughby James Gyll, esq. his son, we are indebted for the above interesting narrative and pedigree, which is also recorded in the College of arms.*

1667. Edward Noakes, glazier, contracts with the vestry to maintain and keep whole, all the windows about the parish church for fifteen years, commencing from Michaelmas 1667. The said Edward, undertaking to repair, and now make two

* Collectanea Topographica et Genealogica, vol. viii.

windows every year during the said term until the whole are repaired or new made, and to leave them in sufficient repair at the end of the term, in consideration of Mr. Edward James, the present churchwarden, paying him the sum of three pounds, and himself and successors paying the said Edward Noakes the sum of 30s. a year, during the said term.

Circ. 1670.   Stage coaches began to run through Dartford from Canterbury and Dover.   In the records of the corporation of Gravesend, one Thomas Tilley, a Canterbury coachman, is stated to be sworn a freeman of that borough A.D. 1673.

The earliest Stage Coach which I have seen noticed, is one which ran from Coventry to London in May, 1659; but at that time the chief mode of travelling for females was by waggon. In Sir William Dugdale's Diary, is the following entry— "1660, March 13th, My daughter Lettice went to London by the Coventrie waggon." Men generally travelled on horseback. In the reign of Richard II., Reginald Shrewsbury and Thomas Athekot were specially licensed to provide travellers passing between Southwark and Dover, through Dartford, Rochester, and Canterbury, with horses called hackneys. Their charge was 1s. 6d. from Southwark to Rochester, and a like sum from Rochester to Canterbury; but as there were some persons who took daily advantage of their horses, and travelled thereon against the will of their owners, paying little or nothing for them, frequently ruining; and sometimes riding away with them; to remedy this inconvenience, a further grant was obtained from the crown, directing that henceforth they should only charge for the hire of one hackney from Southwark to Rochester 12d. and from Rochester to Canterbury 12d. and from thence to Dover 6d. and so from town to town at the same rate per mile; but the said owners not to be compelled to let the said horses, unless the hire be first paid down—and for the security of the said horses, they are to be branded with an heated iron instrument; and any person stealing the said horses and disfiguring them by cutting off their ears and tails shall be amerced at the pleasure of the king. Or should the contractors provide horses *incapable* of performing the proposed journey, the parties letting them shall deduct a proportionate sum in respect of such insufficiency.—

Pat. 19 *Ric.* II. *p.* 2. *m.* 8. Such was the only accommodation for travelling by land, (besides those offered by carts or waggons,) which persons could obtain, till stage coaches were established.

On the Brent are the outlines of "the Deserter's grave" cut in the turf, formerly frequented by the scholars of Hall Place school; the sod of which is still continued to be cut away by the country people in memory of the unknown, traditionally said to have been shot in the adjoining pit. But it is most probable the following entries in the churchwardens account refer to him :

1679. Payed the coroner for setting on a soldier that hanged himself	13s. 0d.
Payed for a stake to drive through him	0s. 6d.
Drink for the Jury	1s. 6d.

1680. January 12th. On the decease of Thomas Harwood, the parishioners of Dartford in vestry assembled, elect, nominate, and appoint, Robert Thompson, of the said parish, taylor, to execute the office of PARISH CLERKSHIP, and from thenceforth during their pleasure, to be and continue PARISH CLERK. It was moreover agreed, that he should demand for his perquisites and duty for ringing the great bell at every funeral and digging the grave, the sum of 12s. ; of which the said clerk is to receive by virtue of his office 7s., and the parish 5s. For ringing the fifth bell and digging the grave 6s. ; whereby the clerk is to have 4s., and the parish 2s. But for breaking the ground in the church as it doth wholly belong to the parish of Dartford, the clerk shall receive nothing for the same. It is also concluded, that the said clerk shall pay half the charge of the bell ropes, and to have what he can get for the ringing of the other four bells. Upon every Easter monday, he shall render an accompte of those burials at which the fifth and sixth bells have been rung during the past year; and also of every person desiring the ground to be broken, to bury in. Whenever this shall be done in the south chancel 10s. shall be paid to the churchwardens;

and in the body of the church 6s.; and the whole shall be charged to their account upon the churchwardens leaving office.*

1686. October 10th. The contract for repairing the church windows having expired at Easter this year. The vestry renew it with George Swift, glazier, Dartford, for seven years, commencing from Easter last, during which time the said George shall repair, new-make, amend, and maintain the glass windows, in and about the parish church, for two pounds per annum, payable in equal portions, at lady day and michaelmas. The contract expired 1693.

1687. Paid for ringing 28th January, the day of thanksgiving for the queen (Mary de Este,) wife of James II., being with child   ...   . 2s. 0d.

1688. Paid the apparitor for a proclamation for altering the prayers for the (pretended) prince of Wales   ...   . 1s. 0d.

Dec. 13. King James on returning from Feversham to London, when passing through Dartford, finds the waters out; and he is carried by men to the corner of Bullis Lane, when the women spread their aprons for him to walk thereon.

1689. King William and queen Mary proclaimed in Dartford, amidst much ringing and rejoicing.

1690. Nov. 5th kept as a great holiday in consequence of the landing of the prince, now king William, and the great deliverance from the powder plot: the ringers have 10s. given them.

1691. The king was so desirous of prosecuting the French war, that he attempted proceeding to Flanders during the Christmas festivities, but the weather became so inclement that after passing through Dartford on the 6th, having reached Canterbury, he was forced to return to Cobham Hall, where he remained till the 9th, when he again passed through the town on his return to Kensington, where he staid till the 15th, and then again proceeded through this place to Gravesend. He returned from Flanders the same year, October 6th, 1691.

1692. The king again passed through the town on his journey to Holland, and returned the same way from Flanders, October 13th.*

1694. The key of the "Magazine" afterwards known as the "armoury" above the vestment room, formally delivered by each retiring churchwarden to his successor, being filled with the accoutrements of the train band.†

1694. May 1st. Queen Mary accompanies the king through the town to Gravesend; and meets him at Margate, on his return.

Globular lamps first introduced.

September 18th. Ringing for the good news of "Peace being signed."

1696. Nov. 15th. King William returned through Dartford on his way from Flanders, not arriving however until after it was dark, the churchwardens caused him to be lighted down the hill, and through the river with links and candles, amidst much ringing and rejoicing. The 4th December, 1698, the king again passed through the town, for the last time, on his return from the same country, at each of which periods the ringers received a gratuity of 10s.

1702. Queen Anne proclaimed.

Sept. Paid for meat and drink when the Duke of Marlborough came	5s.	0d.
The bells recast, and the middle and south aisles new leaded		
1706. Paid ringers upon the news of taking Bruges, Brussels, and Ghent	10s.	0d.
1712. Paid for ringing when the duke of Ormond passed through the town from Dunkirk.‡	10s.	0d.

---

* King William's frequent journeys through Dartford proved highly productive to the ringers, who received 10s. each time.

† *Churchwarden's and Vestry Book, No. 1.*

‡ *Churchwarden's Account Book* The whole of the foregoing and subsequent memoranda in the "Annals of Dartford," where the authority is not given in the margin, has uniformly been taken from these books. For which I express my best thanks to Mr. Churchwarden Snowden.

1713.   The rivulet called the Cramford running along Low-field street being turned out of its antient course opposite the mansion house of John Twisleton, esq., by his planking, boarding, and piling the same; and thereby preventing its running down the said street, according to its antient course, and benefit of the queen's highway.   The vestry order the Surveyors of the Highway to remove the obstruction and undertake to indemnify them.   *Poor Rate Book.*

1714.   P'd for tolling the bell when queen Ann died   ...   1s. 6d.
        20th Oct.   P'd for ringing on king George's coronation day ...   .   10s. 0d.
        17th Nov.   P'd for ringing when we took the rebels at Preston   ...   .   10s. 0d.

1716.   An agreement between the vicar and parishioners respecting the vicarial tithes.   *See p.* 82.

1716.   P'd Mr. String for the use of the M'ket house when the soldiers were in town ...   .   4s. 0d.

1717.   The vault or charnal house, under the late St. Edmund's chapel, in the upper burying ground had now fallen in and 'old Simmons' employed to fill it up.

        P'd John Hudson for paving the church   ...   £34 17s. 0d.

1724.   *Memorandum.*   The charge of maintaining the poor having become excessive by reason of their idleness and improvident management; the churchwardens and overseers resolved to erect an House of Industry in Lurchin's hole,* for their maintenance and employment.   In March, 1728, the house was built by Richard Brandon under the direction of Mr. Blackwall; Rowland Fry and his wife were appointed master and mistress; and in October, 1729, Mr. Chambers, the vicar, preached and published a sermon on the opening, eulogising these establishments.†

1729.   The prayers read by the vicar at the workhouse, of his own composition, censured by the trustees, for omitting

---

* Named from Richard Lurchin whom the parish permitted to build a cottage in the chalk-pit.   † Vestry Book, vol. 2.

petitions for the king and royal family, in the same words as those used in the Book of Common Prayer.

1736. March 3rd. Mrs. Deakins of Dartford, having for sometime past lost the use of her limbs, is advised to be sweated in a horse dunghill, where she continued two hours and a half;—when she fainted; and was taken out dead.*

1738. April 10th. Gill Smith, late an apothecary in Dartford, executed on Kennington Common, for the murder of his wife in St. George's fields;—published with his solemn declaration relative to the several crimes charged upon him of having poisoned Mr. Polhill's family at Horton.†

1740. The parish visited with a " sore disease " (supposed to be the Small Pox,) which carries off a great number of the inhabitants. Seventy-eight funerals are entered in the Register.

1741. The disease vastly increased, insomuch that one hundred and twenty-eight persons fall victims thereunto, and the country people become so much alarmed that the market was nearly deserted, and did not recover for some years. At this period Dartford was one of the chief agricultural marts in the county; and in trade, and in buildings, far surpassed Gravesend.

1746. An extraordinary number of strollers and vagabonds infest the town; and a person appointed to remove them.

1748-9. Twenty-five pounds, the gift of the late Rev. C. Chambers, late vicar, settled upon trustees as a nucleus for the formation of a charity school.

1754. The remains of the Trinity Hospital taken down; the bridge over the Darenth widened, and partly rebuilt.

1756. The churchwardens remove the gates of the lower church yard to the south end of Cranwell's (now Stidolph's) house, and spike them, to stop the passage through the burying ground.

1760. The small pox rages this year, and again in 1766.

* *Gentleman's Magazine*, vol. 40. p. 355. The late Miss Pettit said that it was reported Mr. Brown of Horsman's Place had seen the experiment successful in foreign countries. † *Genuine History, &c.*

1762.　A volunteer rate levied to hire substitutes for those drawn in the parish to serve in the militia.

1769.　The old market-house, etc. taken down, and a new one erected on the garden belonging to the house, or estate of the grammar school on the south side of the same street, the feoffees neglecting to take the precaution of securing an annual rental for the market ground to benefit that institution.

1772.　Messrs. Pigou and Andrews apply to the justices for leave to convert Horton corn mill into gunpowder works : the parish of Dartford oppose it, on account of its contiguity to the public highway, lest the applicants should deposit their gunpowder in a warehouse, or on board vessels, so as to endanger the navigation.

Joseph Law and his wife, prosecuted by direction of the vestry, for keeping a disorderly house in Spital street, and sentenced to stand in the pillory.*　They were the last persons who underwent that punishment in this town.

1773.　A gallery built on the south side of the church.

1776.　Owners of stage horses assessed to the repair of the highways pursuant to act of parliament.

1777.　Mr. Stackpoole shoots John Parker, esq., an absconding debtor, at the Bull inn, Dartford ; is afterwards tried for the same and acquitted by the jury at Maidstone, on the ground of the gun going off accidentally.†　The bullet mark is still visible in the wainscot of the room where the accident occurred.

1778.　The vestry order that no further money be paid out of the parish rates for finding substitutes for persons drawn for the militia, but every person so drawn to find one at his own expense.　The result was that in 1781, the parish officers undertook to receive subscriptions from all persons whether housekeepers, lodgers, or servants, between the age of 18 and 45.

1784.　The pulpit removed to the North-east pillar of the church.

---

* The pillory was usually kept in the belfry, and on this occasion placed opposite the entrance of the new market place.

† *Short-hand Notes of the Trial.*

1793. An organ purchased for the church.

The entrance to Lowfield street widened by setting back the houses on the west side, at an expense of £450 paid to Mr. Tasker by the parish.

1795. An act passed (35 Geo. III.) for raising men for the navy in every county, when Dartford parish agrees to raise five men, and to pay them a bounty not exceeding twenty guineas premium each man. And the following year pursuant to 39 Geo. III., the parish raised nine men.

1796. Sept. Upon a remonstrance of the parishioners against the conveyance of gunpowder through the streets of Dartford, the surveyors make a good road through Frying-pan street, that it may be conveyed to Robin's Hole.

1797. May. Captain Dyke with a troop of West Kent Cavalry stationed at Dartford during the mutiny at the Nore.

1804. A new bridge erected over the Darenth leading to the vicarage.

1807. An act of parliament obtained this year for the establishment of a Court of Requests for the more easy recovery of small debts under five pounds, to be held alternately in Gravesend and Dartford. Defendants for any debts in the hundred of Dartford and Wilmington are not to be summoned to Gravesend, nor are those in the hundreds of Toltingtrough to be summoned to Dartford.* The sum to be sued for, must not exceed five pounds. Mr. Jardine exerted himself greatly in the establishment of these courts.

---

* Present Dartford Commissioners, 1844:

Barrell, James
Cann, George
Cavell, Thomas Devereux
Dunkin, John
Dunkin, Alfred John
Elwin, Thomas
Hadley, Thomas Robert
Hammond, Simmonds
James, John Wheeler
Jardine, Joseph

Kerr, Thomas
Landale, John
Miskin, James Black
Sharp, William
Sharp, James
Snowden, James
Ward, George
Wheatley, Ralph
Willding, John

1812. Four men hired to watch the town, (who were super-intended each night by certain inhabitants,) in consequence of the general alarm spread by the murders in Ratcliffe highway.

1813. An act of parliament procured for lighting, watch-ing, and removing nuisances from the town of Dartford.

1814. The allied sovereigns passed through Dartford to London on a visit to the prince regent.

1815. 23rd Jan. The first steam boat (the Margery, 70 tons, 14 horse power,) first runs from Gravesend to London.

At this time seventy-two coaches pass through Dartford every twenty-four hours.

1816. The vestry determine upon establishing a school for the education of the poorer classes, upon Dr. Bell's system.

21st Dec. On granting an 18*d*. rate for the relief of the poor, (there being an acknowledged outstanding debt of £800,) the farmers and others in vestry undertook to employ only the poor of their own parish, and the parishioners sub-scribe for the purchase of bread, meat, and soap, to be sold to the poor at a reduced price.

Edward Barker* buried March 28th, aged 76.

1817. May 29. A new organ purchased of Mr. Russell.

---

* This individual was currently reported in the town and neighbour-hood, to be the lineal heir of one of the oldest baronetages in the kingdom. The tradition is, that the father of Edward Barker mentioned in the text, had been educated at Oxford, and being the only son, was disinherited and discarded by his father for marrying a tenant's daughter, who there-upon settled the family estates upon his eldest daughter. She carried them in marriage to Abraham Tucker, of Beechworth castle, from whom they descended to the present St. John Mildmay family. Mr. Barker had a family of four sons, Edward, John, Brian, and Richard, and two daughters; one of whom married a barrister of Bloomsbury-square, named Sheppard; and the other, captain Marsh, of the India service; each of whom had a separate fortune of £1,000. Edward, the eldest son betook himself to trade, and for some years successfully carried on the business of a butcher at Farningham, from whence he retired to Sutton at Hone. His only daughter married Mr. Jardine, the father of the present respected linen draper at Dartford. In advanced age, Mr. Barker married again, and left issue two sons. We believe he died in London, and was brought to Dartford for interment.

1818. A new organ gallery erected, *see p. 46.*

1818. Jan. The inhabitants of Dartford present the Rev. Mr. Caporn with a silver cup, value twenty guineas, on his being dismissed from the lectureship.

1820. A select vestry established in the parish.

1822. In the autumn of this year, George IV. was grossly insulted while changing horses at the Bull inn, by a working currier named Calligan, who thrusting his shaggy head into the carriage window, looking the king in the face, roared out "you are a murderer," alluding to his recent treatment of queen Caroline:—the man was instantly seized by one Morris, dragged away and felled to the ground. The carriage window was hastily pulled up, and the post boy ordered to drive on as fast as possible; on passing a paved crossing in the High-street, the valet was precipitated from the carriage, but providentially, fell, without injuring himself.

1825. The road on East Hill greatly lowered, and a new carriage road made up to the cemetry thereon.

1826. The Dartford Gas Light Company established with a capital of £4,000 in two hundred shares of £20 each. On the first of November the company contracted with Mr. W. Walker for the erection of the whole works at £3,224 subject to such deductions or additions which the directors might order.*

-----

* On the 30th October a contract was entered into with the commissioners under the act, for the providing and lighting sixty-eight public lamps at the yearly sum of £245 per annum.

At the first annual general meeting of the proprietors held at the Bull Inn, Dartford, on Monday, August 13th, 1827, it was stated:

"That the works being in a sufficient state of forwardness, they commenced lighting on the 24th June last, but that owing to several minor parts not being finished, the surveyor has not yet delivered in his certificate of the whole being completed according to contract: so that the directors are at present unable to close the accounts of the whole expenditure, but they have every reason to think that the following will not be very wide of the result.

From the incompleteness and inefficacy of the apparatus after the contractor had, what he termed, finished his contract, it was found indispensably necessary to augment the capital to £5,000 by increasing the number of shares.

The apparatus at present consists of sixteen retorts, capable of carbonizing one hundred and twenty-eight bushels of coals in twenty-four hours. Two gas holders capable of containing fourteen thousand cubit feet of gas. The number of lights, including the manufactories, is about six hundred, and the annual rental is upwards of £1,000.

The company consists of nine directors, a treasurer and manager.

1831. The parish cottages on the Waterside, now greatly out of repair, ordered by vestry to be sold.

Cr.	£	s.	d.	Dr.	£	s.	d.
Balance in the Treasurer's hands ...	244	17	0	Remaining due to Contractors ...	1300	0	0
First Call of £5 per share, remaining unpaid on 17 shares	85	0	0	Suppose for extras...	100	0	0
Second Call of £7 10 on 22 ditto ...	165	0	0	Purchase money for land (deducting deposit)	170	0	0
Seven pounds per share remaining due on 189 shares	1323	0	0	To Mr. E. Cresy, surveyor ...	150	0	0
Eleven Shares now untaken	220	0	0	Law expenses, etc., suppose!! ...	300	0	0
				Messrs. Dunn, account books ...		11	4
	£2037	17	0		£2020	11	4

"The directors cannot close their report without particularly noticing the liberality of Thomas Caldecott, esq., who soon after the establishment of the Company, sent a donation of £50."

Since the first construction of the works, there has been added from its own increasing resources, a new house for the residence of the manager; the small retorts replaced by larger, and their number doubled; the retort-house has been enlarged; the hydraulic main lengthened; a new perpendicular condenser fixed; a new lime vessel added; the boundary wall heightened; a new gas holder twenty-seven feet in diameter, and eight feet in depth fixed; the coal shed enlarged to nearly double its size, and a new lime shed, smithery, etc., been built. The company's mains have also been extended in every direction, and a variety of minor alterations and improvements been made.—Mr. William Green is manager.

1831. Nov. 10th. Great fears being entertained of the cholera extending its ravages to Dartford, the inhabitants establish a Board of Health, consisting of the following persons: Rev. F. B. Grant, Messrs. T. B. Fooks, David James, John Tasker, James Hards, Tippetts, Elgar, Jardine, Cooke, J. Snowden, Hadley, and A. J. Dunkin, who much exert themselves to devise means for arresting its progress, and recommend the immediate burning of decayed rags, cordings, and old clothes; the removal of filth of every description; clothes and furniture to be washed and boiled in strong lye; drains to be cleansed, by running water; gutters and privies with chloride of lime, and woodwork in confined rooms washed with strong lye, etc.

On the 25th, Committees were formed for superintending the Lowfield, Waterside, Overy, Spittal, and High-streets. Mr. Capper was appointed the first honorary secretary, and on his resignation, he was succeeded by Mr. A. J. Dunkin.

1832. On the 29th May "The Lords of His Majesty's Council appointed certain of the before-mentioned individuals to form a Board of Health, and directed them "to proceed in the duties required of them." (signed,) W. L. Bathurst.

The date of the first case of clearly ascertained Cholera occurred on the 24th May, and the last on the fifth of June; the duration of the disease was fifteen days, in which, the Returns state, that 116 cases occurred in Dartford and Greenhithe; that thirty persons died of the complaint, and eighty-six recovered, out of a population of 1328; constituting about three and a sixteenth of the population. *Dublin Journal.* 1840.

———

At a Special Court Baron, held May 3rd, ... acres of land on Dartford-heath were granted to the churchwardens for a certain number of years by the lord of the manor, and the major part of the persons in number and value, having right of Common thereon. *Manorial Court Rolls.* The churchwardens immediately commenced enclosing the land, when in consequence of some unfavourable representations made to

Sir Charles Morgan, bart., he commissioned Mr. Rawlings the steward of the manor, to prevent their proceeding.

1833.   Died at the Bull Inn, Dartford, Richard Trevithick, a celebrated Cornish engineer; he was buried in the upper church yard, 26th April, aged 62.*

---

* This engineer was originally a captain or foreman in the Cornish mines, but by his improvements in the steam engine, (a model of which was exhibited in London,) acquired such fame, as in 1815 to be selected for an assistant to Don Peter Abadia, and Don Jose Arimani, to drain the richest silver mines in Peru, then totally drowned. So great were the expectations from his skill, that, on reaching Lima, 20th October, 1817, he was immediately presented to the viceroy, the Marquis Concordi; and his arrival officially announced in the Gazette. Such was the importance attached to Trevithick's personal superintendance, that the lord warden of the mines was ordered to escort him to the mining districts with a guard of honour; and that dignitary proposed to ERECT HIS STATUE IN MASSY SILVER, but it does not appear to have ever been carried into effect. The first engine was erected on the Santa Rosa and Yariacocha mine in Pasco, and such consideration was attached to his name and mission, that when he boldly went and applied to the superior of a convent of the strictest order, wherein no male had ever been suffered to enter, for permission to examine and measure a water course which flowed through the court, to the inexpressible surprise of all, leave was granted. His journal gives a most amusing account of the schemes adopted by the secluded nuns to get a peep at him and his men, while employed in the works;—a proof that the feelings of nature are still paramount to all artificial religious restraint. The next accounts received from that country (in the following year) announced him in the enjoyment of wealth and distinction, and stated that his emoluments at a moderate estimate amounted to £100,000 a year. — *Geological Transactions of Cornwall.* But, alas! riches and honour are often evanescent. Buenos Ayres and the Chilian republic had remarked that the ignorance of the people engendered under the superstition of the priesthood, had attached a considerable part to the cause of Old Spain, and prevented the progress of independence. In 1819 they therefore dispatched Bolivar as general of the land forces, and lord Cochrane as commander of the navy, to invade Peru. The insurgents of Upper Peru, including Potosi, joined them, and the country was speedily overrun. The agents of Old Spain fled; the mining machinery was destroyed, and thrown into the mines, and Trevithick and the rest of the Englishmen compelled to flee for their

1836. August. Fissures appear in the church tower, which is considered in danger, and the bells discontinued to be rung: after a careful examination and some slight repairs, Mr. Cresy, the architect, pronounced the structure stable.

The Commissioners under the New Poor Law Act unite Dartford with the following parishes: *Ash near Ridley, Darenth, Eynsford, Farningham, Fawkham, Hartley, Horton-Kirby, Kingsdown, Longfield, Lullingstone, and Lullingslane, Ridley, Southfleet, Sutton at Hone, Swanscombe, and Wilmington.*

1837. A new valuation of the parish effected.

1838. The celebrated linguist Thomas Manning, esq. resides at Orange Grove. He was educated at Cambridge, and became master of fifteen languages. He was particularly desirous to explore China and attempted entering it through Thibet, where he had an interview with the Grand Lama, whose blessing he received. As a Commissioner he accompanied lord Amherst's embassy to China. Shipwrecked on his return from the east, he landed at St. Helena, where he was favoured with a long audience by Napoleon, to describe the customs and manners of China. His large and valuable Sinanese library was given after his decease to the royal Asiatic Society. A memoir of his life written by A. J. Dunkin appeared in the Gentleman's Magazine for July that year.

1840. The Church Houses in Overy-street proposed to be

---

lives without securing any provision for their future support. *Ann. Reg.* From this period the name of Trevithick seldom occurs in the annals of his time, though he still maintained his celebrity as an engineer. About 1832, having proposed the propulsion of vessels on rivers and canals by steam ejection of water in lieu of paddle wheels, the late Mr. Hall invited him to Dartford to try the experiment on a vessel lately built; but after repeated trials, in which it is said upwards of £1,200 was expended, the scheme was abandoned from the impossibility of obtaining pipes of sufficient strength to resist explosion.

The body of Mr. Trevithick was deposited on the south side the grave of Henry Pilcher. A subscription was commenced to erect a cast iron monument over his remains, sufficiently elevated to be seen by passers by, but the funds raised were inadequate.

taken down and an Infant School erected on their site. Great
excitement in the parish, and the scheme opposed. That the
poor might not be deprived of the antient charity Mr. Storey
offered to give a piece of ground to erect an Infant School rent
free for twenty years ; see p. 43, ante.

1842. Nov. 10th. Queen Victoria, Prince Albert, the infant
Princess royal, and the Prince of Wales, pass through the
town on their way to Walmer Castle.

Many coaches discontinued running the Dartford road, in
consequence of the opening of the line of the Dover railway.

1843.   An Infant school erected on a plot of ground heretofore part of the rectory farm, Waterside.*

A Mechanic's Institute established in Dartford.

1844. Jan. Mr. Robins publishes a letter to the vicar of
Dartford on Puseyism.

---

* A professional gentleman told the writer that he gave the following
reasons to one of the founders of the school for declining to become an
annual subscriber. "When first you proposed an Infant School, I promised a donation of £5, that I will give, but will not allow my name to
appear as a supporter, for having since well considered the subject, I am
satisfied the school will do more injury than good. At present there are
many poor old women in different parts of the town who are only able to
pick up a scanty living, by taking the charge of poor children, while their
mothers go out to a day's work ; all these are sufficiently learned to teach
children their letters, and easy words of one or two syllables—and most
of these in some way contrive to assist another infirm relative chiefly
dependant upon them   My profession calls me to visit such, and I know
the statement is true.—All these your school would drive into the Union
House. Besides, I should like to know how the mothers of those little
creatures, who live in the Crescent, St. Ronans, the upper end of
Lowfield, or the top of Spittal-street, who go to work at 6 or 7 o'clock in
the morning, and don't return before 6 or 7 at night, are to take their
children to school at 9, and fetch them home at 4 in the afternoon.
Why, they would lose their places were they to attempt it --And, as for
one poor person taking another's children to school and fetching them
home for nothing, I know too much of human nature to expect such a
thing. For all these reasons I decline subscribing to the Infant School."
—These observations apply to children from two to five years old. They
can then enter the National or other Schools.

BENEFACTIONS TO THE CHURCH.

1368. William Shepherd of Dartford, gave a rent-charge of seven flaggons of oil for the sustentation of a lamp to set before the High Cross, from a messuage in Lowfield. Lost.

1448. Robert Taylor of Dertford, by his will, gave to Isabella his wife, for her portion and good behaviour, twenty shillings clear yearly rent, out of his meadows and marshes, during her life, and after her decease gave all of the aforesaid meadows and marshes to the church of Dartford, paying 8*d.* yearly to the vicar to pray for his soul.

> A part of these lands was said to be given towards the repair of the clock. The marshes consist of 6*a.* 1*r* 22*p.* and were in 1834, let to T. W. Parkhurst for 21 years at £10 per annum. *Parish Records.* No. 40. *Landale,* 952.

1465. John Dowse, of Mersh street, in Dertford, gave by will, four acres of arable land lying in Southfield, for the use of the church in Dertford, for ever, to buy wax lights.

> In 1776 these lands were a part of Cooper's farm, belonging to Mark Fielder. In 1832, let on lease for 21 years to Alexander Solomon, for £6 clear of taxes. *Par. Rec.* 36. *Land.* 53.

1504. William Ladde, by will, dat. 22nd Nov. gave a messuage in Lowfield, with the appurtenances, to Edward Bernard, clerk, vicar of Dertford, Andrew Auditor, and John Star, as trustees, to the use of the parish church of Dertford, held of the lord of the fee by the accustomed services.

> In 1814, these premises were exchanged with Mr. John Tasker, for a piece of Marsh land in Dartford Fresh-marsh level, and let in 1838, for 21 years to T. W. Parkhurst, for £10 per ann. clear of land tax and wallscot. *Par. Rec.* 29. *Land.* 9 *Churchwardens' Accounts.*

1533. John Morley, by will, dat. 10th Nov. gave his tenement, adjoining his mansion, in Overy street, after the decease of Denys his wife, to Robert Derby, and charged it with providing a 4lb. wax taper, to set before the sepulchre in Dertford church, at Easter every year, directing in case the taper was not found that the churchwardens should enter upon and hold the said premises. It seems the conditions

were not complied with, and the churchwardens did enter
upon the premises, and appropriated them for the habitation of
the poor in all succeeding generations.

> In 1815, the messuage was converted into two dwellings, and is
> still employed for the same praiseworthy purpose. See p. 14
> and 15. *Reg. Test. Episcop. Roffen.* ix. lll.

1599. William Gailor of Dartford, yeoman, by deed, dated
Nov. 2nd. 2 Eliz. gave a messuage and piece of land in Spital
street, the whole containing about 37 feet in length, and 10
feet in breadth, sometime part of the back of a tenement in
the occupation of Robert Watts, to the reparation and amend-
ment of Dartford church for ever. In 1622, the messuage
was down, and the site and land was let to Robert Oakes,
saddler, for 21 years at 6s. 8d. a year.

> This tenement lies on the west side of that given by Jerome
> Warren, for the use of the poor, and was during a part of the
> last century let with it, as one estate, to John and William
> Budgen. John Budgen erected a stable on that part whereon
> the messuage stood.—There is now a kitchen and water closet
> on the site; a lease was granted to Alfred Russell, esq. at £3
> 10s. which is now transferred to Mr Evitt. *Par Rec.* 46. *Land.*
> 24. *Churchwardens' Book.*

The same benefactor also gave another piece of land in the
BULL'S HEAD YARD (now unknown,) to repair the church.

1739. Joshua Allen, gave by will, dat. 7th April, to the
churchwardens of Dartford, £5, to purchase such a piece of
plate as they should think needful for the communion table.

1745. The Rev. Charles Chambers, vicar of Dartford, by
will, dat. 1st Oct. gave £25, for new casting the communion
plate, and purchasing a commodious chest with partitions
proper to contain the same.

Also £10, to purchase and set up in the church four tables
whereon the benefactions to the parish be inscribed.

Also two brass branches of £10, value, to contain twelve
candles each, one to be hung above, and the other below his
grave.

And £20, to purchase a silver bason to receive the alms at
the communion service. *Book of Benefactions.*

BENEFACTIONS TO THE POOR.

1344.   Richard Sone of Dartford, gave one acre in Loampit field, to the use of the poor in Dartford for ever.

> This benefaction although called but one acre, was subsequently found to contain nearly one acre and three quarters, and called two acres in some leases; in 1660, John Twisleton gave the remainder of the field in exchange for the Poor's acre to the Spittal house.—The Loampit field is let to Mr Hodsoll, for £12 a year; two thirds of the rent ought to be paid for the use of the poor, and one third to the Spittal house. *Par. Rec.* 106, 142, 391. *Land.* 18, 34, 25, 45. *Ch. Wards'. Accts.*

1440.   Dennis Swetseir, gave the yearly rent of one acre on Spittal-hill, called Chalkdale to the use of the poor in Dertford, for ever.

> In 1445 the churchwardens of Dartford granted a lease for four years of the house and garden on Chalkdale, to John Grey and John Vynor at 18s. a year, the tenants to build a new lime oast capable of burning eight quarters of lime at once.   The premises were continued to the same use for nearly three centuries, when they were let to Robert Lawrence, mason, for 6s. 8d. a year.   In the reign of Charles II., the premises lay waste, and the parish officers permitted one Richard Lurchin to build a cottage thereon, and the vast pit was called Lurchin's hole.   In 1729, on the expiration of Blackwell's lease, the parish built the workhouse on the site.   The Union House now stands thereon, and it is let by the parish for £40 per ann.   *Custum. Roffen. Par. Rec.* 39, 30, 132.   *Land.* 8, 26.   *Churchwardens' Book.*

1563.   Martin Merial of Swanscombe, gave twenty shillings payable yearly out of his house called Daniels, at Swanscombe, 18s. to be paid to the poor, and 12d. a piece to the churchwardens for their trouble on Good Friday.   This benefaction is lost.

Custumale Roffense. 32.   *Lib. Test. Epis. Roff.* xiii. 102.

1569.   William Vaughan, yeoman of the chamber to queen Elizabeth, gave a house on the south side of the High street, nearly new, with its garden, to the use of the poor, the rent to be distributed by the overseers at their discretion, according to the statute 5 Eliz.

> In 1611 the house was let to the justices for a House of Correc-

tion, and continued to be applied to the same purpose until a new one was built in Lowfield street, A.D. 1720. It is now let to Robert Kemp at £20 per ann. *Par. Rec.* 1. *Land.* 10.

1570.   Catherine Bam, gave a rent of twenty shillings yearly charged on Derland Farm, in the parish of Gillingham, for the use of the poor at Dartford.

Parish Records 102. *Landale.* 27. 68.

1570.   Jerome Warren, surgeon of Dartford, by will dated 3rd Dec. bequeathed to the poor, all his house and garden, in Spittal street, the rent to be given by the vicar and church-wardens to them evermore.

> These premises adjoin to the western side of the estate given by Gailor to the church, in Spittal street; the house is down, and both the parish and church estates now form only an appurten-ance to Mr. Evitt's premises to whom they are let. Mr. Snowden has, very properly, let each estate separately. The yearly rent of that belonging to the poor is £6 10s. *Par. Rec.* 17. 73. 16. *Land.* 15. 38. 67. *Informat. of Mr. Snowden.*

1613.   John Burton citizen and grocer, gave by will £130 the interest to be laid out in bread, to be distributed by the vicar and churchwardens to the poor of Dartford, his native town, for ever; with part of this sum was purchased, in 1623, of John Kettle and Rachael his wife, a house in Spittal street, and two acres of marsh land in Crayford parish, called the Harp piece; and with the remainder of the money was pur-chased of Francis Goldsmith eleven and a half acres of marsh land in Crayford parish.

> In 1815, the lands sold by Goldsmith, and the Harp piece, were let to Robert Weatherhog for 14 years, clear of taxes, at £20 a year, but in June, 1820, on the enclosure of waste lands in Crayford parish some exchanges were made, and they now con-sist of five pieces, marked Nos. 14. 15. 16. 17. 18. in Landale's plan B; and are said to contain together 11a. 3r. 33p. now let to the said R. Weatherhog, at £16, per annum. *Par. Rec.* 47. 67. *Land.* 17. 23. 72. 78. *Churchwardens' books.*

1623.   Francis Goldsmith, esq. abated £15 of the purchase money of the Crayford lands, upon condition, that £1 should be given yearly to the poor of Dartford out of the rents on Shrove Sunday as his free gift.

Parish Records, 52. *Landale.* 23. 74. *Book of Benefactions.*

1624. William Reynolds of London, goldsmith, gave by his will £50, and William Harris his executor £10 more, with the interest thereof to distribute 2s. worth of bread to the poor of Dartford, by the vicar and churchwardens, every Sunday; with which two sums (amounting to £60,) were bought of John Kettle and his wife, a house in Spittal street, afterwards known as the Blue Anchor, and since divided into two tenements. This house was taken down in 1764, and four cottages built on its site.

> The house named as purchased from Kettle in the first sale, is in the occupation of William Lucas Pearce, as under-tenant, and together with the four cottages, let to Thomas Elwin, for 21 years, at £50 a year. *M.S. Book of Benefactions.*

1629. Jonathan Brett, of Barking, Essex, gave to certain trustees, a piece of arable land containing four acres, more or less, called Brent Plantation, the rent to be bestowed on the relief of the poor of the parish of Dartford.

> It is now in the occupation of William Pankhurst, at £16 per annum. *Churchwarden's Accounts.*

1629. Thomas Cooper gave 20s. a year rent charge, payable out of a piece of woodland in Bexley, to be distributed in bread.

> The present owner is T. W. Malcolm, esq. Lamb Abbey.

Robert Rogers of Sundrish, knowing that it was the intention of his deceased father, Francis Rogers of Overy street, to convey a messuage with its appurtenances, over against the church of Dartford, for and towards the relief of the poor for ever, but before the pious and charitable intention was executed, the said Francis Rogers died seized of the said messuage and premises, by which it descended to the said Robert, who together with his son Thomas, for the consideration above-named grants and assigns to certain trustees named in an Indenture made for that purpose, the said messuage and appurtenances to hold in trust, that the rent may be bestowed by the churchwardens for the time being, toward the relief of the poor of the parish of Dartford.

> The house is now let to Mrs. Mitchell, yearly rent, £10. *Book of Benefactions.*

1635.   Anthony Poulter gave, by will, 20s. a year, payable out of the Dolphin inn, to be distributed amongst the poor on Easter day.

> The rent-charge is payable from the premises now occupied as the Bank ; the residence of Mr. Pelton, and the brewhouse of Messrs. Fleet ; heretofore the Dolphin inn—and the rent-charge is paid by the latter. *Churchwarden's Books. Landale,* 96.

1682.   John Round gave a rent-charge 20s. a year, payable out of the Bell inn, to be distributed amongst the poor of Dartford on Christmas day.

> This is now paid by J. and W. Tasker to whom the Bell belongs. *Book of Benefactions. Landale, ibid.*

1704.   Dr. Plume by will, gave 10s. a year, to the vicar of Dartford, to be divided amongst the indigent and godly poor, who attended most frequently upon his alternate weekly lectures.

> *Ibid. See also Landale,* 103   This legacy is paid by the trustees of the Stone Castle estate, to the vicar.

1745.   The Rev. Charles Chambers, vicar of Dartford, gave by will, a legacy of £50 consols for the benefit of 24 poor people on Christmas day ; and also £25, for a charity sermon ; and another £25, as a nucleus toward the formation of a charity school, the interest of the sums to be applied as directed.

> The dividend for use of the poor is received and duly applied. In 1748, a Charity School was formed in Dartford, and afterwards held in the vestry.   The school has been subsequently enlarged by donations, annual subscriptions, and collections at church.   In 1816, was united with the Sunday School, and ordered to be conducted on Dr. Bell's system.

1771.   John Randall of Dartford, gave by will, the interest of £200 to the vicar and officers of Dartford, that 5s. may be given to as many poor widows as will amount to ; also the interest of £100 towards the schooling and clothing as many poor boys as it will admit of ; and the interest of another £100 towards the augmentation of the bread given to the poor on Sundays.

> In 1774, with these sums and the interest, were purchased £495 2s. 7d. three per cent. annuities.   The interest is regularly received and applied according to the donor's will.

1795. Mary Pettit of Dartford, spinster, gave £2,000 three per cent. reduced annuities, to the vicar and churchwardens of Dartford, to pay the annual interest of £1,000 to the charity school and the dividend arising from the remaining £1,000 unto such of the necessitous poor persons not receiving relief out of the rates of the said parish.

Sixty pounds per annum are received from this benefaction.

1809. Edward Pierce of Greenwich, gave by will, dat. 13th Oct. £500 three per cents, to the churchwardens to pay the interest unto the poor in the workhouse, and the poor women in the alms-houses in Dartford for ever.

Fifteen pounds a year is received from this benefaction. The trustees are John Tasker and John Landale.

Three cottages now demolished formerly stood on the east side of Hithe street. The donor is unknown.

The ground is now let to —— Gee, at £1 10s. a year.

1841. Grace Say, of Gartley house near Dartford, in the county of Kent, spinster, gives and devises unto Henry Vint, of Lexden, near Colchester, in co. Essex, esq. ; Alfred Head Bailey, of Cornhill, in the city of London, bookseller; Mr. Edward Deere, of No. 1, Gartley place ; and Henry Young, of Essex-street, Strand, in the city of Westminster, gent., and their heirs, UPON TRUST, all her freehold estates, monies, plate, &c., for certain specified purposes, then after disposing of £6,000 Old and New South Sea annuities, and £6,000 three per cent. Reduced Bank annuities, and upwards of £21,000 three per cent. consols, in legacies to divers persons and institutions,* she gives "£500 to the minister and churchwardens of Dartford, upon trust, to apply the dividends

---

* Miss Say gave £1,000 to the Sea Bathing Infirmary, at Margate; £1,000 to the school of the Indigent Blind, St. George's-field ; £100 to the Old Liverpool Infirmary; £200 to the Deaf and Dumb School; £200 to the London Orphan Asylum, Clapton ; £200 to the Foundling Hospital ; and £400 to the Refuge for the Destitute, in the Hackney Road ; besides £500 to Mr Grant, the vicar of Dartford, and £100 to the vicar and churchwardens of Bexley, to the repair of the New Church, on Bexley-heath.

at their discretion, for the benefit of the National School of
the parish of Dartford;" and then after enumerating sundry
other bequests, directs her executors, hereafter named, to
transfer all the said several sums of stock into the names of
the said respective legatees or trustees, within one month
after the first half-yearly dividend of such stocks shall become
due after her decease, it being her intention, that the first
dividend shall become part of her residuary estate, and that
the expenses of transfer and legacy duties shall be paid out
thereof. Then, after directing her trustees to collect and
call in all such parts of her estate as shall be invested in
mortgages or other securities, and invest them in parliamentary stocks, she gives the interest of the residue, real and
personal, not heretofore disposed of, or which she may not
dispose of by any codicil to her will, (subject to the payment
of her debts, testamentary expenses, and the pecuniary and
specific legacies and annuities, herein-before given,) to her
niece, Ann Bailey, wife of John Bailey, of Dorset Square,
London, to her separate use, not to be subject to his debts,
controul, or interference, and after the decease of the said
Ann Bailey, to John her husband, if he should be the survivor
during life. And after their decease to be equally divided
among their children, who shall be living at the time of
testator's decease, their heirs, administrators and assigns.

The will is dated, 22nd February, 1841; and witnessed by
John Audley, Dartford, pattern drawer, and James Allen,
Dartford, Kent.

By a Codicil attached to this Will, bearing also the same
date (22nd February 1841,) after devising sundry other additional sums, amounting to upwards of £2,650 three per cents,
consols, Miss Say states, that having erected and partly
finished eight Alms Houses on the Crayford-road and nominated certain persons to reside therein, provides for their
perpetual endowment, in the following words, "I give and
bequeath to the trustees named in my will, the sum of £5,000
three per cent consols; and the two houses numbered 3, and

4, Gartly Place, Dartford-road, UPON TRUST, to pay and apply the dividends arising from the stock, unto and between the eight inmates of the eight Alms houses I am now having erected, in equal proportions, and by weekly payments ; and also to pay and apply the rents of the two houses numbered 3, and 4, in Gartly Place, to the repairing and upholding the said two houses, and also the eight Alms Houses. And it is also my wish that Mr. John Audley, and Mr. James Allen, be allowed to remain in them so long as they are willing, at the rent they now pay ; it being my particular wish that their rents be not raised."

The residuary devisee or her husband, (very unlike the eldest son of Francis Rogers, as shewn in the preceding benefaction, p. 411,) have availed themselves of a legal objection, and entirely *deprived the poor* of the ALMS-HOUSES intended to be established by Miss Say, for the benefit of future generations, and immortalizing her own name. Certainly there was no clergyman in Mr. Rogers' family, to offer any opposition to the bequest. In Miss Say's case it was confidently asserted that latterly, her constant and almost only prayer was, that her life might be prolonged for another twelvemonth, to place the endowment beyond the controul of her heirs. Soon after her funeral, the then parish officers reported that an offer had been made them of preserving the Alms-House-charity in case they would pay £1,000 to the devisees or their heirs. This sum they were unable to raise ; and some time after Miss Say's decease, the inscription of "Gartly Alms Houses" was changed to "Gartly Cottages." Miss Say in her life-time had prepared an inscription, painted by Mr. G. Cavell, to the following purport : "Let the occupier of this cottage never forget to give thanks to Almighty God for having provided a friend in their necessities."

Miss Say also gave £1,000, 3 per cent. consols, to apply the dividend to providing each poor inmate of Dartford Union Workhouse, above sixty years of age, with one pint of porter more or less, according to the number of such inmates, on every sabbath day for their dinner.

The regulations of the poor law commissioners prohibit the introduction of beer into Union Houses, unless ordered by the medical attendant. But there is little doubt that if the *charity* of Mr. Bailey induced him to bestow the amount of the legacy in small sums, or in tea and sugar, the act would be overlooked by the guardians, and received with gratitude by the inmates. At present they receive nothing—Or if the residuary legatee would transfer this £1,000 to the parish officers, they might undertake the payment of this legacy in perpetuity, and pay over to her or him, the £1,000 demanded, on condition of Mr. Bailey carrying Miss Say's intended establishment of the Alms Houses, into effect.

APPENDIX.

—

No. 1.

———

Gravestones.   Abstone, Elizabeth, d. 3rd Jan. 1785, a. 84.

Bamford, Richard, (Ashford,) d. 16th May, 1800 a. 38.

He left issue by his wife Charlotte, Mary Bamford.

Charlotte, his relict, afterwards wife of Stephen Day, who d. 20th April, 1804, aged 37, also four children.

Richard, d. 15th May, 1793, a. 2 years.

Ann Clarissa, 12th Sept. 1794, a. 18 months.

John, d. 19th Feb. 1800, a. 5 years.

Richard, d. 27th April, a. 3 yrs. 6 mo.

Barnes, William, (Dartford,) d. 17th June, 1795, a. 59.

Mary, his wife, d. 30th Sept. 1794, a. 64.

Benwill Ann, d. 28th June, 1822.

Bert, d. 7th April, 1840, a. 9 m. 2. w.

Tomb.   Bilke, Edward, of Hertford-st., (May Fair,) d. 5th April, 1828, a 68.

Mary, his widow, d. 28th Feb. 1840, a. 82.

Gravest.   Binkwell, or Blackwall, William, d. . . 1773, a. 80.

Bothell, Joseph, d. 13th Aug. 1781, a. 50.

Thomas, Son of Joseph & Sarah Bothell, d. 24th Mar. 1795.

Tombs.   Brames, Peter, d. 12th Feb. 1812, a. 74.

Brames, Matthew, his son, d. 3rd Aug. 1810, a. 42.

Sarah, his wife, d. 29th Ap. 1824, a. 84.

Gravest.   Brand, William, (Dartford,) d. 17th June, 1795, a. 59.

Mary, his wife, d. 30th Sept. 1794, a. 64.

Mary, wife of Wm. Brand, jun. d. 27th Jan. 1778, a. 39.

Three children, Sarah, Mary and Elizabeth.

Left issue, Jane, William and Mary.

Ann, wife of the above W. Brand, d. 4th Dec. 1785, a. 40.

Brand, Polly, d. 2nd Jan. 1828, a. 56.

Elizabeth, dau. of above, d. 23rd Ap. 1823, a. 25.

Gravest. Bradin, Thos. gent. (Chatham,) d. Aug. 10th, 1810,
             a. 63.

Bradley, Thos. gent. (Chatham,) d. 5th Aug. 1810, a. 63.

Brandon, Thomas, d. 3rd May, 1778, a. 68.

Mary, wife of Thos. Brandon, d. 28 May, 1811, a. 89.

Brandon, Thomas, d. 4th Sept. 1810, a. 72.

Mary, wife of Thos. Brandon, d. 6th Jan. 1781, a. 38.

James, son of the above, d. 7th Mar. 1775, a. 10 mo.

Brandon, John, d. 1st April, 1819, a. 52.

Mary, his first wife, d. 20th Aug. 1800, a. 28.

Brandon, Philip, d. 26th Dec. 1821, a. 51.

Brown, Elizabeth, d. 9th Aug. 1713, a. 19.

John and William, children of John and Elizabeth
Brown.

Brown, Richard, d. 17th July, 1822, a. 37.

Mary, relict of the above Richard Brown, afterwards
wife of Samuel Stratten, d. 24th Mar. 1786, a. 56.

Stratten, Samuel, d. 8th Oct. 1802, a. 51.

Buckland, James, d. 20th Dec. 1826, a. 77.

Mary, his wife, d. 9th Sept. 1815, a. 74.

Buckland, Wm. d. 18th May, 1801, a. 20.

Budgen, John, d. 5th Feb. 1780, a. 71.

Elizabeth, his relict, d. 17th June, 1782, a. 67.

Elizabeth, dau. of Thos. and Eliz. Budgen, d. 24th
May, 1755, a. 4.

Tomb. Budgen, Thomas, d. 26th Dec. 1809, a. 70.

Ann, wife of Thos. Budgen, d. 1st Jan. 1827, a. 82.

Budgen, John his son, d. 18th Feb. 1820, a. 44.

Budgen, James Terry, d. 31st Dec. 1823, a. 14.

Budgen, William, esq. d. 27th April, 1826, a. 75.

Mary, his wife, d. 31st July, 1805, a. 51.

John, son of W. Budgen, esq., d. 26th Nov. 1827,
a. 38.

Gravest. Bullock, Roger, d. 14th Nov. 1823, a. 46.

Ann, his wife, d. 28th June, 1823, a. 45.

Emma Sarah, their dau. d. 28th July, 1831, a. 22.

Burkett, John, d. 30th June, 1836, a. 74.

Mary, his wife, (relict of Joseph Wellard,) d. 27th
Oct. 1808, a. 38.

Callow, Adam, d. 28th April, 1812, a. 90.

Alice, his wife, d. 18th Oct. 1765, a. 35.

Mark, son of Adam, d. 16th Nov. 1818, a. 60.

Gravest. Callow, Mark,* d. 5th June, 1810, a. 82.

        Catherine his wife, d. 23rd March, 1784, a. 43.

        Three children, Mark, Catherine and

Callow, Mark Fielder, d. 29th Feb. 1791, a. 20.

        Maria, sister of above, daughter of Mark and Catherine Callow, d. 11th Sept. 1804, a. 20.

Cann, Sarah, wife of John, d. 24th June, 1832, a. 53.

        Caroline, their daughter, d. 31st June, 1831, a. 12.

Carrington, Richard, d. 19th Nov. 1798, a. 63.

Clarke, George, d. 10th Sept. 1817, a. 42.

        Mary, his wife, d. 22nd April, 1833, a. 56.

        Child. Mary Ann, dau. a. 10 months.

        George Fisher, d. 25th Feb. 1804, a. 6 months.

        William, d. 26th June, 1807, a. 3.

        Geo. Bromley, d. 18th Aug. 1807, a. 2 yrs. 7 days.

        Ann, d. 16th Dec. 1815, a. 1 yr. 7 days.

        Oliver, d. 2nd April, 1804, a. 3 months.

Clark, Oliver, d. 2nd April, 1804, a. 30.

Clark, Richard, eld. son of Richard and Rosine, d. 4th Oct. 1830, a. 13.

Claxton, William, d. 12th Jan. 1812, a. 40.

        Patience, his wife, d. 17th Nov. 1812, a. 42.

        leaving issue Mary Ann, Mary, Elizabeth & Martha.

        Child. William, d. 13th Jan. 1796, a. 5 months.

        George, d. 6th April, 1798, a. 7 months.

        Francis, d. 28th Nov. 1803, a. 1 yr. 11 mo.

Coles, William, d. 4th Jan. 1745-6, a. 47.

Colyer, Henry, d. 21st April, 1839, a. 65.

        Hannah, his relict, d. 25th Nov. 1839, a.

Connell, Thomas, d. 10th July, 1800, a. 35.

Cook, John, d. 15th Nov. 1763, a.

        Mary, wife of John Cook, (Welling,) d. 19th March, 1775, a. 46.

Cox, Webb, Elizabeth wife of, d. 25th Oct. 1839, a. 68.

        Elizabeth, her dau. d. 10th Oct. 1788, a. 5 months.

---

* Mark Callow was partner with Mr. Fielder, a linen draper, and is said to have died worth £60,000. Adam Callow was a tailor and draper, Mark Fielder and the two Callows are reported to have been worth nearly £300,000. Mr. Fielder left most of his property to Mrs. Henley, his sister.

Gravest.   Cresy, Edward, d. 11th Feb. 1789, a. 87.
  Elizabeth, his wife, d. 10th June, 1776, a. 76.
Cresy, John, d. 31st Jan. 1787, a. 54.
  Ann, his wife, d. 3rd Dec. 1783, a. 43.
Cresy, Jas., son of John and Ann, d. 9th April, 1796, a. 18.
Cresy, John, jun., d. 22nd Oct. 1779, a. 17.
Cresy, James, d. 4th Nov. 1767, a. 1 yr. 9 mo.
Davis, John, d. 12th April, 1812, a. 42.
Day, Lucy Eliz. wife of Xtopher, d. 13th Ap. 1827, a. 23.
  William Robert, his son, d. 18th Sept. 1826, a. 9 weeks.

Tomb.   Deane, Francis, d. 11th Aug. 1790, a. 66.
  Alice, his wife, d. 24th Sept. 1780, a. 55.
  Elizabeth, wife of Ambrose Warde, (Stone,) d. 8th March, 1798, a. 32.
  Warde, Ann, d. 18th Dec. 1833, a. 48.
  Mary died in infancy.
        left issue three sons and three daughters.

Gravest.   Dear, Joseph, d. 3rd Ap. 1739, a. 73.
Dingley, *children of Samuel and Ann.*
  William, d. 6th Feb. 1803, a. 27.
  Samuel, d. 22nd Ap. 1809, a 4 yrs.
  Samuel, d. 20th Oct. 1814, a. 1 yr. 9 mo.
Dixon, Flora, d. 21st June, 1825, a. 33.
  George Clarke, and Richard their sons.

Tomb.   Dorman, John,* (Dartford,) yeoman. d. 19th June, 1800, a. 66.
  Elizabeth, his relict, d. 8th Oct. 1831, a. 80.
  Elizabeth, their dau. d. 21st Aug. 1807, a. 21.
  Sophia, dau. of above, and wife of Edmund Hodgson, citizen of London, d. 19th Aug. 1823, a. 34.
  Dorman, Chas., son of above J. D. d. 27th July, 1828, a. 29.
  Dorman, Thos., son of J. D. d. 3rd Oct. 1781, a. 5 m.
  William his brother, d. 12th Nov. 1803.
  Pope, Sarah, sister of Eliz. wife of J. Dorman, d. 31st July, 1820, a. 66.

Gravest.   Edwards, Samuel, 40 yrs. in the service of Mr. Richard Davids, of Crayford, formerly Calico-printer, d. 30th March, 1807, a. 60.

---

* See tomb of Sharp.   The Dormans came from Sutton-at-Hone.

Gravest. Edwards, Susanna, wife of John, dau. of Richard
and Ann Webb, d. 8th Jan. 1829, a. 32.

Elgar, Richard, d. 1st Nov. 1746, a. 65.

Elliott, John, d. 12th March, 1776, a. 50.
Elizabeth his wife, d.   1775, a. 56.

Elliott, Ann, d. 13th Dec. 1826, a. 71.

Ellis, Henry, (Dartford,) d. 20th Aug. 1809, a. 72.
Jane, his wife, d. 23rd April, 1814, a. 73.
Child. Henry, d. 2nd July, 1772, a. 2 yrs. 6 mo.
William, d. 2nd July, 1774, a. 1 yr. 3 mo.
William French, d. 27th March, 1780, a.
6 yrs.

Ellis, Henry, (p.) d. 26th May, 1838, a. 60.
James, son of above, d. 31st July, 1834, a. 18.
Children who died in infancy, William French,
Jane, Henry, John, Rose, Ann and Henry.

Emerey, Sarah, d. 12th May, 1768, a. 60 yrs.

Emery, Robert, Ann wife of, (p.) d. 10th Feb.
1745, a. 42.
John, son of Robert and Ann, d. 1740, a. 2 mo.
Ann, dau. of above, d. 5th Sept. 1749, a. 11 yrs.

Emery, John, of Camberwell, many years an
inhabitant of this parish, d. 23rd March, 1836,
a. 80.
Martha, his wife, d. 21st March, 1805, a. 49.
Child. Mary, d. 3rd Aug. 1799, a. 7 yrs. 4 mo.
11 days.
John, d. 8th May, 1790, a. 15 days.
Harriet, d. 1st Nov. 1793, a. 1 mo. 11 days.
Martha, d. 23rd Mar. 1802, a. 5 yrs. 2 mo. 7
days.
Richard, d. 2nd Oct. 1795, a. 7 mo. 8 days.

Everest, John, d. 28th March, 1842, a. 33.
Eliza Ann, his daughter, died in infancy.

Farmes, Jos., Elizabeth wife of, d. 31st Jan. 1838,
a. 50.

Fear, William, d. 21st June, 1810, a. 46.
Charlotte, his wife, d. 25th June, 1805, a. 38.
William, their son, d. 23rd Aug. 1819, a. 12.
Mary Ann, their dau., d. 28th Aug. 1810, a. 19.

Finch, John, (Dartford,) d. 19th July, 1768, a. 36.
Martha, his wife, d. 5th Nov. 1775, a. 45.

Finch, Wm., son of above, d. 14th Nov. 1830, a. 70.

Finch, John, d. 2nd April, 1842, a. 84.
Mary, his wife, d. 23rd Jan. 1796, a. 35.

Gravest. William, son, of J. F. d. 11th June, 1825, a. 42.

Foard, Joseph, (Dartford), d. 8th April, 1763; a. 74.

Elizabeth, his wife, d. 6th Feb. 1761, a. 73.

Frame Richard, d. 14th Sept. 1833, a. 61.

Tomb. Gardiner, Rev. Wm. (Kingsdown,) near Sittingbourne, and fellow of St. John's College, Oxford, eight years curate of this parish, d. 9th May, 1754, a. 32.

Gravest. Gatland, Edward, d. 1st July, 1799, a. 11.

Gibson, John, son of Charles and Mary, bapt. 13th Nov. 1704, in the parish of St. Mary Virgin, Dover, resided many years in Dartford, d. 26th Feb. 1810, in the 106th years from his baptism.

Godier, John, many years writer in the East India Company's service, d. 23rd Sept. 1825, a. 66.

Mary, his wife, d. 5th September, 1825, a. 68.

Goddard, Richard, d. 30th Oct. 1830, a. 62.

Phillis, his wife, d. 3rd Oct. 1839, a. 74.

Gold, Moses, d. 9th Dec. 1792, a. 30.

Susanna Rawlinson, d. Aug. 1812, a. 59.

Green, Edward, d. 13th Oct. 1812, a. 81.

Green, George, of this parish, d. 4th April, 1839, a. 36.

William Whitmore, his son, d. 12th July, 1836, a. 1 yr. 9 mo.

Gregory, Charles, d. 7th Dec. 1789, a. 30.

Griffiths, Elizabeth, wife of Thomas, of St. Mary, Islington, dau. of Chas. Pearce, Dartford, d. 7th March, 1812, a. 23.

Also one of her children died in infancy.

Griffiths, Mary, wife of Wm., d. 3rd July, 1798, a. 29.

Mary Ann, her dau. d. 5th Jan. 1791, a. 7 weeks.

John, her brother, d. 11th Aug. 1790, a. 26.

Gurney, David, (St. Sepulchre, Snow Hill, London,) Tallow Chandler, d. July, 1772, a. 34.

Halford, Thomas, (Greenwich,) d. 15th Nov. 1821, a. 50.

George, son of Thomas and Mary Halford, d. 4th Nov. 1810, a. 7 yrs. 4 mo.

Tomb. Hall, John, millwright and engineer, d. 7th Jan. 1836, a 71.

Gravest. Hall, James, d. July 5th, 1798, a. 30 yrs.

Gravest. Hall, William, (Dartford,) d. 15th May, 1835, a. 61.
Frances, his mother, d. 12th May, 1836, a. 89.
Hall, Sarah, wife of William, d. 19th Jan. 1780, a. 29.
Hall, Edward, son of Edward and Charlotte, d. 18th Dec. 1810, a. 3 yrs. 7 mo.

Tomb. Hammond, Simmons, Mary Ann, wife of, d. 7th Sept. 1828, a. 46.

Gravest. *Child.* Elizabeth, d. 17th April, 1805, a. 2 yrs. 21 days.
George, d. 6th May, a. 1 yr. 4 mo.
Simmons, d. 7th Aug. 1807, a. 2 yrs. 11 mo.
Hanwell, John, (Dartford,) d. July, 1769.
Elizabeth, dau. of John and Sarah H. d. 18th April, 1753, a. 2 yrs. 4 mo.
Hards, John, (seedsman,) d. 8th Dec. 1817, a. 77.
Mary his wife, dau. of J. Loader, d. 3rd Aug. 1802, a. 58.
Hards, James, (Miller,) d. 4th Feb. 1838, a. 59.
Martha, his wife, d. 25th April, 1817, a. 38.
Two children, Frederick and Henry Warren.
Hards, George, jun., d. 25th April, 1761, a. 26.
He left two children.
Harman, Charlotte, wife of James, dau. of John Wellard, d. 15th Feb. 1827, a. 40.

Tomb. Harwood, Rev. James, vicar of Dartford, and rector of Cliffe, d. 15th Feb. 1778, a. 63.
Rebecca, his wife, d. 3rd June, 1839, a. 70.
Child. Ann, d. 29th July, 1781, a. 25.
Charlotte, d. 20th Ap. 1768, a. 6.
Mary, d. Feb. 13th 1776, a. 12.
Francis, d. 26th Feb. 1768, a. 5 mo.
James, d. 24th Oct. 1782, buried at Lisbon.
Rebecca, d. 1st Jan. 1839, a. 81, *she caused this tomb to be erected to her family.*
Judith, youngest dau. of above, d. 13th Mar. 1842.

Gravest. Hartwell, John, (Dartford,) d. July 26th, 1760, a. 60.
Elizabeth, dau. of John and Sarah Hartwell, citizen of London, now of this parish, d. 16th April, 1755, a. 2 yrs. 4 mo.
Hibben, William, d. 31st Dec. 1760, a. 63.
Elizabeth, his wife, d. May, 1768, a. 69.

Gravest. Hibben, William, (Dartford,) d. 11th Oct. 1768, a.

Hicks, Anthony, eldest son of Anthony and Sarah, (Stoke Nayland, co. Suffolk,) d. 18th Dec. 1828, a. 23.

Hill, Abraham, d. 1st Dec. 1716, a. 38.

Hodsoll, Thomas, d. 27th Feb. 1816, a. 67.

Sarah, his wife, d. 28th Nov. 1814, a. 66.

Child. Sarah, d. 21st April, 1808, a. 26.

Elizabeth, d. 10th Dec. 1804, a. 14.

Hester, d. 15th May, 1799, a. 12 yrs.

Samuel, d. Sept. 3rd, 1798, a. 2 yrs.

Maxfield, d. 2nd May, 1800, a. 5 yrs.

Holdsworth, Robert, (Dartford,) surgeon, d. . . . a. 53.

Holmes, Richard, d. 4th March, 1792, a. 58.

Elizabeth, his wife, d. 18th October, 1810, a. 73.

Hooper, Frances, wife of Matthias, (Lower Brook-street, Grosvenor-sq.,) and dau. of William and Frances Wakeford, of Dartford, d. 3rd July, 1828, a. 38.

Huggett, Charles, (Dartford,) tallow chandler, d. 18th Sept. 1813, a. 50.

Mary, his wife, d. 20th Sept. 1810, a. 39, leaving issue, Mary, Charles, Elizabeth, Frederick and James.

Huggett, Henry, d. 20th Dec. a. 5 yrs. 9 mo.

Emma, d. 19th April, 1811, a. 10 mo.

Humphrey, John, (Dartford,) d. 12th Oct. 1829, a. 52.

Jardine, Joseph, (linen draper,) d. 14th March, 1832, a. 75.

Sarah, his wife,* d. 17th Dec. 1816, a. 49.

Child. Edward James, d. 18th May, 1794, a. 4 yrs.

Edward, d. 14th Oct. 1796, a. 5 mo.

Elizabeth, d. 24th Nov. 1803, a. 2 mo.

Jardine, Sarah, only dau. of Joseph and Sarah, d. 5th Sept. 1831, a. 34.

Jegon, Mary, d. 28th Aug. 1824, a. 78.

Jennings, Mellicent, wife of John, (Dartford,) d. 30th July, 1809, a. 37.

John, their son, d. a. 11 mo.

---

* Only daughter of (Sir) Edward Barker, of Sutton-at-Hone, lineally descended from the Barkers of Bocking Hall, baronets. Her father lies buried in an adjoining grave without any memorial. *Note p.* 400.

Gravest. Kemp,* William, d. 21st June, 1696, a. 65.

    Mary, his wife, d. 21st June, 1705, a. 70.

    Kettlewell, John, d. 21st Sept. 1810, aged 48.

    Elizabeth, his wife, d. 8th July, 1831, a. 70.

    William, son of John and Elizabeth Kettlewell, d. 13th Feb. 1809, a. 24.

    Kettlewell, John Round, (Dartford,) d. 17th March, 1821, a. 31.

    Mary, his wife, d. 17th July, 1815, a. 27.

    Jane Eliz. their dau., d. 24th May, 1815, a. 1 mo.

    Kettlewell, Henry Round, son of John and Elizabeth, d. 18th Nov. 1806, a. 5 yrs.

    Latham, Elizabeth,† dau. of John and Ann, (Dartford,) d. 12th Jan. 1763, a. 7 mo.

    Mary, her sister, d. 16th Dec. 1767, a. 3 weeks.

    Lardner, Richard, (Ramsden,) near Witney, Oxfordshire, clerk to Mr. John Pettit, brewer, Dartford, d. Jan. 27th 1752, a. 43.

    Lear, George, (Dartford,) d. 4th May, 1813, a. 71.

    Mary, his wife, d. 25th Oct. 1834, a. 79.

    William, their son, d. 3rd Aug. 1834, a. 37.

    Lee, Peter, (Dartford,) d. 21st April, 1839, a. 87.

    Susannah, his wife, dau. of Wm. and Jane Hounsted, d. 12th March, 1825, a. 75.

    Loader, John, d. 20th Oct. 1763, a. 64.

    Loader, John, d. 14th Dec. 1787, a. 49.

    Ann Loader, his wife, d. 15th Dec. 1787, a. 51.

    Loader, William, d. 14th Nov. 1810, a. 70.

    Mary, his sister, wife of John Hards, d. 3rd August, 1802, a. 58.

    Lowe, Albinus, d. 31st   1823, a. 17 mo.

    Loweth, Robert, (Dartford,) miller, d. 26th August, 1731, a. 69.

    Elizabeth, his relict, d. 14th Jan. 1741, a. 74.

    Luddington, William, d. 3rd March, 1766, a. 45.

    Margaret, his wife, d. 3rd March, 1763, a. 37.

    Makey, John, d. 6th Jan. 1792, a. 60.

---

* The oldest gravestone in the Burial ground.

† Children of John Latham, the celebrated naturalist. *Note p.* 8

Tomb. Manguad, John, esq., (Brixton place, Surrey,) d. 24th
April, 1810, a. 87.

Gravest. Marshall, Henry, mason, (Dartford,) d. 12th November, 1831, a. 36.

William Robert, died in infancy.

Martin, Samuel, d. 20th Sept. 1803, a. 59.

Ann, his wife, d. 23rd Nov. 1825, a. 76.

Martin, Henry, (Dartford,) d. 24th June, 1825, a. 55.

Elizabeth, his relict, d. 2nd Jan. 1836, a. 80.

Merchant, Benjamin, d. Christmas day, 1783, a. 46.

Esther, his wife, d. Jan. 8th, 1799, a. 70.

Messenger, Ann, d. June 11th, 1821, a. 51.

Messenger, Charles, Mildred, wife of, d. 2nd Jan.
1839, a. 42.

Charles, their son, d. 11th Jan. 1842, a. 24.

Ann, their dau., d. 16th Aug. 1824, a. 18 mo.

Harriet, d. 7th Sept. 1833, a. 2 yrs.

William, d. 15th Jan. 1837, a. 19 yrs.

Louisa, d. 28th Aug. 1837, a. 18 mo.

Metcalf, Thomas, d. 19th April, 1808, a. 58.

Frances, his wife, d. 2nd Nov. 1799, a. 45.

Elizabeth, their dau. d. 7th April, 1786, a. 6 weeks.

Thomas, their son, d. 29th June, 1795, a. 5 yrs.
4 mo.

Thomas Metcalf, their nephew, d. 1st Jan. 1800,
a. 17.

Mombo, William, bapt. 1803, a. 39.

Momroo, William, 30th April, 1803, a. 29.

Nettlefold, William, d. 28th Sept. 1789, a. 45.

Elizabeth, his wife, d. 21st Jan. 1804, a. 54.

Child. Amy, d. 25th April, 1783, a. 18 mo.

Elizabeth, d. 29th Aug. 1789, a. 6 yrs.

John, d. 4th Sept. 1789, a. 4 mo.

Sarah,* dau. of Wm. and Eliz. Nettlefold,
d. 16th Dec. 1820, a. 42.

Nettlefold, William, d. 30th July, 1834, a. 61.

Ann, his wife, d. 15th Aug. 1830, a. 51.

Norman, William, (Dartford,) d. 26th Feb. 1825,
a. 24.

Alice, his wife, d. 8th November, 1832, a. 72.

---

* Said by some to be married to Mr. James.

Gravest. Norris, John, (Dartford,) d. 28th Jan. 1799, a. 44.
    Ruth Chalk, his relict, d. 8th April, 1832, a. 84.
    Maria, their dau. d. 17th April, 1789, a. 12 mo.
    North, John, d. Feb. 1819, a. 62.
      Elizabeth, his wife, d. Mar. 1831, a. 72.
      Thomas, their son, d. Nov. 1827, a. 30.
    Notley, Eliz., wife of George, d. 25th Mar. 1796, a. 44.
    Notley, Charles, d. 2nd July, 1802, a. 81.
      Susan, d. 11th April, 1802, a. 83.
    Okill, Thomas, son of Thomas and Jane, d. 20th Nov. 1802, a. 12.
    Orme, Thomas, d. 17th March, 1836, a. 41.
      Elizabeth, his wife, d. 25th June, a. 50.
      Elizabeth, their dau. d. 6th Feb. 1819, a. 7.
    Parker, William, (Dartford,) freeman of London, d. 22nd Nov. 1744, a. 57.
    Ann, his wife, ... also 7 children.
    Parker, William, (freeman of Gravesend,) d. 1778.
    Parkhurst, William, d. 26th Feb. 1796, a. 71.
      Elizabeth, his wife, d. 26th May, 1805, a. 71.
    Parkhurst, Thomas, d. 15th Aug. 1822, a. 27.
      Elizabeth, his wife, d. 8th Dec. 1819, a. 38.
    Parkhurst, William, d. 1st Sept. 1827, a. 62.
    Parkhurst, Thomas, (Stone,) Sarah, wife of, d. 4th June, 1804, left issue, 1 boy and 4 girls.
    Pearce, Charles, (Dartford,) smith and farrier, d. 17th April, 1813, a. 66.
      Elizabeth, his wife, d. 14th Aug. 1820, a. 66, also their five children, Charles, Whittenton, Ann, Thomas, and Elizabeth, wife of Thomas Griffith, of the parish of St. Mary, Islington.
    Peirce, Edward, (Dartford,) d. 10th Feb. 1771, a. 58.
    Sarah, his wife, d. 28th Aug. 1781, a. 68.
    Sarah, their daughter.
    Peirce, Hester, (Dartford,) d. 24th June, 1750, a. 22.
    Peirce, Mary, (Dartford,) d. 8th June, 1775, a. 22.

Tomb. Peirce, Edward, (late of Greenwich,) d. 17th Oct. 1809, a. 66.
    Mary, his widow, d. 14th Jan. 1819, a. 77.

Gravest. Peirce, Thomas, (Dartford,) ironmonger, and livery-
man of London, d. 3rd March, 1831, a. 53.

Mary, his wife, d. 24th June, 1828, a. 44.

Child. Mary, d. 9th Jan. 1828, a. 1 yr. 6 da.

Elizabeth, d. 23rd July, 1811, a. 1 yr. 11
mo.

Frederick, d. 18th Ap. 1824, a. 7 mo. 6 da.

Thomas, d. 27th Jan. 1832, a. 21.

Peirce, Elizabeth, (Dartford,) d. 30th Nov. 1766.

Pelton, Jane Elizabeth, wife of Richard Pelton, originally of Brentford, now of Dartford, daughter
of John and Margaret Weekes, of Chatham, d.
11th Sept. 1841, a. 49.*

Perkins, John, (Dartford,) d. 19th April, 1812, a. 36.

Ann, his wife, d. 28th March, 1815, a. 33.

Philcox, Elizabeth, formerly of Wye, d. 12th May,
1834, a. 83.

Pike, Sarah, d. Nov. 1804, a. 62.

Pilcher, Henry,† d. 29th June, 1838, a. 36, *erected
by the Amicable Society, of which he was long
the Sec.*

Potter, Edward, (Dartford,) d. Nov. 3rd, 1828, a. 59.

Powell, John, "a long and respectable inhabitant of
Dartford," d. 23rd March, 1805, a. 53.

Puplett, John, d. 5th March, 1809, a. 53.

Ann, his wife, d. 1st March, 1831, a. 78.

T. P. d. 12th May, 1836.

Quait, William, of Sullington, co. Sussex, 30th Sept.
1822, a. 65.

Hannah, his wife, 26th Feb. 1815, a. 62.

Quait, Richard, d. 6th Nov. 1830, a. 43.

Caroline, his dau. 24th April, 1820, a. 7 m. 2 d.

Amelia, 26th Oct. 1821, 8 m. 12 d.

Quelch, William, paper maker, d. June, 1775, a. 96.

Quelch, Mary, d. 1774, a. 92.

Quelch, Elizabeth, d. 19th April, 1741, a. 22.

Eleanor, wife of John Terry, d. 23rd Oct. 1773,
a. 61.

---

* This inscription is the most complete in the burial ground, inasmuch
as it states the names of the deceased's parents, their residence, and the
former abode of her husband.

† On the south side of Pilcher's grave, without any memorial, lies
Richard Trevithic, a Cornishman and a celebrated engineer; *see also p
404, ante.*

Graves. Quelch, William, d. 9th May, 1797, a. 72.

Hannah, his wife, d. 12th June, 1762, a. 51.

Raisback, William, d. 30th Sept. 1805, a. 64, *he conducted Dartford workhouse fifteen years.*

Grace, his wife, d. 3rd August, 1813, a. 75.

Randall, John, d. 1st Feb. 1772, a. 59.

Rawlings, Edward, (Dartford,) d. 10th Dec. 1783, a. 50.

Elizabeth, his wife, d. 27th July, 1786, a. 54.

Ray, Elizabeth, d. 11th June, 1821, a. 77.

Reason, James, d. 19th March, 1767, a. 38.

Richards, William, late surgeon, (Dartford,) d. 14th Jan. 1812, a. 60.

Ann, his wife, d. 17th Nov. 1813, a. 60.

Robinson, Thomas, d. 20th July, 1782, a. 64.

Robinson, Francis, esq., d. April 28th, 1793, a. 43.

Margaret, wife of above, d. 19th Feb. 1806, a. 58.

Round, Mary, late of Shoreham, d. 5th Jan. 1786, a. 18.

Sarah, dau. of Wm. and Sarah Round, of Shoreham, d. 10th May, 1794, a. 2.

Round, Mary Ann, dau. of John and Elizabeth, (Dartford,) d. 13th June, 1814, a. 19.

Salvett, Daniel, d. 18th Sept. 1811, a. 81.

Sanham, Richard, d. 23rd Nov. 1796, a. 72.

Jane, his wife, d. 16th Nov. 1778, a. 52.

Richard, son of the above, d. 25th May, 1777, a. 25.

and six other children.

Sanham, James, d. 21st Jan. 1807, a. 75.

Frances, his wife, d. 1st April, 1779, a. 49.

Rebecca, his second wife, d. 16th April, 1792, a. 47.

Sanham, James, builder, d. 9th Dec. 1831, a. 49.

Martha, his daughter, d. 26th Aug. 1827, a. 19.

Six children of Henry and Mary Sanham—*the stone erected by their son Henry.*

Sanham, Jane, d. 24th May, 1836, a. 72.

Seagur, Sarah, spinster, (Bishopsgate-st., London,) d. 29th April, 1779, a. 24.

Seagur, Elizabeth, wife of Nathaniel, d. 6th Feb. 1804, a. 41.

Nathaniel, son of above, d. 20th May, 1803, a. 7 mo. 7 d.

Gravest. Sears, Henrietta, wife of Thomas, d. 19th Feb. 1836, a. 63.

 Mary, dau. of the above, d. 26th May, 1799, a. 18 mo.

 Eleanor, their dau. d. 18th Sept. 1824, a. 19.
 The grave is adorned with shrubs, and surrounded by iron rails.

Searson, George, d. 31st Jan. 1826, a. 77.

 Mary, his wife, d. 9th Feb. 1828, a. 87.

Tomb. Sharp, Elizabeth, wife of Charles, d. 23rd Aug. 1760, a. 38.

 Mary, his second wife, d. 10th April, 1772, a. 47.

Sharp, Charles, the above, d. 24th Sept. 1773, a. 50.

 Charles, son of Charles and Eliz. Sharp, d. 23rd Oct. 1779, a. 21.

 Dorman, John, yeoman,* (Dartford,) d. 19th June, 1800, a. 66.

 Dorman, Thomas, son of above, d. 3rd Oct. 1781, a. 5 mo.

 Dorman, William, his brother, d. Nov. 1803, a. 23.

 Sarah Pope, d. 3rd July, 1820, a. 66.

Gravest. Sharp, Charles, son of Joseph, builder, d. 1st Nov. 1811, a. 30.

 Ann, his wife, d. 7th July, 1832, a. 46.

 Sheppard, John, (Dartford,) d. 19th March, 1803, a. 61.

 Elizabeth, his wife, 24th May, 1800, a. 51.

Tomb. Sheppard, William, (Dartford,) 8th Jan. 1831, a. 58.

 Sheppard, Elizabeth, d. 14th Sept. 1807, a. 34.

Gravest. Sherren, John, d. 19th May, 1783, a. 67.

 Ann, his wife, d. 5th March, 1772, a. 52.

Sherren, John, d. 16th March, 1789, a. 34.

 Elizabeth, his wife, d. 18th Oct. 1786, a. 34.

Short, Mary Ann, wife of William, d. 28th Jan. 1840, a. 29.

Sibley, Ann, wife of Robert William, d. Aug. 1841, a. 65.

 Three children died in infancy, Hannah, John, Naomi.

Smalley, Thomas, d. 2nd June, 1773.

Smalley, Ann, (Dartford,) d. 4th April, 1770, a. 35.

Snowden, Harriet, wife of James, d. 7th March, 1840, a. 50.

---

* He married Elizabeth, their daughter, who survived him thirty years.

Gravest. Solomon, Thomas, (Dartford,) d. 1st Dec. 1770, a. 73.
 Elizabeth, his wife, d. 30th April, 1773, a. 72.
Stains, Charles, d. 7th Aug. 1837, a. 42.
 Sarah, his dau. d. 10th July, 1832, a. 13 mo.
Southgate, John, d. 18th June, 1808, a. 27.
 Two children died in infancy.
Stevens, Thomas, d. 4th April, 1710, a. 25.
 Also two children.
Storey, Ann, dau. of James and Mary, (Dartford,) d.
 1st Feb. 1804, a. 6 mo.
 James, his brother, d. 25th April, 1807, a. 10.
 Thomas Edward, brother of above, d. 23rd June,
  1814, a. 13.
Storey, Charles, son of Charles and Ann, d. 21st
 March, 1840, a. 3 yrs. 6 mo.
 Barbara Ann, sister of above, d. 21st March, 1840,
  a. 8.
Street, Lydia, d. 1st July, 1770, a. 74.
Stretton, Martha, dau. of Benjamin and Mary, d.
 13th Dec. 1835, a. 19.
Stratton, Samuel, d. 8th October, 1802, a. 65.
 Elizabeth, his wife, d. 27th November, 1816, a. 51.
Stubbs, Thomas, d. 13th June, 1763, a. 69.
 Ann, his wife, d. 14th Dec. 1741, a. 37.
Swaisland, Amos, (Crayford,) d. 30th Dec. 1810,
 a. 72.
 Ann, his wife, d. 10th Feb. 1824, a. 73.
 Six children died in infancy.
Sykes, John, d. 10th May, 1803, a. 22.
Taylor, John, d. 24th August, 1833, a. 53.
 Elizabeth, dau. of John and Sarah Taylor, d. 17th
  Sept. 1826, a. 18 yrs. 2 mo.
Taylor, Thomas, d. 9th Nov. 1820, a. 2 yrs. 5 mo.
Tee, Robert, (Horndean, co. Southampton,) d. Easter
 Sunday, 1805, a. 32.
Terry, John, d. 12th July, 1766, a. 53.
Terry, Eleanor, d. 23rd October, 1773, a. 61.
Terry, Elizabeth, d. 24th Dec. 1759, a. 24.
Terry, John, d. 12th July, 1775, a. 23.
Terry, James, many years an inhabitant of Graves-
 end, d. 31st Oct. 1770, a. 60.*

---

* A carpenter, and brother of John Terry, who married Eleanor Quelch.

Gravest. Terry, James, son of John and Eleanor, late of this parish, d. 1st Nov. 1788, a. 31.

Thackara, Elizabeth, dau. of James and Mary, (Dartford,) d. 27th July, 1786, a. 11.

Elizabeth, dau. of above, d. 17th Dec. a. 11.

Tinsley, Joseph, builder, d. 3rd November, 1836, a. 70.

Elizabeth, his wife, d. 9th Nov. 1836, a. 64.

Tinsley, Thomas, his son, millwright, d. 21st June, 1815, a. 20.

Charlotte, his sister, d. 15th July, 1796.

Tippetts, Richard, "26 yrs. surgeon in Dartford," d. 11th Dec. 1824, a. 50.

Tippetts, Elizabeth, wife of Richard, (Dartford,) d. 8th April, 1813, a. 38.

Anna Maria, dau. of Richard and Elizabeth, d. 6th May, 1830, a. 18.

Child. Louisa Ann, d. Jan. 19th, 1806, a. 2.

Edwin Berriman, d. Ap. 13th, 1806, a. 2 yrs.

Frederick, d. 31st July, 1802, a. 6.

Emily, d. 7th April, 1813, a. 3.

Trusson, William, d. 25th Nov. 1791, a. 35.

Tomb. Umfrey, Finch, esq., barrister at Law, d. 13th July, 1743, a. 43. he married the only daughter of John Jervis, of this parish. *This tomb is erected by his wife, Elizabeth Umfrey.*

Varnfield, Ann, wife of Edward, d. 17th Feb. 1825, a. 33.

Varnfield, Thomas, son of Edward and Ann, d. 17th Feb. 1825, a. 33.

Wakeford, William, d. 31st March, 1826, a. 38.

Elizabeth Ann, his wife, dau. of James and Mary Ann Storey, d. 20th Jan. 1818, a. 26.

Three children died in infancy.

Wakeford, William, d. 14th June, 1812, a. 57.

Frances, his wife, d. 10th Oct. 1808, a. 40.

Mary, their dau. d. 5th Sept. 1792, a. 4 mo.

Wakeford, Edward Howes, d. 31st March, 1827, a. 30.

Wakeford, Frances, dau. of Wm. and Frances, wife of Matthias Hooper, of Lower Brook-st., Grosvenor sq., d. 23rd July, 1825, a. 38.

Gravest. Walker, Thomas Grant, son of Thomas and Elizabeth Walker, d. 20th . . . . 1807, a. 6.

Walker, John, son of T. and E. d. 18th, Jan. 1810, a. 2.

Walker, Ann, dau. of T. and E. d. 29th July, 1822, a. 16.

Tomb. Walker, Thomas, esq., d. 13th Mar. 1828, a. 60.

Gravest. Warcup, John, d. 3rd May, 1815, a. 63.

Hester, dau. of John and Hester Warcup, d. 24th Mar. 1825, a. 43.

Tomb. Warde, Elizabeth, wife of Ambrose, (Stone,) d. 8th Mar. 1798, a. 32.

Mary their daughter, left issue three sons and three daughters.

Warde, Ann, d. 18th Dec. 1833, a. 48.

Gravest. Ward, William, d. 10th June, 1803, a. 83.

Elizabeth, his wife, d. 14th Nov. 1809, a. 81.

Flat St. Wardale, Ann Harriet, dau. of George, (Wisbeach, Cambridgeshire,) merchant, d. 19th March, 1815, a. 26.

Gravest. Warman, Elizabeth, relict of William Tresson, d. 25th Nov. 1771, a. 35.

Warns, Sarah Maria Miller, dau. of Robert and Esther, d. 6th April, 1841, a. 14.

Tomb. Warton, Thomas, (Dartford,) d. 26th April, 1819, a. 65.

Mary, wife of James Titmers, (Hackney,) sister of the above, d. 26th March, 1818, a. 63.

Warton, Thomas, nephew of the above, eldest son of Henry Warton, of Chatham, killed by a fall from his horse, 12th March, 1828, a. 24.

Gravest. Watson, Richard, d. 16th July, 1842, a. 63.

Weekes, John, son of John and Mary, d. 26th Jan. 1837, a. 2 yrs. 5 mo.

Welch, Sarah, wife of Joseph, (Crooked Lane, London,) daughter of John Hartwell, d. 17th Feb. 1766.

Wellard, John, (Dartford,) d. 2nd Dec. 1830, a. 83.

Elizabeth, his wife, d. 4th March, 1825, a. 72.

James, his son, d. 14th Sept. 1781, a. 4.

John, d. 15th Jan. 1792, a. 11 mo.

James, d. 20th Oct. 1792, a. 33.

Charlotte, dau. of above, and wife of James Harman, d. 15th Feb. 1827, a. 40.

E*

Gravest. Weston, John, d. 28th June, 1744, a. 49. *Latin Inscription.*

Weston, Jane, wife of William, d. 30th Aug. 1794, a. 51.

Wheatley, Paul, (Rochester,) d. 9th Aug. 1767, a. 46.
Paul, his son, d. 1786, a. 57.

Whitehead, Henry, d. 4th May, 1807, a. 83.

Whitsey, Stephen, d. 14th Nov. 1833, a. 73.
Ann, his wife, d. 7th June, 1818, a. 48.

Tomb. Wildding, John, d. 30th Dec. 1829, a. 78.
Anna Maria, his wife, d. 10th Sept. 1836, a. 79.
Hannah Charlton, dau. of John and Anna Maria W. d. May 11th, 1828, a. 32.

Tomb, iron rails. Williams, John, esq., (formerly of this parish, but late of Willcroft House, near Hereford,) d. August 14th, 1823, a. 69.
Grace, his wife, d. 7th July, 1799, a. 44.

Gravest. Winter, Edward, d. 10th Mar. 1830, a. 57.
Mary, his wife, d. 20th May, 1834, a. 59.

Wood, William, d. 20th Dec. 1821, a. 47.

Woodham, John, late of Greenwich, baker, formerly of this parish, d. 8th May, 1778, a. 45.
Five children of John and Elizabeth Woodham.

GENERAL DIETARY FOR THE POOR, IN DARTFORD UNION.

No. 2.   Ordered by the Poor Law Commissioners.

		BREAKFAST.	DINNER.	SUPPER.
Sunday ...	Men	6 oz. bread 1 oz. cheese	16 oz. Meat Pudding with Veg.*	6 oz. bread 1 oz. cheese
	Women	5 oz. bread ½ oz. butter	10 oz. Meat Pudding with ditto	5 oz. bread ½ oz. butter
Monday ...	Men	6 oz. bread 1 oz. cheese	7 oz. bread 1 oz. cheese	6 oz. bread 1 oz. cheese
	Women	5 oz. bread ½ oz. butter	7 oz. bread 1 oz. cheese	5 oz. bread ½ oz. butter
Tuesday ...	Men	6 oz. bread 1 oz. cheese	16 oz. Suet Pudding with Veg.	6 oz. bread 1 oz. cheese
	Women	5 oz. bread ½ oz. butter	10 oz. Suet Pudding with ditto	5 oz. bread ½ oz. butter
Wednesday	Men	6 oz. bread 1 oz. cheese	7 oz. bread 1 oz. cheese	6 oz. bread 1 oz. cheese
	Women	5 oz. bread ½ oz. butter	7 oz. bread 1 oz. cheese	5 oz. bread ½ oz. butter
Thursday	Men	6 oz. bread 1 oz. cheese	7 oz. bread 1 oz. cheese	6 oz. bread 1 oz. cheese
	Women	5 oz. bread 1 oz. cheese	7 oz. bread 1 oz. cheese	5 oz. bread ½ oz. butter
Friday ...	Men	6 oz. bread 1 oz. cheese	16 oz. Suet Pudding with Veg.	6 oz. bread 1 oz. cheese
	Women	5 oz. bread ½ oz. butter	10 oz. Suet Pudding with ditto	5 oz. bread ½ oz. butter
Saturday	Men	6 oz. bread 1 oz. cheese	7 oz. bread 1 oz. cheese	6 oz. bread 1 oz. cheese
	Women	5 oz. bread ½ oz. butter	7 oz. bread 1 oz. cheese	5 oz. bread ½ oz. butter

* The Vegetables are extra, and not included in the weight.

The following officers are appointed to carry the New Poor Law into effect and afford medical assistance, &c. at the undermentioned salaries per annum.

Three Commissioners at £3000 each. DARTFORD UNION, John Hayward, *clerk*, £100. Thomas Patten, *Auditor*, £30. Mrs. Medhurst, *Schoolmistress*, £20. Mr. and Mrs. Farmer, *Master and Matron*, £80. R. Symon, *Porter*, £20. Samuel Levens, *Relieving Officer*, £100. R. Beard, *ditto*, £100. *Medical Officers.* R. Tippets, *No. 1 District*, £150. Edwin Cottingham, *No. 2 District*, £100. Frederick Hunt, *No. 3 District*, £100. *Chaplain*, F. B. Grant, £100. *Total*...£895.

The *New Poor Law* was introduced under pretence of reducing the rates, but has not done so, though it has greatly increased the sufferings of the poor, and "*The Times*" newspaper of April 26th, 1844, says "the law affronts men's understanding whilst it picks their pockets, and treats them like fools while it legalizes an extortion, which out of every shilling it professes to raise for the *relief* of the poor, gives *tenpence* to some otiose* salaried officer or absentee inspector."

OLD PEOPLE above 60 years of age are allowed the weekly addition of 1 ounce of Tea and milk, and also an additional meat-pudding dinner on Thursday in each week, in lieu of bread and cheese, for those whose age and infirmities it may be deemed proper and requisite.

CHILDREN have bread and milk for their breakfast and supper, or gruel when milk cannot be obtained; also such proportions of their dinner as may be requisite for their respective ages.

The SICK : whatever is ordered for them by the medical officer.

. *There are generally about 260 inmates in the Union, and a great mass of children and aged persons.*

The above diet is said to be amply sufficient for children and aged persons, but hardly enough for able-bodied working men. However, these but rarely apply for admission; during the summer of 1843, as but few Irishmen came to this neighbourhood to assist in getting in the harvest, several farmers in the vicinity directed the master of the union house, to send them all the applicants for temporary relief, promising them work for some time. Strange to say, out of more than three hundred only about three or four presented themselves, as willing to accept employment.

It is an invariable practice to separate married men from their wives on admission; and in one instance, where an elderly woman was a little irritated at the circumstance, the governor ordered a strait-waistcoat to be put on her,—when, in a few hours, the *poor wretch became quiet and resigned ?*

---

* From Otium *Lat*, living at ease ; not working.

THE DARTFORD MARKET QUESTION.

No sooner was the dispute settled with Mr. Pearce, [*vide* p. 252] and that individual had been induced to resign all claim to the lease of the Tolls of Dartford Market and Fair, than the following notice appeared:—"All persons desirous of holding stalls and shambles in the market, must apply to my office for particulars, since the Shamble market heretofore held in the High-street, Dartford, aforesaid will be discontinued." (*Signed,*) JOHN HAYWARD,

Agent to the lord of the manor.

Simultaneously was issued a printed hand bill announcing that by virtue of an order made by the Commissioners appointed by an Act of Parliament, passed in the 54th Geo. III, for lighting, watching, and improving the town of Dartford, in the county of Kent, in which notice was given,

"That all persons who shall obstruct, or in any ways incommode the free passage of any or either of the said several streets, lanes, or other public passages or places, within the said parish, or suffer any boards, stalls, booths, goods, wares, merchandize, or other thing or things whatsoever to be laid or placed and left to remain in any of the said streets, ways, lanes, or other public passages, or places during the night or for any longer time that shall be necessary for removing or housing the same, will be prosecuted according to the provisions of the said act and the penalties of the said act will be strictly enforced."

(Signed,) JOHN HAYWARD,

"Clerk to the said Commissioners."

Dated, Dartford, 2nd April, 1843.

In this way was a local act strained to meet the exigency, although it contained a special clause respecting the reservation of the rights of the lord of the manor; loud and deep were the mutterings that ensued amongst the hucksters and market-followers; yet, no one seemed inclined to dispute the ordonnance, except Mr. Arthur Colls, a butcher, and John Clifford, a baker; who were immediately denounced by Henry Bourner, a police constable. A magistrate astonished at the consummate wickedness of the age, immediately granted a summons for the delinquents to attend at the next *justice-* [?] day; during the week Mr. Colls sought advice from counsel, whom he also engaged to attend and defend him on the occasion.

On Saturday, May 13th, the case was appointed to be heard before the Justices in Petty Sessions;—Present, Sir P. H. Dyke, bart., and the Reverend Messrs. Davies and Renouard. Mr. Horn, the barrister, assisted by Mr. Fenton, attended on behalf of the delinquent, and Mr. Hayward, of Dartford, supported the prosecution, and appeared in the quadruple capacity of solicitor to the Commissioners, agent to the lord of the manor of Dartford, legal adviser to the Magistrates, and clerk to the feoffees of the Grammar School, when the following proceedings took place, as reported in the newspapers:

THE COMMISSIONERS FOR LIGHTING, ETC. OF DARTFORD
v. COLLS.*

Mr. Horn informed the court that he not only appeared for the defendant A. Colls, but also for the tradesmen of Dartford, and others, who felt aggrieved at the lord of the manor's demands— on which, Mr. Hayward immediately rose, and said he was much surprised at the presence of counsel with whom he felt *unable* to cope.—He must therefore request the magistrates *to postpone* the case till the next bench day.

Mr. Horn said it must be perfectly well known to the bench, that the defendant had been at great expense in bringing a counsel and solicitor, the one from London, and the other from Gravesend, on this occasion; and Mr. Hayward, who was clerk to the commissioners and agent to the lord of the manor, must be now, as well acquainted with the facts of the case as he could possibly be a fortnight hence. The learned gentleman then stated, that this was a summons against Mr. Colls, a butcher in Lowfield-street, Dartford, for suffering his stall to remain in the High-street on a Market day, and involved the right of holding a market. He would ask the bench what there was on the face of such a complaint to require a postponement. If Mr. Hayward had not his witnesses, there might be a ground, but it was the same in principle whether a counsel or an attorney attended, and he apprehended that the bench would not postpone a case, merely because one party had a supposed advantage of such a nature. Mr. Hayward having chosen to make this a criminal prosecution was now bound to enter into his case since he, (Mr. Horn) never heard in the whole course of his existence, of a criminal proceeding being postponed on the plea "that the prosecutor was not ready at the time he had himself fixed for the trial." He trusted the court would not accede to the application.

Mr. Hayward said he considered himself incompetent to cope with Mr. Horn.

---

* Reported by Mr. Fenton in the following week's Kentish Independent.

Mr Horn replied, that, without meaning any disrespect to the Bench, it was manifest theirs was not a tribunal before which so important a question ought to be argued. At all events, Mr. Hayward was bound to pay the expenses incurred by the delay, which the learned counsel stated would amount to upwards of £15.

The magistrates agreed with Mr. Hayward as to his incompetency and granted the postponement, but refused Mr. Colls his expenses, "thus showing" says the Kentish Independent, "that had the unfortunate butcher chosen to employ a 'nincom' he might have saved his money and lost his cause in a regular manner, but here he was punished for having too good a chance of winning, and is an example of the truth of the saying 'a man may have too much of a good thing.'"

Another week elapsed, Mr. Colls kept his station in the street, and as he was becoming a martyr, was pitied and patronized.

On the Tuesday following, a notice was served upon Colls that Mr. Hayward did not intend to proceed further upon this tack, but would try an indictment.

On June 10th, some of the stall keepers who had been terrified into the new building, finding they could not take enough *to pay even the tolls*, resumed their old places in the street, consequently, during the ensuing week, appeared the following fulmination, which was duly proclaimed by the town crier, as well as printed in the form of a hand bill, lugging into the battle, "The Priory Manor" an hitherto untried combatant.*

"DARTFORD MARKET.—Whereas the Rev. Charles Augustus Samuel Morgan, Clerk, lord of the manor of Dartford Priory, in the County of Kent, and owner and proprietor of the Market, has found it expedient for the public convenience, that the Market for the sale of meat and other goods, wares and merchandize, should be *removed* from the place *where the same has hitherto been set down and exposed for sale in the High Street of the town of Dartford* aforesaid, to the newly erected market and shambles, adjoining the said High-street of the said town. Notice is hereby given by the said Charles Augustus Samuel Morgan, on Saturday, the 17th of June, 1843, and henceforth *on every other* market day following, the Market for the sale of meat and other goods, wares, and merchandize, will be removed to, and held in, the said newly erected market and shambles, and the same is hereby removed accordingly."

(Signed,)   JOHN HAYWARD, Attorney and Agent
for the Rev. Chas. Augustus Samuel Morgan.

Dartford, June 16, 1843.

---

* Nundina Cantiana, A, p. 20.

On Saturday, June 17th, all the market attendants became contumacious, and stood, in utter defiance of the preceding notice in the open street. The town crier was again employed to re-proclaim it, which he did; Mr. Colls appended the following additional paragraph:

"The lord of the manor of Dartford Priory has no right to erect buildings on the estate of the feoffees of the Grammar School, without benefiting the estate, for holding the market. The feoffees had not the power of granting a *permanent right*; and there is no Act of Parliament to compel persons to remove thither with their goods."

June 17th, 1843.   (Signed) A. S. COLLS.

The roars of laughter with which the above addenda was received, would have benefited the worst hypochondriac. The gentlemen and farmers of the corn market heartily entered into the spirit of the joke, for fun it appeared to them, many not having the least doubt Mr. Colls would ultimately beat his opponents.

On the 10th of September following, Mr. Colls summoned Henry Bourner, a police constable of Dartford, to the Gravesend and Dartford Court of Requests, in consequence of his (Bourner's) solicitor, Mr. Hayward, having thought fit to abandon proceedings against him before the magistrates in Petty Sessions, at the Town Hall, Dartford, to show cause why he created an obstruction in the street by exposing his goods for sale on a market day, when he had attended with counsel and his attorney, and recompence was now sought in this court for the damage sustained.

COLLS v. BOURNER.*

The Commissioners present were Messrs. Snowden, (chairman,) Sharp, J. Dunkin and A. J. Dunkin. Messrs. Kerr and Cann, who sat on the previous cases, declined acting, the former, because on his wife's side he was related to plaintiff, expecting a similar delicacy would actuate Mr. Snowden, who had superseded Bourner as the prosecutor in this very case at the then ensuing Maidstone assizes. Mr. Hayward attended as clerk to the Commissioners.

Bourner pleaded not indebted, and called Mr. Hayward as a witness.

Mr. Hayward, when sworn, stated that he was clerk to the magistrates, who had already decided upon this case, and whose minute

---

* Dover Chronicle.

book he produced, to show that the magistrates had refused to allow expenses; therefore he submitted, that the present tribunal could not entertain the question. The magistrates ordered the case to be postponed, because the plaintiff brought counsel to the Petty Sessions.

Mr. Colls in reply, said, that the reason why the magistrates would not entertain the application for the expenses, and *then, allow them,* was, because they considered the whole case would be fully argued and considered the next Bench-day,—but which, Mr. Hayward instead of trying, had thought fit to abandon,—thus, giving him no opportunity of getting a verdict, and as the costs already incurred, amounted to fifteen pounds, he had reduced them to five pounds, and now summoned the defendant who was his then ostensible prosecutor, to the Court of Requests for that sum.

Mr. Hayward stated, that had he been certain of the fact of a barrister's attendance, he should have employed Mr. Deedes to oppose Mr. Horn. Mr. H. then told the Commissioners they would be exceeding their powers if they adjudicated upon the case.

Mr. Alfred John Dunkin said, this was a Court of Equity. The question which the court had to consider, was, had any damage been sustained? If there had, to what extent? His opinion was, that the powers granted the court by Act of Parliament would not be exceeded by deciding upon the case. Of the proceedings in Petty Session, this court could not take cognizance. From the evidence adduced, it appeared the plaintiff had expended five pounds to combat proceedings instituted against him by the defendant, who had thought fit to abandon the prosecution of the cause before the day of hearing, and damage had therefore been sustained to that amount. The only remedy for the plaintiff was, through the mediation of a Court of Equity.

The chairman refused to put the question to the Vote; he would sit there all the week first.

Mr. A. J. Dunkin begged to tell the chairman the question must be put. His office in that respect was purely ministerial. He could vote afterwards as he pleased.

Mr. Hayward, as clerk to the Commissioners, said Mr. Snowden must put it to the vote, whether the verdict should be for plaintiff or defendant. The Commissioners would decide on their own responsibility, if they exceeded the powers granted them by the Act of Parliament which constituted them a body.

Mr. Kerr declined voting. Messrs Snowden and Sharp voted for defendant and the Messrs. Dunkin for the plaintiff. The votes being equal, Mr. Snowden gave a casting vote, which settled the affair, the plaintiff being non-suited.

Matters remained in this state until the Lent Assizes at Maidstone, 1844, when the question was again brought forward by Indictment of Mr. Colls.

On Saturday morning March the 17th, however, when the
case was called for hearing before Baron Alderson, the indictment was, on application, allowed to be withdrawn, the prosecutor undertaking to pay all expenses.

———

At the same Assizes a trial took place respecting the Dartford
Creek Navigation, in which Mr. Allen, the occupier of a farm at
Crayford, alledged that the cuttings of the new canal were so
unskilfully and negligently executed, that the banks were unable
to resist the pressure of the water, by which a breach was effected,
and his farm flooded, causing the most grievous injury to his farm
and crops.   The nature of the complaint against the commissioners was as follows :—In December, 1840, a contract was entered
into with a Mr. Button, for the performance of certain works,
which were to be executed under the control of the commissioners' engineer, Mr. Easton.   The old cut was thought to be too circuitous, and the object of the new works was to make a more
direct passage.   The canal proceeded for some distance by the side
of the plaintiff's land.   The soil through which it passed was
composed of a surface of peat, below which was clay for 15 or
20 inches, and then peat earth again.   The cut was made, and the
banks formed out of the soil excavated.   It was complained by
the plaintiff, that looking to the character of the soil, negligence
had been shown not only in the structure, but in the position of
the banks.   It was contended that a table of land should have
been left between the excavation and the bank outside, forming a
protection to it.   This, in fact, had been suggested during the
progress of the works, by a person of great experience in such
matters, who predicted, that unless this was done, the banks
would not stand.   In fact, this prediction was verified before the
completion of the works, and the commissioners caused the banks
to be rebuilt with a foreland, as it was called, for a considerable
distance, but not down to the point where the breach complained
of took place.   On the morning of the 19th of July, the bank
gave way, the water flowed into Mr. Allen's land, and caused
vast injury to the crops, for which he now sought compensation.   The amount of damage, it was agreed, should be settled
by arbitration ; the only point therefore which the jury would
have to consider was, whether the defendant as the representative of the commissioners, was liable to be sued for the injury
which had been sustained, for the compensation for which, if
it should be decided that he was, the commissioners themselves
would not be personally responsible, but the tolls and funds
under their control.

The jury returned a verdict for the plaintiff.

The CASTLE of EYNSFORD and CHURCHES in the NEIGHBOURHOOD of DARTFORD.

EYNSFORD CASTLE.

AN erebean gloom rests upon and encircles Eynsford Castle, undeniably the most interesting relic in the Valley of Holmesdale, both in the magnitude and venerable antiquity of its ruins, combined with the historical recollections connected with its decadence. One historical fact is known: within those time-hallowed walls the first opposition was organized to the overweening ambition of Thomas a Becket, which finally ended in his murder, in the temple, and before the holy altar of God.

From the day when the mason laid the first stone of the foundation, till the present, the pile has attracted the eye of every passer-by,—in its youth, the serf gazed with fear and trembling on its frowning form—in its state of discrepitude, the antiquary and tourist regard its mouldering and crumbling ruins with intense curiosity.

Thorpe in the Custumale Roffense says, the Keep is a square building and still makes a venerable appearance, mantled with ivy; and when he was in it in the year 1783, some part was then made use of for a stable and kennel for fox-hounds.

Half a century has passed away since this visit, and those barbarous excrescences, which actually polluted this hoary fabric, have been removed; and the ruins now [1844,] present the appearance depicted at the head of this article.

The accompanying engraving has been kindly drawn by Mr. JARDINE, of Dartford, from THE RESTORED MODEL of "Eynsford Castle in the olden times," made by the Rev. Mr. BURNSIDE, of Farningham, from the appearance of the existing ruins, and the remains of the foundations which presented themselves on digging. The model was shewn at a meeting of the *Society of Antiquaries*, and excited much interest amid that learned body; at the same time, several Plans and Drawings were exhibited, and a paper by E. CRESY, esq., of South Darenth, was read, illustrative of the structure, from which the following account of the discoveries made at the excavation has been extracted.

"After clearing away to the depth of eight or nine feet, the vast heap of earth and rubbish that had accumulated, the entire plan of the building was visible.

"*The outer or curtain wall*, unquestionably one of the most perfect specimens in this country, is an irregular polygonal oval, or horse shoe, formed of unequal sides, the entire girth of which is about five hundred and twenty feet. One of the peculiar characteristics of this external wall is *not having*, as was common to Norman fortresses, *any small tower or buttresses*, where the sides unite; *nor any loop holes* or openings for the discharge of missles. Its *original height*, nearly throughout is preserved, which, from the level of the meadows to the passage or walk upon the top, three feet wide, *is thirty feet.*

"Eight feet from the ground, (externally,) the wall is battered or tumbled in, about eight inches above which, up to the walk around, *its thickness is uniformly five feet four inches.* The wall of the battlement remains in some places, and near the opening, afterwards described as the original entrance, may be distinctly traced. The apertures or openings on this outer wall are few, and exhibit in their construction Roman tiles. *The two at the south end* have the character of having been used as *sally ports;* they are much broken away, but their sides are in part covered with rough stucco. The small

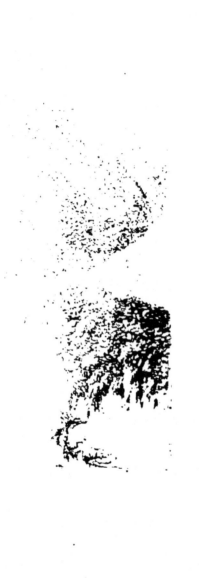

circular hole served only as a drain or outlet for the water which fell in the court yard.

" *The principal opening*, and which has every appearance of having been one of the principal entrances into the castle, *is .on the north side*, and in a very perfect state, *situate about twenty-five feet above the level* of the present ground on the outside. The wall here, as in one other division on the south side, is made of extra thickness, as if to contain some arrangements not required in other portions of it. The opening or door-way, is *three-feet wide*, and *six-feet high*, and *externally the corbel stones remain, which supported a timber platform or landing place, from whence a ladder was dropped, to enable anyone to mount,* and get admission within. On passing this door-way, you arrive at a small chamber, hollowed out of the wall, six feet long, and four feet six inches wide ; on one side of which is a small hole or recess, covered with two courses of Roman tiles, and which seems to have served as a lodgment to a stout wooden beam that secured the door when shut. This chamber is six feet high, and vaulted semi-circularly ; the whole has been covered with rough stucco ;— it commands a fine view of the valley towards Farningham, as well as the whole causeway, which is within bow-shot of any one stationed to overlook or guard the passage across the river. *Another opening occurs at the back of the keep*, on the outer wall, in all respects corresponding in level and dimensions with those already described at the southern angle, and has *been used in modern times to draw water from a well*, constructed since the river has been diverted to a mcre westerly course."

THORPE conjectured, the present breach *was the original entrance, and that it was approached by a Drawbridge*, but CRESY states there is no authority for the conjecture, the yard internally being considerably below the wall, which is continued through the breach. The present entrance in all probability, he says, was therefore made when the castle was first used for stables.

THE KEEP is a parallelogram in its plan, its walls five feet in thickness, strengthened with five buttresses of unequal projection. Possibly the most eastern of these buttresses might indicate the position of fire places in the upper rooms, or a look-out chamber which rose above the curtain wall. The interior is divided into two rooms one considerably larger than the other. The width of the Keep is half its entire

length, like most of the buildings constructed in the middle ages.
The entrance-door to the Keep is through a small tower, supposed to be the guard-chamber, on the right of which is a
doorway of Reigate stone, where the hooks remain on which
the door turned: the precise way which led to the chief portal
has not been decided. Its general character, entrance, etc.,
bears a strong resemblance to that erected by Gundulph at
Rochester, though upon a much smaller scale.

"At the north angle of the principal room is an entrance
conducting to a winding staircase, that led to the upper-room;
below, was another apartment, which served for the kitchen,
the fire-place of which is still remaining; the smoke escaped
through an aperture in the wall. To this room, however,
there is no apparent entrance, and it must have been approached
by an aperture from the floor.

"The walls, are constructed of flints, with the occasional
introduction of tiles,* and the whole has the appearance of
being carried up on caissoons with mortar composed of coarse
sand and lime, well grouted as the works went on. The surrounding country abounds in flints; the quantity required,
however, for even the outer wall, containing as it does upwards
of three hundred rods of reduced work, could not have been
collected without vast labour, and the keep and other buildings
must have required more than a similar quantity.

"The portal is not in the middle, and, externally, its width is
six feet three inches. The wall being destroyed about eight feet
from the foundation, there is no trace of its arch or lintel. The
sill is two feet above the level of the floor, and the entrance must
have been by a descent of two or more steps. The right jamb
is of Reigate stone, built at the same time the guard-room was
constructed; the other jamb is *original*, and formed of tiles."

Few particulars of the individual history of William de
Eynsford have been chronicled, except the fact of his excom-
munication by Archbishop Becket, and his subsequent absolu-
tion by that prelate. It is evident that he assisted in the
erection of the cloisters of Canterbury Cathedral, by his shield
adorning one of the escutcheon bosses.

His appointment as sheriff of London, and his friendship
with Henry II., and his queen Eleanor, are alike indisputable.
The northern chapel of Eynsford church appears to have been
used as a burial-place of the family of de Eynsford; and every

---

* A proof there must have been *then* the remains of some antient
Roman building in the vicinity from which they were taken, perhaps an
antient Roman British church.

successive antiquary, down to Mr. Carlos, agrees with the suggestion of Mr. Thorpe, that the last word of the inscription—

𝔍𝔠𝔦 𝔤𝔦𝔰 . . . . 𝔩𝔞 𝔣𝔢𝔪𝔢 𝔡𝔢 𝔩𝔞 𝔔𝔬𝔟𝔢𝔯𝔤 𝔡𝔢 𝔈𝔠𝔥𝔦𝔰𝔣𝔬𝔯𝔡.

in "wondrous* antique characters" [Lombardic] engraven around the verge of the stone, should be read *Eynsford*.

William de Eynsford seems to have been the last of his race —the family extinct,—superstition flung her mantle over the pile, and man therein abode no longer. The estate then passed into other hands.

Subsequent possessors erected a mansion-house within the adjoining moated precincts. Of this interpolation, no trace remains; the ruthless hand of time has swept it away, like its successor the dog-kennel.†

DARENTH CHURCH.

From time immemorial the chancel of Darenth Church, (as shown in the wood-cut above,) had traditionally been said to be a genuine remain of the work of the Saxons; and, as such, a most elaborate article was written thereon, by Mr.

---

* Weever, 331.

† *Vide* Introductory chapter to Mr. A. J. Dunkin's WILLIAM DE EYNS-FORD, in his Legenda Cantiana, A.

Denne, a well-known antiquary, and published in the Custumale Roffensis, p. 90—95. This opinion has however,
been since controverted by Mr. Carlos, (Gents. Mag. Sep.
1837,) who considers it "a very early Norman work, of which
the simple vaulting, groined in the Roman fashion, the confined windows, and the thickness of the walls, (above three
feet,) are so many indications. The vaulting is also worthy
of notice, not only from the absence of ribs at the interseo-
tion of the groins, but from its springing at once from the
face of the wall without any impost. This portion, it may
be fairly supposed, was erected *soon after the Conquest*, the
antient nave being repaired and the addition made of a choir
and chancel, a mode of management common to the early
Roman churches.

"The introduction of the pointed arch led to the next
alteration ; an aisle was added, in which, the Roman character
was still retained, in combination with the newly introduced
arch. This part, judging from the state of the remainder, may
be of the age of Henry II., or perhaps of Stephen. The tower
was erected shortly after, and coeval with it, are the windows
of the choir." The oldest portion is evidently the nave,
which shows in its walls remains of a building constructed
during the Roman dominion in Britain, or shortly after its
discontinuance, and, was originally erected as a church,
although the Domesday record is silent with regard to the
existence of such a sacred fane in this village, which, may be
easily reconciled by the actual appearance of the building,
which may have been a ruin at the time of the survey—laid
waste, in some of the combats with the Danes, which took
place in the neighbourhood, and on that account was unnoticed
by the compilers.

PAUL'S CRAY CHURCH.

"An old and valued correspondent," says the editor of
the Gentleman's Magazine (April, 1841,) "gives it as his
opinion, that the nave of Darenth church was constructed
during the Roman dominion in Britain, or shortly after its
discontinuance, his arguments are grounded on the employment of Roman tiles at the angles, and in courses, and
strengthened by the constructional evidence, whereby, the

chancel of the earliest Roman work, is proved to be an addition
to the nave." The writer of the present article examined both
edifices, within a few days of each other, and is decidedly of
opinion, that both are the work of the same era, and probably
of the same hand; Darenth is a larger and more perfect
specimen, but both exhibit the same mode of construction.

When the Romans had taken their final departure from this
island, it was overrun by hordes of Pagan barbarians, who
speedily demolished the churches and monuments of architecture which their predecessors had universally raised. Christianity was banished for about 150 years, when its introduction
by Augustine at the close of the sixth century, renewed an
acquaintance with the previous style of Architecture,* and the
first churches of the humble christians were erected from those
ruined materials, which lay *scattered everywhere* in such dis-
astrous *profusion*. The rude Architects perhaps received their
instructions from the learned men who were daily arriving
from Rome, and we are thus indebted for such edifices as those
now under notice. The age of Paul's Cray church can moreover be affixed with a greater degree of certainty, from its
being dedicated to a Saint, who was bishop of a diocese, till
his death, A.D. 654.

It may not be assuming too much, to suppose the small
chapel on the north side now used as a vestry room, was
originally an oratory raised in honour of Paulinus; the nave
was shortly after added, forming a primitive church of one pace
without chancel or bell tower, it was in this state at the time
of the Domesday compilation, and existed without alteration,
five or six centuries, during which period, the Saxon Dynasty
had risen, flourished and decayed: a foreign race swayed the
English sceptre, by whom, new institutions and new styles
had been introduced. About the reign of John, addition was
made of a chancel, tower, and aisles. Succeeding centuries
have not passed over without imparting the whims and fancies
of different tastes, till, at the present day, divested of all
proportion, and humble even to meanness, few travellers feel
sufficient inducement to examine closely the remains of a
structure over which a "thousand years have passed away as
it were a tale that is told."

---

* It is now generally acknowledged, that the form of the Christian
churches was taken from the Basilica, or Justice Halls and Markets of

STONE CHURCH.

Stone Church is usually considered one of the handsomest churches in the county, and it has fortunately met with an able historian in Mr. Edward Cresy, the architect, who has done full justice to its merits, both in the elaborate drawing of its details, and its historical particulars, from which the following account is extracted.

Stone church is dedicated to St. Mary. In the 15 Edward I., the Rectory was valued at 30 marcs, and the vicarage at 7 marcs. There was a good parsonage house, and 8 acres of glebe land worth £170 per annum, in Cromwell's time.* The edifice, at different periods, has undergone various alterations, but the plan remains as the result of one design. The foundation walls of the tower are the most antient. The upper part is more modern, and was once surmounted by a lofty spire, steadied by flying buttresses, whose mouldings are in a style so late as that of Edward III., and may be attributed to John Lombard, the elder, who died 1408.

Omitting the chancel, the church with the tower included, is nearly square, clustered pillars support the arches, which separate the side aisles from the nave. Beyond the richly decorated arch on the eastern side, and between the nave and chancel, once stood the rood-loft, approached on the south side by a small plain pointed arched doorway, now walled up, and some traces of the stairs may still be seen. The Rood-loft extended 17 ft. 19 inches in length, and was 7 ft. 6 in. in depth and was over a screen, the vestiges of which no longer remain; it was probably of wood and destroyed at the Reformation. Wiltshire's chantry, with a small chapel or muniment room are attached to the north side of the chancel. The former appears to have communicated with the north

---

the Romans, the first of which was afterwards known as St. Giovani Laterano given by Constantine, to the Christians, for a place of public worship, which, being found to admit ample space for a large assemblage or congregation *under one roof*, the form has ever since been adhered to in the formation of churches. The antient Pagan temples were not calculated for an assemblage of the population as worshippers together in one edifice. Their sacrifices were generally offered on an altar in the open air, which stood in a court or enclosure of the temple, around which, the votaries usually assembled. Many Temples had no windows, but were dimly illumined by a solitary lamp, placed before the Statue of the Deity to whom they were dedicated, and like the Jewish temples, were entered only at stated seasons by the officiating priest.

* Parliamentary Surveys, Lambeth Library, vol. xix.

aisle of the nave. In this, is a canopied monument erected for Sir John Wiltshire, who rebuilt the splendid mansion of Stone Place (mentioned p. 372) and his son-in-law Sir R. Wingfield entertained Cardinal Wolsey, on his embassy to France. A few years since, his monumental chapel was so dilapidated, that the bones of the founder were visible ; it is now converted into a Vestry room.

The polished Petworth marble columns had their delicately carved capitals above those of the nave, and when sustaining the cross springers of the vault, left nothing to render this chancel a beautiful model of the early pointed style.

On the north side of the nave a Moor's head is introduced to bear the most eastern label. Possibly the sculptor intended to commemorate some interesting event which happened in the Holy wars, especially, as the eastern label of the central window of the northern aisle is supported by the head of a queen, bearing a castellated crown, not improbably that of Eleanor of Castile, the high-minded consort of Edward I. She died 1290.

About the time, (1272,) that this part of the church was finished, the King, then prince, was absent at Acre, on a crusade, and while sitting loosely-robed in his tent, was wounded by the poisoned dagger of a Moor, sent as a messenger from the Emir of Jaffa. Perchance the sculptor by the introduction of these heads intended to emblematize the favourite story of the affectionate attentions of Eleanor towards her husband.

Mr. Cresy supposes that around the wall of the nave, beneath the row of windows, a dado or series of arches, similar to those of the chancel, perhaps rested upon the seat or plinth, which projects so considerably, and was contrived for the purpose of supporting them.

In Mr. Cresy's work are twelve beautifully engraved plates, illustrative of the details of the church, particularly valuable to students in Architecture.

The three main arches which separate the side aisles, are light and well-proportioned, the height of the clustered pillars from the pavement to the top of the mouldings is 27 ft. The pillars are arranged with great regularity, and their lightness is equal to many of the classic age. The foliage on the capital of the pillars is in the style of many in Sicily, and bear the impress of an oriental origin.

The chancel has undergone several alterations, and at present has two distinct styles of Architecture. The earliest is

in harmony with the body of the church, and is confined
principally to that part, which is below the stone moulding, on
which the windows rest. Above this, the building is of later
date, constructed at the beginning or middle of the fifteenth
century. Previously to the construction of these windows, the
chancel had a double groined vault which rested on clustered
Purbeck marble pillars, and though more elaborately ornamented, partook of the same style as the nave. Above the
dado or trefoil arches, were three lancet windows under each
division of the groining, and probably, at the east end, a larger
one of four bays similar to that at the east end of the north
aisle.

The church has lately undergone a complete repair* under
the judicious superintendence of the Archdeacon,† which has
been effected in strict accordance with the original character
of the edifice, and in the northern and southern divisions of the
east window are paintings of St. Matthew and St. John, by
Mr. Miller, of 32, Brewer-street, London. The figures of St.
Mark and St. Luke painted by Miss Wodehouse, will fill the
two remaining compartments; a fine toned organ has also
been erected in a gallery under the tower, in front of which,
sit the female children of the school, uniformly attired, forming a respectable choir. In the central window of the north
aisle, are, gorgeously emblazoned on glass the arms of King,
the present venerable Archdeacon, and Lawrence, the late
Rector.‡ Many ornamented tiles remain in the chancel floor.

Several Roman tiles in the walls of the edifice, indicate that
they were partly constructed of some more antient Roman-
British edifice.

The accompanying engravings of Stone Church and the
Door on the North side, have been kindly executed by Miss
Wodehouse expressly for this work.

---

* On the 14th of January, 1638, the church was damaged by a violent
storm of wind, thunder and lightning,—the roof and the steeple were
burnt,—and the bells melted as they hung.

† And agreeably to the "Instructions to Churchwardens, and Observations on the Duties of their Office, by Walker King, Archdeacon of
Rochester, 1841"—The Rev. W. King is also now Rector of Stone.

‡ Afterwards Archbishop of Cashel.

DOOR ON NORTH SIDE OF STONE CHURCH.

EPISCOPAL CHAPEL, BEXLEY HEATH.

This Chapel originated in the increased population of the parish, which at the time of its erection was supposed to contain 4,000 souls, while the parish church was capable of containing not more than 600 persons, and being considered from its age incapable of sufficient enlargement. A donation of £350 by two individuals, unconnected with the parish, formed the nucleus of the subsequent contributions. On Oct. 7th, 1835, the archbishop of Canterbury laid the first stone of the building. The ground for the site of the chapel having been given by John Smith, esq. The contract for building the chapel, was £1,180, besides furniture, fencing, and the formation of the road. The wood-cut above, shows the first appearance of the Chapel, but since this was taken, alterations have been made, and the buttresses carried up above the roof. Ultimately the whole expenses amounted to £2,197 13s. 0½d.

A Burial Ground has since been attached.

———

At Lamorby, in the same parish, another Episcopal Chapel has been erected, by the exertions of the present Vicar, the Rev. Mr. Harding; to whom, Bexley is likewise indebted, for the elegant National Schools lately built.

ST. JOHN'S CHURCH, SIDCUP.

ON Tuesday, the 16th of April, 1844, the new church dedicated to St. John, at Sidcup, in Chislehurst parish, the building of which has been in progress since the latter end of the year 1841, was consecrated by the Right Rev. Dr. Murray, the Lord Bishop of Rochester. The effect of this imposing ceremony was much increased by the numerous attendance of the clergy of the surrounding parishes, by whom, together with the principal families in the neighbourhood, including a large proportion of those who are intended to form the congregation, the body of the church and the galleries were completely filled.

Although some of the minor details of the works were not entirely finished, the building in all essential parts was in a complete state of preparation for the performance of the service. The Bishop having proceeded to the Vestry, received the Petition for consecration from the hands of lord Viscount Sydney, and having taken his position near the altar, delivered the Petition to the Registrar, by whom it was read. The prescribed consecration service with the appropriate prayers and blessing were then gone through by the Bishop and the assistant clergy in the most impressive manner. The Deeds of Endowment and Conveyance of the site of the church and parsonage were next read by the deputy Chancellor, after which, the regular morning service

was performed by the Rev. Samuel Holmes the newly
appointed minister of the church, with the occasional assistance
of the Bishop; his chaplain, the Rev. Francis Murray; and
the Venerable Walker King, archdeacon of the diocese. Mr.
Cox of Footscray, (organist of Charlton,) was at the organ, and
the chaunting of the Te Deum, and Jubilate, with the singing
psalms, (the Old Hundredth and St. Matthew's Tune,) were
admirably performed by the youthful choir from North Cray,
under the direction of Mr. Reeves, whose services were
obtained by the kind permission of the Rev. E. W. Edgell.
After an appropriate Sermon by the Bishop, the consecration
of the church-yard was proceeded with in due form, which
was the conclusion of a ceremony which will long live in the
recollections of the neighbourhood.

Those who are acquainted with the locality in which
this building has been erected, will be aware of the necessity which has long existed for additional means of attendance on the service of the established church. That part
of the parish of Chislehurst in which the New Church is
placed and which is called the Lower Borough, is separated
by a considerable interval from the other portion of the
parish called the Upper Borough, its inhabitants being
considered as belonging to Footscray, rather than to Chislehurst, and, in consequence, the small church of the former
village, has been inconveniently crowded by the attendance
of those, who, (as well by the distance, as by want of sufficient accommodation,) are debarred from attendance in their
proper parish. A sense of these inconveniences induced
some of the residents in the district, and especially the
lords Sydney and Bexley, and Mr. H. Berens of Sidcup,
to make an effort for their removal, and accordingly, a proposal for a subscription with this object, was circulated
in the beginning of 1841. Towards the end of that year,
however it was found that the amount of subscription
afforded little prospect of an early completion of the building
on an adequate scale, therefore in accordance with the wishes
of the other promoters of the work, Mr. H. Berens undertook to carry it into effect on his personal responsibility.
This he has been enabled to accomplish with the assistance
of the above-named noble lords and other friends, especially by the munificence of lord Bexley, who not only contributed largely to the building fund, but has also supplied the

whole of the funds for the endowment and erection of the Parsonage house.

In his report on the completion of the church, sent to the subscribers previously to the consecration, Mr. Berens states, that owing to the contributions of friends, he is also enabled to report the fitting up of the interior in a far more complete state than he had anticipated.—The whole of the windows have been filled with ground plate glass, presented by Mr. Wollaston, of Welling;—a beautiful service of plate and other appendages, for the communion, has been presented by members of the family of Footscray-place;—a finger organ of great power and sweetness, and also a peal of six bells, by a member of his own; a complete set of books of the handsomest description, by his relation the Rector of Buckland, Surrey;—an altar canopy of antient carved oak, by the Rector of Northcray;—the pair of handsome carved oak chairs, for the east end, by John Hayward, esq., of Dartford; and a very curious antique alms-dish of embossed silver, beautifully illustrated with inscriptions in Gothic letters by H. Jeremy, esq., of Chislehurst.

As this little church offers a good deal that may be considered novel, both with regard to its external structure and to its internal arrangements, it has been thought that, in these church building days, it might be acceptable to offer some authentic explanation of the objects with which the building has been completed, externally and internally, in its present form; and the writer has accordingly been favoured by the gentleman under whose superintendence the whole of the work has been executed with the following particulars.

As to the exterior,—the general object being to produce a building, which, although limited in point of dimensions, and constructed of the most ordinary material, (namely the brick and flint of the neighbourhood,) should still be appropriate in character to the purposes for which it was designed, and also to the situation in which it was to be placed; it was thought that this object might be effected without incurring that expense which is frequently applied to the purpose of mere ornament, and especially to the purpose of giving to the building an appearance of antiquity, which does not belong to it. With this view, there has been considerable deviation from most of the plans of the recently-erected district churches or chapels, — the most striking features of this deviation are,—Firstly, the arcade or cloister round three sides of the church,—Secondly, the two towers at the west-end instead of a single tower or steeple.

With respect to the first, those who look at this part of the edifice with the eyes of a builder, will see that the piers between the arches are of remarkable strength and solidity, and will understand, that they effectually answer all those purposes of strength and support to the building which are usually sought to be obtained, either by the extended thickness of the external walls at the base, or by the application of numerous external buttresses. It has been also intended that this arcade should be conducive to various other purposes deserving of attention, in the construction of buildings of the nature in question—amongst them it may be stated, that it completely obviates the necessity of any projecting appendage, (so frequently inconvenient and unsightly) for the purpose of a porch, or a vestry; that it offers the convenience (which is usually so much required,) of a vestibule or antichapel, where there is sufficient space under cover for persons coming to church to pause for a moment, and prepare themselves before stepping into the part appropriated to divine worship;—that it is always ready for shelter in bad weather, occurring before or after service, and will be constantly useful as a place of waiting for those engaged in the occasional duties of the church:—the walls of the cloister are also intended as a suitable place for the erection of monumental tablets or inscriptions, affording an opportunity which is so generally thought to be desirable of excluding those appendages from the part of the church appropriated to worship. It may be added, that this arcade, besides answering the above, and several other objects of convenience, must be considered at least as effective for purposes of architectural ornament as the generality of the external additions which we see applied to buildings of a similar description with that object.

Secondly. The same combined motives of practical utility and architectural ornament, which led to the adoption of the cloister, led also to the erection of the two towers at the western end—these towers it will be observed, are not in any part detached, but are worked into and form part of the external wall, and it will be at once seen, that the increased solidity and thickness which is thus given, especially at the foundation to two of the exterior angles of the building, must form a most important support and abutment to the whole structure. These towers have also afforded a convenient situation for the staircases leading to the galleries, without interfering with the interior. In point of architectural appearance, it has been thought, that in a building comparatively of such small dimensions, towers of moderate size and height at the two angles, whilst they at once form a more imposing and handsome western front, than could in the usual manner be obtained, contribute also much more to the general symmetry and proportion to the building, than a single tower, which, in order to be made effective as an architectural feature, is usually constructed of a size disproportionate to the body of the church. The double tower in question may also be referred to, as increasing the picturesque effect of the building, by the variety of its position as seen from different points of view. In conformity with the general character of Kentish churches, the steeples or roofs of the towers are covered with heart of oak shingles obtained from the neighbourhood of Sevenoaks.

The peculiarities of the interior arrangement, are principally those on which the following explanations are offered. Firstly, the whole area being intended to be devoted indiscriminately to free sittings, whilst at the same time, there was a necessity for reserving a considerable portion of the building for appropriated seats; the only mode of effecting these objects was by galleries, and as great objection was entertained to the usual mode of disfiguring the interior by having these appendages projecting from one or more of its sides, it was an additional motive for the adoption of the cloister, that the galleries might be formed over it, with convenient means of communication, and without interfering with the interior,—an example of a similar mode of construction may be seen in the Chapel of the Foundling Hospital.

Secondly. The usual modes of constructing the inclosed pew or reading desk for the officiating minister, have been in some respects deviated from, under the impression, that the effect and dignity of the service would be promoted (in conformity with the practice in cathedrals,) by the person officiating being more in view of the congregation than is commonly the case, when the partition and desk by which the minister is surrounded, leaves little more visible than his head, and in great measure prevents the people from being made aware of those changes of position as to standing and kneeling which are enjoined by the rubric. With this view, a detached standing desk has been provided, with a contiguous fald-stool or kneeling desk; this, with a desk for the assistant, and also the pulpit being placed on the raised platform which occupies the east end of the church—it should be added, that this part of the arrangement is less complete than it ought to have been, in consequence of the original intention having been, to place the pulpit and desks within the balustrade, in front of the altar; the rails were accordingly so placed in the first instance, but objections having been made to this disposition by authority, the rails were subsequently removed to their present position, which brings them rather inconveniently near to the communion table.

A departure from the usual plan has also been applied, (and as is generally thought successfully,) to the placing of the organ,—these instruments are usually placed in a gallery at the western-end, when they obstruct in a great degree the light and space that would otherwise be obtained in that part of the church, the performer sitting with his back to the congregation; to obviate these inconveniences, the organ in question, has been constructed, so, as to have a great part of its front, and nearly the whole of its works brought below the front of the west gallery, where it forms no obstruction, being supported on the top of the enclosed door-way, and constituting a very ornamental appendage to that end of the church, with comparatively but little interference with either light or space, the performer being conveniently placed at the back of the instrument looking towards the congregation. At a time, when the disposition to do away altogether with the use of inclosed pews* has become so prevalent, it may be hardly considered as a peculiarity, that there is no enclosure of any kind in this church, the seats being either plain benches, or for those which are to be appropriated, open rows of stalls as in cathedrals.

---

* Pews—the seats in churches; these were not enclosed before the Reformation, but were open seats, or fixed benches of wood with backs; the ends are frequently raised, and are then called Poppies—a fine one still exists at the end of a pew in the chancel of Dartford church Weever, the Rector of Erith, in his Funeral Monuments published during the reign of Elizabeth, bitterly attacks "the pewes" and says, they "are *made high and easie*, for parishioners to sit or *sleepe in*, a fashion of no long continuance, and worthy of reformation."

A good deal of pains and research having been bestowed on some of the interior ornaments or appendages to the service, a few minute details relating to them, may be thought desirable.

The font is a very elegant specimen of modern sculpture. It is formed of the purest white Carrara marble, and is a hexagon with bas reliefs on each face as follows: 1.—The Baptism of our Saviour. 2.—St. John, the Evangelist. 3.—St. Luke, the Evangelist. 4.—A figure of Faith bearing the cross. 5.—St. Mark, the Evangelist. 6.—St. Matthew, the Evangelist.—Beneath these compartments, a wreath of lilies supported by cherub heads at each angle; the execution of this wreath and also of the ornamental scroll work on the pedestal, is deserving of peculiar notice.

It was intended that the marble of the font should receive the water for baptisms, but there is reason to believe that the hard spring water of this country would corrode and discolour the statuary marble, and therefore an internal vessel or lining with an ornamental cover of the new electro gilt metal, has been added to it.

The Bas relief over the altar, (also of Carrara marble,) is a copy of the celebrated painting of Lionardo da Vinci, usually called "La Cena," at Milan; it is very accurately modelled from the most esteemed engravings of the picture, especially that by Raphael Morghen.

The delicacy of workmanship displayed in this tablet has been justly admired, nothing can exceed the finish of the minutest vessels upon the table, as well as of the drapery of the figures, the table cloth, and the arabesque ornament on the walls of the chamber—the perspective has also been attended to with great care, and by a skilful management of the chisel, the open window at the back of the table, is made to show, (when the light is strong and favourable,) the hills in the neighbourhood of Jerusalem. The distinctive characters in the countenances of the Saviour and his followers, as shown in the original, have also been preserved in a degree, which, when the comparative smallness of the figures for a work in marble is considered, must reflect great credit on the skill and labour of the artist.

Both of the above works, and also the marble balustrade in front of the altar, and the marble tablets on each side,— the one inscribed with the Lord's prayer and Apostle's creed, the other with the Ten Commandments, were executed by Vincenzo Bonanni, a sculptor at Carrara; from designs suggested to him by Mr. Berens.

Each of the three marble tablets which thus form the appropriate ornaments of the east end, is enclosed by a handsome frame of carved oak, the centre of which is coloured with a bright mazarine blue, for the purpose of receiving inscriptions referrable to the subject of each tablet in gilt letters of the old English character;—the upper part of each frame bears an extract from Scripture, the lower part an invocation or prayer in accordance with it, thus: over the Pater-noster, our Lord's words, "𝔚𝔥𝔢𝔫 𝔶𝔢 𝔓𝔯𝔞𝔶 𝔰𝔞𝔶" beneath it, the scriptural petition "𝔏𝔬𝔯𝔡 𝔱𝔢𝔞𝔠𝔥 𝔲𝔰 𝔱𝔬 𝔭𝔯𝔞𝔶,"—over the Creed, the words from the same divine lips, "𝔅𝔩𝔢𝔰𝔰𝔢𝔡 𝔦𝔰 𝔥𝔢 𝔱𝔥𝔞𝔱 𝔥𝔞𝔱𝔥 𝔫𝔬𝔱 𝔰𝔢𝔢𝔫, 𝔞𝔫𝔡 𝔶𝔢𝔱 𝔥𝔞𝔰 𝔟𝔢𝔩𝔦𝔢𝔟𝔢𝔡," beneath the Petition also from the Gospel, "𝔏𝔬𝔯𝔡 𝔍 𝔟𝔢𝔩𝔦𝔢𝔟𝔢, 𝔥𝔢𝔩𝔭 𝔗𝔥𝔬𝔲 𝔪𝔦𝔫𝔢 𝔲𝔫𝔟𝔢𝔩𝔦𝔢𝔣,"— over the Last Supper, our Saviour's Injunction, "𝔇𝔬 𝔱𝔥𝔦𝔰 𝔦𝔫 𝔯𝔢𝔪𝔢𝔪𝔟𝔯𝔞𝔫𝔠𝔢 𝔬𝔣 𝔐𝔢"—beneath, the invocation of the Liturgy, "𝔇𝔯𝔞𝔴 𝔫𝔢𝔞𝔯 𝔴𝔦𝔱𝔥 𝔣𝔞𝔦𝔱𝔥 𝔞𝔫𝔡 𝔱𝔞𝔨𝔢 𝔱𝔥𝔦𝔰 𝔥𝔬𝔩𝔶 𝔖𝔞𝔠𝔯𝔞𝔪𝔢𝔫𝔱 𝔱𝔬 𝔶𝔬𝔲𝔯 𝔠𝔬𝔪𝔣𝔬𝔯𝔱,"—over the Commandments, "𝔊𝔬𝔡 𝔰𝔭𝔞𝔨𝔢 𝔱𝔥𝔢𝔰𝔢 𝔴𝔬𝔯𝔡𝔰 𝔞𝔫𝔡 𝔰𝔞𝔦𝔡" beneath the comprehensive petition, also from the Liturgy, "𝔏𝔬𝔯𝔡 𝔥𝔞𝔟𝔢 𝔪𝔢𝔯𝔠𝔶 𝔲𝔭𝔬𝔫 𝔲𝔰 𝔞𝔫𝔡 𝔴𝔯𝔦𝔱𝔢 𝔞𝔩𝔩 𝔱𝔥𝔢𝔰𝔢, 𝔗𝔥𝔶 𝔩𝔞𝔴𝔰, 𝔦𝔫 𝔬𝔲𝔯 𝔥𝔢𝔞𝔯𝔱𝔰 𝔴𝔢 𝔟𝔢𝔰𝔢𝔢𝔠𝔥 𝔗𝔥𝔢𝔢."—These texts have been selected as assistants to devotional feelings, as well during intervals of the service, as at other times when the tablets to which they are attached, may be subjects of attention from occasional visitants to the church.

The pulpit is an elaborate specimen of antient carving in oak or chesnut, obtained from Flanders; four of the panels of the hexagon, contain effigies of the four Evangelists in bold relief,—on the fifth, which was blank, from having been next to the wall, in its former position, a carved figure of Hope has been placed,—the sixth is the door. It bears date, Antwerp, 1651.

The analogium* or reading desk consists of an antient open-work brass frame, supported on a boldly carved pillar, with a tripod base, being surmounted with the Imperial

---

* The Analogium is a metal reading desk, surmounted with an eagle It was sometimes taken for the Martyrology, or Necrology, because that book was always laid upon it, to read from it what belonged to the service of the day.

eagle, it probably belonged to one of the suppressed convents in the Austrian Netherlands. It seems to have been a present from the prior to the choir of the convent, from the following inscription on the front:—Cura zeloque reverendi patris Antonii Prioris erectum, concentibus exultandum ferventius. Decorantes excelsum vocibus excolendum. On the other front: Exacto fervore Pulpitum decorate. Cuncti. exultemus Deo. Exaltamus pectore jucundo et laudibus excellamus. Round a star in the centre: Orietur stella ex Jacob N. N. M. 34. The letters and style of these inscriptions have an appearance so grotesque, that one is surprised at the comparatively recent date of the remaining inscription: Pid. Largille, me construxit, Anno Dom. 1776.

The two kneeling desks are also of antient carved oak, ornamented in front, with the effigies of the four Evangelists within Roman or Saxon arches.

The rails in front of the communion table, which extend from side to side, consist of a balustrade, which has been much admired for its proportions and workmanship, the balusters are of a veined white marble; the base and cornice on the top, of the highly polished black marble, called Bardiglio.

The communion table is supported by a handsome frame of antient carved oak, and covered by a curiously embroidered cloth of old brocade, having in the centre a representation of Christ's Ascension, worked in silver.

The various articles or appendages to the service above described, it should be remembered, are all of them presents from different friends to the undertaking, and therefore, the ornamental character and costliness of some of them, should not be considered as inconsistent with that simplicity and plainness which it has been the intention to maintain in every part of the structure to which the sums contributed to the building fund have been applied. In conjunction with such simplicity, it has been the object, that all the materials as well as the workmanship should be the best of their kind;— as is before stated, the brick and flint of the exterior walls are remarkable for their quality, and for the attention bestowed in placing them, the ornament or relief attempted has been by giving variety in their colour and disposition—the only adventitious ornament consists in the Portland stone, keystones, capitals and copings, which it was found would contribute greatly to the solidity, as well as the appearance of the building. The building was intended to be covered in with the excellent tiles made at Wrotham, but it was found that the pitch of the roof required for tiling, would have occasioned so material an increase of expense in the necessary timber, and would also have been so inferior a protection against the weather, that a slated and boarded roof with a parapet, was substituted.—The interior of the roof is left open, and though of the most simple construction, has been much admired for the extent of the span and the skill of the workmanship.

The fittings up of the interior both in the galleries and area, with the benches, desks, kneeling boards and banisters to the galleries, are of seasoned wainscot oak; the west end is fitted with wainscot panelling, and pilasters of the same material are carried to the cornice of the galleries on each side, the intervals between them being of stucco, which in this, as well as in the other parts of the interior walls is painted in oil of a subdued Roman red colour, calculated to give effect to the natural colour of the oak, which has been merely polished and oiled.

The timbers of the roof are coloured with a simple mixture of red ochre, which has been fixed with a double coat of varnish.—The only ornament attempted to this part of the interior, is, by the addition under the ends of the tiebeams, of twelve antient carved figures of the Apostles, in the way of brackets or corbels.

In concluding this description of St. John's, Sidcup, the inhabitants of that neighbourhood, cannot but congratulate themselves on the completeness of the provision which has been made by the erection of this church, and of the appropriate and well contrived Parsonage adjoining it, for the religious worship and pastoral superintendance of the district;— and it must be a matter of sincere satisfaction to the distinguished prelate under whose spiritual jurisdiction this additional benefice has been placed, to have witnessed, in the period of the last seven years, the complete establishment of seven new churches within a circuit of less than that number of miles distance from the Episcopal palace at Bromley:— Namely, the new chapels or churches at Sydenham, Penge, Bromley common, Black-heath hill, Bexley-heath, Lamorby, in the parish of Bexley, and Sidcup in that of Chislehurst,

The architect has been G. B. Wollaston, esq., a grandson of the former rector of Chislehurst; and the builders, Mr. D. Mandy of Footscray, for the carpenter's work, and Messrs. E. and B. Francis, for the flint and brick-work.

BEXLEY.

FOR some ages after the Conquest of England by the Normans, the manor and demesne of Bexley remained appendant to the See of Canterbury, and in 9 Edw. II., Walter Reynolds, the archbishop, obtained the Charter for a Market and Fair, as given in the note below.* Gradually certain portions of the demesne were granted to the archbishop's knights to hold the same in fee, for the military defence of the lands belonging to the archbishoprick, on which those chieftains erected mansions, as Blendon, Lamorby, Hall Place, etc.

ROT. CART. 9 EDW. II. No. 49.

* Rex Archiepiscopo. &c , Salutem. Sciatis nos concessisse et hâc cartâ nostrâ confirmasse venerabili patri Walteri Cantuar' archiepiscopo totius Angliæ primati quod ipse et successores sui in perpetuum habeant unum Mercatum singulis septimanis per diem Martis apud manorium suum de Bixle, in com' Kantia; et unam Feriam ibidem singulis annis per duos dies duraturum: videlicet, in vigilia et in die Exaltacionis Sanctæ Crucis. Nisi mercatum illud et feriæ illæ sint ad nocumentum vicinorum mercatorum et vicinarum feriarum. Quam volumus et firmiter præcipimus pro nobis et hæredibus nostris quod prædictus Archiepiscopus et successores sui in perpetuum habeant prædictum mercatum et feriam apud manorium suum prædictum cum omnibus libertatibus et liberis consuetudinibus ad hujusmodi mercatum et feriam pertinentibus. Nisi mercatum illud et feriæ illæ, &c., sicut prædictum est. His testibus venerabili patre T. Norwicien' episcopo; Thomâ, comite Lancastriæ; Joanne de Britanniâ, comite Richmond; Humphrey de Bohun, comite Hereford et Essex; Johanne de Warren, comite Surriæ; Roger de Mortui Mari de Cheke; Philippo de Vyme; Johanne de Croumbewell, seneschale hospitii nostri, et aliis   Data per manum nostram apud Lincoln primo de Septembre, per breve de privato sigillo residens in filariis.

[TRANSLATION:]

The King to the Archbishop, &c., Health. Know ye that we have granted and by the present charter confirmed to the venerable father Walter, Archbishop of Canterbury, primate of all England, for himself and his successors, for ever, that they shall have a Market upon Tuesday in every week at their manor of Bexley in the County of Kent, and one Fair every year during two days in the same place; namely, on the vigil (or eve) and on the day of the Exaltation of the Holy Cross. Unless the fair should be to the injury of the neighbouring markets or fairs. And we will and firmly enjoin for ourselves and our heirs, that the aforesaid Archbishop and his successors, shall have the aforesaid market and fair, with all liberties and free customs appertaining to a market and fair of this sort, unless that market and fair &c., as is before mentioned. The following are witnesses the venerable father T. Bishop of Norwich; Thomas, Earl of Lancaster; John of Britanny, Earl of Richmond; Humphrey Bohun, Earl of Hereford and Essex; John Warren, Earl of Surrey; Roger Mortimer, of Cheke; Philip Vyme; John Croumbewell, Steward of our household, and others. Given under our hand at Lincoln, the first day of September, by writ of privy seal hereunto appended by the string.

HALL PLACE, BEXLEY.

HALL PLACE.

HALL PLACE is an antient and stately mansion; of late years renowned as the principal seminary in this part of Kent for the education of young gentlemen. It stands in the northern part of the parish of Bexley, and was the inheritance of a family who assumed their name from it, being called At-hall. A member of the family in the 41 Edw. III., sold it to Thomas Shelle of Gaysum in Westerham, (A.D. 1366,) who is said to have erected a castellated mansion on the site of Hall Place, a part of which still exists, particularly the tower on the south side. Mr. Cottingham the architect, is decidedly of opinion, that some of the present windows are characteristic of the age of Edward the Third. In this family it continued to John Shelly who resided here and died in possession, 20 Henry VI., (1441); William, his son, sold it 1537, to Sir John Champneis, Knight, Lord Mayor of London, 26 Henry VIII. Sir John died at Hall place, and was buried in the church; Sir John married Meriell, daughter of John Barrell, of Belhouse, co. Essex, by whom he had seven sons and two daughters. Of the sons, Justinian, the youngest, became the only survivor, and possessed this estate in the 25th of Elizabeth.*

He rebuilt great part of the mansion with stone, particularly the hall, now used as a school-room, which is universally regarded as one of the most splendid and perfect apartments of that description in England. Indeed the whole mansion is an unique example of the residence of a gentleman of the Elizabethan era. In 1582, Justinian was sheriff of the county. He married Theodora, daughter and co-heir of John Blundell, of Steeple Aston, in Oxfordshire, and died 1596. There is a handsome monument affixed to the north wall of Bexley church, to the memory of himself, his lady and their family. His son Richard Champneis, was employed with Sir Arthur Weldon, (vide p. 203, ante,) by the court of chancery to settle the dispute between the proprietors of Horsman's Place and the parish of Dartford, respecting the Spital House estates, and

---

* Hasted's Kent, with Dr. Latham's additions, vol. i. p. 160.

many others in the county. He eventually sold it to Robert Austin, esq., who added the vast pile of brick building to the former mansion, which exists on the eastern side, and was afterwards created a baronet. Sir R. Austin died 30th October, 1666. Sir Robert, the 4th baronet died 1743, without issue, and left the mansion and estate to Francis lord Le Despenser, who on his decease, left them to Francis Dashwood, esq., his natural son. This gentleman while residing at Hall Place, in 1793, married lady Anne Maitland, daughter of James, seventh earl of Lauderdale. Here he resided some time, kept his coach and six, was very gay, and greatly impaired his fortune, but eventually obtained an appointment in India, where it is believed he died. Lady Dashwood, on her return to England, fitted up the seat in the immediate vicinity, now called Halcot, where she continues to reside with her son, Francis Dashwood, esq.*

About 1784, Hall Place was the residence of Richard Calvert, esq., who married Mary, widow of John the eldest son of Ralph, 1st earl of Verney,† and mother of Lady Ferma-

---

* Manuscript account of Bexley, drawn up from original documents, by Frederick Holbrooke, esq.

† Ralph 2nd earl of Verney, built a splendid mansion with a magnificent front, in the Italian style, at Middle Clayton, Buckinghamshire. The principal entrance was through a saloon, comprising a cube of 50ft., containing a circle of lofty columns of artificial jasper, with white marble bases and capitals, supporting an entablature and gallery with an iron balustrade, lighted by lofty windows in the tympanium, and crowned with a dome, which above the roof of the saloon was enclosed with a balustrade of stone, and contained a circular belvidere, the windows of which commanded very beautiful views of the surrounding country to a great distance. It was the admiration of the neighbourhood. When the mansion came into the possession of Lady Fermanagh, not being considered of sufficient stability, the saloon, ball room and belvidere were taken down and their glories still furnish the theme of many a long winter evening's tale to the old people in that part of the country; Lady Fermanagh gave Mr. Harenc the ball which surmounted the dome of her mansion, who affixed it to the top of the dome of the house he was then building in Footscray, and it still ornaments the mansion of Lord Bexley, at Footscray Place. *Information of the late B. Harenc, esq.* Mrs. Potts (*Moonshine*, vol iii) in her pleasant gossip of the neighbourhood, describes Lady Fermanagh in her younger days as a very beautiful and amiable woman, and has many anecdotes respecting her, the members of the Calvert family, and the other residents at Bexley, whom she visited [circ. 1780] Mr. Thorpe her father, (the celebrated author of the Custumale Roffense,) *then* resided in the large mansion near Bexley church

nagh, who died 1789. After her decease, Lady Fermanagh who had been brought up at Hall Place, wished to reside there, but Mr. Dashwood unwilling to remove, refused to let it, although she offered to expend £10,000 on its repair. She then took May Place, Crayford, and made it her residence. Mr. Dashwood some time afterwards, let it on lease for a school to Mr. Jeffreys of Margate, who after three or four years' occupation, parted with his interest therein, to the Rev. Mr. Wilson, in 1801; Mr. Stone succeeded Mr. Wilson, in Jan. 1804; and Mr. Stone resigned it to Mr. John Barton, at Midsummer, 1832.*

The accompanying engraving of Hall Place, has been executed expressly for this work, by Mr. SHEW, a highly talented professor of the establishment.

---

* Communication by Mr. Stone.

HALL PLACE, BEXLEY, FROM THE PLAYING FIELDS.

INDEX.

—

Lightning Source UK Ltd.
Milton Keynes UK
UKOW05f0607170717
305461UK00006B/457/P

9 781175 226075